LITTLE,
BROWN

LB

**LARGE
PRINT**

Also by Chuck Todd

*How Barack Obama Won: A State-by-State Guide
to the Historic 2008 Presidential Election*
(with Sheldon Gawiser)

THE STRANGER

Barack Obama in the White House

CHUCK TODD

LITTLE, BROWN AND COMPANY

LARGE PRINT EDITION

Little, Brown and Company
Hachette Book Group
1290 Avenue of the Americas, New York, NY 10104
littlebrown.com

First Edition: November 2014

Little, Brown and Company is a division of Hachette Book Group, Inc. The Little, Brown name and logo are trademarks of Hachette Book Group, Inc.

The publisher is not responsible for websites (or their content) that are not owned by the publisher.

The Hachette Speakers Bureau provides a wide range of authors for speaking events. To find out more, go to hachettespeakersbureau.com or call (866) 376-6591.

ISBN 978-0-316-07957-0 (hc) / 978-0-316-24520-3 (large print)
Library of Congress Control Number: 2014940632

10 9 8 7 6 5 4 3 2 1

RRD-C

Printed in the United States of America

To my late father, Steve Todd, and my cousin, friend, and brother from another mother, Bob Balkin. I can still trace my fascination with politics and the presidency to your late-night debates.

The passion, the fun, the knowledge, the espresso (and the extra little something in the espresso) made a lasting impression on the fourteen-year-old me.

CONTENTS

THE STRANGER

The Stranger

A president's legacy takes years, even decades, to fully reveal itself. Historians are still fighting over some of our earliest presidents and their proper places in the more than two-century-old American experiment. This book is an attempt to bring readers behind the scenes to understand both who Barack Obama is and who he isn't, what he strives to be and what he actually is. The careful portrait painted by Obama's handlers, and to an incredible degree crafted by the president himself, has created an image in the eyes of his fans and his detractors. But that image is hardly representative of the president and the administration he has built. He is neither the liberal his allies had hoped for nor the one his enemies belittle. Americans rarely rush a nobody to the presidency, and when they do, it's usually out of a combination of frustration and anticipation — think Jimmy Carter post–Watergate/Vietnam. Obama was rushed into the White House by an American public fed up with Washington and frustrated by America's position in the world after 9/11. Obama's was still one of the more remarkable rises in American history and one this book sets out to understand.

In January 2007, just before her husband formally launched his campaign, Michelle Obama sat down for breakfast at a restaurant in Hyde Park, the family's neighborhood in Chicago, with Jan Schakowsky. Schakowsky, a short, fiery, and loyal liberal Democrat who represented a nearby congressional district, had helped Barack Obama at the beginning of his career, lending her support during Obama's run for state senate; she recalls seeing the rookie candidate standing alone at the entrance to a local Democratic event, handing out literature, and she stood next to him to lend a little credibility. So Schakowsky, like anyone who watches a former pupil succeed, was now excited by the prospect of an Obama presidential run, but also a little worried. "He needs security," Schakowsky said. "Are you worried about the family?" Michelle Obama just smiled as Schakowsky continued. "You know, there are people in the community, and even some in the family, who are really afraid for him," she explained. Schakowsky was expressing a fear many supporters her age and older would constantly be thinking during Obama's historic presidential run that first time. After all, Schakowsky lived through the 1960s and that era of political assassinations. For baby boomers of a certain age, it was not a matter of if but when some wacko was going to take a shot at the young African American candidate. It set up a lot of interesting friendly editorial battles in newsrooms between baby boomer–era senior editors and producers and younger reporters. For older baby boomers the fear was real, but for tweeners like Barack and Michelle Obama and their contemporaries, while they had been alive at the time of those tragic killings, they were very young. Barack was not yet seven in 1968, the year that saw lone gunmen take the lives of Bobby Kennedy and Martin Luther King Jr.; Michelle was even younger. She told Schakowsky they had held a family meeting to discuss the pros and cons of running for president: "We decided, what if Barack Obama is the president of the United States, and what if he's able to do all these great things for our country? And we decided, absolutely, it's worth going through all these what-ifs."

In part, Obama's meteoric rise reflected a hunger Americans were feeling at the time, a deep-seated need for change after almost two decades of Washington partisan warfare. Bill Clinton, George W. Bush, Newt Gingrich, Tom DeLay, Al Gore, John Kerry, impeachment, the Iraq War — American politics had been doing nothing but disappoint, left and right alike. And since those disappointments were being overseen by white male baby boomers, it was easy for Americans to picture Obama representing change. Perhaps a young, energetic black man from the tail end of that generation, one influenced more by the 1980s and '90s than by the Vietnam War and the civil rights movement, would change the way Washington worked—it's a sentiment many Obama loyalists tried to remind the president of from time to time. Robert Gibbs, the president's first White House press secretary, never believed voters were sending the message that the country was ready for a black president in 2008; he always believed the country was so desperate for change that many overlooked their own prejudices and simply wanted Washington to understand: "We so want you to change the way you do business, *we'll even* send a black man to the White House," so Gibbs would regularly remind his colleagues

But Obama's rise also came at a moment when the cynical media that had covered all those flawed candidates was changing dramatically. The thirst for someone different, especially among a newly partisan media, gave Obama the candidate exposure, even in 2004 when he first came to national prominence, when he could be contrasted with the stiff and stale Kerry. The rise of YouTube and social media gave the candidate unfettered access to the activists and voters he was trying to reach. And Obama received fawning coverage—which drove opponents from Hillary Clinton to John McCain to Mitt Romney crazy at times—due in no small part to the baby boomers who ran America's newsrooms, all of whom had grown up during the civil rights era and many of whom were drawn to the notion of America's first black president—even as they all feared the worst.

Like several of his recent predecessors, the president came to office with a clear mandate to change the city and its governing institutions. Unlike his recent predecessors, he was fairly new to national politics, a factor that aided him with a public desperate to change the way Washington works but has served as a severe handicap as he's attempted to govern. Not since Jimmy Carter's election, in 1976, had voters been so angry that the outsider they had sent to the Oval Office was so inexperienced.

In many ways, the country's anger and cynicism in 2008 mirrored 1976. Instead of Vietnam fatigue, it was Iraq, and instead of Watergate, it was polarization that was frustrating Americans and making them lose faith in government in general. Voters were tired of Washington, tired of politics as usual, so they sent a relative political stranger to Washington, someone who hadn't even served a full term in the United States Senate. Obama had never held an executive office—or an executive position in anything larger than his own campaign—and had been the first non-governor or non–vice president to win the presidency in nearly two generations. It appears that

Obama had never even fired anyone of consequence before becoming president. That's how little executive experience he brought to the office.

To understand a legacy, one must understand the man behind the legacy, and despite two national campaigns, an insatiable media machine that measures its news cycles in minutes rather than days, and as much reporting as any president has ever received, Barack Obama the man remains shrouded in the carefully maintained image cultivated over his entire career.

While there's no ordinary path to the White House, Obama's is more extraordinary than most. Most of what we knew about his childhood and his psyche in 2008 came thanks to his memoir, *Dreams of My Father.* And while it may be hard for most Americans to relate to a guy born in Hawaii to a white mother and a black Kenyan father, there has always been something about his unusual upbringing that explains many of his best and worst personality traits. Despite being born in Hawaii, he was not raised as a child of privilege. He saw his share of poverty while living in Indonesia as a child. And when he was sent back to stay with his grandmother in Hawaii as he became a teenager, home was an unremarkable apartment building in Honolulu, which could easily be mistaken for some nondescript medical office building that houses a handful of doctors. It was not exactly how many Americans dream of life for their own children, let alone in a supposed paradise—no big backyard, no tree-lined streets with kids playing ball. It's hard to picture the eventual plaque that will go up on that Honolulu apartment building to note its historical importance—it's certainly no log cabin.

As is the case for many Americans, the president's unusual upbringing shaped him to be the person he is today. He's a very present father to his two daughters, the opposite of what he experienced; he's extremely self-reliant, perhaps to a fault, but that self-reliance has also served him well as an ambitious politician. He is very comfortable being alone, an attribute that actually is the opposite of successful politicians in the modern era, who seem to crave public affection and the company of others. This is both an asset and a liability for Obama in Washington, because the town is filled with people he just doesn't get. Being the son of an anthropologist gave him instinctive observational skills that have allowed him to read and understand folks better than most politicians, who usually need polls to help them understand people who grew up differently than they did.

And, of course, growing up biracial, and specifically being raised by white grandparents who were a constant reminder that he was different from others, infused in him the temperament and patience that have marked his presidency both positively and negatively. What else explains his ability to never take the bait of the most racist and hateful rhetoric that some spew at him?

Of course, in 2008 the country didn't really give either candidate a personality test before it elected Obama. It simply did what it has done every time it's elected a new president from the opposite party — it hired the candidate who most possessed the qualities it thought the previous president lacked. Jimmy Carter won in 1976 because he projected an image that was the opposite of what the country despised about Nixon. Ronald Reagan's optimism and charisma were the pluses to Carter's biggest malaise minuses. Bill Clinton's hands-on "feel your pain" style won out over the patrician George H. W. Bush. And of course, Dubya's 2000 campaign was all about projecting a wholesome moral image, even using the political tagline "restoring honor and integrity to the White House" as his not-so-subtle reminder that he didn't have Clinton's libido issues.

With Obama, the professorial, nuanced, thinking candidate seemed like everything George W. Bush wasn't. If Bush saw everything in black and white, as he seemed to do when he'd say things like "wanted dead or alive," Obama seemed to see only gray areas. And while Bush certainly was intelligent, the perception of our forty-third president was that he wasn't intellectually curious. The bookish Obama emphatically checked that box.

But no presidency ever goes the way the winning candidate hopes it will go. Despite trying to run as someone different, like his predecessors Obama has struggled to shape his own presidency. Instead, his battles with Washington institutions—Congress, both political parties, the military, the media—have shaped his presidency for him. In moments of unintended frankness, he shows clear disdain for almost every institution that defines the Capitol. In turn, many who have been part of Washington's governing culture far longer than he has been in office show clear disdain for Obama himself. The two factions—the change agent and the agents to be changed—have never seen eye to eye because they fail to understand each other, and rarely try.

To candidate Obama, "change" didn't just refer to policy—it referred to the ways of Washington: the manner in which decisions were made; the emphasis on the trivial instead of the crucial; the means over the ends; the subordination of figuring out the right way to resolve spiteful quarrels over who had right-of-way. Obama's desire to replace that with something better, idealistic as it was, was also staggeringly naïve. He may have been correct to see the process as deformed, counterproductive, and sometimes corrupt (it would be hard to find many

Americans on either side who would disagree), but there was a game that had started before his arrival, and no matter the hard fouls and trash talk, his sitting on the sidelines was not going to dictate the style of play.

You can't simply hope things change, you have to make change happen; and in order to create a new set of rules, you have to succeed by the old ones — all lessons Barack Obama may end up taking away from the presidency, but lessons he may wish he had learned before taking office.

Breaking Washington's addiction to partisanship was one of the basic promises of Obama's first campaign, and he meant to keep it. Since his childhood, he had been forced to negotiate his life as an outsider and an exception, a child and then man between worlds and expectations. This sometimes required looking for common ground, showing those who might discount him (be they black community activists who saw him as an elitist, drop-in Ivy League outsider, or white Americans who could not see past the color of his skin) that they shared a concern, perspective, or goal, and building out from there. But Washington was not a small conference room or street corner or the *Harvard Law Review,* and his inability to fulfill that campaign promise sat poorly with him.

Every presidential campaign has a phrase or two that defines it, and before "Hope and Change" defined Obama, there was another phrase that he developed during his epic primary fight with Hillary Clinton that defined the president he *wanted* to be but has failed at: "It's time to turn the page." It was a very clever motto: it could mean many things to different audiences. To Democrats fearful of the partisan battles of the 1990s that the Clintons led, it meant turning the page from the Democratic Party's past. To independents, it meant turning the page from cheap and sometimes corrupt partisanship. To some Republicans who didn't like the in-your-face tactics of African American leaders like Jesse Jackson or Al Sharpton, it meant turning the page on the more divisive racial issues of this country's past. To others, it meant turning the page from the me-first generation of baby-boom politicians.

And of course, "turning the page" also was code for "not of Washington." It's rare for any campaign to develop a phrase so successful at truly meaning all things to all people.

Running against Washington is an increasingly effective campaign strategy, even for those who have been on Capitol Hill for decades. ("*I'm* a good guy, but *everyone else…*") This sort of campaigning was even easier for Obama because he clearly *wasn't* a congressional veteran, which made him confident that the turmoil would change under his watch. Yeah, the Republicans had attacked him without mercy during the campaign, but that was *then*—now, he was *president*. Surely, he thought, when given the choice, enough good people in Congress would jump at the chance to shed corruption and extremism.

And Obama had something else going for him in those first days of his presidency: coattails. The American public didn't just hand him the keys to the presidency, but gave Democrats huge advantages in the House and Senate. They gave him a mandate like no presidency since Reagan's in 1980 and before that LBJ's in 1964. It was a once-in-a-generation gift. And that resounding message was something Obama thought would mean cooperation — not just from Washington Democrats but all of Washington, even Republicans who he assumed would be in a mood to cooperate.

As it would turn out, Obama's logic had no place in an age of ferocious unreasonableness, or in D.C.'s thicket of congressmen, executive branch rivals, lobbyists, and movers and shakers, all with their own interests. His inability to successfully transform Washington was due to the resilience of the Washington ecosystem, then magnified by his own strengths and weaknesses. At times both passive and arrogant, this is a president who is brilliant at communicating with voters and miserable at communicating with the folks they voted for. It's no secret he despises the glad-handing, backslapping necessities of his chosen profession. It took less than two years before many in official Washington simply treated him as they had treated other presidents: just another officeholder who would be gone as quickly as he came, powerful only for the shortest period of time. These Washington elites had outlasted previous cycles of reform, and they'd outlast this one. He was president, but not the first and not the last, and many of those he had to lobby and cajole had been in Washington long before him and would be there long after him. They didn't report to him, and he couldn't fire them when they tried to undermine him and his policies. Similar to most presidents, Barack Obama (just like George W. Bush, like Bill Clinton, like George H. W. Bush and Ronald Reagan, and on and on) celebrated the democracy that had brought him to the Oval Office, and yet sometimes he wished his power to get things done did not require the consent and approval of more than five hundred elected representatives or the moneyed interests behind them. There's no joke this president loves to make more when he's in a country that has either no legislative branch or a weak one, and he gets to wish he had no Congress to deal with. He tells it so much, it's an eye-roller for those reporters who cover him nonstop.

The fact of the matter is, presidents succeed when the other party cooperates, and many a political strategist has figured out that the best tactic to bring down an initially popular leader of the other party is to simply oppose everything. This trend has metastasized since the mid-1980s. And both parties blame the other for starting this path to mutually assured political destruction.

Republicans point to the Democratic Party's treatment of Robert Bork, Ronald Reagan's conservative Supreme Court pick who was defeated in a surprisingly bitter and partisan confirmation fight. Democrats like to point to the tactics of Newt Gingrich and how he bullied House Speaker Jim Wright out of office in the late 1980s. The truth is, both parties have seen that total and complete obstruction can bring the presidency to a near halt and reward the party that's out of power. And arguably, Republicans have perfected the strategy.

When the Republican leader of the Senate declares that his number one job is to make certain the president's agenda so utterly fails as to doom his re-election chances, you're not starting from a productive place. Then again, Mitch McConnell would not be a very popular Republican leader if he didn't verbally promise to use his position to either rein in or undermine the president of the opposite party. His political base would expect nothing less. Indeed, Obama would find the GOP members of Congress opposing policies they actually supported, just because Obama supported them, too. Yet Obama's management style would make his war against Washington a multiple-front assault—and ultimately a chaotic defense against too many besieging parties. And that's why these battles with Washington are defining his years in office.

Perhaps over time the squabbles that have come to dominate the conversation in Washington and the headlines around the country will fade into historical footnotes.

In the nostalgia of later generations, future studies of Obama's terms in office might well gloss over his feuds with John Boehner and Mitch McConnell with throwaway lines: "As was typical of many presidents, Barack Obama faced a recalcitrant Congress, but he eventually got his way." Of course, for that last line to ever be written will depend on money and the all-out effort to stamp his legacy via postpresidential work and such monuments as his library. But he'll also have to have quite a few of his big policies, namely health care, vindicated by the only thing that ultimately matters when it comes to presidential legacies: time.

If years from now our government is still lurching from crisis to crisis, fixing issues on a temporary basis and gridlocked to the point at which long-term solutions are all but out of the question, then the biographies yet to be written will have a different tone and a different take on what happened in the Obama era. His foreign policy achievements and any grand legislative accomplishments will be seen as lightning bolts rather than sunshine. Much of the mess came before him, but he will be judged a failure, seen as a full participant in the partisan wars.

"The thing that's sort of almost bizarre about Obama in the current context is, here is a guy who built his political cachet and experience around being nonideological. That was I think very important to his identity," observes one West Wing insider who thinks Obama overpromised because you can't push progressive ideas and also sell nonpartisanship. "So he's the guy who's a brainiac, nonideological. He's a guy who says let's put the facts on the table, let's respect each other, let's not get too hung up on ideology. Let's not get too hung up on political philosophy. There are commonsense answers to these questions. And yet the political structure now has driven him into a very different modus operandi." "He likes the policy side. He likes the intellectual side," a longtime advisor says to me. "What he just doesn't like is sort of what you and I think of as politics." Most of those closest to him echo this assessment. "He's the polar opposite of Bill Clinton," notes one longtime Obama staffer who worked on Hillary Clinton's 2008 campaign. "I've never met two people who are so different and have had the same job, let alone be in the same party. They are like the exact opposite people. Everything Obama hates about politics, Bill Clinton loves."

Thus one of the great conundrums of Barack Obama: How does one of the most successful politicians in American history, a man whose entire career seems to be blessed by Providence, appear to be so bad at practicing the basics of politics in the back rooms of Washington, whether on Capitol Hill, on K Street, or at the Pentagon? This book attempts to answer that basic question. But it also studies Obama's administration in terms of where it will land in the history books. Have Obama's days been truly historic, delivering the kind of transformation of the American political system he has promised since the moment he burst onto the national stage?

Every president, when first elected, believes he will be a transformational leader. But the vast majority end up as transitional, simply paving the way for one of the rare men who changes the way we think about government. It's an observation Obama himself made, in a 2008 interview during his brawl with Hillary Clinton for the Democratic presidential nomination. "I don't want to present myself as some sort of singular figure," Obama told the *Reno Gazette-Journal.* "I think part of what's different are the times....I think Ronald Reagan changed the trajectory of America in a way that Richard Nixon did not and in a way that Bill Clinton did not. He put us on a fundamentally different path because the country was ready for it....He just tapped into what people were already feeling, which was we want clarity, we want optimism, we want a return to that sense of dynamism and entrepreneurship that had been missing."

At the time Obama made those comments, the media focused on the explicit insult to the Clinton family. Bill Clinton, Obama meant, was merely a transitional figure rather than a transformative one. (Putting Clinton in the same context as Richard Nixon must have further enraged the forty-second president, who at the time was in the middle of a self-destructive spiral as he tried to rescue his wife's faltering presidential campaign.) According to one former Clinton insider who ended up in the Obama White House, no specific Obama comment made Hillary madder. "It sent her over the edge," remembers a confidant.

But the important point is that Obama himself set the high bar for historians. He *must* be transformational, period — anything less would be a disappointment, at least to himself. Times of economic disaster and international crisis, Obama argued in 2008 — and would argue today — demand a transformational vision to guide the country, even the world, through a time of unusual peril and turbulence. But perversely, it might have been less challenging to save the world than to manage the 202 area code. History books rarely focus on the routine, laborious, and even boring details of managing an office, even one shaped like an oval. Ignorance on this front—how to actually manage people, and himself—would be another obstacle to Obama's success. At times he was all telescope and zero microscope.

It's notable that Obama, perhaps the most liberal president to take office since Franklin Roosevelt (in campaign pronouncements, at least), would compare himself to Ronald Reagan, the most conservative Republican to hold office in the twentieth century, and not to Roosevelt, John Kennedy, or Abraham Lincoln. Reagan's presidency is not measured by legislative successes, nor even by consistency. His lasting achievements were to change the country's perception of, and relationship to, government; to change the perception of the Republican Party; and to change the country's perception of itself. To put it in ideological terms, Ronald Reagan shifted the country from a center-left ideology to a center-right ideology. There was no clearer evidence of his success than the moment in January 1995, a decade and a half after Reagan was first elected, when a Democratic president stood before the United States Congress and declared the era of big government over: Reagan was so transformational, he even changed the core identity of the Democratic Party.

How transformational would Obama be?

The country Obama governs is at a crossroads. Fifty years from now, historians will look at this era as a moment of irreversible change, a moment in which the economy moved away from an industrial, manufacturing-based model toward an information and service-based one, a reckoning with a world in which American dominance is colored by the rise of opposing semi-superpowers and a devolution of authority and control. As the world shrinks, America's old ways of influencing events around the globe are not as effective, and that presents its own set of challenges. Obama had the bad luck, perhaps, to be the first American president in an eventual series that will find controlling events around the world so much harder than it was in the twentieth century. Of course, this will be an argument for future presidential candidates to debate as the very nature of American diplomacy is being forced to change by the day thanks mostly to technology.

Historians will look upon the election of Barack Obama as a wonderful shattering of an American glass ceiling, that only decades after the lynchings, beatings, bombings, and assassinations of civil rights leaders, a black man had become president of the United States. There is no doubt about the significance of Obama's accomplishment. Yet the demographic change at 1600 Pennsylvania Avenue is far from the only one faced by the nation.

Barack Obama inherited a country going through its most turbulent period since the Great Depression, when the national economy underwent a similar transition from rural, agrarian dependence to a growing urban, industrialized core. And our politics are just as turbulent; as in the 1920s and '30s, when fifty- or sixty-seat swings in the House of Representatives were commonplace, recent elections in 2006, 2008, and 2010 have brought about their own form of political whiplash. The existential crisis has gone beyond the wallet: Obama came into office in the midst of two failing wars, the threat of continued terrorist attacks, a rising China, a reassertive Russia, North Korean nuclear bullying, and an Iran busily spinning its own centrifuges, among other foreign policy challenges. Voters are anxious; they worry about their future and their children's future, and they don't see their politicians as willing, or able, to overcome the challenges the country faces. America is in therapy, trying to figure out what it wants to be in the twenty-first century.

Such was the backdrop when Barack Obama came to Washington. This book could rightfully be called *The Outsider, The Savior, The Impostor,* depending on which side of this fractured city you hang in. I am calling it *The Stranger* because it seems most true to the man and the president I've observed these past years. This book tells his story, the story of what Obama has achieved so far and how that fits — or doesn't — with his own measure of success, and of the carefully crafted image he's created during his

career. It seems everyone is still trying to get to know
Obama, to figure him out, from Democrats on Capitol Hill to Republicans, the media, and even some
of his own staffers. He's known to have loved playing poker in his pre-presidential years (the card game
spades is his game of choice now), and like a good
poker player, he can be a hard guy to read. He came
to Washington on the strength of being a stranger
to the city and to the political elites, but it hasn't
always served him well. His has not been an easy
presidency, if such a thing exists. In the age of Obama,
both Washington and the president have the scars
to show just how tough the battle has been.

CHAPTER ONE

A Not-So-Fresh Start

O n June 7, 2008, Hillary Rodham Clinton, member of the most powerful family in Democratic politics since the heyday of Camelot, conceded that a freshman senator named Barack Hussein Obama had beaten her for the party's presidential nomination. A woman—a former First Lady and senator—who had been in the national eye for nearly two decades had lost to someone that the late Senator Ted Kennedy had introduced just three years before as "Obama Baraka," someone whose very skin color promised a freshness, a rejuvenation, a different kind of politics.

The Clinton team was flummoxed. Their insinuation that Obama wasn't up to the job—that he wouldn't be able to handle an international crisis, a portentous "3 a.m. phone call"—hadn't convinced voters to cast a ballot for someone more experienced. The Republican nominee, John McCain, would try and fail to make a similar point stick in the general election. Neither the Clinton team nor the McCain team understood it was Obama's freshness, newness, even strangeness, the fact that he hadn't been tainted by years building his Washington résumé, that appealed to voters. The inexperience was the asset. This was an America desperate for change, not just wanting to hear the words but to *see* the change with its own eyes.

So it surprised John Podesta that he was one of the first people the new Democratic presidential nominee called after Clinton conceded.

The speed with which Barack Obama rose to national prominence meant he had to build a network faster than most other presidents. His predecessors had had time to amass allies across the country. George W. Bush had been a prominent figure in the Republican Party for two decades, going back to his father's tenure as Ronald Reagan's vice president, before he ran for national office. Bill Clinton had been a governor for more than a decade and a leader in reestablishing the Democratic Party's centrist ranks through prominent think tanks like the Democratic Leadership Council, well before he took the oath in 1993. George H. W. Bush, Reagan, Richard Nixon, and Lyndon Johnson—each had run in national political circles for decades before ascending to the highest office in the land.

But Obama's background was more like Jimmy Carter's. Carter had gone from peanut farmer to two terms in the state senate, then in a surprising upset became governor of Georgia. He had some experience with national politics, having chaired the Democratic National Committee's campaign wing during the 1974 elections, but his emergence on the national scene during the 1976 Democratic primaries—at the expense of more seasoned politicians like Morris Udall, Henry "Scoop" Jackson, Lloyd Bentsen, and Frank Church—was swift, and not the least bit expected when the campaign kicked off.

Similarly, Obama ascended from the depths of the Illinois state senate to a U.S. Senate seat he wasn't supposed to win. Even before he won election to the Senate, some Democrats believed he would be president of the United States one day. And when "one day" turned out to be just four years down the line, Obama found himself with some catching up to do if he had any chance to build a team competent enough to run the country.

Podesta, as much as anyone who claimed to share party affiliation with the newly crowned nominee, was part of what Obama had been railing against, one of the "Professional Democrats" who'd figured out how to accumulate a healthy living whether his party was in or out of power. He'd started on Capitol Hill in 1979 as a young lawyer, assisting the Senate Judiciary Committee and its chairman, Ted Kennedy. Over the next two decades, he held just about every important job in Washington, working as the top lawyer to the Senate Agriculture

Committee; as a top advisor to Senate majority leader Tom Daschle; as the founder, with his brother Tony, of the Podesta Group, still one of the most influential Democratic lobbying firms in the city. He was Bill Clinton's first staff secretary, a job that gave him intimate access to the president. In 1998, as Clinton faced impeachment, he hired the wiry and physically unimposing Podesta, by then well known to Democrats and Republicans alike, to be his chief of staff. Podesta lasted until the end of Clinton's second term and then invented his own kind of permanent Washington perch in 2003, founding the Center for American Progress, a liberal think tank that today is one of the party's power centers—ironically, at the time of its founding, because of Podesta, CAP was viewed as Hillary Clinton's campaign and government-in-waiting, whenever she decided to run, be it 2004 or 2008.

At exactly the moment when Podesta's influence appeared to be on the wane, the junior senator from Illinois was on the phone. Barack Obama wanted John Podesta to begin planning his administration. So Podesta—certainly not of the new generation Obama had been promising to bring with him to the White House—was surprised. After all, he believed the Obama team saw him as a Clinton insider, which made him an enemy in the eyes of some Obama loyalists. Indeed, two of Obama's most trusted lieutenants in particular—David Axelrod, his chief political strategist, and Robert Gibbs, his longtime press secretary—earned a reputation for blocking Clintonites from the Obama inner circle, both in the general election campaign in 2008 and eventually in the White House itself. But here was Obama, reaching out.

They met the following month, in July 2008. And despite (or perhaps because of) the fact that the two men—one a longtime insider, one an outsider who had promised to shake up the insiders—had little in the way of a preexisting relationship, there wasn't much chitchat in their first encounter. It was, Podesta later recalled, all business. "We were way into the nuts and bolts right from the get-go," he said. Of all the former Clinton insiders, Obama was told, Podesta was the least Kool-Aid drinking. During the Clinton years, there was a group of Democrats who didn't comfortably call themselves FOBs (Friends of Bill). Most of them ended up very close to the congressional wing of the Democratic Party, confidants of folks like Dick Gephardt, onetime leader of the House Democrats, and Tom Daschle, Senate Democratic leader from 1994 to 2004. And Podesta straddled that world well. Daschle, who had become close to Team Obama throughout 2008, essentially signed off on Podesta as a Clintonista who could be trusted.

But part of Obama's outreach to the Clinton old guard was out of necessity. Unlike most folks who run for president, Obama didn't have a network of people to reach out to, whether the subject was foreign policy or health care. He was that new to the scene. And the prospect of filling a government meant Obama had to have an open mind about Clinton veterans. Who else was there, really? There were only so many Democrats in 2008 who had zero ties to the Clintons, and just about every one of them was already involved with the campaign. And of course the incoming president had been in Washington only a few years, far too short a time to develop his own network of qualified candidates. Eventually he would fill numerous positions with Washington outsiders, but at the beginning, if Obama had limited himself to those who had no ties to the Clinton White House, he might not have been able to fill every job in the West Wing, let alone an entire executive branch.

As the months went on, Obama began taking the transition planning more seriously—the job is actually so big post-9/11 that it is now expected that major presidential nominees start the process, even knowing that there's a good chance they might *not* be elected. Podesta, with Obama's consent, pulled together a roster of Professional Democrats who'd served with him in the Clinton administration, to begin collecting résumés and putting together names of friends, former colleagues, and rising stars to fill out the next Democratic administration.

Through the Democratic and Republican conventions, the presidential debates, and especially after the early September 2008 tailspin that started with the collapse of Lehman Brothers and the first Troubled Asset Relief Program (TARP) bailout of big banks later that month, the economy increasingly became *the* big issue. Here Obama got an assist from rival John McCain, who stubbornly continued to claim that the fundamentals of the U.S. economy were sound — even saying it again on the Monday after the Lehman collapse. That flew in the face of what many voters were witnessing, and with each McCain declaration of confidence, it began to look more probable that the first Obama administration would be taking office the following January. And as this change in focus for the campaign came to be, so did Podesta's focus on the transition. Suddenly, putting together a top-notch economic team that seemed ready to deal with a huge challenge was a necessity. And this is where Podesta's ties to the Clintons gave him more cachet with candidate Obama, since the Clinton era was viewed by the public as an economic success. And whether Obama believed the Clinton '90s economic team was the right way to go, it didn't matter at this point; Podesta's experience meant the list of folks he would present Obama to choose from would be veterans of the Clinton years.

*   *   *

Obama came to the U.S. Senate in January 2005, after winning a difficult Democratic primary election through more than a little bit of luck—his wealthy primary opponent's embarrassing divorce records happened to leak to the press (a leak that some in Illinois Democratic politics still believe Obama aides engineered). His general election matchup followed the same pattern: Republican Jack Ryan, a potentially strong opponent, imploded, thanks to embarrassing divorce records. (Ryan reportedly asked his wife, a famous actress, to have sex with him in swinger clubs; he may be the only politician in history whose sex scandal boiled down to his wanting to have sex with his own wife, not another woman.) When Ryan dropped out of the race, Illinois Republicans cast their lot with former radio host and frequent presidential candidate Alan Keyes. Obama rolled up more than seven in ten voters to win a seat previously held by a Republican.

Senator Tom Daschle recognized a political talent when he saw one—as did those who had been watching the Democratic National Convention three months earlier. There, Obama had been chosen by John Kerry's campaign to make the keynote address, and, writing the speech himself, Obama knocked it way out of the park and essentially became *the* rising star of the Democratic Party.

As Obama was cruising toward that Senate win,

Daschle was in the fight of his life as he sought to keep his seat in South Dakota, a state George W. Bush was going to win by twenty points or more in that year's presidential election. When Republican John Thune beat him by just a handful of votes that fall, Daschle's Capitol Hill days were over. Meanwhile, Barack Obama's were just beginning.

Daschle's defeat was a loss for the party, but he would leave a legacy within Democratic circles. In party politics over the past two decades there have been a few camps to which the best party activists remain loyal. The Clintons own a cadre of top strategists. So did House Democratic leader Dick Gephardt. Nancy Pelosi, who would become the first female Speaker of the House in American history after the 2006 Democratic landslide, owned the friendship and devotion of most of the party's major fund-raisers and donors on the two coasts. And though there were a few other clans—the Ted Kennedy clique, the Paul Wellstone veterans, the Bill Bradley acolytes—only one group could legitimately take on the Clinton machine in a political street fight: the Tom Daschle gang.

In Washington, Daschle had come to power by putting in his time. He patiently worked his way up the seniority ladder, courted the votes of his colleagues, and eventually took over when Maine senator George Mitchell quit as Democratic leader in 1994. On his way to the top, Daschle collected a staff that reads like a who's who of Democratic insider politics of the twenty-first century—names unknown outside of the Washington metro area but backroom and cloakroom celebrities within it. They were the muscle.

No one better embodied the Daschle staffer, the powerful but soft-spoken insider, than his long-time chief of staff, Pete Rouse. Rumpled, a tad over-weight and understated, Rouse never seemed to revel in the amount of power he wielded. When Daschle led the Senate Democratic Caucus, observers called Rouse the 101st senator, for his ability to deal directly with the principals necessary to get a bill passed, an amendment adopted, or a procedural hurdle overcome. It is rare for a staffer to be able to deal directly with a member of Congress, much less an egomaniacal senator; the unassuming Rouse had no trouble doing so.

After Daschle's loss, Rouse was determined to get out of government and go through Washington's revolving door to make some money. Daschle himself thought his old friend was burned-out, ready to take a break from Capitol Hill. But as Daschle spoke with Senator-elect Barack Obama, he became convinced that the new guy had a future and that he needed an experienced chief of staff to navigate the pitfalls that threatened a freshman senator, especially one who might have his eye on national office down the line. He needed Pete Rouse. So Daschle persuaded Obama to give his chief of staff a call. Obama did; Rouse wasn't interested.

That changed with a little help from the outgoing Senate Democratic leader. Daschle and Rouse talked; if only they could get Obama off on the right foot, they thought, the sky might be the limit for the Illinois freshman. Encouraged by Daschle's efforts, Obama came at Rouse again. "Barack worked on Pete for a long time," Daschle later recalled. "[Pete] and I both had such an affection for Barack and thought he had so much potential." Rouse agreed to take the job for six weeks, until Obama had a staff and his feet had hit the ground. Then Rouse agreed to stay a few more months. Rouse would finally leave Obama's employ toward the end of 2013, nearly nine years after agreeing to be Obama's chief of staff for six weeks. It actually became a running West Wing joke for those four-plus years Rouse was around: he was always leaving in about six months.

Rouse's hiring is particularly revealing in light of the presidency to come. One of Obama's first acts in Washington, kicking off a career that would ostensibly be dedicated to changing the way the Capitol works, was to hire—and then keep—one of the most plugged-in Democratic insiders the city had to offer. Rouse, and the insiders who would later join him, were Obama's acknowledgment that he lacked the expertise to navigate the Washington thicket. But there was more to it than just that. Obama saw himself as a Washington change agent — as he does now — and yet there was a devil to deal with. One could win an election running as an outsider, someone uncorrupted by the Washington swamp, but once there, the outsider finds there is no way into the rooms where decisions are made. Before you can teach the town to speak a foreign language you have to be fluent in its native tongue. This dilemma dogs Obama today: how to be out while in, how to be in while out. Obama knows this intellectually but in practice struggles with it. And he's terrible at faking it. He expects folks to rationally view a problem the way he views it. And when they don't, he assumes they're simply playing politics and loses patience quickly. For instance, at the start of his second term, the president hosted a series of dinners with Republican senators. It was an idea his new chief of staff at the time, Denis McDonough, came up with. Obama agreed in principle, but the practice was not nearly as rewarding for these senators as it could have been. While all who attended acknowledged the president was serious about reaching out and about figuring out how to do something big, the follow-through wasn't there. A few senators even softened their anger toward the president, but because these Republicans got the distinct impression he was there under pressure from McDonough and not because he wanted to be, the occasions didn't do what they should have done—make new potential frenemies. It really served as an opportunity for Denis, as chief of staff, to make key connections in the Senate, which just doesn't produce the results a presidential relationship could.

From the moment he hired Rouse, back in 2005, Obama had designs on the leadership of the Daschle gang. As it turned out, most of that gang, from the senior operatives to the most junior members, would follow Rouse's lead. Just a year into Obama's term in the Senate, Anita Dunn, like Podesta a veteran of Daschle's Senate office and a permanent member of the Professional Democrats, came on board Team Obama to help advise his political action committee. Rouse, whose job was to keep Obama's options open, asked her to get involved. "We don't know what we're going to do with this thing," Rouse told Dunn; the idea that Obama might run for the governorship of Illinois in 2010, or even president in 2008 or 2012, went unspoken.

Now, almost four years later, 1600 Pennsylvania in sight, Obama was sending Podesta, his transition chief, mixed signals. On one hand, he wanted to make it clear that his election signaled a new and different way of doing business in Washington; a part of that was bringing in a new and different cadre of government officials. Longtime Obama friends such as Valerie Jarrett, Michael Froman, and Julius Genachowski would be occupying the top ranks of his administration. But at the same time, Obama's ideas for other, more prominent positions— positions that might find themselves defending Obama administration policy on Sunday morning talk shows—seemed decidedly establishmentarian. And whenever an acolyte would bring up this contradiction to Obama himself, his answer would be the same: *I'm* enough change.

For many who served under him, that claim would prove both insubstantial and detrimental. "Obama thinks he is the agent of change," concluded one disappointed insider. "So he gives a lot of leeway to having establishment people around him sometimes. He thinks that as long as he's president, he'll drive that change." But "he hasn't always used personnel to do it."

Of course "always" doesn't mean "never," and hardly anyone in the Obama administration proved that point better than the vice president—a loyalist first.

New York congressman Anthony Weiner was not well liked among his fellow House Democrats, even before the salacious scandal that erupted when a self-portrait of Weiner's nether regions, mistakenly posted to Twitter, cost him his career in Congress. Weiner was loud and confrontational, less a legislator than a bomb-thrower; a made-for-twenty-first-century-cable-TV officeholder, not an old-school legislator. He was known among colleagues for angry, accusatory speeches on the House floor; he was known among his legions of fans for his take-no-prisoners rants on the cable news channels. (Weiner was one of the few Democrats who would willingly, almost gleefully, take on any Fox News host who came his way, angling for a YouTube moment.)

There had been a time early on in Obama's first term when a group of angry congressional Democrats were up in arms over what they saw as the president's spineless capitulation to Republican talking points and position papers in an attempt to gain support from a GOP out to destroy him. With his colleagues watching, Weiner decided to confront Joe Biden and treat him like Sean Hannity, bellowing that the president needed to change his whole approach. Obama was acting like a "negotiator in chief," Weiner snapped, instead of acting like a leader.

His comments found the end of Biden's rope. "There's no goddamned way," Biden roared, losing his temper. In front of the assembled Democrats, his face flashing red before he detonated, he told Weiner (and by extension all gathered), "I'm not going to stand here and talk about the president like that!"[1]

On the surface, such an outburst from the man first in line for the presidency could have seemed reckless, possibly undermining his own reputation and relations between the White House and fellow Democrats. But to those who knew and worked with Joseph Robinette Biden Jr., it was a moment that clarified the way he saw himself in an administration in which his position had not always been clear: Biden was choosing sides, and the side he chose was Barack Obama's. It was steel reinforcement for what had become an already good, loyal relationship with the man in the Oval Office.

The moment a presidential candidate chooses a running mate, his campaign begins peddling an awkward, tortured, and almost entirely false narrative. The two ticket-mates, as the campaign will tell it, are thick as thieves. They get along famously, there are no policy differences between the two of them, and if elected, they'll govern in complete harmony.

In reality, that's almost never the case. Ronald Reagan and George H. W. Bush were barely on speaking terms after a bitter 1980 primary season that pitted two of the Republican Party's best-known faces against each other. Bush wasn't even Reagan's first choice for the job; he was the compromise after former president Gerald Ford refused to join the ticket. Bush picked Dan Quayle, a little-known senator whose verbal gaffes delighted the media and embarrassed the White House. Bill Clinton made a counterintuitive choice in Al Gore, tapping someone from a neighboring state; but their constant side-by-side campaigning forged a personal bond, and the image the two baby boomers projected was one of generational change that resonated with voters. Gore never felt fully like an insider once the presidency began. But only after Clinton was impeached by Congress and Gore's thoughts turned to his own presidential chances, which he believed were hurt by Clinton's personal shortcomings, did the relationship truly turn sour.

Where Clinton and Gore had demonstrated a generational harmony and some ideological common ground (remember that Al Gore, circa 1992, was considered a moderate-to-conservative classic Southern Democrat), the difference in age between the younger Obama and the older Biden couldn't have been more stark; the *New York Times* once noted that they were farther apart in age (nineteen years) than their West Wing offices were in steps (seventeen).

During the 2008 primaries, when Biden ran an underfunded shoestring bid, he had been critical of Obama's lack of experience. And at one point, he inadvertently insulted not just Obama but African Americans in general, calling him "the first mainstream African American who is articulate and bright and clean and a nice-looking guy." It had been the prototypical Biden gaffe, a well-intentioned effort at a compliment that had come across as boneheaded, belittling, even racially tinged. Biden, who counts himself a champion of civil rights, called to personally apologize; Obama accepted, and promised there were no hard feelings. And as the primary campaign wore on and the candidates spent more time together at a slew of debates, Obama found himself impressed with Biden's nimbleness when the spotlight was on. Arguably, Biden won (at least on points from actual debate coaches) just about every debate he participated in during the 2007 portion of the 2008 campaign. And Biden did it without belittling Obama on the most public of stages. Of course, those debate victories did nothing for Biden with the voters, but they left an impression with the one person who would ultimately matter.

When Obama began narrowing his choice of a vice president, Biden's was the name on the short list that at first looked most out of place. No way a guy campaigning as the change candidate picks the guy with the most congressional experience. But Team Obama had a "do no harm" strategy when narrowing their VP choices. The biggest reach on the short list was Virginia governor Tim Kaine, the first major Democrat to endorse Obama in the primary campaign and the closest in age; picking Kaine would have been akin to Clinton's 1992 choice of Gore—a generational, change ticket. And Kaine was seen as someone who would also help lock in a state in a year when some Democrats actually doubted Virginia's place in the swing state category. But Kaine would have reinforced the inexperience talking point, something the campaign was still a tad nervous about.

The poster boy of the "do no harm" short list was the lone centrist on the list, Indiana's Evan

Bayh—also young, but after four terms in state-level office, including two as governor, and two terms in the U.S. Senate, someone with much more governing experience than Obama had. Bayh, however, was just a tad too conservative and, well, underwhelming for Obama's taste. Indeed, his legislative footprint was about as nonexistent as Obama's, and yet Bayh had been there twice as long.

Biden certainly had negatives. If Obama was running against Washington, how did it make sense to choose a man who had spent his entire adult life in public office and more than three decades in the United States Senate? Biden's undisciplined side was legendary; even before he became vice president, the term "Bidenism"—a dopey, quotable gem that tumbled from Biden's never-still mouth—was routinely used by the Capitol Hill press corps.

But Biden brought to the table what Obama couldn't: unassailable foreign policy credentials, deep relationships with some of the United States' most important allies across the globe, and long-standing relationships with members of Congress—Republicans and Democrats—whose votes would be necessary to advance the president's agenda. In short, Biden was a player, and if picking a running mate is about filling a void the nominee has, Biden filled the "Washington insider" void.

"The day that Clinton picks Gore, he's in third

place in a three-way race for the presidency. Not first, not second, third," said Ron Klain, the longtime Democratic operative who served as chief of staff to both Biden and Gore. "Within a week of the time he picks Gore, he's gone from third place to first place. As a result, from the start, the concept of the Clinton-Gore ticket was, partners." Gore got a similar boost from his running mate pick in 2000, when Joe Lieberman's selection coincided with a surge of enthusiasm for the Democratic ticket that brought the race back to even for the duration.

Obama, on the other hand, was firmly in the lead by August 2008, when he needed to pick a vice president. His advisors didn't want to do anything to change the fundamental structure of the race. "They didn't want a game-changing choice. They liked their game," Klain said. "I honestly believe, if they could have found a thing in the Constitution that said, 'You don't have to have a vice president,' they didn't need one."

Biden himself harbored doubts. After all, he had made the decision to run for president because he believed he would make the best president. That feeling was hard to let go; he believed even after accepting the invitation to join the ticket that he would have made a better president than Obama. Biden's closest aides told him to knock it off, but in his mind that feeling persisted.

His sense of being unfairly diminished wasn't

helped by the Obama team's practice, almost from the beginning, of keeping Biden at a distance. Aside from a brief bus tour, a joint appearance at the Democratic convention, and the odd moment when they happened to be in the same state at the same time, the two men didn't spend much time getting to know each other. And Obama's advisors were certainly wary of another Bidenism that would reflect badly on the ticket. Nobody was more leery of the Biden pick from the get-go than the chief architect of the Obama campaign apparatus, David Plouffe. It was a skepticism that would never truly go away.

As the economy cratered in the late summer and early fall of 2008, and as it became clearer that Obama would be the next president, he spent hours every day on the phone with Hank Paulson, Bush's treasury secretary, receiving briefings on an economic disaster he would inherit. When John McCain suspended his campaign in September, ostensibly to return to Washington to deal with the crisis, and the two candidates joined a briefing at the White House, Biden saw a sullen, withdrawn McCain contrasted with the engaged, animated Obama. At the height of a crisis, one neither of his making nor his responsibility, Obama was acting like a leader, Biden thought. Then after the pair had won, when economic advisors made clear to Obama just how bad the economic recession they faced would be, a thought crossed Biden's mind, according to those close to him: they got the order of this ticket just right. At that point, Biden abandoned any misgivings he harbored about Obama during the campaign.

Biden had developed on the stump his own peculiar mannerisms during his four-decade career in politics. Anyone who had seen him speak to an audience more than once almost certainly heard some old saying that his mother, father, grandfather, or grandmother had used. He took to heart the lessons learned in his hometown of Scranton, Pennsylvania, building a kind of guiding morality based on old-fashioned American Rust Belt values. And while politicians earned a reputation for making promises they couldn't or wouldn't keep, that morality required Biden to pledge — repeatedly — that whatever he said, he would do. He routinely gave his "word as a Biden," a phrase that assumed an intimacy with his audiences.

Those quirks, that intimacy, were key elements of Biden's natural skill as a politician. What Obama brought to the ticket in soaring rhetoric and the sheer ability to give a speech, Biden brought in retail political skills. The man who hated the backslapping nature of politics in Washington had picked the consummate backslapper to be his vice president. Walk into the Oval Office with your family and the president will be very courteous, give you a warm handshake, perhaps say something fun to your kids. Walk into the vice president's residence and get ready for a

lot of touching. If you have young kids, Biden immediately picks them up and treats them like his own
grandkids; for the adults, man hugs, and kisses for
the women. It's just in his DNA—just as much as
being less huggy and kissy is in Obama's.

Biden had watched eight vice presidents of the
United States from his perch as a Delaware senator,
beginning with Spiro Agnew, who resigned nine
months into Biden's first term. Unlike for the office
of president, there is little guidance for what a vice
president ought to do, save casting the occasional
tie-breaking vote in the Senate. And Biden's predecessors had traveled dramatically different paths. Dan
Quayle had been relegated to the sidelines in George
H. W. Bush's White House. Bush himself had routinely been the last advisor in the room with Ronald
Reagan before Reagan made a critical decision, hiding his own views from others so that the staff never
quite knew where he stood (a trait that Obama's
first defense secretary admitted he wished Biden
would adopt). Al Gore had worked more hand in
glove with Clinton than had any VP of the modern
era, and Cheney, of course, one-upped Gore and
was put in charge of large swaths of George W. Bush's
White House, from an energy task force to an aggressive foreign policy—at least in the first term, until
that relationship soured late in the second.

Biden wanted to learn from his predecessors, to
adopt their best practices. Before he'd agreed to serve

on the ticket, he'd thought of the office in about the same terms as had John Nance Garner, the Texan who served two terms as Franklin Roosevelt's vice president. Garner quit because the office wasn't worth "a bucket of warm piss." In fact, Biden actually turned down the job when Obama first offered it.

Obama aides on the White House staff, most of them veterans of the campaign, had worried about the prospect of Hillary Clinton serving as secretary of state. Robert Gibbs and David Axelrod had even argued against choosing her. And some felt a similar distrust toward Biden, albeit nowhere near the level of their distrust of Clinton. But as Biden proved again and again, that distrust was misplaced. In Secret Service terms, Biden was the type of guy who in politics, once you earned his loyalty, would take a bullet for you. There would be no greater defender of the Obama brand, no one who would so readily subsume his own reputation in an effort to protect the team, than Biden.

Biden made clear that he didn't want a portfolio — primary responsibility for a specific area of policy — like Dick Cheney had carved out for himself. But he told Obama he wanted his opinion considered; he wanted to be the last person in the room. In hindsight, Biden couldn't believe he'd almost resisted Obama's offer and was relieved he was asked a second time. He regularly told anyone willing to listen that even he was astonished at how little a part he played, as a sitting senator, in running the government's operations. He now believed there was no job other than vice president that prepares anyone to be president — not forty years in the Senate, not ten years as a governor, nothing. And, typically for Biden, he said this wholeheartedly and with the best of intent, without realizing what it might say about his boss's qualifications for the job.

During the first two weeks of their term, Biden committed two trademark Bidenisms that made Obama aides nervous about their vice president. During the inauguration, Chief Justice John Roberts had flubbed his lines while he administered the oath of office to President Obama. What hadn't seemed like a big deal at the time made some in the White House nervous; if Obama hadn't said exactly the right words in exactly the right order, did that mean he wasn't president? Some extreme Obama-haters had already begun to spread rumors that Obama's Hawaii birth certificate was fake, that he had been born in Kenya and was thus ineligible to serve as president. And while Team Obama would pretend publicly the whole birtherism stuff was crazy noise and not a serious concern, they did show some sensitivity. So to assuage any possible doubts, the White House invited Roberts to administer the oath again, in a private ceremony.

And just as Chief of Staff Rahm Emanuel was

reaching out to the Supreme Court to extend the invitation to Roberts, Obama and Biden were administering the oaths of office that White House senior staffers would take in front of the public. In a meeting room in the Eisenhower Executive Office Building, the ornate, many-columned warren of offices that stands between the White House and Seventeenth Street, Obama asked Biden to read the oath.

"For the senior staff, all right," Biden said, asking for a card with the oath's text. "My memory is not as good as Justice Roberts', Chief Justice Roberts'." The thirty or so staffers in the room understood Biden's dig, and they laughed at the joke. A smile broke out on Biden's face. But Obama flashed irritation he hadn't shown before; he blanched, as one person in the room described it, scowled, and shook his head. He reached out to Biden to cut him off. Later, he admonished Biden, who called Roberts to apologize.[2]

The second Bidenism happened a few weeks later, when Biden addressed House Democrats at an annual retreat. He confessed that crafting a stimulus measure that would spend hundreds of billions of dollars in a bid to revive the stagnant economy carried with it political risks, and that even a perfect bill wouldn't insulate them completely. "If we do everything right, if we do it with absolute certainty, there's still a 30 percent chance we're going to get it wrong," he said.[3] This was a classic "Washington gaffe," as defined by longtime liberal columnist Michael Kinsley, when a politician accidentally speaks the truth but ends up causing a political headache. At a press conference the following day, Biden's boss, who saw the question coming, took a verbal poke at his own vice president.

"I don't remember exactly what Joe was referring to, not surprisingly," Obama said. "But let me try this out. I think what Joe may have been suggesting, although I wouldn't put numerical — I wouldn't ascribe any numerical percentage to any of this — is that given the magnitude of the challenges that we have, any single thing that we do is going to be part of the solution, not all of the solution."[4]

Biden was incensed. It was the first time Obama had made a joke at his expense, and in a nationally televised press conference, at that. The two men then sat down in the Oval Office, where each made clear to the other that he wasn't happy with the situation.

While this was the first time Obama had dialed back Biden publicly, it was the second time he'd done so since selecting him as his running mate. In the fall of 2008, Biden had defended Obama's lack of foreign policy experience to a group of reporters. He had answered a question by saying that what the Democratic candidate lacked in experience, he made up for in vision. As far as Obama was concerned, in saying this, Biden had agreed with the premise *too* much. Obama promptly called up his running mate and privately let him know that it was not Biden's job to defend his inexperience. Biden was used to dealing with self-assured politicians—after all, he was one himself—so he took the rebuke in stride. But his takeaway from the incident was that one thing Obama didn't do well was accept even the mildest of friendly critiques.

At around the same time, Obama brought up the subject of Hillary Clinton to Podesta one day early in the fall of 2008, two months before he offered her the job, suggesting that his old rival might be the perfect person to take over as secretary of state. Podesta actually saw Clinton as a potential secretary of defense, but Obama had another idea. He had already told Rahm Emanuel, the Illinois congressman and Clinton administration veteran who had barely concealed designs on Pelosi's speakership—and who was the personification of partisan warfare in Washington—that he wanted him to serve as his chief of staff. Biden was in place, and, based on a few conversations he had had with one of his few real friends in Washington, Obama began trying to find a way to keep another insider— this one a bona fide Republican—on board. Just a few weeks after he became the Democratic nominee, Obama decided he was going to attempt to convince Robert Gates to stay on as secretary of defense.

The idea to keep George W. Bush's Pentagon chief on the job began to germinate in July 2008, when the candidate traveled to Iraq, Afghanistan, and a few other Middle Eastern countries. The stated mission of the trip was to give Obama, a member of the Senate Foreign Relations Committee, and his companions a view of the situation on the ground. The real reason, one formulated more by his campaign in Chicago than by his Senate office in Washington, was to give the Democratic presidential nominee a chance to bolster his foreign policy credentials at a moment when voters were just beginning to tune in to the fall's presidential contest.

Obama, clearly cognizant of his own perceived inexperience in foreign policy matters, had asked Rhode Island senator Jack Reed to organize the trip. The two men could hardly have come from more different backgrounds. One was a community organizer who spent his formative years engaged in social justice campaigns in hardscrabble areas of Chicago. The other was a northeastern Catholic who graduated from West Point and served as a U.S. Army Ranger. But the two got along; in fact, while few people in Washington count themselves as true friends of Barack Obama, he and Reed hit it off so well from the beginning of Obama's time in the Senate that today many see Reed as one of the few conduits to the White House. (Although Reed, like many folks identified as "close Obama confidants," admits that the two, while friendly, aren't particularly close.)

So when Obama asked Reed to organize the trip,

he was turning to the closest thing he had to a friend in the U.S. Senate. Such congressional delegation expeditions—CODELs in Washington-speak—are paid for with taxpayer money, and are thus required to include members of both political parties. To fulfill this requirement, Reed turned to a friend of his own, a fellow army veteran named Chuck Hagel. Obama, who knew Hagel from the Foreign Relations Committee and was aware of his relationship with Reed, could have easily guessed the choice—in fact, he was counting on it; Reed and Hagel were thick as thieves. A tour of Reed's Senate office shows nearly as many photographs of Hagel as it does of Reed. The two traveled overseas together a lot when they were serving in the Senate.

The company wasn't bad politics, either. Obama had yet to pick a running mate, and some news outlets speculated that Hagel—a close friend of McCain's and, eventually, of Obama's—was on the Democrat's vice presidential short list. For the obvious political gain, the Obama campaign did nothing to dissuade people from thinking this. Hagel's wife was a prominent late endorser of Obama, attended a debate as a guest of Michelle Obama in 2008, and was a donor. It was toward the end of his Senate career in 2008 as a Republican that Hagel started to publicly break from his party, particularly on Iraq.

The trip itself was a study in generational—or perhaps cultural—differences. Reed and Hagel, both veterans of military service and of the U.S. Senate, spent their time on the military aircraft swapping stories, trading jokes, playing cards, and gossiping about fellow senators. Obama, the youngest of the three and the newest to the senatorial club, spent his time studying notebooks on policy and doing good old-fashioned debate prep. "He was very disciplined about doing some work," Reed recalled years later. "We were less so, more like old guys hanging out together."

The possibility—perhaps the likelihood—that he would assume the presidency was clearly on Obama's mind at the time, which also explains why he was less than good company during this trip. A meeting with General David Petraeus, then the commander of allied forces in Iraq, turned unusually formal and slightly tense. "You've got to understand, as I think I understand, my role versus your role" in crafting war policy, Obama told the general.

For his part, Petraeus was just as formal, and decided to use his time with his potential new boss to persuade him about the surge and try to convince the country's most famous Iraq skeptic that progress was being made. Using PowerPoint, Petraeus didn't quite seem to get the hint that his presentation was coming across more as a lecture than as an explanation. Later claims that the two really got off on the wrong foot were probably overstated, but it was clear during this first meeting between Obama and Petraeus that each was sizing up the other, the way two alpha dogs might. And that lecture/debate that the two had in front of Reed and Hagel drove the perception for years that these men never saw either major war the same way.

It was on this trip that Obama began discussing his administration with Reed, the colleague he trusted most on issues of war, peace, and the Pentagon. No soldier himself, Obama knew he would face trouble relating to generals who had spent a lifetime in the military, fighting wars and building the bureaucracy of a Washington establishment that had been growing at a rapid pace for more than half a century. When Dwight Eisenhower gave his famous speech warning of the growing power of the military-industrial complex in 1961, Barack Obama hadn't even been conceived.

So, during the trip overseas, Obama asked Reed what he thought should happen at the Pentagon. This was actually Obama's way of sizing up Reed himself for the job. Whether or not he realized that the president-to-be was sorta, kinda interviewing him, Reed shifted the discussion immediately in another direction. Reed said he believed that the two ongoing wars, plus the deepening economic crisis at home, meant there had to be some continuity within the ranks of the military. That moment of instability abroad and at home was no time to go about inflicting new instability where there need be none. Reed made it known he wouldn't just support the idea of keeping Robert Gates on the job—he wanted it to happen.

But that was no simple task, and only recently have presidents asked members of the opposition party to serve in their cabinets. Yes, George W. Bush asked Norm Mineta, a former Democratic congressman from California and Bill Clinton's last commerce secretary, to stay on as head of Bush's Transportation Department, hardly a high-profile assignment. To ask Gates, the head of Bush's war-planning department, to stick around in the same position for a new president who'd won the Democratic primary by being farther to the left, more opposed than any of his opponents to the war in Iraq, was another leap altogether, one even Obama's most dedicated supporters would have trouble understanding.

And yet the request was very much in line with Obama's sense of self—political and personal. He had always straddled lines—part black, part white; a childhood overseas and at the very edge of America; Barry to Barack—and knew that labels could be a barrier, not a blessing. He also had a sense of historical grandeur. As part of its sales pitch to some key political elites, his campaign leaked (in such a way that it would become widely known) that in preparation for taking office he read Doris Kearns Goodwin's *Team of Rivals,* an account of how Lincoln

gathered into his cabinet several of his fiercest antag-
onists. Bringing Hillary into the administration
would follow such a formula, and the idea of retaining Gates might have been even more appealing in
terms of the "Obama as transcendent" narrative.
And yet it was about more than the precedent set by
an earlier Illinois politician: Obama was following a
presidential term that had gotten the rap, fairly or
not, of being not-ready-for-prime-time in certain
areas, from FEMA to the Pentagon to a sometimes
rogue office of the vice presidency. Given that issue,
and Obama's own perceived inexperience, there was a
focus on trying to bring in big personalities in the
cabinet or, in the case of Gates, keep one. In keeping with the spirit of the postpartisanship brand
Obama had been creating for himself since 2004, it
would have been odd if he couldn't find places for
political rivals and even Republicans in his cabinet.
He had to show he could walk the walk on building
a real bipartisan team. Gates's agreeing to stay on
would send that message loudly.

It fell to Reed to make the sale. A few months
after their trip to Afghanistan and Iraq, Obama's
transition team asked Reed to reach out to Gates to
gauge his interest. Initially skeptical that such a relationship could work, Gates used Reed in the same
manner, asking questions about the arrangement
through the Rhode Islander to see how serious Obama
was. And cognizant of how the politics of Washing-

ton are played, Gates never let the discussions leak. It was quite an impressive feat and is proof that when someone *does* want to keep a secret in Washington, it can be done.

Over several weeks of back-and-forth, Reed made it clear that the Democratic nominee was very serious about keeping Gates on board. But there was another factor at play: Gates wanted to retire. Before being brought back into government service as Bush's SecDef, he had had a comfortable, even joyful, position as president of Texas A&M University. He attended Aggie football games, he showed up at the school's weekly Yell (the rally held on campus before game day), and he even posted anonymously to Aggie football message boards. He would have liked nothing better than to return to the academic sector, according to his closest aides.

But thanks to Reed, Obama knew something about Gates that would serve as his trump card, and more than once: Robert Gates was a patriot, someone with a deep sense of service and duty to country, someone who couldn't say no when a president asked him to serve a little longer. What's more, Gates felt an almost paternalistic obligation to those in the field, the troops he commanded, particularly post-surge and during a time of deep unpopularity of the wars.

Still, Gates was truly conflicted. Recalled chairman of the Joint Chiefs Mike Mullen, "Gates and I

talked about this a lot, and he had very mixed feelings. One of Gates's greatest strengths and a weakness is he's such a public servant. There's nobody
that represents better the cliché in town which is,
you know, if you don't want the president to ask
you, you'd better intercept it before the phone
rings. You'd better get the message over there, please
don't make the call." Gates never asked Obama *not*
to ask, setting the silent signal that he was open to
persuasion.*

Shortly after Obama won the election, the two
met face-to-face for the first time. The clandestine
encounter took place at a firehouse on the grounds
of Washington's Reagan National Airport—perhaps
unintentionally symbolic, given that Gates's first job
in the White House with any real seniority had been
in Ronald Reagan's administration.

Gates had given Obama's team a list of questions
before the meeting, a bold move for a prospective
employee meeting a prospective employer, even in a
relationship as sensitive as that between a defense
secretary and a president. The questions were both
stylistic and policy based, according to those familiar with the meeting. Obama pulled the list from
his inside coat pocket, which impressed Gates; they
went over it point by point, and by the end of the

---

* Pre-election, Obama wasn't the only potential president interested in
 keeping Gates. John McCain's team had also let it be known that if
 he won, Gates would be asked to stay on.

brief encounter, they both believed they would make a good fit. One Gates confidant admitted that the minute Obama pulled out his questions was the moment Gates knew he was staying on board— Gates saw it as a sign of respect.

In fact, even before they got to Gates's questions, the secretary of defense was preparing to stay on for the new commander in chief. But he wanted to keep his senior staff, too, at least until new officials could be appointed and confirmed by the Senate. The Obama people disagreed on a few names, including Gates's chief of staff, a longtime committed Republican, and Geoff Morrell, the Pentagon's spokesman, but the soon-to-be president overruled his own staff, and Gates kept his aides.*

Only a few media outlets got wind that Gates might be sticking around for another tour, but what reporters were really concerned with was whether Barack Obama would offer Hillary Clinton a job, whether she would take it, and what that said about

---

* When Morrell, a former ABC News reporter who had left journalism to serve Gates, had asked Bush in an Oval Office meeting on Election Day 2008 whether Gates should stay on in the new administration, the president, in front of Dana Perino, his press secretary, and Ed Gillespie, his political director, told the Pentagon spokesman that he absolutely had to remain to serve the transition. Bush kept bringing up the issue with Morrell's friends, who further conveyed the outgoing president's wishes. Morrell sensed that Bush, who had been Barack Obama's punching bag during the campaign, got a small sense of satisfaction that the new president needed Gates.

the rift between Clinton and Obama, a schism that once appeared to threaten the very fabric of the Democratic coalition.

In fact, Obama had been intent on hiring Clinton for a long time. His staff likes to say he had decided she would make a strong secretary of state during the primaries, presumably as she was ripping into one of his policies on a debate stage or in yet another negative advertisement. But for Obama, bringing Clinton into the fold meant avoiding a pitfall several of his predecessors hadn't: he could co-opt an intraparty rival.

Such an olive branch was something other presidents hadn't been able to stomach (and perhaps other presidents succumbed to staff pressure a tad more easily). After winning the Republican nomination, and then the presidency, in 2000, George W. Bush made no effort to bring John McCain into his administration. (In fact, the bad blood between the two men was so substantial that some Democrats, including John Kerry, believed they might be able to recruit McCain for the VP slot on the 2004 Democratic ticket.)

Jimmy Carter made the same mistake in 1976, when he never paid the Kennedy family its due, never even asked Ted Kennedy to come on board the ticket. Carter, like Obama, was riding a wave of change that had swept a public sickened by the most dramatic inside-Washington scandal, Watergate.

Carter, a bit of a true believer in himself, was moralistic to a fault and thought reaching out to someone like Kennedy would undermine his credibility as a change agent. No name screamed "Washington insider" in the mid-1970s like Kennedy. Carter's snub helped create the first crack in the Democratic Party that would become a full-fledged fracture by 1980, as Kennedy ended up challenging Carter for the Democratic nomination (to this day, Carter believes it cost him the general election against Ronald Reagan).

In turn, the bitterly fought primary campaign of 1980 made Reagan and George H. W. Bush rivals for the same job. But after Reagan picked Bush to become his running mate, in no small part to unite the divided Republican Party, their relationship evolved into something more, into a form of mutual dependency. Reagan, the outsider who defined conservatism for a generation of Americans, needed Bush, the consummate insider, to help him navigate the convoluted contours of governing in Washington. And Bush needed Reagan in order to be successful, and to hand over the legacy that would usher him from the vice presidency to the Oval Office.

Still, that sort of accommodation seemed to be the exception, not the rule. Even Lyndon Johnson pushed Robert F. Kennedy aside as early as was politically feasible, sending the attorney general to New York to win a Senate seat rather than keeping him

in the tent—in hindsight, a mistake. And Bobby's
shadow in 1968 helped convince LBJ not to run.
Hillary's husband had a sense of what might happen if you let an opponent walk away. Bill Clinton's
toughest rival by the end of the 1992 campaign was,
arguably, Nebraska's Bob Kerrey. Kerrey didn't get a
job in the Clinton administration; instead he stayed
on in the Senate, where he turned into the go-to guy
for members of the press looking for a Democrat
who would criticize the young president.

Obama learned the lessons Bush, Carter, Johnson, and even Clinton suffered for; he wanted Hillary Clinton on his side. Yet it was more than history
that had inspired him to pursue the woman he'd
defeated only months earlier. Obama saw something
else in Hillary Clinton: raw grit and determination.
Despite their campaign trail rivalry, Obama came
to deeply appreciate Clinton's tenacity. Even when
the numbers looked daunting, even when she would
need to win an almost impossible percentage of the
vote to catch Obama in the delegate count, Clinton
hadn't given up. If the roles had been reversed, Obama
sometimes wondered, would he have done the same?
Or would he have thrown in the towel? Short answer:
he probably would have folded a lot sooner than she
did.

Since she was interested in the vice presidency
only if she was guaranteed the job, that left secretary of state, a position that gave her the potential to

bolster her credentials abroad and that gave Obama two huge advantages: On one hand, Clinton was a global superstar in her own right, someone who would command attention and respect from friends and enemies alike, someone who could give a rookie president instant credibility on the international stage. On the other, secretary of state is a traditionally apolitical position; Clinton would be precluded from offering her take on domestic politics, robbing the media of a juicy Obama-versus-Clinton story line. Picking Clinton to be his secretary of state would put her in "a box," explained one veteran of both the Obama and Clinton administrations, albeit "a very impressive, dignified, special box."

What's more, while the administration may not have seen the true calamity the Great Recession was about to bring on, Obama knew his first term would be dominated by trying to fix a broken economy. His focus would need to be on the home front, though in his campaign he had promised a more humble America, willing and able to work with the rest of the world. Only someone with an international stature as great as his own could speak for the United States as Obama dealt with domestic issues; that someone was Hillary Clinton.

Her international status allowed Obama to delegate; if a world leader was upset that Obama couldn't personally visit, or wasn't giving the respect that leader felt he deserved, Hillary would be dispatched. While she hadn't spent her life training to be an international diplomat, her two decades in the highest echelons of American politics—as First Lady and as a senator serving on the Armed Services Committee—gave her a broad range of connections with foreign leaders. Clinton would enter office with more international relationships than most of Obama's predecessors could have claimed, with the possible exceptions of George H. W. Bush, Richard Nixon, and Dwight Eisenhower.

Initially, Clinton was skeptical of taking the job in Foggy Bottom. She would be working for someone else, executing his policies, and leaving behind a Senate career that still had promise. There were moments when Clinton saw herself as the logical successor to Ted Kennedy, the next liberal lion of the Senate. But Obama's appeal to her sense of patriotism was a strong pitch. And behind the scenes, Harry Reid, the Senate Democratic leader, was making another thing clear: the Senate still worked on a hierarchical system, and a junior senator with little more than a single term under her belt shouldn't be comparing herself to Ted Kennedy just yet. Reid had no interest in seeing Hillary become the biggest star in his Senate. Such were the ironies of Washington: it was easier for Barack Obama to become president than to become leader of the Senate, and easier for Hillary Clinton to enter the cabinet than somehow take over running the Senate, or even step into leadership.

So Clinton would have returned to the Senate much as she'd left it — as a senator who made headlines but who had little real power in the committee system, not exactly a backbencher but somewhere in the middle, and certainly not someone who had any real chance of climbing the leadership ladder, especially not when Reid and Clinton's senior colleague, New York's Chuck Schumer, were still around. Without a piece of actual Senate real estate to run, she would be relegated to become either a White House Senate ally or one of its chief critics in order to fulfill her own ambitions. Leaving the Senate started to have a lot more appeal.

And then there was the mounting public pressure to take the job, especially from some of her biggest supporters. Private appeals from Podesta, from Obama, and, perhaps most important, from Bill Clinton, were pushing her in the same direction. Reid's coldness only made Clinton's decision easier. The night before accepting the job, she went to bed convinced she would stay in the Senate; by the next day, she had changed her mind. Obama's chief rival would join his cause.

The role of national security advisor is as important and as close to a president as that of chief of staff; it also explains why the national security advisor's office is the only other one in the West Wing, besides the chief of staff's, that has a conference table and a fireplace. It's a plum job and is almost always reserved for someone very close to the president. But Obama didn't have a wise old hand on his foreign policy campaign team who fit the part; Biden was the closest thing, and his position was settled. The folks he would most come to rely on for foreign policy during the campaign were all extremely young. The freshman's top Senate advisor, Mark Lippert, was a Hill staffer who had worked on the Senate Appropriations Committee and served in the Navy Reserve, and he was all of thirty-two years old when he went to work for Obama, in 2005.[5] When Lippert was called up to active duty in 2007, he recruited a senior fellow at the Center for American Progress, another longtime Hill staffer named Denis McDonough, to replace him. McDonough was also a former member of the Tom Daschle mafia, and he was a rising star in Democratic foreign relations circles, but he had been a professional advisor for half as long as some of Clinton's allies.

The third member of Obama's inner circle on foreign affairs had even less experience. Ben Rhodes had been a speechwriter for Lee Hamilton, the former Indiana congressman who cochaired both the 9/11 Commission and the Iraq Study Group during George W. Bush's administration. Rhodes had wanted to get involved in campaigns, and he'd even traveled to New Hampshire with Virginia governor Mark Warner, who was thinking about running in 2008. After Warner decided not to run, in October 2006, Rhodes tried to get on board Obama's campaign, months before a campaign even existed. He pitched in where he could, writing floor statements on foreign policy to help Jon Favreau, Obama's top speechwriter. His big break came in April 2007, when Favreau had to write the candidate's first foreign policy speech. Another speechwriter wasn't getting the job done, so Favreau helped the campaign kill two birds with one stone—they hired a better writer and found someone who understood foreign policy better than the policy staff did. Rhodes spent 2007 backfilling for both teams.

A small number of better-known foreign policy and national security types with Clinton ties chose Obama over Clinton during the campaign, and some even served as prominent surrogates on TV: Susan Rice, who had been a rising star in the State Department back during the Clinton administration; Samantha Power, another veteran of Obama's Senate office and a growing voice advocating a more robust U.S. role in stopping genocide from her perch at Harvard and as author of a prizewinning book on the subject; and Greg Craig, a classmate of both Hillary's and Bill's when they attended Yale Law School in the early 1970s (he even sublet his apartment in New Haven, for seventy-five dollars a month, to the not-yet-married couple).[6] Craig, who had defended Bill Clinton at his impeachment hearing (and who desperately wanted a job in Obama's State Department), sided with Obama over Clinton. So, too, did Tony Lake, Bill's former national security advisor; Lake was the single biggest Democratic foreign policy grand pooh-bah to pick Obama over Clinton, though he played only a small role in actually forming the candidate's foreign policy.

If you thought the general public was putting way too much stock into what an Obama presidency was going to look like, folks in the liberal foreign policy world were taking it to another level. After the Bush era, many of these people thought serving overseas for Obama would be the closest thing they would ever experience to working in an international Utopia (though it sounds naïve in retrospect, the Bush era was viewed that negatively in foreign service circles).

By the time he won the Democratic nomination, the number of folks claiming to be Obama foreign policy advisors had swelled to three hundred, including some of the same Clintonites — such as former secretary of state Madeleine Albright — who, just weeks earlier in one of those end-of-the-campaign desperation hits, had questioned Obama's readiness. To deal with the huge number of so-called advisors and make sure all of them felt they were being used in *some* form, McDonough broke the crowd into about twenty groups and subgroups, divided by region or issue, so their input could be sought at a moment's notice if the candidate needed to react to some new development on the world stage.[7] Many of those on the roster were there merely for show, to demonstrate that Obama had united the Democratic Party; he was only really close to Craig, Rice, and Scott Gration.*

That made for a very short list of actual close aides to serve as national security advisor, made shorter when Power quit during the primaries after she was quoted calling Hillary Clinton a "monster." Craig had so angered the Clintons with his defection, and the language he used as an Obama surrogate attacking his former friends, that he would never be allowed to serve in Foggy Bottom while Clinton was secretary of state. The only campaign surrogate who got a look for national security advisor was Susan Rice, but Obama ultimately felt she fit best as ambassador to the United Nations. "We had huge decisions on Iraq, Afghanistan, and terrorism," Rhodes recalled. "That was going to dominate, even though we had a whole agenda that we were going to push out on a range of other issues like nonproliferation and resetting our relations in the world. We had a

---

* When Gration, Obama's first pick to run NASA, clashed with Senator Bill Nelson, a former astronaut and the chairman of the subcommittee that oversees the space agency, Gration was shifted to the Sudan portfolio, a position that didn't require Senate confirmation.

lot of military decisions to make, so I think the president's thinking was, let's put Susan in a prominent diplomatic role. That's where her experience is rooted in. And I want someone who has military experience in the national security advisor's role because I'm going to have these big decisions to make on defense and I'm going to have less time to focus on this myself because I've got so many domestic agenda items to take care of." Left unsaid but widely known in Obama circles, Rice and Clinton might not work well together. And one thing that *never* works well in any administration is when the national security advisor and secretary of state are at odds. Both believe they should have the most influence on America's foreign policy. The reality is that the person who briefs and meets with the president the most is usually the most influential, and that's what makes the National Security Council (NSC) role so sought after.

Oddly, back when Hillary Clinton and John McCain were claiming that Obama couldn't handle that 3 a.m. phone call, there must have been at least one person who took that attack—or at least the perception it created—to heart: Barack Obama himself. Even with Gates and Clinton secured, the president wasn't finished attempting to tap establishment figures to round out his national security team. Sensitive to the fact that neither he nor his vice president wore the uniform, Obama wanted some high-profile generals on the team, even if it was simply for the sake of appearances. Two big military names that he got to know—a little bit—were former marine corps general Jim Jones and former navy admiral Dennis Blair.

Obama had met Jones, who had served as supreme allied commander in Europe, back in 2005, when Lippert arranged a sit-down.[8] During the campaign, Jones had offered Obama advice in private while publicly appearing with his old friend John McCain. Meeting secretly with Jones in Richmond, Virginia, during one of Obama's campaign swings through the battleground state, Obama brought up the possibility of Jones working in his administration; Jones said he would be better suited to serving as secretary of state than as national security advisor, a prospect that at the time wasn't wholly out of the realm of possibility.[9] On those two occasions Obama and Jones had clicked, and Obama liked the way Jones presented information.

It didn't matter to Obama that he barely had any relationship with Jones, aside from the few conversations they had had over the preceding three years. As one advisor remembered, "Jones presents well." Added another, "Jones gives good meeting." Perhaps a stronger advocate for Jones was Biden, and Obama, according to one of the longtime aides who would put together the foreign policy team, liked the fact that Jones was cut from the same cloth as Chuck

Hagel and Bob Gates, "kind of this moderate Republican realist, alliance-internationalist tradition" that was the dominant strain of Republican foreign policy through the first President Bush. These were responsible Republican foreign policy elites—they hadn't rushed to war in Iraq and Afghanistan, and they understood, in the same way Obama did, America's delicate position in the world.*

The first time Jones showed up at an Obama campaign rally in the early summer of 2008, one of Jones's closest friends, none other than John McCain, was taken by surprise. In fact, when first alerted to Jones's appearance, some of McCain's friends thought the press reports were mistaken. After all, Jones and McCain were close, having talked almost weekly for years. No way Jones would be playing national security prop for Obama, or so swore one of McCain's closest confidants. But prop he *would* play—with a nice reward: when President-elect Obama announced his national security team, on December 1, 2008,

---

* Obama, to this day, loves that his foreign policy doctrine gets compared favorably to George H. W. Bush's. The comparison is tinged with more than a bit of irony, given that he won the presidency by presenting himself as a polar opposite of George W. But the greater irony was to come: as Obama's presidency progressed, he would continue many of his predecessor's national security policies and see significant backlash. But that was in the future—at the time, his search was for those who saw the world through steady, veteran eyes, more *E-Ring* than evangelical.

Jones stood next to Clinton, Gates, Arizona governor Janet Napolitano (who would head the Department of Homeland Security), and Eric Holder (who would be attorney general) as the incoming national security advisor.

To balance the establishment-pleasing Jones, Obama loaded up the national security team inside the West Wing with his young true believers, folks like Rhodes, McDonough, and the now-back-in-good-graces Samantha Power, all of whom had independent and better relationships with the commander in chief than did Jones—a fact Jones would realize only once it was too late.

The last major piece of the puzzle was perhaps the most delicate: Wall Street and the economy were in free fall. In a single September day, after the House voted down the nine-figure bank bailout known as the Troubled Asset Relief Program (TARP), the Dow Jones Industrial Average lost 778 points, nearly 8 percent of its total value. To calm the markets as much as possible, and to chart a course to recovery, Obama needed a treasury secretary of stature and gravitas, and as with Defense, he needed someone who would immediately create a bipartisan consensus.

But picking a treasury secretary Wall Street would trust was a delicate task at the moment. Average Americans blamed the Street for destroying their

401(k)'s, their job prospects, and perhaps their children's futures. On top of that, almost every prominent Democrat on Wall Street had at one time or another worked for Robert Rubin, Clinton's second treasury secretary. Rubin began his career on the Street and had served as a board member, and briefly as chairman, of Citigroup, and picking a Rubin acolyte would mean choosing someone tainted by the Street's most unsavory business practices. Voters wanted to see someone from Wall Street frog-marched off to jail, not to the ornate office building across Executive Drive from the White House.

Obama's short list came down to precisely two names: Larry Summers, the former secretary who took over for Rubin, an Obama advisor who desperately wanted to be chairman of the Federal Reserve but would take Treasury if it meant a shot at the Fed, and Timothy Geithner, a low-key former Summers aide who served as governor of the New York Federal Reserve Bank, the Treasury Department's unofficial embassy on Wall Street. (There actually was a third name on the short list before the Lehman collapse, former Goldman Sachs CEO and governor of New Jersey at the time, Jon Corzine. But his Goldman ties made Corzine a nonstarter politically.)

Both Summers and Geithner were well known on the Street. Both had Obama's confidence. But Summers struck many Obama aides as too brash for the moment; he was known for bullying subordinates and equals alike, and he had a history of getting himself into trouble. He had been fired from the presidency of Harvard University after making pseudoscientific statements about the differences between men's and women's brains. And how this person played in public mattered at the time. While many treasury secretaries in the past could be seen and not heard, that was *not* going to be the case for the first Obama secretary. Digging out of the Great Recession was going to put this one under the klieg lights, and the person needed to be a good fit temperamentally. That wasn't Summers. He'd gotten into trouble at the World Bank for signing on to a report that claimed it made economic sense to export pollution to Africa. (He later admitted he'd not read the report through and simply promised to be smarter about reading something thoroughly before he signed on to it. An assistant classified the idea as "an ironic aside."[10]) Oh, and Summers was *too* easily connected with the Clintons—after all, he was being considered for the same job he'd inherited back then. Obama had been fine with drawing from the pool of Democratic veterans, but a direct repeat was too much for someone who wanted to maintain that his was a new generation. Never mind Summers's rocky time at Harvard, which earned him a reputation, fairly or not, of not being particularly sensitive to women in leadership roles.

Geithner, on the other hand, had an unquantifiable advantage, one that positioned him well for the inside track. His ability to communicate ideas in a clear, concise way had grabbed the attention of his superiors throughout his career; one reason Summers had promoted Geithner through the ranks of his own Treasury Department during the Clinton years was because Summers liked the way Geithner presented briefing materials. Obama and Geithner had met only once, a private get-together after a campaign fund-raiser in New York City, but the two hit it off, and Obama liked the way Geithner cut to the chase—a very personable guy who loves to crack jokes and would later earn a reputation for using the f-word more often than Rahm Emanuel.

Geithner was also close to the Street without being too close. As president of the New York Fed, Geithner knew all the players. He had dealt with the heads of the big banks as an equal, sometimes as a savior. He even looked the part: even though Geithner's salary was a tiny fraction of even a junior Wall Street partner's, he dressed well, ate at the right restaurants, and knew the language and nomenclature. In fact, he appeared to be such a creature of Wall Street that, later in his tenure at Treasury, some opponents would accuse him of being a former banker himself, even though he hadn't worked in the private sector.

Geithner, over the objections of Obama's new chief

of staff, Rahm Emanuel, got the job. Emanuel, who was a Summers acolyte, did convince Obama to hire Summers as chairman of the National Economic Council. Summers took the lesser position because he saw it as a way to earn the trust of the new president so he could then get appointed to his real dream job: chairman of the Federal Reserve.

By picking three establishment favorites—Clinton, who was popular among both Democratic and Republican senators; Gates, who had already won bipartisan backing; and Geithner, who had good relations on Capitol Hill and who had been on both John McCain's and Barack Obama's short lists for treasury secretary—Obama had hired qualified, competent managers of three key departments, all while avoiding a fight that might cost him political capital.

That latter part, *avoiding a fight,* was another lesson learned from a prior administration. It took Bill Clinton three tries to find an attorney general, thanks to a few missing tax payments that upended both Zoë Baird and Kimba Wood. When the nomination of former New York City police commissioner Bernard Kerik as the second secretary of the Department of Homeland Security had to be withdrawn, after even a basic vetting by a rookie FBI agent would have turned up plenty of red flags, it foreshadowed the beginning of a long period of weakness for the Bush administration.

Obama's picks were by no means without controversy. Several other choices for key cabinet roles—Tom Daschle as health and human services secretary; Penny Pritzker, then Bill Richardson, then Judd Gregg as commerce secretary—either withdrew their nominations or withdrew themselves from consideration because of personal or political considerations. But in the three departments that would make the biggest difference to Obama's presidency, he avoided early self-inflicted wounds. With several important votes coming up before his inauguration or shortly thereafter, Obama was going to use his political capital on issues rather than on personnel. But the cabinet was hardly looking like change; then again, the Obama mantra throughout the transition and even during the VP selection process was that being America's first black president was change enough.

The transition period is an awkward time for a president-elect and an outgoing commander in chief. For the two and a half months between Election Day and Inauguration Day, there are in effect two leaders of the United States, and at a moment when one party is handing power to another, their policies can differ dramatically. Few presidential transitions in the nation's history have had the potential to be as fraught as the transition between George W. Bush, the man who orchestrated and authorized the wars in Iraq and Afghanistan, and Barack Obama, the man who campaigned against one and only barely accepted the necessity of the other. But after the September 11 attacks, during which one of the hijacked aircraft was apparently destined for the White House, Bush had made a smooth transition a priority, regardless of which party would take power once he left. Obama's team, Bush told his staff, was to be given full access, to ease their path to power so there wouldn't be so much as a hiccup when the old guard handed power to the new.

That didn't mean the transition period wasn't a confusing time for the incoming president's personnel. They had spent two years in a virtual bunker together, working around the country against—and beating—some of the most established names in Democratic politics. They had rallied for hope, for change, for a new way to do business in Washington. But as the unadulterated glee of winning a national campaign wore off, some of the illusion that they would truly be able to change Washington right off the bat went with it.

For one thing, once campaign aides had recuperated for a few days and started considering their positions in the White House, they found the beginnings of a team already in place. And instead of reuniting entirely with those who had helped the candidate win the election, they were meeting senior members of the transition who had long careers in Washington, and even stints of employment in the Clinton administration and the Clinton campaign, behind them. Of course there was John Podesta, who had by now been leading the transition effort for months. Carol Browner, who had headed the Environmental Protection Agency in Clinton's White House and was a veteran of Washington politics, had been brought in early to help staff several agencies. Federico Peña, Clinton's HUD secretary, was on the advisory board; so was Bill Daley, Clinton's old commerce secretary. Old keys opened old doors, while campaign foes became friends. Tom Vilsack, who had run briefly in 2008 and then endorsed Hillary Clinton, was tapped to run the Agriculture Department, an important outreach position the president could use to woo voters in farm-heavy midwestern states. And so it went.

Sometimes the exclusion was quite literal. Dan Pfeiffer, an Obama aide since his old boss, Senator Evan Bayh, had made it clear he wouldn't run for president, left Chicago in a daze after helping elect the nation's first African American president. The Monday after Election Day, he walked into the transition office's headquarters, a run-down government building halfway between downtown Washington and Capitol Hill, with an aging McDonald's facing the street. But no one had told the Secret Service that Pfeiffer, who would direct communications for the transition office, was allowed in the building. While he waited for the oversight to be fixed, Pfeiffer watched in amazement as Jamie

Rubin, a Clinton administration State Department veteran and a vocal surrogate attacking Obama during the primaries on behalf of Hillary's campaign, breezed right through security, his credentials already taken care of.

This was change they could believe in? To Obama aides and outside observers alike, the evidence was suddenly pointing in the other direction: longtime Washington hands crowded transition team meetings and would eventually hold the more important posts in the White House. And just as mind-boggling to the campaign staff, a Bush Republican, Obama's chief primary rival, and an emissary from Wall Street occupied the three most important cabinet posts Obama would fill.

But, Obama would argue, he wasn't selling out his ideals. Sure, the true believers who had been with him from the beginning ended up with lower-level political jobs, or at least positions that didn't require Senate confirmation. He was merely demonstrating a pragmatic side, one that would reveal itself time and again during his first four years as president, sometimes at moments when pragmatism was seemingly at odds with the idealism that had carried Obama into office.

His favoring of establishment insiders and veterans of presidencies past demonstrated to those who had been up close with Obama something they'd known was there but had hoped might fade come arrival at 1600 Pennsylvania. They saw the supreme self-confidence, at times bordering on arrogance, that defined Obama, the assuredness that allowed him to sit in a room with four-star generals, heads of state, senior senators, or business icons and believe himself their intellectual equal or superior. Obama wasn't concerned about bringing big names, pillars of old Washington, on board an administration bent on change; as always, he saw himself as the change.

Only months before, Obama had accepted his party's nomination by proclaiming that "the change we need doesn't come *from* Washington. Change comes *to* Washington." He'd meant it—but perhaps not, it seemed, in the way his acolytes had imagined, since the only change apparent to them was him.

CHAPTER TWO

Getting Rolled Early

The 3 a.m. phone call Obama was most likely to receive, as it turned out, didn't have to do with foreign threats. In fact, it was more of a 3 p.m. call than anything else, word from the world of business and the economy of an impending market crash, or some other catalyst that could deepen the spiral of falling consumer confidence, falling demand, and rising unemployment numbers.

Rhode Island senator Jack Reed had been the first to warn that the economic crisis would suck up Obama's time. He wasn't the last to make the case. This meant the president needed an experienced team that could work through most issues by themselves. Regarding foreign policy, Gates represented continuity. Clinton and the team she and Obama installed at the State Department represented competence. Jones was chosen less for his rapport with the president than for his strong résumé, knowledge, and relationships, and his ability to navigate the world of the uniformed service chiefs.

The economic team, by the same token, was designed to show off the capable hands in charge of the recovery. Geithner had credibility on Wall Street; Summers was a known commodity, in both New York and Washington. Even Christina Romer, the outsider in the group whom Obama tapped to chair the Council of Economic Advisers, was a choice made to send a message: the University of California, Berkeley, professor's academic background was in the Great Depression.

On December 16, 2008, a little over a month before being formally sworn in to office, Barack Obama's economic team gave him some bad news: his entire first term was about to be swallowed whole by an economic crisis the depth of which they were only beginning to comprehend.

Just as everyone remembers where they were when they heard that John Kennedy had been assassinated or when the *Challenger* blew up, everyone who was on the incoming president's transition team, gathered just a few days after the euphoria of Obama's victory speech in Grant Park, will never forget where they were when given the dismal economic update. They have vivid recollections of the thoughts that flooded into their minds as the numbers—eye-popping, jaw-dropping numbers so huge as to be fantastic—and the scope of the disaster they faced came into view. It was when everyone in the room began to feel the weight of the task at hand. This wasn't a campaign anymore, this was the real thing. Outside, snow fell. An unseasonably warm weekend had given way to single-digit temperatures. Inside, in the transition team's conference room, the president-elect sat at the end of a square table. Biden sat at Obama's side. They faced the team they had selected to oversee the economy: Tim Geithner, Christina Romer, Peter Orszag — a onetime congressional budget guru the president was tapping as his budget chief — Biden's chief economic advisor Jared Bernstein, and Larry Summers. Axelrod, Gibbs, and Emanuel also were there. The message the economic team had for the president-elect was as blunt as it was succinct.

"Mr. President, this is your 'holy-shit moment.' It's worse than we thought," said Romer, who would head the Council of Economic Advisers.

The new administration would have to throw its weight behind a stimulus package aimed at rescuing an economy on the verge of spiraling out of control. Whether they would muscle a stimulus package through Congress was not the question; the question was how big that package needed to be. Summers and Romer presented their options and debated the merits of a $600 billion option and an $800 billion option. Romer even mentioned, in passing, that she believed something bigger — north of $1 trillion—would be needed to have a real impact.*[1] In truth, the two had been squabbling over whether Romer's bigger option should have been laid out in their presentation; she had a nagging feeling that the stimulus should have been much higher, perhaps $1.6 trillion. Summers, whose experience in Washington made him a better operator than the politically naïve Romer, talked her out of that position—a short-term win for him, but ultimately, in the minds of some economists, a mistake for the country.

Jared Bernstein called the presentation the economic equivalent of shock and awe. "At one level, you're sitting there with the first African American president, who's just run a deeply compelling and resonant campaign about hope, about change. And you're part of this new team, and the excitement is palpable," he recalled later. "At the same time, the economy is headed off a cliff. The juxtaposition was really quite wrenching."

Axelrod's mind was filled with decidedly non-economic thoughts: *This is going to be politically tough.* For the first time, just six weeks after Obama had won a sweepingly historic election, Axelrod considered the possibility that the Democratic

---

* Several participants in the meeting recall that Summers became uncharacteristically quiet when Romer brought the word "trillion" to the table, a sign that he wanted to be sure Romer had enough rope to hang herself with.

majority in Congress would be short-lived, given the tough economic times ahead, and the amount of spending it would take to dig out of the hole was going to be hard to sell politically. Axelrod's mind was wandering to what he thought could be a horrible place for the president politically, the 2010 midterms.

Rahm was having a different thought: how the response to the economic crisis could be used for maximum political gain. Most staffers during Emanuel's twenty-one-month tenure would see him as a capable manager, someone with the knowledge and ability to run the unwieldy White House. Emanuel's thesis on governing was evident throughout the first term. He believed that political power, like chips in a poker tournament, could be multiplied only if it was exercised: make a bet, win the bet, and gain more power. Political power unused would eventually be whittled away.

Emanuel's collection of colloquialisms — "Put points on the board," "In politics, you're either pitching or catching" — emphasized the necessity of driving the conversation, lest the conversation drive you. And for a president who had promised the hope of changing the way Washington ran, Obama recognized he needed someone who could drive that conversation. With big Democratic majorities in the House and Senate, who better to install as his chief of staff than someone who had been in House leadership and who had deep, abiding relations with senators who mattered, like Harry Reid and Chuck Schumer?

"I think Obama saw the presidency the way historians probably judge presidents, which is, it's a function of being able to command the legislature. Pass big bills," said Podesta. "And he saw Rahm as the guy with the guts and the know-how and the smarts to be able to do that."

While Emanuel would eventually become frustrated with what he saw as the president's inability to centralize internal power, thus depleting the chief of staff position of its potential, others would come to believe that Emanuel was running the White House with an iron fist. He clashed with many people at all levels of the staff, and occasionally a story would hit the papers that suggested that the White House was a sexist boys' club — the clear implication being that it was Rahm who had fostered such an environment. Obama, who did think Emanuel fought too much with his coworkers, bought into some of that criticism. He especially thought Rahm didn't get along well with senior female members of the staff, Valerie Jarrett first and foremost among them. But the president also didn't mind the tension, as long as it wasn't a complete distraction. In Rahm, Obama saw the ultimate means-to-an-end guy he needed, whether he liked him or not, which is why Rahm never would be punished, per se, for any internal staff transgressions. Rahm's defenders maintained that he yelled just as loudly, and swore just as much, at men as he did at women; he didn't care, in the end, about the gender of the person on the other end of a "fuck you," usually reserved for someone who had screwed up. He only cared that they had screwed up.

Emanuel would also regularly end up at odds with Gibbs. Gibbs had led Obama's press operation since his Senate campaign, after running communications for the Democratic Senatorial Campaign Committee, not to mention serving as John Kerry's press secretary during his presidential bid in 2004. He was a true believer, someone in Rahm's eyes who had wholeheartedly partaken of the Kool-Aid that said Obama had come to Washington to change things. His insistence that Obama transform business as usual in the Beltway swamp, which one former coworker described as putting on the white hat, grated on the more pragmatic Emanuel. The two would stand farthest apart on an early test of change versus status quo.

At the moment, however, Emanuel must have been thinking about his own reversed circumstances. In September 2008, when he was a member of the House Democratic leadership, he, Speaker Nancy Pelosi, and majority leader Steny Hoyer had urged President George W. Bush to put forward a $150 billion stimulus package to reverse the economic slide. It was thought of as a huge ask of a Republican president, but the fear that the economy was collapsing was very real, and Bush was actually ready to go along with what was at the time historically a fairly large number. Turns out that number looked like pennies on the dollar, compared to what Rahm was about to ask Congress for just six months later.

After the meeting broke up, Emanuel huddled with the economic team to finalize their plan. Heads nodded, pens scratched over notepads. The transition team would ask Congress for $775 billion in stimulus spending, a number that could make it through the Democratic-controlled Congress. Axelrod drifted out of the room, still wondering just how long Democrats could keep Congress in their control. Passing this thing was going to be a struggle as it was. *But passing it with the GOP in control?* Now that would be scary—and neither Axelrod nor anyone else in American politics had heard of the Tea Party yet.

The next two months began one of the most frenzied legislative scrambles that anyone with experience in politics can remember. Throughout December and into January, even before they had moved into the White House, staffers furiously calculated programs that cost multiples of any they had ever helped fund before.

There are areas of the resulting stimulus in which Barack Obama's imprimatur is clear: the Department of Energy's Advanced Research Projects Agency, which aimed to use stimulus dollars to create the next great innovation in energy research, or what became one of the president's pet projects he'd campaign on, advanced battery manufacturing; and Race to the Top, a grant program that would reward states that came up with innovative ways of reforming their education systems, which eventually received more than $4 billion in funding—nearly a third of the funding George W. Bush's No Child Left Behind law added to education and with virtually none of the controversy or attention.[2] But in large part, once they found their White House offices, Obama's transition team, and eventually his legislative staff, allowed their allies on Capitol Hill to write significant portions of the stimulus bill. The theory was that involving Congress early would, in effect, win their buy-in, and once they had bought in, they couldn't help but vote for the bill.

No matter the politics, no matter the president, when so much money is at stake, it's almost certain that some will be misspent. With a Republican minority eager to label the stimulus package laden with waste, fraud, and abuse (a favorite expression of penny-pinching politicians everywhere), the administration wanted to be doubly certain that every dollar was accounted for. Obama put Joe Biden in charge of keeping tabs on how the money was spent.

Biden would end up devoting a significant part

of his first two years as vice president to conference calls with local elected officials, watching over their shoulders to make sure the money went toward creating jobs or accomplishing other aspects of the bill's myriad goals. The good news, for such a big bill, was that it didn't lead to any major spending scandals. Of course, there is still debate about whether the stimulus was as effective as it could have been.

Even as Obama's economic advisors urged him to spend big to calm the markets and provide stability, his political team was worried about a different demon. Republicans were sure to accuse the administration of exploding the deficit, so Obama's team had to do all they could to convey the notion that the stimulus bill would be only a short-term fix rather than a permanent expansion of government spending. A split emerged in the economic team; Peter Orszag, in particular, worried about the impact of the federal deficit, both on the markets and on the country's economy as a whole, while others like Bernstein and Romer believed short-term spending was crucial to long-term stability, regardless of how big the deficit became.

Conscious of the politically negative "optics," administration officials, from Obama to advisors who spoke to reporters only on condition that their names not be revealed, constantly used a four-word refrain when characterizing the stimulus: the money they spent was supposed to be "timely, temporary, and targeted," and the administration would pursue only so-called shovel-ready projects, directing money to infrastructure programs and other investments that would lead to immediate job creation.

Of course, as they were bandying about all these massive numbers—a billion here and a billion there, and soon you're talking about real money—the White House staff had to make sure they could win over the votes necessary to secure passage in Congress. The House wasn't a problem; with 255 Democrats and just 178 Republicans in office, Speaker Nancy Pelosi would be able to round up the votes to pass the bill.

But there were already signs that the White House would have a difficult time winning over congressional Republicans to pass a bill with bipartisan support. Staff in the White House Office of Intergovernmental Affairs, essentially the president's state liaisons, were hearing from Republican governors all over the nation desperate for any stimulus money Washington could send their way. The states were facing steep budget cuts, and they needed help from the federal government. But when the office asked the governors to write letters to that effect, to come out publicly in favor of the stimulus, many demurred for obvious political reasons. Only four Republicans serving at the time—Vermont's Jim Douglas, California's Arnold Schwarzenegger, Connecticut's Jodi Rell, and Florida's Charlie Crist—were willing to say publicly that they backed the bill. None of them were considered pillars of the conservative wing of the GOP.

The White House tried to entice Republican votes by including exactly what the GOP was most inclined to vote for — tax incentives. The final bill included $288 billion, more than a third of the total package, in tax breaks, including a payroll tax credit of $400 per worker, an expansion of the child tax credit, a huge homebuyer tax credit to help spur the struggling housing industry, an expansion of tax credits for home energy use and college tuition costs, and the earned income tax credit. Bernstein, among various advisors, argued that too much of the stimulus was weighted toward tax breaks, which he saw as a terrible way to use the money, since tax break dollars didn't necessarily get used the way stimulus dollars were supposed to be used. A tax break takes too long to get back into the economy, and what this recession needed, in Bernstein's view, was fast cash. A family that gets a tax credit in a recession is more likely to save the money or use it to pay down debt than to spend it. Even if they do spend it, given general American consumption patterns, the money is likely to go toward purchasing an import, which means American tax dollars are making their way overseas anyway. These tax breaks just weren't stimulants for an economy in a tailspin.

But others on the economic team, and within the

legislative office, disagreed. They said repeatedly that they needed to include the tax breaks to get the final bill over the finish line; to do so, they needed Republicans who would be attracted to the idea of more than a quarter of a trillion dollars in tax cuts.

On Capitol Hill, House Democratic leaders were on Bernstein's side. Hoyer in particular was angry with the White House for including the tax breaks; he wanted to see the money go toward longer-term projects so that the effects of the stimulus would last more than a few months. "If we had put that [$288 billion] into infrastructure, and not worried about the 18-month shovel-ready projects, we'd be spending it now, creating jobs now and economic growth now," he said in a 2012 interview. Ultimately most of Obama's economic advisors would agree with Hoyer that the stimulus bill spent too much on the front end, without a long-term investment that would keep the government juice flowing. If they had planned better for the longer term, the recovery might have been steadier, rather than petering out over a shorter time frame. But Obama's goal wasn't to build the perfect bill; it was to build the best bill that could still pass Congress.

What the White House didn't know was that a number of senior Republican strategists had already determined to make life difficult for the White House—very, very difficult. If Obama understood pragmatism as short-term compromise for the sake of long-term evolution, Republican leaders understood pragmatism in a very different manner. On the very evening Obama was inaugurated, more than a dozen top Republicans met to talk strategy at the Caucus Room, a high-priced Washington steak house (since closed) owned by former Republican National Committee chairman Haley Barbour and Democratic lobbyist Tommy Boggs. The group included House Republican whip Eric Cantor; his deputy, Kevin McCarthy; House Budget Committee ranking member Paul Ryan; five senators; former House Speaker Newt Gingrich; and Republican pollster Frank Luntz. For four hours they talked strategy aimed at ways to cut down the new president, even before Obama had finished his appearances at the inaugural balls.

One of their conclusions: they had to oppose Obama wherever they could, and they had to be unified. "If you act like you're the minority, you're going to stay in the minority," McCarthy said, according to an account by the journalist Robert Draper. "We've gotta challenge them on every single bill and challenge them on every single campaign."[3] What was pragmatic to the men in the room? Actions that helped the Republican Party get back into power. Obama might have won the November battle, beating McCain soundly, but for these Washington Republicans, the ones who survived two straight Democratic landslides (in 2006 and 2008), it was time for the party to reinvent itself. And with an era of big, activist government coming in with the new president, there was no time like the present to begin reshaping the GOP back to its small-government roots. The GOP wouldn't be credible as a small-government party if it began helping Obama too much, and thus was born their early obstruction strategy.

Eight days later, on January 28, just a week after Obama was inaugurated, the bill came to the floor of the House. Cantor, the Republican whip, did his job and kept the caucus in line; not a single Republican voted for the bill. Cantor had gone the distance in keeping his conference together: Representative Ahn "Joseph" Cao, a Louisiana freshman elected in a fluke over a Democrat who was found to have tens of thousands of dollars in bribes stored in his freezer, had nearly voted for the bill but had been stopped in the Republican cloakroom by Cantor's staff and browbeaten until he agreed to vote against it.[4]

The results stunned the White House; even on the day the bill was put before the House, Phil Schiliro, the top liaison between the White House and Capitol Hill, suspected they would receive as many as 15 Republican votes in the House. After all, there were provisions in the bill that were put in specifically at the request of a few of those 15 Republicans Schiliro thought would support the measure.

Schiliro had been a creature of the House for decades and saw firsthand members of the minority party always voting for big spending bills, especially if they got a specific provision they asked for. It was standard congressional operating procedure. Or at least it was pre-Obama. There was a sense in the White House that House Republicans had betrayed their duty. The economy was circling the drain, depression loomed, and Republicans were saying the government was spending too much. "It seemed as though we were in crisis and we needed to take action," said Valerie Jarrett, who had just assumed her first job in Washington as a senior advisor to the president. "Most of what we were proposing had received bipartisan support in the past, and the fact that we were having a really hard time getting enthusiasm on the Republican side for what seemed so obviously necessary to do was frustrating." Of course, what the Obama White House believed were bipartisan ideas were actually ideas that only a handful of less conservative Republicans had agreed to decades earlier when House Republicans and Bill Clinton regularly did business together. This was a new Republican Party and a new mind-set.

While the White House was slack-jawed over what had happened, House Democrats had seen the vote margin coming. The Republican tactic, Democratic leadership surmised, was the same as it had been in 1993, the last time a young Democratic president had tried to win over reluctant Republicans: they would stand united in opposition to the White House, just as Republicans had done over Bill Clinton's tax overhaul that year.

The unity of the House GOP was a punch in the gut, but because the Democrats controlled the chamber, the measure passed; at that point, Republicans in the House were in such a deep minority that they couldn't expect to play a major role in actual policy making. But in the Senate, Republicans held 41 of 100 seats, enough to sustain a filibuster and prevent a bill's passage. The White House initially believed it could get as many as 70 votes for a stimulus package—all 57 Democrats, both left-leaning independents and almost a dozen Republican votes. Obama had, after all, made a campaign promise—based his entire political life on the promise—to move beyond partisan politics as usual.

There were certainly Republicans willing to vote with Obama in some cases, when it served their political interests—on a January 29, 2009, vote to extend the State Children's Health Insurance Program, or SCHIP, 9 Republican senators voted with the Democratic majority.[5] But this time the White House focused on only 3 Republicans in particular—Pennsylvania's Arlen Specter and the 2 Republicans from Maine, Olympia Snowe and Susan Collins. Aides to Senate majority leader Harry Reid had told Obama's legislative strategists that they should be reaching out beyond those 3, to members like George Voinovich of Ohio, Lisa Murkowski of Alaska, and Lamar Alexander of Tennessee. But the White House seemed interested only in building a coalition just over the bare minimum number of senators it would take to pass the bill. Frustrated, Reid's team could do little to change course. This would be the first disagreement about how to reach out to Senate Republicans, but not the last.

The White House was particularly sensitive to those House Democrats who were concerned that too much Senate GOP outreach would water down the bill unnecessarily. So the White House chose the bare-minimum approach in order to keep the peace with the House leadership. Had the White House made its goal, say, ten Senate Republicans, it would have shrunk the size of the bill, perhaps by a good $200 billion, an unnecessary compromise, or so believed folks in the West Wing.

Biden began reaching out to Snowe, Specter, and Collins as early as December, a month before he and Obama would take office, to gauge what they needed to support the bill, and the White House went to extremes to make sure they won over all three. Both Reid and Pelosi had insisted that the bill come in under $1 trillion, so as to make it politically palatable to their own caucuses. Snowe and Collins wanted the bill's price tag to be smaller still. Snowe even brought a list of proposed cuts to one meeting with the president—one of several one-on-one sit-downs the two held in the Oval Office—that she had received from the Republican Policy Committee, which was filled with the House Republicans' most conservative members. Obama took the list, impressing Snowe by seriously considering her proposals. Several of those cuts ended up in the final version of the bill.

The price tag was still shockingly high, at $787 billion, but it won them over: on February 10, all three moderate Republicans voted for the Senate's version of the bill.[6] Three days later, a compromise between members of a conference committee passed the Senate again, by a 60–38 margin; again, all three Republican moderates voted for the bill.[7]

For a candidate who preached hope and change, Obama was off to an inauspicious start. He had signed a stimulus bill that would give Republicans every excuse they needed to accuse him of exploding the deficit. Far from drawing up a truly bipartisan bill, Obama would claim the veneer of bipartisanship with only Snowe, Collins, and Specter for cover.

Adopting, in some cases co-opting, Washington insiders was part of a larger strategy that drove Obama's early days. Many of the new president's top advisors, most notably Rahm Emanuel, had been a part of, or studied, Bill Clinton's early days in the White House, and they were determined not to repeat his mistakes. Throughout his tenure as chief of staff, Emanuel took pains to consult and involve Congress—the stimulus bill was written in close consultation with Democratic leaders (and even with Republican input); the White House would take pains to include every relevant committee while crafting a health care reform bill; and while Obama himself wasn't great at reaching out to members of Congress, Rahm kept in close contact with leaders and rank-and-file congressmen alike. Still, it hadn't helped win more support for the stimulus.

The administration faced what it referred to as a series of five-alarm fires in its earliest days. During the two and a half months between Obama's election and when he took the oath of office, some presidential advisors sat in on meetings with top economists and wondered just what they had gotten themselves into. The new president would inherit the deepest economic recession in eighty years, guaranteeing that his early agenda would be all but shelved until he could make sure those fires didn't spread. Franklin Roosevelt's bold agenda in his first hundred days in office had become something of an artificial measuring stick the media would use to judge every president who followed. Obama had so many crises to deal with in his first hundred days—the economic stimulus, bailing out the American auto industry, a second round of TARP funding—that he would be lucky if he could get to *any* item on his own agenda within that period. The Obama agenda would eventually begin, and Emanuel suspected he knew what the first item on that agenda would be: health care reform, the same issue that had tripped up Clinton and caused an electoral wipeout for Democrats in the subsequent 1994 midterm elections. This time around, Emanuel hoped to get a better outcome, either a smaller bite of the health care apple or an actual passed bill.

But first, only a week after President Obama signed the American Recovery and Reinvestment Act at an elaborate ceremony in Denver, his two presidential personas—the rational, pragmatic politician and the ideologue whose purity of purpose was determined to change Washington—had their first true clash. On Tuesday, February 24, during his first address to a joint session of Congress (it wasn't technically a State of the Union but delivered at a similar time and a tradition now for first-year presidents), Obama stood up for a pledge he had made during the Democratic primaries, a pledge to do something he and his top advisors believed would signal an important change in the way Washington did business: he defended his call to eliminate earmarks, the long Washington tradition of congressmen adding special projects to benefit their districts to bills that often have little or nothing to do with those projects.

"I'm proud that we passed the recovery plan free of earmarks, and I want to pass a budget next year that ensures that each dollar we spend reflects only our most important national priorities," Obama told Congress.[8] It was a line that Robert Gibbs and David Axelrod—the two advisors most concerned with keeping Obama's core image intact—were immensely proud of and one all of the old Washington hands thought screamed naïveté.

The very next afternoon, 229 Democrats and 16 Republicans took Obama's lecture on earmarks so seriously, they voted for the Omnibus Appropriations Act of 2009, an earmark-laden bill that lumped the annual budgets of all but three executive departments into one single package (it was actually a leftover spending bill that probably would have been signed by President Bush had it been sent to his desk in time). The $410 billion spending measure, on top of the $787 billion in the stimulus package and the billions more that would soon be spent on TARP and the auto company bailouts, was laden with pork. The conservative Heritage Foundation counted 9,287 earmarks stuffed into hidden corners of the bill, accounting for $12.8 billion of its final price tag. The earmarks included more than $1 million to combat Mormon crickets in Utah, $200,000 for a tattoo removal program in California, and $190,000 for a museum dedicated to the memory of Buffalo Bill in Cody, Wyoming—to say nothing of the $75,000 for a Totally Teen Zone in Albany, Georgia.[9]

Obama was incensed. He had made clear his position against earmarks, had taken his stand in front of an audience of tens of millions of people — not to mention the 435 congressmen and 100 senators who attended his address before the joint session of Congress — and now his own party had delivered a bill so stuffed with pork that his Republican opponents would have a field day. And make no mistake, congressional Democrats purposely waited until Obama got into office to send this bill to his desk, not as some test but because they figured they had a better shot at getting their way than if they risked sending this spending bill to Bush.

Here was the perfect distillation of Obama's battle with a Washington establishment — in this case, his own party. Democrats on Capitol Hill had tried to talk Obama out of his anti-earmark stance. Democratic leaders on Capitol Hill, including the chairmen of the committees Obama's health care proposal would have to go through, had a way of doing business they didn't want to see upset. Earmarks were considered a key vote-organizing tool. Vetoing a bill would anger a number of senior members, some of whom had been on Capitol Hill since Obama was in diapers — members such as Wisconsin's David Obey, the chairman of the House Appropriations Committee, who had already clashed with the administration over stimulus spending, and Montana's Max Baucus, the Senate Finance Committee chairman.

In their first meeting at the White House, Steny Hoyer had spoken up in favor of the controversial practice. "I think your earmark stance is going to get you in a pinch with Congress," the Maryland representative told the president. "I think, first of all, it's our responsibility, constitutionally, [to allocate government resources], and secondly, why do you want to have that fight with Congress, over essentially nickels [and] dimes?" Hoyer later made the same case to Rahm Emanuel, his old House colleague. Earmarks weren't even drops in the bucket of the massive federal budget. Taking a stand against them was too trivial for a president of the United States.

Emanuel agreed, but Obama was unconvinced. His gut reaction was to make his first stand in favor of changing the way Washington did business on the omnibus bill. He wanted to veto legislation that more than 90 percent of the House Democratic Caucus and all but three Senate Democrats had voted for. It would have sent a real message, a "new sheriff in town" kind of message. This could have been his airline-traffic-controller moment (as in Reagan's decision to fire striking air traffic controllers, which did send a message early in his presidency that he was going to be a tougher customer to negotiate with than insiders at the time thought).

But with the fight over health care looming, Obama was choosing what many of his advisors thought was the wrong battle. Emanuel, Jim Messina, Phil Schiliro, and Pete Rouse—the four most senior staffers with significant Capitol Hill experience—all told him not to veto the bill. Messina and Rouse were worried about how much it would anger Senate Democrats and embolden Republicans. Schiliro and Emanuel knew they risked making Pelosi and Hoyer in the House furious. "If you want to lose two months on health care, veto the bill," Emanuel told Obama. "I can't veto a bill and get health care started. Those are the tradeoffs. That's what you get paid the big bucks for." Schiliro, who had the best access to House leadership thinking, was more pessimistic: "You do this and you won't get anything," one former advisor recalls him saying.

On the other side, Gibbs and Axelrod wanted Obama to veto the bill. "We ran a campaign on changing the way Washington works, to change the way Washington does business," Gibbs recalled later. "And our first act was going to be to swallow this big piece of Washington business? I thought it was hugely bad."

The debate raged for days. The legislative liaison's office, headed by Schiliro and Rob Nabors—a former staffer for one of the biggest earmarkers in the House, David Obey, chairman of the powerful Appropriations Committee—kept warning the true believers that rocking the boat to such an extreme degree would hurt relationships with the legislators they needed most. The true believers never gave an inch; they felt they were getting steamrolled by the old-timers on Capitol Hill and their former staffers who now worked at the White House.

To this day, some of the true believers think Schiliro and Rahm had the whole thing precooked, that they had preemptively agreed with Democratic leaders on the Hill, in the president's name, to compromise on the issue without admitting this to the president. In fact, some of these aides believe Rahm cut this deal before the president was even sworn in. Regardless, the old-timers won, and one of Obama's core principles was jettisoned for the sake of expediency. One of the chief criticisms of Obama's Washington is the president's inability to get his way either by force or by compromise. He is also criticized for how he manages Washington: he seems unable either to make the old system work or to create a new system to work better. One of the misconceptions of Obama is that he's not a good compromiser. That's not true: he compromises all the time; he just seems to get more downsides from his compromises than upsides. In this case, he broke an early symbolic promise.

On March 11, as he prepared to sign the omnibus legislation, Obama tried to save face, but even the opening of his remarks that day, in the Eisenhower Executive Office Building, began with an implicit admission that things hadn't gone his way.

"I ran for President pledging to change the way business is done in Washington and build a government that works for the people by opening it up to the people. And that means restoring responsibility and transparency and accountability to actions that the government takes," Obama said. He cited the earmark-free stimulus bill before expressing his solemn disgust at the bill he was about to sign. "Yesterday Congress sent me the final part of last year's budget; a piece of legislation that rolls nine bills required to keep the government running into one, a piece of legislation that addresses the immediate concerns of the American people by making needed investments in line with our urgent national priorities. That's what nearly 99 percent of this legislation does—the nearly 99 percent that you probably haven't heard much about," Obama said. "What you likely have heard about is that this bill does include earmarks."

He went on: "I am signing an imperfect omnibus bill because it's necessary for the ongoing functions of government, and we have a lot more work to do. We can't have Congress bogged down at this critical juncture in our economic recovery. But I also view this as a departure point for more far-reaching change."

Obama next laid out a series of reforms he wanted to see: An earmark should show up on a member of Congress's website before it is enacted. There should be hearings to justify each earmark. Earmarks aimed at private companies should be open to competitive bidding. He went on at some length. And then he signed a bill that added another 9,287 earmarks to the federal budget. What the president didn't truly appreciate about this decision was that he was sending an unmistakable message: he could be rolled.

In hindsight, the administration officials closest to Obama admit that signing the bill was the president's biggest political regret of his first term. "I think he realized that what he wanted to do was tying his hands," Gibbs said later, reflecting on the decision. "It was a decision to go with the flow as opposed to shak[ing] things up," added Dan Pfeiffer, who was present for the debate. Pfeiffer no doubt hopes that the Obama presidency doesn't go down in history as failing to figure out how to shake things up.

The decision not to veto the omnibus bill also highlights another strange relationship the Obama administration struggled with in the first term: Obama had worked closely with Harry Reid during his brief tenure in the Senate; in fact, Reid had quietly rooted for Obama in his fight against Hillary Clinton. But Obama had never been as close to Nancy Pelosi, the House Democratic leader. As a result, the White House had made a calculated decision early on to focus on the Senate. After all, with a huge majority in the House, they expected Pelosi would be able to win over the 218 votes she needed for passage of a bill anytime she wanted. Reid, on the other hand, would struggle to get 60 votes to overcome a filibuster, given that he had to enlist several conservative Democrats and, with Ted Kennedy ailing from brain cancer and absent for most votes, at least two of the moderate Republicans, from Maine or Pennsylvania.

The Senate calendar, too, was a massive obstacle to Obama's agenda; Reid had far less control over what happened on his floor than did Pelosi on hers. The Senate spent a significant chunk of the first three weeks of the 111th Congress debating a bill to allow guns in national parks, rather than the stimulus bill. If Pelosi and Hoyer, who as majority leader technically controlled the floor schedule, wanted a vote on the stimulus, they could simply call a vote on it.

Within a Democratic Party still fractured between the Clintons and Obama, Pelosi held a unique position. She had been active in party politics since childhood, as the daughter of legendary Baltimore mayor Tommy D'Alesandro. She had run for the top position at the Democratic National Committee (and lost to Paul Kirk of Massachusetts, who would replace Ted Kennedy when the legendary senator passed away). Whether a prominent party fund-raiser was an Obama backer or a Clinton backer, he or she was sure to be a Pelosi confidant; one could argue that few have done more to raise money for the Democratic Party since the 1980s than Nancy Pelosi.

But Obama had few ties to Pelosi. Not a single person in the White House could be considered a true Pelosi acolyte; Schiliro, a former chief of staff to California congressman Henry Waxman, a Pelosi ally, and Nabors, as David Obey's former top aide, each had conduits to the Speaker's office, but those conduits were one-way streets headed up Pennsylvania Avenue. They could easily understand or find out what Pelosi was thinking, but they couldn't necessarily get their message to her.

Pelosi suffered, in some respects, in contrast to Reid. When asked whether they could cobble together the votes necessary to pass a bill, Pelosi would tick off the coalitions she would have to put together and what it would cost to build those coalitions; Reid would simply give a yes or no answer. That approach, on a personal level, appealed to Obama much more than Pelosi's did. Fairly or not, Obama sometimes believed Pelosi was using her explanations to gain leverage.

For her part, Pelosi minced no words when it came to achieving the president's agenda. After eight years of George W. Bush, she was thrilled that a Democrat had taken back the White House. And she believed she never wanted, or asked, much of

Obama, though it was clear she felt disrespected. As time went on during 2009, Obama's decision to focus on the Senate became more evident especially at the staff level; Pelosi felt that disrespect increasing— and, unsurprisingly, she hated it. They took her for granted, something former Obama aides now realize. And as the debate over health care reform loomed, Pelosi's growing dissatisfaction, her feeling that the White House was overlooking her House of Representatives domain, would prove costly.

CHAPTER THREE

Unplanned Legacy

Barack Obama was something of an unlikely champion for health care reform. During his tenure in public office, he had toed a traditionally Democratic line on the subject, which was some version of being in favor of universal health care, though he had never stepped out ahead of the issue. (He had been chairman of the Public Health Committee in the Illinois state senate, though with few results to brag about.) He had personal experience with the byzantine insurance system; he frequently invoked his mother, a cancer victim who had had to deal with paperwork from her hospital bed. But as a member of the Illinois Senate and a candidate for the U.S. Senate, he preferred and perhaps had to focus on other things. After all, as a junior senator in Washington, what could he do that Ted Kennedy could not? What could he do that Hillary Clinton had not?

Thus it is ironic that the initiative that defined much of his tenure in office — and will likely be the basis for his postpresidential reputation — was never his highest priority, and that its two key elements were proposals advanced by other candidates, proposals Obama himself had attacked on the campaign trail.

But the story of health care reform and Barack Obama begins with a throwaway line in a last-minute speech concocted by aides not thinking about the presidency.

The Hillary Clinton factor took on added importance in late 2006 and early 2007, when Obama and his top advisors began taking formal steps toward a run for president. Policy-wise, Clinton had been defined by her health care task force during her husband's first term in the White House. She had credibility within the far-flung liberal policy community, even though that experience had left scars. Among other potential candidates, John Edwards had spent his career before politics as a trial lawyer, combating the insurance industry on his clients' behalf; he, it was clear, would try to carve out a position on health care that was to her political left, something closer to universal coverage than perhaps even Clinton herself advocated.

Not surprisingly, some of Obama's top advisors were concerned about how their candidate would differentiate his health care position from those of two well-established politicians. Adding urgency to the question was an early scheduling hiccup that laid bare just how unprepared for the rigors and stresses of a presidential campaign the Obama brain trust truly was.

On January 16, 2007, Obama appeared in a web video to announce he would explore the prospect of running for president. He said he would have discussions with potential supporters, friends, and family, then make a final decision in his home state on February 10, almost a month later.

An exploratory committee is something of a formality these days—few politicians who start one are actually undecided about running. Very few who explore the possibility of running for something ever decide against taking the final leap. In fact, in the eyes of the Federal Election Commission, there is no legal difference between an exploratory committee and a formal campaign committee. Just the name on the paperwork. Ditto in the eyes of official Washington.

That fact became a problem for Robert Gibbs and Dan Pfeiffer, two of the exploratory committee's earliest employees. As they examined the calendar, the two men realized that Obama's campaign and his Senate office had neglected to compare notes. Pete Rouse, Obama's Senate chief of staff, had months earlier, pre-campaign, promised Ron Pollack, the influential head of the liberal health care group Families USA, that Obama would give the keynote address at the group's annual meeting in Washington—a perfectly reasonable thing for an up-and-coming U.S. senator to do.

Both Gibbs and Pfeiffer were experienced operatives, and they knew that everything Obama said after January 16, during the exploratory phase, would be scrutinized, parsed, analyzed, and picked apart to a much higher degree than anything he had said before he made his announcement. Every speech he gave would suddenly be measured against Clinton, who would announce her own campaign five days later, and Edwards, who for all intents and purposes had been running for president since just after the 2004 elections. Going to Families USA to give a speech was an important stop for any Democratic senator; going as a presidential contender was another matter altogether, one that presented both a challenge and an opportunity for the nascent campaign.

"You can't go, 'I bring greetings from the U.S. Senate' sort of thing. You're a full-fledged presidential candidate. We had to, like, do something," Gibbs said. But while the exploratory committee had signed up a campaign manager, prominent Democratic lawyers, and other top operatives for key posts, they hadn't hired a policy director.

There was no question Obama would have to offer a grand health care proposal during the campaign. Doing so, David Axelrod later said, "became a sine qua non of the Democratic primary. There was almost a requirement in the primary to have a strong health care position."

But they hadn't even started formulating what that policy might be. Doing so, at the level of a professional presidential campaign, requires input from key constituency and stakeholder groups. Obama's campaign didn't even have someone who could pick up the phone and introduce him- or herself as the staffer in charge of policy oversight.

One of Obama's first stops as a presidential candidate, in other words, would be before a group that cared deeply about health care reform, and the candidate didn't have much to say about it. And instead of a check-the-box event, one any Democratic senator is obliged to do, the speech itself, by dint of its prescheduled spot on the calendar, proved an early hurdle.

Gibbs, Pfeiffer, and speechwriter Jon Favreau came up with a way to make the speech resonate: they would have Obama promise to pass health care reform by the end of his first term in office. It seemed like the perfect solution for a candidate who didn't have a plan — don't highlight a plan; instead, highlight a mission.

"On this January morning of two thousand and seven, more than sixty years after President Truman first issued the call for national health insurance, we find ourselves in the midst of an historic moment on health care. From Maine to California, from business to labor, from Democrats to Republicans, the emergence of new and bold proposals from across the spectrum has effectively ended the debate over whether or not we should have universal health care in this country," Obama told the Families USA audience. "... In the 2008 campaign, affordable, universal health care for every single American must not be a question of whether. It must be a question of how. We have the ideas, we have the resources. Now we have to find the will to pass a plan by the end of the next president's first term."[1]

The decision to call for universal health care was a practical short-term solution for the new campaign. Little differentiated Obama from Clinton and Edwards; the Democratic primary electorate was in no mood for a centrist, and Obama wasn't about to wear the moderate label. The only thing that was different was the concrete pledge to action — it certainly was a promise Clinton would not have made. But his declaration demonstrated just how much the new presidential candidate and his team had to learn about running for the highest office in the land. Within ten days of launching his campaign, almost on a whim, Obama had committed himself to a position that every Democrat in Washington would hold him to. "We hadn't exactly sat down and plotted out that this would become a core campaign process," Pfeiffer said. In fact, he added, the lack of a process became something of a running joke inside the campaign. "There really wasn't any approval process for speeches at that point," Pfeiffer recalled later. "He just went out and said it. And it became a staple of his stump speech for the next two years." For Pfeiffer and his fellow Obama true believers, it was akin to fastening the wings on a plane that was already taking off. But the staffers were fine with this—there was a "what the fuck" mind-set for those Democrats who made the decision to snub Clinton and the establishment and work for Obama.

The Democratic establishment—especially in Hillary Clinton's camp—took notice. Clinton, who had been burned by health care once before, had been circumspect about the prospects of passing a bill so soon after taking office. Her top aides made clear they thought pledging health care reform in the first term was insane, a demonstration of the young senator's political naïveté. Yet that speech began Obama's long and winding path to a final product, a massive bill that would engender a political storm that swallowed the House Democratic majority, lead to a government shutdown, and, once implemented, spark the greatest crisis of Obama's presidency.

The Affordable Care Act can hardly qualify as the universal health care Obama promised. Instead, almost from the day he proposed such a bill, Obama began moving toward the center in what would become a familiar Obama pattern: grandly proclaim a bold new direction, then move to the establishment middle.

During the 2008 primary, Clinton's proposal most closely resembled the lofty ambitions of universal coverage. Her plan advocated an individual mandate to purchase health insurance; Obama's advocated a mandate for children only. In fact, Obama even attacked Clinton's plan, and its individual mandate, as unenforceable and philosophically misguided. "Their essential argument is the only way to get everybody covered is if the government forces you to buy health insurance. If you don't buy it, then you'll be penalized in some way," he said in Iowa in November 2007, just ten months after calling for universal coverage.

Paul Krugman, an arbiter of liberal policy proposals who the next year would win the Nobel Prize for economics, was savage. Obama was using "right wing talking points," Krugman wrote in the *New York Times*. "Mr. Obama's caution, his reluctance to stake out a clearly partisan position, led him to propose a relatively weak, incomplete health care plan."[2]

Obama's fight over health care reform made its way into the November presidential campaign, too. The Obama campaign pounded John McCain for months over a proposal that would have offered individuals a $2,500 tax credit, or $5,000 for a family, to help them afford private health insurance. As a partial offset for the lower revenue to the federal government as a result of the credits, families would no longer be able to claim insurance coverage provided by employers as a tax write-off. To the Obama team, that opened a window of political opportunity—an opportunity to get to McCain's right on health care reform as well as taxes.

"Senator McCain would pay for his plan, in part, by taxing your health care benefits for the first time in history. And this tax would come out of your paycheck," Obama said during an October 2008 campaign stop in Newport News, Virginia. "But the new tax credit he's proposing? That wouldn't go to you. It would go directly to your insurance company—not your bank account. So when you read the fine print, it's clear that John McCain is pulling an old Washington bait and switch. It's a shell game. He gives you a tax credit with one hand—but raises your taxes with the other."[3]

The Obama team had always worried that McCain would use health care as a cudgel, a weapon Republicans had been wielding for decades to portray Democrats as big-government ideologues willing to take over such a mammoth part of the American economy. Taxes gave Obama an opening to blunt that argument, to present himself as the candidate most interested in cutting taxes.

Though health care reform was never the core of his campaign, Obama's team would find themselves reverting to two overarching principles during the year-and-a-half battle that would follow: First, they believed that Obama's appeal to voters rested with his resolve to govern on issues he had run on during the campaign. His staff was determined to stick to the script and stay true to Obama himself, rather than to have the candidate seen as just another opportunistic flip-flopper. Second, they were determined not to repeat the mistakes Bill Clinton had made, mistakes that cost Clinton not only the Democratic Congress but also any shot at reforming the system itself.

In 1993, Clinton had tried to ram health care through the Senate, where he had few relationships and fewer true allies. He made an enemy of New York senator Daniel Patrick Moynihan, at the time the chairman of the Senate Finance Committee, by keeping deliberations over health care reform legislation behind closed doors in the White House. Moynihan had been particularly offended that Hillary Clinton, who was leading the strategy sessions, hadn't consulted him; consequently, he turned against the bill and helped kill his own president's top initiative.

Rahm Emanuel would not let another Democratic president make the same mistake. The White House Obama and Emanuel were building would avoid such blunders by taking the opposite tack. Even with healthy Democratic majorities in both the House and Senate—once Arlen Specter, the Pennsylvania

Republican, switched parties on April 28, 2009, Democrats held a majority large enough to overcome a Republican filibuster—Congress's input would be solicited and incorporated. Instead of dictating the legislative language that Congress would take up, the Obama White House would cede much of the actual bill writing to Congress itself, based on a series of principles the president would lay out. Again, all designed to make sure the Obama White House was doing business with the Democratic Congress differently than Bill Clinton had. (By the way, in the pre-2010 Obama White House the easiest way to get the president or many members of this West Wing staff to do something was to claim that Clinton didn't do *X,* so we should. After the 2010 elections, there was a newfound respect for the Clinton way, but that lesson would take time to learn.)

To help guide the bill through Congress, Obama had initially turned to Tom Daschle and Neera Tanden, a former Hillary Clinton hand who had served as the campaign's policy director during the general election, to work together to craft the bill.

Tanden, another Democrat with decades of experience crafting policy for her party's most senior members in Washington, had caught Obama's eye during the primary. Obama believed Clinton's campaign had actually offered more detailed, well-thought-out policy proposals than his had, and those ideas had come from Tanden. During a Democratic primary debate just before the Nevada caucuses, Obama had spotted Tanden trailing along with Clinton's entourage. "When I win," Obama told Axelrod, "I want her on my team."

Once Clinton had bowed out of the race, Axelrod asked Tanden to come to Chicago. Behind the scenes, Obama's campaign team hadn't been thrilled with the idea of bringing a committed Clintonite so far into the fold. Some leaders quietly tried to overrule the boss and hire Melody Barnes, an executive vice president at the Center for American Progress. Barnes had been an Obama surrogate during the primaries, and Obama staffers made the case that she would be a better fit within the already-existing system. But Obama overruled them. "Hillary was better than me on policy," he said. "I've decided we're hiring Neera."

His comments put her in an awkward position. What Obama had meant as a compliment, some of her new employees took as a slap at them: they hadn't been as good as she was, and now she was their boss. But Tanden was smart and proved her loyalty, and eventually much of her staff came around.

On December 11, 2008, just a month after winning election, Obama tapped Daschle to serve as health and human services secretary and as the director of the new White House Office of Health Reform. The idea in giving Daschle the dual titles was to create a point person to shepherd Obama's health care reform—a CEO of sorts. Before agreeing to do the job, Daschle had elicited promises from Obama: that he would have a desk in the West Wing, and that health care reform would remain one of the president's top agenda items.

"I've talked to too many cabinet people over the years who feel so isolated," Daschle told Obama. "I've got to have an opportunity to have regular access. I've got to be in the West Wing if this is going to work."

Obama agreed. "Health care will be my legacy," he prophetically told Daschle.

But before he got to the White House, Daschle would have to get through the Senate. A former majority leader would ordinarily have had no trouble getting confirmed to a cabinet-level post. But Daschle was also one of Washington's foremost big names, one on a long roster of former elected officials who, while not technically registered as lobbyists, were employed by major lobbying firms to offer "strategic advice," Washington-speak for lobbyist-in-disguise. Daschle's connections led him to work with Leo Hindery, a major Democratic donor and New York–based investment guru who gave Daschle access to a limousine and a chauffeur—benefits he hadn't declared on his tax returns.

A Senate Finance Committee check into Daschle's background discovered the unpaid taxes. Unfazed,

Daschle had written a $140,000 check to the IRS even before he was nominated, and he expected the unpaid taxes to represent no more than a speed bump.

He was wrong. On January 30, Daschle was in Boston visiting his brother, who was suffering from terminal brain cancer, when he started getting phone calls from reporters. A scathing editorial in the *New York Times* the following weekend pushed Daschle to the brink. He became more frustrated, angrier with the process than he had ever been. A closed-door meeting with the Senate Finance Committee made matters worse. The committee had its own vetting process for certain cabinet members, and it's easily the most excruciating process any Senate body puts nominees through—so burdensome, many feel, that it drives folks away from serving in government. The president has been vocal for years since about the Senate Finance Committee's process. But at the time Obama was too new to argue.

By February 2, Daschle was considering withdrawing his nomination. On February 3, he called Rouse, his old chief of staff, to tell him to pull the plug.

Obama came on the line—in fact, Obama called him three times that day. The president wasn't trying to talk Daschle out of withdrawing, but he was clearly making it known that the White House would fight for its chosen lieutenant if Daschle was up for the contest. Obama wanted Daschle, the man who arguably had been the most important early supporter of Obama's Washington rise, to be certain of his own decision before he would accept the withdrawal. Daschle said he was, and formally dropped out on February 4. Years later, there's not an Obama veteran from that era who doesn't believe this wasn't the ultimate "butterfly effect" moment of the president's first term, that most of the problems that followed with health care could have been either mitigated or eliminated had Daschle been in place. No way Daschle doesn't get GOP buy-in, no way Daschle doesn't get this bill passed before the end of 2009, and no way Daschle doesn't have a team ready to launch a website. Or so many Obama staffers choose to believe today.

At that point less than a month into his administration, Obama seemingly had enough to deal with. The economy had shed 800,000 jobs during the month Obama took office. The stimulus bill was still three weeks away from passing. There were, in short, more pressing problems for a president still finding his way around his new home. It would have been easy for Barack Obama to wait, to shelve a controversial and politically costly debate over health care until the markets stabilized, the recession healed, and the country was headed in the right direction. Indeed, in several meetings to plot the administration's early legislative strategy, there was considerable discord among senior White House staffers. Several of Obama's top wise men, including Emanuel and Axelrod, urged Obama to use the Daschle exit as a time to rethink health care and scale back his plans and promises for a grand overhaul, in the process saving his points for later.

Political capital was very much on the White House's mind. The economic crisis had forced the president to push through a nearly $800 billion stimulus package—a sum that even a Republican president would likely have spent to avert disaster. The administration had to devote even more money to saving big banks, through a second round of TARP funding. Then there were American automakers, who needed their own multi-billion-dollar bailout to avoid going out of business and taking a few million jobs with them.

Not until the late spring of 2009, after months of near-frantic reaction—more than a few White House staffers likened their jobs to those of firemen constantly racing to put out new blazes—did it begin to seem as if the president might have an opportunity to advance his own agenda.

Emanuel, Summers, Geithner, Rouse, and Axelrod, among others, debated what the administration should tackle first. Three items stood out: health care reform, climate change—by way of cap-and-trade legislation—and reforming the financial sector.

Emanuel was an advocate of financial regulatory

reform. He was obsessed with spending—the administration had spent its first five months writing checks nonstop, committing trillions—and even though the money had to be spent, Emanuel saw it as an issue tailor-made for Republican attacks. He could also read poll numbers.

"Why don't we do financial [reform]?" Emanuel asked at one of many meetings in which he urged Obama to put off health care reform. "It has no money associated with it, the financial scandal is still there, we can get some Old Testament justice done."

On the other hand, Geithner and Summers argued against advancing financial regulatory reform in Obama's first year. The banks were still recovering, they explained. Introducing uncertainty now would slow the financial sector's return to normal—something that would reverberate through the housing market, the construction sector, and just about every industry that needed a loan to operate and create jobs. What's more, they said, waiting until the banks got their bearings wouldn't cause any damage; their weakened financial state meant no bank had the financial wherewithal to do anything nefarious before reform took place. Geithner and Summers also didn't want to pick a fight with Wall Street while they were still trying to coerce them to change some of their ways.

Cap-and-trade legislation, on the other hand, was

going to happen. Henry Waxman, chairman of the House Energy and Commerce Committee, was prepared to move the legislation himself, with or without the administration's involvement. It was also one of Pelosi's highest priorities.

Few senior White House officials favored advancing climate change legislation, for simple political reasons: while the House Democratic Caucus was dominated by liberals from urban and suburban districts, the ranks of Senate Democrats included many from energy-producing states such as West Virginia, Montana, Alaska, and the Dakotas—senators whose constituents were predisposed to oppose any kind of cap-and-trade legislation. As a result, the House could pass as many environment-friendly bills as it liked, but they would languish in the Senate without the 60 votes necessary to overcome a certain Republican-led filibuster.*

Emanuel wanted to pass legislation that could get signed into law; no one at the White House could envision how to get cap-and-trade through the Senate, where geography would trump ideology on the Democratic side.

---

* Some in the White House faulted Schiliro for failing to talk Waxman, his old boss, out of moving cap-and-trade legislation before health care; others saw Pelosi's not-so-hidden hand behind the legislation's advance—a signal, during complex negotiations with the Senate over health care, that the House was not to be taken for granted.

*   *   *

Obama's own view of power in Washington argued for pursuing health care reform: Democrats held a huge majority in the House, 60 votes in the Senate, and the White House. If Obama was going to succeed on health care, the first year of his first term, under such favorable political circumstances, was the time to do it.

In the end, health care reform was the most viable option the White House could pursue if it wanted to begin advancing its own agenda. Yet that decision, to pursue health care reform over other big legislative priorities, was more out of the White House's control than it would admit.

The White House kicked off its push for health care reform with a summit that brought together congressional leaders, industry stakeholders, think tank experts, and union leaders on March 5, 2009. Obama promised to have a bill passed by the end of the year, just nine months away.

Internally, the White House was far more ambitious: it hoped to have legislative language prepared by late spring or early summer, final passage in the House and Senate by the end of July, and negotiations to reconcile any differences between the two bills finished over the August recess or, pessimistically, by the end of September. The White House wanted a fall bill-signing ceremony.

In Daschle's absence, the White House split his

two job titles between Kathleen Sebelius, the governor of Kansas who would become health and human services secretary, and Nancy-Ann DeParle, a longtime reform advocate who had experience running Tennessee's health care system and the federal Health Care Financing Administration under Bill Clinton. DeParle would take over the White House Office of Health Reform, where she would prove instrumental in driving Obama away from his original proposal and toward the version Hillary Clinton had originally pitched.

It was DeParle who spearheaded the push to include an individual mandate—the cornerstone of Hillary Clinton's plan—in the final bill. She and her allies pitched it as a substantive way to cover millions of uninsured Americans. Obama, who had blasted Clinton for the same language, ultimately adopted her proposal.

Of course, the final bill itself, the language that would ultimately require congressional votes to pass, wouldn't be written by one person or one group of people. It required the input of Congress, which meant, despite overwhelming Democratic majorities, winning over skeptical centrists. But if they did it right, the White House could rely upon nearly all the main Democratic players on Capitol Hill—Ted Kennedy, Nancy Pelosi, Charlie Rangel, George Miller, Henry Waxman—all over seventy years old, for whom this would be their last chance before retirement, Emanuel calculated, to work on something so key to the Democratic platform. "They were going to get this done, because for their entire lives now they were writing the last chapter of the book. This had been a twenty-five- to thirty-year journey for everybody." And, Emanuel figured, it would make these elderly liberal members more open to compromise in order to get centrists (or even Republicans) on board.

If only.

A year after he'd arrived in Washington, Barack Obama tried to keep a low profile. Reporters and pundits had tapped him as a rising star, a would-be presidential candidate even before he was sworn in to the Senate. But before his national ambitions played out, Obama knew he needed to build a reputation in Washington, to show he was about more than just fluff and soaring rhetoric.

Obama had promised to change Washington, to work across the aisle to get a dysfunctional city moving again. And in an era of steadily increasing partisanship, he saw an opportunity to do that: he would work with a man he saw as his counterpart on the Republican side, a longtime senator who was held in similar esteem by the national media, someone who knew the pitfalls of Washington, someone with a history of working to change the system. So one day on the Senate floor, Obama wandered up to John McCain, the senior senator from Arizona.

Early in his career in the Senate, McCain had been caught up in scandal. He was the only Republican among the five senators (the "Keating Five") implicated in an investigation the Federal Home Loan Bank Board was conducting into the Lincoln Savings and Loan Association and its chairman, Charles Keating. After Lincoln's collapse, which cost taxpayers $3 billion, the Senate Ethics Committee found that three Democratic senators had improperly intervened; the panel rapped two others, McCain and John Glenn, the Ohio Democrat, on the knuckles for exercising poor judgment in the case.

The scandal set McCain, until then a rank-and-file member of the Senate Republican Conference, on an unexpected path. He began crusading for campaign finance and ethics reform, having come to believe that the explosion of money in politics had a significant negative impact on government and on the image of those who governed. At a time when most Republican senators were looking for new ways to allow their allies in the business community to spend more on advertisements, McCain began searching for ways to shut off the spigot.

So when Obama came to McCain that day in 2006, McCain saw a potentially valuable, like-minded ally. If the two of them could work together on lobbying and ethics reform, the combination of their individual star power, plus the fallout from the scandal involving disgraced lobbyist Jack Abramoff, could lead to a real shake-up.

"I like him," McCain told his top aide after Obama broached the subject of working together. "He's probably got a great future. We can do some work together."[4]

At the time, Abramoff had already cost his party dearly. An investigation into his conduct surrounding the payoffs Abramoff and his employees had delivered to members of Congress, an investigation spearheaded by McCain himself, had added to the GOP's mounting electoral woes — the party had lost control of both chambers of Congress in the 2006 elections, after Democrats had made ethics and governance a key issue.

Needing a quick fix to show voters that they were doing something about the ethics problems, the GOP realized that McCain's reputation as a good-government crusader would help. They now turned to McCain to begin drafting an ethics bill. Democrats, hoping to double down on their electoral advantage, turned to Obama to come up with their version. If the two could work together, they might be able to get some truly sweeping reforms passed.

McCain invited Obama to a bipartisan gathering of senators who met on February 1, 2006, to discuss reform. Some Republicans present took note when Obama delivered what sounded like a campaign speech without discussing the actual specifics of a bill. The next day, McCain received a letter from Obama that caught him off guard. "I appreciate your willingness to reach out to me and several other Senate Democrats to discuss what should be done to restore public confidence in the way that Congress conducts its business," Obama wrote, in an unusually formal tone that didn't seem to adhere to the collegial atmosphere of the previous day's meeting.

"I know you have expressed an interest in creating a task force to further study and discuss these matters, but I and others in the Democratic Caucus believe the more effective and timely course is to allow the committees of jurisdiction to roll up their sleeves and get to work on writing ethics and lobbying reform legislation that a majority of the Senate can support," Obama went on. "Committee consideration of these matters through the normal course will ensure that these issues are discussed in a public forum and that those within Congress, as well as those on the outside, can express their views, ensuring a thorough review of this matter."[5]

McCain was incredulous, more so when Obama's letter promptly showed up in Capitol Hill newspapers. The letter looked as if it had come straight from the desk of Harry Reid, the Senate Democratic leader. "He's sending you a press release/letter for his leader," Mark Salter, McCain's chief of staff, told his boss.

McCain told Salter to throw an inside fastball in

response, to "brush him back," Salter recalled later. The letter that went out under McCain's name, dripping with sarcasm and oozing contempt, caused much of official Washington to sit up and take note.

"I would like to apologize to you for assuming that your private assurances to me regarding your desire to cooperate in our efforts to negotiate bipartisan lobbying reform legislation were sincere. When you approached me and insisted that despite your leadership's preference to use the issue to gain a political advantage in the 2006 elections, you were personally committed to achieving a result that would reflect credit on the entire Senate and offer the country a better example of political leadership, I concluded your professed concern for the institution and the public interest was genuine and admirable. Thank you for disabusing me of such notions," Salter wrote for McCain.

"I understand how important the opportunity to lead your party's effort to exploit this issue must seem to a freshman Senator, and I hold no hard feelings over your earlier disingenuousness. Again, I have been around long enough to appreciate that in politics the public interest isn't always a priority for every one of us. Good luck to you, Senator."[6]

Asked about McCain's response, Obama dug the hole deeper: McCain, Obama said, "has served here in Washington for 20 years, so if he wants to get cranky once in a while, that's his prerogative." A reporter asked him whether he had just called McCain cranky. "You got my quote the first time," Obama snapped.[7]

Both Obama and McCain realized they had taken their feud too far, too fast. They spoke by phone the next day, and McCain told reporters the two were moving on. "We're still colleagues. We're still friends. I mean, this isn't war," he said. A few days later, at a Senate Rules Committee meeting where McCain and Obama testified about their respective ethics proposals, Obama began by thanking McCain, "my new pen pal." The laughter in the committee room defused any lingering tension.[8]

But the once-promising partnership had turned stone cold. A Washington relationship depends on trust, and both McCain and Obama felt that trust had been broken. In an institution in which the effusiveness with which one senator praises another is inversely related to the general loathing they feel for each other — the higher the compliment, the lower the esteem — McCain and Obama would be friends only on the Senate floor. The dustup with McCain was the first hint Obama received that Washington wasn't going to be like Harvard.

Sixteen years before he and McCain traded letters, Obama was an audacious Harvard Law School student who had barged into the office of Lawrence

Tribe, a hero in liberal legal circles, to seek a mentor. By the end of his second year, Obama had decided to run for president — of the *Harvard Law Review.*

He didn't campaign terribly hard for the job, but others did. The *Review,* run by eighty editors, was starkly divided along partisan, and even racial, lines. But Obama didn't fall into any particular category — or at least he seemed to simultaneously occupy several of them; he was hard to pin down. Conservatives thought that the guy from Hawaii in the skinny jeans and the leather jacket would listen to them, though they preferred Brad Berenson, later a leading conservative and one of the top lawyers in George W. Bush's White House. But when it became clear that Berenson couldn't win, the conservative bloc joined with a group of African American law students to back Obama.

"They had a sense that he was more open-minded and would listen to the conservatives, and would value and accept their contributions in a way that some of the other candidates would not," Berenson later recalled. "He ended up upsetting many more of his colleagues on the far left than those of us who were on the right, in part because the bottom line for him as president of the law review always remained putting out a first-class publication."[9] That experience shaped Obama's approach to legislating — working across the aisle meant listening to one's opponents, he came to believe, even if that's *all* he did. Some longtime Washington hands believe the president's ease at working across ideological lines at Harvard Law gave him false self-confidence that burns in him — and burns him — to this day.

But it wasn't only his Harvard experience that gave Obama a false sense of self-importance when it came to working with Republicans. Obama's early political experiences bolstered that notion. He worked with Kirk Dillard, a Republican state senator, to pass campaign finance and ethics reform in a state capital that had been long known for its lax approach to ethics rules. Six months into his tenure in the U.S. Senate, Obama accompanied Senator Richard Lugar, the Indiana Republican, on a trip to Russia, Azerbaijan, and Ukraine to inspect nuclear facilities in the old Soviet bloc; after their trip, the two pushed nuclear nonproliferation legislation that became law in 2007.

Personal connections, Obama seemed to learn, were important to success in Washington. Just after he won election to the Senate, Obama made a new friend: Tom Coburn, the conservative Republican from Oklahoma.

The two men met in December 2004, during an orientation for new members of the Senate. Their wives became fast friends, too. Obama and Coburn spent time together at weekly prayer breakfasts. Together they addressed a gathering of young college leaders. They even made a bipartisan push to install a chief financial officer to oversee federal funds spent on rebuilding the Gulf Coast after Hurricanes Katrina and Rita.[10]

When he ran for president, Obama made those bipartisan credentials, and the potential for more bipartisanship to come, a cornerstone of his campaign. Dillard showed up in his campaign's first television ad. Lugar's image followed close behind. At his first joint address to Congress, Obama very publicly hugged Coburn on the floor of the House of Representatives. The promise of Barack Obama, in short, was the promise of a new era of bipartisanship.

And that's how his administration kicked off its first two years in office—with an actual effort to cross party lines. Politically and in the policy arena, the first quarter of Obama's eight-year tenure in office will be remembered as a time when the White House, perhaps naïvely, stretched an arm across the aisle.

Just as early on, there were signs that Republicans wouldn't follow the presidential Pied Piper to postpartisanship.

The very night Obama was inaugurated, as he danced with Michelle at celebratory balls around the city, the cadre of top House and Senate Republicans and the political strategists who hoped to guide them back to power met at that high-priced Washington steak house, concluding: stymie Obama at every turn, attack the administration where it was weak, and give no quarter. Instead of working with the administration, which would only give Obama the victories he needed to further consolidate his political success, Republicans would hold the line and make every Obama win a polarizing, partisan moment. They wouldn't make the same mistake they had with Clinton in the '90s.

At this point, his first term just beginning, there was no way to know just how overwhelming GOP opposition would end up hampering not only the president's agenda but the basic functioning of the federal government. Right now, a bipartisan health care bill seemed well within the realm of possibility: with the House firmly in Democratic hands and 59, then (with Arlen Specter's party switch) 60, Democratic votes in the Senate, the administration needed only a handful of committee chairmen to advance their proposal and a small number of Republican votes to give the massive overhaul at least a veneer of bipartisanship, enough to get wavering centrist Democrats on board.

To help make this happen, Obama was willing to sacrifice some Democratic sacred cows in hopes of winning over Republican votes.

The administration focused on two key relationships. The first was between Senate Finance Committee chairman Max Baucus, a centrist Democrat, and Chuck Grassley, the ranking Republican on the panel. The two had a long history of working together and running the finance panel harmoniously; if Baucus and Grassley could strike a deal, the reasoning went, Grassley would bring a handful of Republicans with him and score a legislative coup for Obama's signature initiative.

Baucus wanted to bring his partner Grassley along, and Jim Messina, Baucus's former chief of staff turned deputy chief of staff for Obama, was convinced his old boss could do it, so the White House made the decision to wait for Baucus to negotiate with Grassley over some of his key concerns.

And wait they did. In less than a month, between late April and mid-May, Grassley and Baucus held three roundtable events with stakeholders and business leaders, then published three sets of policy options. The Finance Committee as a whole gathered several more times, and by mid-June a bipartisan Gang of Six—Baucus, Grassley, and Senators Kent Conrad, Jeff Bingaman, Olympia Snowe, and Mike Enzi—started meeting almost daily when Congress was in Washington to try to hammer out a bill. Before breaking up in mid-September, the Gang had convened a total of thirty-one times—without coming up with legislative language.[11]

June came and went, then July. Remember, according to the initial timeline, the White House thought it would be passing bills in July, not still writing them. In the White House, the long slog toward a bill took its toll on senior officials. Tensions ran high among key decision-makers; Sebelius, DeParle, Tanden, Geithner, Summers, Orszag, Messina, and economic advisor Jason Furman didn't even hold a major meeting of key West Wing players between the end of April and the end of July. Time was running out: the longer health care took, the less likely were the prospects for the rest of the agenda. Sensing the vacuum, DeParle, a skilled political operator, aggregated ideas and strategy memos under her own name and won praise from Obama. Yet the president seemed preoccupied with other initiatives, according to several aides.

One issue he seemed to be struggling with was his own performance. Throughout the grueling year, Obama grew frustrated by his inability to communicate his own plans better. In interviews and in private, he would frequently cite communications as the issue he needed to work on most. At times, that trickled down to staffers, who believed they simply needed a better message rather than a better bill. At one Oval Office meeting Obama stopped a debate between Emanuel, the political operative, and Axelrod, who retained a sense of purity about the president he had helped elect. "You know, I'm usually a pretty good communicator, and I'm not communicating this very well," Obama said.

"One of the problems is, we've made all these

deals, so people don't understand. We used to attack the insurance companies, and now we're making deals with them," Axelrod said.

"We decided to make these deals because we wanted to pass a bill," Emanuel shot back.

Obama repeated his frustration with the message and communications strategy. Axelrod and Emanuel repeated their points. Neither picked up on the president's frustration; another participant in the room was embarrassed at their behavior. Many aides later recalled that they never held any political meeting to discuss a policy problem on any issue, health care or otherwise; it was always a "communications" problem. If only they could sell it themselves, if only they could cut Congress out, cut the press out, and communicate the health care plan *directly* to the people, only *then* would they get it and simply love it! So goes the assumption of every single elected official in history.

Meanwhile, fissures between the two chief legislative strategists emerged. Emanuel grew frustrated with Baucus, who insisted on working with Grassley in hopes he would come around. Reid argued in favor of giving Baucus time, but that time was also allowing opposition to the bill to coalesce. Republicans who weren't at the negotiating table—that is, almost everyone except Grassley and a handful of others—were winning the public relations battle, while a new rump group of conservatives who called themselves the Tea Party started getting national media attention.

By the time Grassley went home to Iowa for the August recess, he and plenty of his fellow members of Congress were confronting growing crowds at town hall meetings who were furious over the bill's language. Grassley himself, at a session in Winterset, Iowa—home of Iowa's famous covered bridges as well as the birthplace of John Wayne—embraced a growing conspiracy theory that held that the House version of the health care bill included what he called "death panels"—a moniker McCain's running mate, former Alaska governor Sarah Palin, and a few other prominent conservatives had latched onto to grab attention. (The section of the bill in question was actually an alteration suggested by a Republican, in this case Georgia senator Johnny Isakson. It would have required Medicare to provide end-of-life counseling sessions, on a voluntary basis. Palin, in comments on her Facebook page, bastardized the language to suggest the bill would give the government the power to decide to euthanize patients, a notion Isakson himself called "nuts.")[12]

To some Democrats, Grassley's Winterset comments were a warning bell. Jim Manley, Reid's communications director, recalled his cell phone ringing just hours later, while he was on a golf course. It was the majority leader's first indication that the August recess ahead was going to be particularly rough for his caucus.

If the White House didn't get the same message, that Grassley was no longer a viable negotiating partner, they needed only another five days to understand. On August 17, Grassley appeared on MSNBC, where he was asked just what it would take for him to support the health care bill. If he had gotten everything he wanted but was one of just a few Republicans backing the bill, I asked Grassley, would he still vote for it?

Grassley said no. "I am negotiating for Republicans. If I can't negotiate something that gets more than four Republicans, I'm not a good negotiator," he said. "It isn't a good deal if I can't sell my product to more Republicans."[13] The White House realized then that Baucus's negotiating partner had left the table. Grassley had a very pragmatic reason to walk away. He had seen his own political future, had he signed on to a deal, and it was bleak. He was up for re-election in 2010, and the Iowa conservative grass roots was potentially restless. He clearly made the rational political decision that if he wanted another term in the Senate, he was going to have to walk away, a choice he made after precious time had been lost.

With town hall meetings threatening to derail the bill even farther, the White House turned to its single best asset, the president himself. Obama began holding his *own* town hall meetings to pitch the aspects of the bill that polled best—keeping children on a parent's health care plan until age twenty-six, prohibiting denial of coverage for preexisting conditions.

But while the staff accompanying him enjoyed getting out of Washington, with each stop their malaise grew. Before one town hall meeting in Belgrade, Montana, Obama came across a morose Gibbs. He asked why his press secretary looked so glum.

"I feel like we're getting the shit kicked out of us," Gibbs said.

"We've been through a lot worse than this," Obama chuckled. "Do you think Reverend Wright wasn't as bad as this? Come on, man, we're fine."

As bad as this. ABC *World News* had first aired the videos that made Jeremiah Wright famous, but at the time, it seemed like another Chicagoland figure was Obama's big problem. Hillary Clinton's campaign was raising questions about businessman Tony Rezko's ties to Obama—about the ten-foot-wide strip of property the candidate had purchased from Rezko to expand the footprint of his Kenwood home, or the campaign contributions Rezko had provided the up-and-coming politician, or the letters Obama had written to city and state regulators backing a low-income-housing project Rezko wanted to build. At a debate almost two months earlier in South Carolina, Clinton had asked Obama about the "slum land-lord" with whom he associated. Rezko's close ties to Rod Blagojevich, the governor of Illinois, would eventually land both men in jail; Clinton's team was hoping the Rezko connection could bring down Obama's presidential campaign, too.

But with regard to Obama's presidential campaign, Rezko would turn out to be a minor hiccup com-pared to the short man in the video. In a preacher's frock, his mustache and close-cropped hair framing his glasses, Jeremiah Wright, pastor of Trinity United Church of Christ, blamed America for the Septem-ber 11 terrorist attacks with his now-infamous "chick-ens coming home to roost" line.

"The government gives [African Americans] the drugs, builds bigger prisons, passes the three-strikes law, and then wants us to sing 'God Bless Amer-ica,'" the preacher shouted, his face contorting with rage. "No, no, no! Not God bless America. God *damn* America!"

Wright had played a major role in Obama's life. He had helped introduce the candidate to the black church, an experience Obama hadn't had while grow-ing up in Hawaii. He had officiated at Barack and Michelle's wedding, and baptized their children. The title of Obama's bestselling book *The Audacity of Hope* had come from one of Wright's sermons.

Now Wright was on television screaming about the evils of the U.S. government and giving voice to many discredited conspiracy theories. Suddenly the Obama campaign had a much bigger problem than Tony Rezko.

The campaign had worked so hard to thread a needle—capturing the electoral benefit that came with being the first front-running black candidate in a party in which blacks made up such a big percentage of the coalition, while simultaneously trying to downplay the candidate's race for a general election in which winning over white voters was critical. Now the intemperate statements of someone not even involved in the campaign threatened to undo a year or more of their hard work, thanks to speeches that were readily available on the Internet. Indeed, it wasn't as if ABC had sneaked into Wright's church—his sermons were available for purchase!

Some inside the campaign had known that Wright would be a problem from the start. Obama had invited his old pastor to give the invocation at his campaign kickoff, on a cold morning in early February 2007. But when Obama's team got wind of the reverend's penchant for controversial comments, some of which first appeared in a *Rolling Stone* article that hit newsstands that very month, they had to disinvite him.[14] Obama's opponents—Clinton first, then the Republican noise machine—kept pushing opposition research on Wright. But nobody found the tapes until ABC came calling.

Obama was furious: how could the campaign not have known that video was out there? A communications aide had drafted a statement to hand out to a sympathetic media outlet. Obama hated the statement. He wrote his own, calling Wright's language "inflammatory and appalling."[15] And then Obama went a step farther: he said he needed to address race on his own, to confront head-on the elephant in the room.

His opponents would never say it outright, but the message they had pushed about Barack Hussein Obama was clear: he's not one of us. It wasn't just Republicans delivering the subtle dog whistles; those came from Democrats, too. And it wasn't just whites who wanted to drive a wedge, but blacks as well.

And the fact was, they were right: Obama didn't fit neatly into any category. His skin color set him apart from his white grandparents, with whom he spent several years as a teenager in Hawaii; even his grandmother, he pointed out, would occasionally look at other races with skepticism. He didn't fit neatly into a black political community that had grown up fighting for civil rights in the 1960s, either; Obama had been born too late for those battles, which bred some distrust among icons like Jesse Jackson and Al Sharpton. His father was from Kenya, not from the United States; Obama didn't have any relatives who had been slaves. The experience of growing up in Hawaii, the eclectic melting pot where Obama learned from a multiethnic group of friends for whom race was hardly a factor, set him further apart from identifying with any individual group.

Though he's wary of wading into the debate, Obama views race through a lens inspired by his mother, Stanley Ann Dunham. Dunham had received a PhD in anthropology from the University of Hawaii, where she spent years researching household and community manufacturing in Indonesia. Her thesis, which weighed in at a robust 1,000 pages, detailed local blacksmithing work in the island nation, where she also worked for the United States Agency for International Development and the Ford Foundation.[16]

Obama was his mother's son. His own remove from any one single community led him to view the world through the lens of an anthropologist, an observer who stood apart and analyzed some tribe or culture—a philosophy that has gotten him in hot water. While Americans like to view their country as a melting pot of ethnic identities, Obama has at times acknowledged the differences between our tribes. Most famously, he offered his own view of how his campaign was performing among white voters in early Democratic primary states, and why he fared worse in some Rust Belt states than in other states he won. "Here's how it is: In a lot of these communities in big industrial states like Ohio and Pennsylvania, people have been beaten down so long. They feel so betrayed by government that when they hear a pitch that is premised on not being cynical about government, then a part of them just doesn't buy it. And when it's delivered by—it's true that when it's delivered by a 46-year-old black man named Barack Obama, then that adds another layer of skepticism," Obama said at a fund-raiser held in San Francisco in early April 2008. At that point the Pennsylvania primaries were the next big contest on the horizon.

"You go into these small towns in Pennsylvania, and like a lot of small towns in the Midwest, the jobs have been gone now for 25 years and nothing's replaced them. And they fell through the Clinton administration and the Bush administration, and each successive administration has said that somehow these communities are going to regenerate and they have not," Obama continued. "And it's not surprising, then, they get bitter, they cling to guns or religion or antipathy to people who aren't like them or anti-immigrant sentiment or anti-trade sentiment as a way to explain their frustrations."[17]

Clinging to guns or religion. Obama's comments weren't meant as a criticism of white rural America, for whom the Second Amendment might as well have been etched on Moses's stone tablets and for whom churches are the center of many communities. They were an anthropological construct, a difference Obama had noticed between struggling communities in the Midwest and their coastal urban counterparts. But this wasn't Obama being out of touch; he was simply being his mother's son—an acute observer. Of course, sometimes those observations came across as condescending, as this infamous "cling" comment did.

His opponents used the remarks to paint Obama as out of touch with mainstream America. Presidential campaigns are about optimistic views of the future, and Obama had suggested, inadvertently, that pessimism was at the root of any opposition to his campaign. At a rally in Philadelphia, Clinton spoke of "people who are resilient, who are optimistic, who are positive....Pennsylvanians don't need a president who looks down on them. They need a president who stands up for them, who fights for them."[18] Yet here, too, was the possibility of language coded in race: who was "they," who was "them"?

Obama's analytical and personal distance proved both an asset and a curse. A generation of civil rights icons like Jackson and Sharpton hadn't been successful at the ballot box; in fact, the legacy they left was of African American politicians being boxed into majority-minority districts, rather than breaking out in statewide races. When Obama ran for the Senate

in 2004, not a single African American held a seat
in that body or led a state as governor. He didn't
want to be the black candidate; the only time he
had tried, back in 2000, to win a majority-minority
district, Obama had been stomped by Representative Bobby Rush, a former Black Panther who held
a majority-black district on Chicago's South Side.
Instead, Obama built his initial campaign for statewide office on a decidedly liberal platform opposing
the war in Iraq, a position he used to contrast himself with his two main rivals in the presidential race
four years later.

But that meant that when he ran for president,
Obama couldn't rely on the natural constituency a
black candidate might otherwise have expected.
Many black leaders wondered aloud whether the
country was ready for a black president, and the
deep divisions of the civil rights era still existed;
white voters, the theory went, were still skeptical of
black candidates. (Again, the evidence being the
fact that by the time he announced his campaign
for president, only one state had a black governor:
Massachusetts, where Deval Patrick had won office
in 2006 with the help of two key consultants, David
Plouffe and David Axelrod.) If votes inside the
Democratic coalition broke down along racial lines,
Obama was cooked: the first two primary contests
would be held in Iowa and New Hampshire, two of

the whitest states in the Union. Not until later, when South Carolina had its say, would a significant number of African American voters be a part of the primary electorate.

Other black leaders didn't believe Obama had paid his dues the way they had. Jackson made those private gripes public when a hot microphone caught his comments during an interview with Fox News: "See, Barack's been talking down to black people," Jackson said into the mic. "I want to cut his nuts off."[19]

But any questions about whether Obama could win white voters disappeared in Iowa. Obama didn't just win a lot of white voters, he won the caucuses, taking 37.6 percent, eight points better than John Edwards and Hillary Clinton. The effect was dramatic. Black voters suddenly found themselves believing that, just maybe, a major political party would elect one of their own. And they started telling pollsters they would cast a ballot for Obama. In December, before the contests began, Clinton and Obama had been running about even in South Carolina; after he won the Iowa caucuses, Obama never trailed in another poll of Palmetto State voters—and still, those polls all understated the huge twenty-nine-point win Obama scored on January 26.[20]

Then came the Reverend Wright. Back in campaign headquarters, Obama's advisors tried to talk him out of a grand speech on race. The subject was still a third rail in politics, especially for a black candidate who was trying to build a postracial brand. But Obama had been thinking about a major address on race for almost his entire campaign; his top advisors had talked him out of it when he brought it up the first time, back in the fall, and again after primaries in Texas and Ohio earlier that same month, when exit polls had shown Clinton winning the white vote by overwhelming margins. But on that March Friday in Chicago, Obama told Axelrod he wanted to give the speech within the next four days.

There was a tightrope to be walked: Obama couldn't come across as patronizing, or defensive, or even apologetic. He told Jon Favreau, his lead speechwriter, that he wanted the speech to be "a teaching moment." He consulted with some of his closest friends — Valerie Jarrett, Marty Nesbitt, and Eric Whitaker, all of whom are black — about how to thread the needle.

Obama wrote the vast majority of the speech himself. He didn't finish it until the early-morning hours of March 18, the day he would give the address at the National Constitution Center in Philadelphia. The final draft floored his top advisors. "This is why you should be president," Axelrod told Obama after he had read the draft. [21]

In Philadelphia, surrounded by American flags and a blue backdrop, Obama condemned Wright's comments, but not the man himself. "I can no more disown [Wright] than I can disown the black community," Obama said. "I can no more disown him than I can my white grandmother.

"The fact is that the comments that have been made and the issues that have surfaced over the last few weeks reflect the complexities of race in this country that we've never really worked through—a part of our Union that we have yet to perfect," Obama said. "If we walk away now, if we simply retreat into our respective corners, we will never be able to come together and solve challenges like health care, or education, or the need to find good jobs for every American."

For thirty-seven minutes, Obama spoke of race through a new prism, the progress America had made and the challenges the country still faced. It was a remarkable balancing act between distancing himself from the accusatory tone many black leaders had used and refusing to disavow an entire community that had fought for decades to secure for people like Barack Obama not only the right to vote, but the right to run for the highest office in the land. What's more, Obama made a point of acknowledging the reason many white Americans might harbor some small manner of racial hostility, effectively offering an olive branch when the two sides were more used to weapons.

"The profound mistake of Reverend Wright's

sermons is not that he spoke about racism in our society," Obama said. "It's that he spoke as if our society was static, as if no progress has been made." Immediate reaction was positive.

"There are moments—increasingly rare in risk-abhorrent modern campaigns—when politicians are called upon to bare their fundamental beliefs. In the best of these moments, the speaker does not just salve the current political wound, but also illuminates larger, troubling issues that the nation is wrestling with," the *New York Times* editorial board wrote of the speech. "Senator Barack Obama, who has not faced such tests of character this year, faced one on Tuesday. It is hard to imagine how he could have handled it better."[22]

Obama had saved his campaign with one speech, thus teaching a (wrong?) lesson to a future President Obama: when in doubt, a speech can fix things. Of course, in campaigns speeches *can* fix things. In the presidency? A different story.

Obama's candidacy came at a moment when race was becoming an increasingly important factor for both electoral coalitions. White voters had been trending away from Democrats since 1968, when Richard Nixon's Southern Strategy pitted whites against minorities, with Democrats representing minority interests. Meanwhile, Nixon's strategy put black voters almost unanimously in the Democratic column. Then in the intervening decades, the Hispanic population, which began as but a small segment of the electorate, began to boom.

Some Republicans did well with Hispanic voters. George W. Bush won 44 percent of Hispanics when he ran for re-election in 2004. But Bush's party, driven by an activist base that increasingly saw strict enforcement-only immigration laws as the way to stem an overstated tide of undocumented migrants they imagined streaming across the border, did serious damage to itself during a bitter intraparty feud over immigration reform in 2005. Though the Bush White House backed a comprehensive solution, Fox News and conservative talk radio stations warned of "amnesty" for those in the country illegally. The more intemperate members of the Republican Party — Rush Limbaugh, Representatives Jim Sensenbrenner and Tom Tancredo and Steve King, and just about anybody who hosted a prime-time show on Fox that year — used language that convinced many Hispanic voters that the GOP simply wasn't interested in their votes. In 2008, John McCain, one of the party's most vocal advocates of comprehensive immigration reform during his time in Congress, got just 31 percent of the Hispanic vote.

By the time Barack Obama climbed atop the national stage, the country's demographics, and the coalitions that made up both national political parties, had changed further. Democrats were relying more on a growing pool of minority voters, spending millions on registering and turning out Hispanics and African Americans—and, increasingly, Asian Americans—who had historically voted at lower levels than whites. Republicans were winning more and more votes from white voters, even as the pool of whites shrank. In 1980, white voters had made up 89 percent of the electorate; by 2008, they were 74 percent of the electorate, dropping to 72 percent in 2012. Even though Obama won just 43 percent of the white vote, he was able to win a sweeping victory because of the increased influence blacks, Hispanics, and Asians held. By 2012, Obama was down to 39 percent of the white vote, but it didn't matter, since the white vote had decreased by nearly the same percentage of the vote Obama lost from 2008 to 2012. In fact, Obama's share of the white vote was nearly identical to the share of the white vote Michael Dukakis received in 1988 against George H. W. Bush. Dukakis's 39 percent of the white vote meant he couldn't even win 200 electoral votes. Obama's 39 percent of the white vote coupled with larger shares of Hispanic and black votes gave him a near-landslide electoral win.

Those demographics may have won Barack Obama the presidency, but they didn't mean much in terms of a sitting President Obama winning the Senate or controlling the House.

* * *

A week after criss-crossing the country trying to tout health care, Ted Kennedy succumbed to the brain cancer he had been fighting since suffering a seizure in 2008. Health care reform had been one of Kennedy's top priorities in a Senate career that spanned parts of six decades; even after he was ready to commit to endorsing the young, untested Obama during the height of the 2008 Democratic primary, after a fierce behind-the-scenes feud with both Bill and Hillary Clinton, Kennedy told the candidate he needed a commitment that he would push for universal health care as a top priority. Obama had agreed.[23]

Kennedy had been too sick to participate in the legislative maneuvering around health care reform; he had even given up the chairmanship of the Health, Education, Labor and Pensions Committee (HELP in Washington-speak) to his close friend Connecticut's Chris Dodd. His death was a blow to Democratic morale; everyone, even those who had backed Jimmy Carter over Kennedy in 1980, venerated the liberal lion from Massachusetts. And to this day, many Senate Republicans who served with Kennedy admit that if anyone could have gotten a bipartisan health deal through the Senate, it was Teddy. But it was not to be, and he would not live long enough to vote for the final bill.

Without Kennedy's seat after his death in the summer of 2009, Democrats had 59 Senate votes, one shy of the number required to break a filibuster. Massachusetts governor Deval Patrick quickly appointed Paul Kirk, a former Kennedy aide, to fill the seat. But the state's legislators had gotten clever in 2004, at a moment when John Kerry looked as if he would win the presidency; the legislature, which is overwhelmingly Democratic, had changed state law to require a special election to fill a Senate seat, so that Mitt Romney, the Republican governor at the time, wouldn't be able to pick Kerry's replacement. This meant that Kirk, who took the oath of office in September, would serve for only four months, until a special election could take place. The best-laid plans... always come back to bite. Welcome to the law of unintended consequences, the one law that does more political damage than any *actual* law politicians have ever passed.

Still, Democrats weren't worried about a special election in deep-blue Massachusetts, a state President Obama had won with more than 60 percent of the vote in 2008. And besides, between September and January, they still had the opportunity to win over a Republican vote — that is, one Republican's vote in particular to become the 60th Senate vote.

The White House was relying on Olympia Snowe. The fact that her name rhymes with "Godot" made the life of more literary-loving headline writers rather easy. Well, that and the fact her last name is also a weather event.

Obama and Snowe were smitten with each other, and though the two hadn't interacted much when Obama was in the Senate, by the time he needed Republican votes as president she was a frequent guest at the White House. During the stimulus debate, Obama had invited Snowe into the Oval Office, just the two of them, on a few occasions. For instance, Snowe had brought a list of cuts she and some of her fellow Republicans wanted in order to make the price tag a little more palatable; she was impressed that Obama acted interested, kept the list, and, in the end, incorporated a number of the suggestions into the bill. For Snowe, that was an important trust-building exercise.

When it came to health care, Snowe was one of the few Republicans willing to entertain the notion of a public option — that is, a new government-run insurance pool for those who couldn't afford private health insurance — if it kept costs down. That gave the White House an opening; Obama took more one-on-one meetings and chatted with her by phone more than half a dozen times. Others in the administration kept in touch, among them Joe Biden and Rahm Emanuel, who called more than a dozen times throughout the year — but Snowe had a soft spot for the president.

While Grassley was starting to worry about his

own politics, Snowe was becoming more engaged with policy. Her participation in the Gang of Six meant that she had her fingerprints all over the bill Baucus was crafting, and she started to seriously negotiate with the White House. Snowe had proposed a "trigger option," which would have given insurance companies a window of time in which to make changes that would result in more Americans receiving health insurance; if the companies didn't meet the requirements within the window, the government would set up a public option. Ultimately, the White House agreed, and Snowe's trigger went into the bill. (Ironically, Snowe's trigger version was the closest the health care bill actually got to a public option had it been kept in, but it didn't survive in the House. So the left is having to lament the demise of a Republican senator's idea on health care. Go figure.)

The nine-month campaign to win Snowe's vote, first on the stimulus bill, then on health care reform, paid off in the short term: on October 13, after a marathon seven-day markup during which the Finance Committee considered hundreds of amendments on virtually every section of the bill, Snowe voted for the America's Healthy Future Act, which passed out of committee by a 14–9 vote.[24] Her vote in committee would be the only Republican vote for any version of health care reform in 2009 or

2010. Usually, once a senator decides to own a bill in committee, they are in. But something changed.

How Snowe went from supporting one version of the bill in committee to opposing the entire bill on the floor of the Senate is a now-familiar story of delicate upper-chamber egos. A little backstory: A bill the size of the health care one was going to get debated and drafted on parallel tracks in various Senate committees. For months, the focus of the White House and much of the health care community had been on the Finance Committee, where Snowe was a member and Baucus was the chairman. There aren't many pieces of major legislation in the Senate that don't find their way to the Finance Committee. Little attention had been paid to the second major Senate committee that had jurisdiction over the health care bill, the Health, Education, Labor and Pensions Committee. At the time, most Washington types never believed Harry Reid's Senate could produce a bill that didn't go through the arduous process of the Baucus-run Finance Committee. But Washington miscalculated, and it all helps tell the tale of how Snowe was lost and, more important, how Snowe herself lost her biggest leverage, being the most cooperative Republican on the most important committee. In the month between October 13, when the bill emerged from the Finance Committee, and November 19, when Baucus, Harry Reid, and Chris

Dodd (who was then chairman of the Senate Health, Education, Labor and Pensions Committee) introduced the Patient Protection and Affordable Care Act, the White House remained eager to keep Snowe in the fold. But suddenly, Reid decided he was tired of waiting for Baucus and Finance in general and decided to move in a different direction. Politically, the White House understood but still wanted to find a way to keep Snowe on their side. But Snowe was beginning to worry that Reid wasn't throwing straight with her, and a trust deficit between her and Reid began to develop. Reid, Snowe, and Ben Nelson, the conservative Nebraska Democrat who was always the most difficult member of the president's own party to win over, met soon after the Finance Committee voted its version of the bill to the floor. At the same time, Reid, Baucus, and Dodd were ironing out the differences between the two versions that had passed each committee. When Snowe saw the final version, which had 1,200 more pages than the version she had voted for, she told her chief of staff she didn't know whether she could cast another vote in favor of the bill. Nelson and Snowe told Reid they wanted an open amendment process — that is, the freedom to offer amendments from the floor of the Senate, without the parliamentary tricks that could shut off debate.

"You're going to have the amendment process that you want," Snowe remembers Reid promising her. "Great," she replied. "Because that's what I think it's all about. [The bill] needs to be significantly improved." But the open amendment process Snowe had been promised never materialized. Reid, Snowe felt, had gone back on his word. But Reid was worried about a larger issue, one that time would prove him right on, and that was giving Republicans too much of an opportunity to gum up the bill and eventually kill it. And it was this rationale that drove Reid to limit the amendments and in turn lose Snowe. Frankly, it's been that rationale for Reid since on how to manage the Senate. He basically has taken the entire amendment process out of the working process of the Senate as a whole. It is a tactic that a former Republican leader of the Senate, Bill Frist, started using during the Bush years, but Reid has perfected it. Called "filling the amendment tree," it's Senate-speak for Reid's guarantee that amendments that he thinks will split his own party or kill the bill altogether don't get offered by the minority.

Still, this early in the new way Reid was starting to manage the Senate, Snowe left the door open to giving the final product a thumbs-up. Her chief of staff, nervous as ever about how Snowe's politics would play among Republicans in Maine, wondered what was going to happen with the bill. "I truly have no idea," Snowe said. "I'm just gonna follow the path. And I will know at the end of the path whether it's right or wrong. If things change, then fine. If not, then I know the answer to the question."

Snowe's bottom line had always been cost. If the final product really could bring down the deficit while insuring enough people, the White House would win her vote. Obama kept calling, and the two had substantive policy discussions, but Snowe was watching the price tag, and she needed assurances from the Congressional Budget Office, the proudly nonpartisan institution that estimates how much any given legislation will cost.

Snowe formally requested a CBO study of the Reid-Baucus-Dodd version of the bill by December 1, about a week and a half after it had been unveiled by the three Democrats. In ordinary circumstances, a senior senator who was also a member of the Finance Committee would get a study in short order. But these were no ordinary circumstances. CBO was working day and night to give cost estimates on various versions of the bill and dozens of amendments, no matter how realistic those amendments' chances of being included in the final bill were. But Snowe thought something else was afoot—that Reid had blocked the final scoring of the bill (in Senate-speak, this means he blocked the final cost estimate from going public) in order to avoid the sticker shock some of his own members were certainly already beginning to feel. Snowe's suspicions grew when Doug Elmendorf, head of the CBO, called her personally to apologize, explaining that she wouldn't get her study at any point during the month of December. While she was appreciative of the call, it was not something he normally did, feeding Snowe's suspicion that somehow an outside force was messing with the CBO's schedule, at a minimum, even if it wasn't influencing the math itself.

Snowe continued talks with Obama, but she was increasingly frustrated that those talks seemed to go nowhere. They'd agree to a deal and then Reid would never include it. The last time Obama and Snowe met on health care, Obama pleaded with her. "We had all these meetings," he said.

"Yes," Snowe replied. "But nothing changed." The White House had lost its last hope of winning over a Republican vote. In many ways, this wasn't on Obama, it was on Reid, or so Snowe chooses to believe.

Republicans weren't the White House's only problem on Capitol Hill. Several moderate Democrats, like Nebraska's Ben Nelson and Louisiana's Mary Landrieu, had their own concerns over the bill's size and scope. Given that Nelson and Landrieu were from red states, they had extra incentive to express their concerns publicly. For Nelson, there was another issue: abortion.

To win over Nelson, Michigan representative Bart Stupak, and a number of other pro-life Democrats concerned over abortion provisions in the bill, the

White House spent three days negotiating in Harry Reid's office. Reid, Nelson, and liberal Democrats Patty Murray and Barbara Boxer met with Rouse, Messina, DeParle, and other senior White House officials. Once the language was finalized, just two weeks before Christmas, Nelson left the office. Reid called the White House and put Obama on speakerphone. "We've got a deal, Mr. President," he said.

But they weren't done with Nelson, who was still nervous over the bill's cost to his state. Given the loss of Snowe in the vote count, the White House couldn't afford to lose any Democrat. Nelson suddenly had maximum leverage, or so he claimed — and so *some* at the White House believed was true. The White House put together a plan that would have given Nebraska a special deal when it came to expanding Medicaid coverage, which has become a major issue in many states since the law's implementation. What Nelson negotiated was a cheaper buy-in for Nebraska — the type of special deal senators have been making for their states for years. It was left to Pete Rouse and Jim Messina to nail down the final details of Nelson's specially designed Medicaid exemption. The two even met Nelson at a home in ritzy Georgetown just days before Christmas to keep him happy. Remember, the White House suddenly realized they had no votes to spare. Every Democrat had to be on board if they couldn't find Republican support.

Rouse and Messina believed the deal had been necessary to secure Nelson's vote; in hindsight, others in the White House now see it as another reason for the bill's delay, not to mention the long-term collateral damage that cutting deals for senators has gotten. Almost immediately, the deal to benefit Nebraska—the "Cornhusker Kickback," critics called it—earned a special level of scorn, the embodiment of all that opponents knew was wrong with Washington, coupled with government becoming bigger and more intrusive. Horse-trading is as old as the Republic itself; the first earmark in American history sent $1,500 to complete construction of the Portland Head Lighthouse in Maine in 1790, a provision that Representative George Thatcher inserted into an unrelated bill, with support from George Washington.[25] But Nelson's Cornhusker Kickback and the "Louisiana Purchase," a similar carve-out for Landrieu's state, drew so much fire that they were ultimately dropped from the bill. Out of embarrassment over being caught publicly trying to use their health care vote as leverage, Nelson and Landrieu both voted in favor of the bill. The lesson senators from both parties took from that episode was that the old ways of winning re-election by touting the special deals and access the state has acquired under your term were disappearing as political benefits. The reverberation from these two deals going south is still being felt, as this Congress still doesn't know how to function without the ability to use carve-outs and special deals to win votes.

But leave out the decision by the oldest of Washington hands in the West Wing — Rouse and Messina — to do whatever it took to get to 60 votes; the real question among some other West Wingers was why cut a *bad* deal, one that could actually hurt the legislation.

"I didn't understand why Rahm didn't recognize that that bill with that deal was the debacle of debacles," said one former insider, still perplexed at how Rahm and Messina so misread the political tea leaves of the moment in creating special deals. "That's where the White House made a clear error. Because you can ask people about the bill today and they still remember [the Cornhusker kickback]. Including Scalia." (This is a reference to the conservative Supreme Court justice who talked about the kickback during the oral arguments about health care's constitutionality in June 2012.)

For the better part of a year, the White House had also still been focused on winning over Chuck Grassley, through Max Baucus and Olympia Snowe and the president himself. But with just days to go before the Senate voted on a final version of the Patient Protection and Affordable Care Act, it had become clear that both relationships had fallen apart. Grassley was conscious of his own political calculus; the town hall meetings he headlined in August in Iowa were enough to make him worry about his career. Snowe had grown increasingly frustrated, first with Democratic shenanigans in merging the two bills behind closed doors, then with Reid's behind-the-scenes tactics in shutting off opportunities to amend the bill.

Obama's end-of-the-year deadline forced members of Congress to work right up until the last minute. The Senate had debated the legislation for twenty-five straight days, as Snowe's report was blocked and Nelson's changes were negotiated. Early on Christmas Eve, 60 Democrats, including Nelson, Landrieu, and Kirk, voted for the bill. All 39 Republicans, including Snowe and Grassley, voted against it—the beginning of a long-term partisan-driven standoff that the country is still dealing with.

CHAPTER FOUR

Triage

Barack Obama had achieved what no other Democratic president since Franklin Roosevelt could claim: he'd passed a major health care reform package through the Senate. What made the achievement more impressive was that he had done it not only in his first term, as he promised, but in his first year in office. After the Christmas Eve vote, almost everyone in the White House could see the finish line—or so they thought. Remember the cliché, the light at the end of the tunnel could very well be a freight train.

But a Senate vote alone doesn't make a bill, and the finish line came after a hurdle called the House of Representatives. Despite a big House majority, led with an almost iron fist by Speaker Nancy Pelosi, the White House was having trouble convincing a number of pro-life conservative Democrats to drop objections over public funding for abortions. Any change in the bill would mean a conference committee, made up of representatives from both chambers, then a vote on the compromise that emerged.

It meant, in short, more time for Republicans to drum up opposition to the bill, rally their troops, raise money with direct-mail campaigns, and swing public opinion to their side. With November's midterm elections less than a year away, the White House staff was beginning to feel as nervous as their fellow Democrats in Congress. To some, even those who had dedicated their entire White House tenure to passing health care reform, a successful outcome was becoming greater than the sum of its parts.

In fact, political expediency—writing a bill that could pass, rather than the perfect bill—had always weighed on the minds in the White House. Some elements of the legislation were included, and others excluded, for the sake of winning votes. "There was never an issue that was in the bill that was more important than just passing the bill," said Neera Tanden, who had a role in crafting both the legislation and the legislative strategy.

President Obama had wanted to include malpractice reform in the legislation, a critical issue to Republicans from the beginning, back when his advisors still believed Republican votes could be won over. Phil Schiliro, the White House's chief liaison to Congress, told Obama that Democrats in the House would never back malpractice reform, given the sway trial lawyers hold over the Democratic Party. So Obama barely even tried, simply agreeing to a few pilot programs, but this was among the bigger missed opportunities for Obama to look like he had the upper hand in trying to win over GOP support. Olympia Snowe's insistence on a trigger, rather than a straight-out public option, caused friction within the more liberal elements of the Democratic Caucus, too, though Obama shouted down his own troops on this one since Snowe was their best chance at getting even a *potential* public plan into the final bill.

But sometimes House Democrats resisted no matter how many times they were told. The issue of covering undocumented immigrants was something the president himself said he was against. He made that commitment in the campaign. And yet it wasn't until a Republican congressman named Joe Wilson yelled "You lie!" during an Obama speech before Congress that the White House and Senate Democrats finally convinced House Democrats to get rid of the provision that would have allowed undocumented immigrants to be covered on insurance policies bought through the exchanges. This was just one of many instances where, if the White House had used a heavier hand in drafting the legislation, they would have avoided some political pain. The issue with immigrants was a self-inflicted wound. Of course, many folks allowed these disagreements between the House and Senate to exist for the short term because eventually the two bills would be merged in something called a conference committee, or so they thought. As far as the White House was concerned, they weren't going to play the role of the heavy until then. But then a new hurdle arose.

As the year 2010 began and the Senate mess was behind them, and some Democrats were preparing for a signing ceremony, Rahm Emanuel and David Axelrod began hearing from friends outside the White House that they might have a more pressing problem than the November midterms. Up in Massachusetts, something was going wrong with what should have been a gimme special election.

Since November, when the two parties had nominated their respective candidates for Senator Kennedy's seat, the National Republican Senatorial Committee had been quietly funneling money to a state senator named Scott Brown; soon, Brown was showing up on Fox News, and conservative commentators and bloggers were touting his chances as the filibuster-preserving 41st Republican vote in the Senate. Meanwhile, kinks were still being worked out of the House bill, and there was no hope that a conference committee would finish negotiations before January 19, when the Massachusetts special election would be held—meaning that there was a very real chance that any major alteration to the

Senate bill was going to have to be voted on in the Senate again, and without a 60th Democratic vote, there would be a problem.

Democrats around Washington weren't worried. They had nominated Martha Coakley, Massachusetts's attorney general, a woman who had won the Commonwealth's top law enforcement job with a whopping 73 percent of the vote. It was a great spot to start from. The attorney general's office is traditionally a routine stepping-stone to higher office. An attorney general gets to collar crooks, fight on behalf of the citizens of his or her state, take on corporations, and, in Coakley's case, take the Environmental Protection Agency to task for dragging its feet on greenhouse gas emissions. It is as close to the perfect political job as exists in the United States — one with a huge number of upsides and only a small handful of pitfalls.

It thus came as an unwelcome surprise to Axelrod and Emanuel when rumors started percolating down from Boston that Coakley's campaign was in trouble.

In fact, Coakley proved to be a disastrous candidate. To start, after winning the Democratic primary in late 2009 she took a vacation, thinking as many in Washington did that the general election was a foregone conclusion; the primary in deep-blue Massachusetts was supposed to be the game. But given how many times Republicans have shocked

Democrats in the state—think Mitt Romney or Bill Weld—smart Democrats should have known better. There has always been a quirky independent streak in the Massachusetts electorate. If Democrats get too cocky, they are bitten by this part of the electorate. The vacation decision was Coakley getting cocky. Then on her first fund-raising trip to Washington, a top advisor bodychecked a conservative reporter into a fence. The footage a Republican tracker had taken quickly appeared in advertising financed by the National Republican Senatorial Committee.

Scott Brown, meanwhile, was no ordinary Republican. Republicans who have had success in Massachusetts in recent decades have been businessmen of the Boston Brahmin type: Paul Cellucci, William Weld, Mitt Romney. Brown was the opposite; his Carhartt jacket and pickup truck demonstrated a blue-collar outlook, and his model good looks—*Cosmopolitan* named him America's Sexiest Man in 1982—gave him an appeal well beyond the traditional Republican base in the ultraliberal state, never mind that his pickup was used to haul his daughter's horse around, or that his wife was a well-known news anchor in Boston.

Quickly, Brown became such a cause célèbre among conservative activists that he began raising massive amounts of money online, literally pulling in cash so fast his strategists couldn't use it all. Brown's campaign ended with more than $7 million in the bank, simply because there hadn't been time to send more direct-mail pieces or buy more advertising on television.

The White House watched in horror as Coakley's campaign flatlined. In early January, White House political director Patrick Gaspard brought a frightening poll to the morning staff meeting, a survey that showed her trailing. The Democratic Senatorial Campaign Committee's surveys showed the same result. Time was basically running out. "We knew, there was just nothing you could do about it. The DSCC knew, we knew," one Obama advisor lamented to me.[1]

Then, too, the media began to take notice, and Gibbs began getting questions, both during the televised daily briefing and in private conversations with reporters, about whether Obama would travel to Massachusetts to campaign for Coakley. The media often reads far too much into special elections, in which a single outcome in one isolated part of the country is extrapolated to the rest of America, but this time the crystal ball was all too clear: if a Republican won a Senate election in a state that hadn't elected a Republican senator since 1972, a state Obama had won with 61.8 percent of the vote, there was no mistaking that the unpopularity of Obama's health care bill—and, by extension, of Obama himself—was at least partly to blame.

Some White House advisors, Emanuel chief among them, didn't want Obama going off to fight a battle he couldn't win. Emanuel resisted the idea of sending Obama to a rally with Coakley if that appearance would make it more obvious that either the president's agenda was partly to blame for Coakley's troubles or that the president had picked a fight and lost.

Gibbs (and others) disagreed. He told the press for a week that Obama had no plans to campaign for Coakley, but he would leave the podium and argue the opposite case in senior staff meetings. "What do you mean, we're not going to Massachusetts?" he remembers asking. "We have to go to Massachusetts!"

In the end, Gibbs and his allies won the fight. "I never lied, but my theory of this was, okay, health care is at stake," Gibbs recalled later. "If she doesn't win, someone's going to say, 'Jesus Fucking Christ, health care was on the line and you couldn't go to fucking Boston for a rally?'"

Obama traveled to Boston to hold a last-minute rally with Coakley on Sunday, January 17, to no avail. That same day, when Emanuel ran into a reporter at a bar on Capitol Hill, he was glum. "Do you think she's going to win?" he asked. The reporter said yes. Emanuel shook his head.[2]

On January 19, Brown won by 110,000 votes, or about five percentage points—enough to deny

Democrats their filibuster-proof 60-vote margin in the Senate. He was sworn in sixteen days later, on February 4, 2010.

Brown's victory was the exclamation point on a sentence written months before. Polls showed a big plurality of Americans thought the White House was spending too much time on health care in the first place; by January 23, four days after Brown was elected, 46 percent of Americans said Obama's health care plan was a bad idea, while just 31 percent thought the opposite.[3]

Reforming such a massive sector of American life was always going to pose a public opinion problem for the White House. After all, the vast majority of Americans already had health care coverage, and by and large they were happy with it. There was an irony in the word "universal" — the only part of the universe that doesn't already have coverage is a slim segment at the margins of society, a.k.a. folks who are not swing voters; in fact, many are not voters at all. That meant the average American was hearing all about a government takeover of a sector they pretty much had come to rely on even if they weren't happy with the rising costs. But as the debate steered away from keeping costs down and instead focused on getting more people covered, those with health insurance began thinking that someone *else* was getting something new, while their *own* coverage was changing in a way that wasn't terribly clear, given the confusing Washington-speak coming from the White House.

And yet, for all their political acumen, there was a certain degree of confusion — especially regarding misreading polling results — that went on among the White House staff as well. During the 2008 campaign, the team had played it perfectly — Obama opposed an individual mandate, which played well among general election voters. He opposed McCain's tax on Cadillac insurance plans, which was also where the country happened to be. But the final version of health care reform included both a mandate, to cover more people, and a tax, to make sure the mandate was paid for.

"His reaction to the mandate was not poll-driven, it was instinctual. He became convinced by the policy people when he got there that there was no other way to achieve the big goal of getting people with preexisting conditions coverage unless everybody was in the pool," said David Axelrod. "Romney [the author of a similar measure in Massachusetts] was right about that." In theory, there is something welcome in a politician who does not make his decisions based on polls, and for better or for worse, this was definitely an "in theory" president. But what was left unsaid was that the president, in 2008 as a candidate, had learned how it is a lot easier to win an argument on health care by being against a proposal than it is about championing one.

Brown's election set the White House scrambling to salvage its yearlong effort. But this new effort looked a lot more like survival mode than anything else. Once again, Emanuel preached caution; he simply wanted to get something, anything, passed, just to get health care off the table. A win, in his mind, would be turning to some other issue—any other issue—and stopping the bleeding on health care. Emanuel considered winning ugly a better option than losing. "Mr. President, you've got the rest of the agenda. This is like seven more months [of work]," he said at one meeting. "Scale it back. You'll get a win."

Obama was open to the concept of something smaller, like health insurance reform—do preexisting conditions, force policies to accept children up to age twenty-six, and that's about it. But Pelosi decided she had had enough. She lobbied Obama furiously, demanding that the White House stick to its guns and take the political risks her own members were taking by repeatedly siding with Obama on big-ticket agenda items.

"We're in the majority," Pelosi told Obama at one point. "We'll never have a better majority in your presidency in numbers than we've got right now. We can make this work."[4] In a conference call with members of the House Democratic Caucus, Pelosi even took shots at Emanuel's approach, dubbing it "Kiddie Care" and labeling Emanuel an "incrementalist."[5]

Though he had been making the case for health care reform for a year, Obama tried one more PR stunt to get public opinion back on his side. He called House and Senate leaders to the White House a month later, on February 25, to try again to find some Republican votes for his proposal. The summit, held at Blair House, across the street, did not go well. Obama had attended a House Republican Conference retreat in Baltimore the week before, and he'd used the opportunity to lecture the GOP while Republican congressmen threw him canned questions. It was a public relations win for the White House and an embarrassment for House Republicans. The second time around, Republicans decided, they would not ask questions; instead, they would outline their proposal and stay respectful, but they would give no ground.

At the meeting, Obama offered an opening statement, then turned to House Republican leader John Boehner and Senate minority leader Mitch McConnell.

"I just want to say again how much I appreciate everybody for participating. And I am going to now turn it over to Senator McConnell so that he can make some opening remarks. And we'll just go back and forth between the Democratic leaders and the Republican leaders, House and Senate, and then we'll just open it up and we'll start diving in. All right?" Obama said.

McConnell threw a curveball. "Thank you very much, Mr. President. John Boehner and I have selected Lamar Alexander of Tennessee to make our opening framing statement, and let me turn to him."

Obama and Alexander went back and forth over the intricacies of the legislation, and in the following months, Alexander, who was no Tea Party conservative by any definition, would use a Fox News clip of one particular exchange — over whether the legislation would cost middle-class families more money — to show off to conservative audiences in his home state. Tennessee Republicans ate it up just as voraciously as Tea Party conservatives around the country.

Once again, the White House learned the hard way that there would be no Republican support for its bill. Any changes in the House bill would lead to a conference committee, which would then require another Senate vote. But while the Senate-passed bill would be the only available vehicle to get reform across the finish line, now that Brown — who took to signing autographs as "Brown 41" — was in office, Democrats couldn't muster the votes necessary in the Senate to overcome a certain Republican filibuster.

It also meant that Stupak and his group of seven pro-life Democrats had new leverage. Stupak had almost derailed the first House-passed version of the bill over concerns about public funding for abortions; Pelosi had salvaged it, and assuaged Stupak, by adopting a last-minute amendment to disallow any such funding.

This time, to win over Stupak's group, White House counsel Bob Bauer went through weeks of agonizing negotiations that would get the pro-lifers' support without requiring a new Senate vote. The solution: Executive Order 13535, which cemented restrictions on public funding for abortions first laid down under the Hyde Amendment. Obama, who won election with support from pro-choice groups that make up part of the Democratic Party's backbone, had to reaffirm one of the pro-life movement's most sacred touchstones just to save his legislation.

In this case, Stupak spent days reviewing drafts of the executive order and negotiating word changes. Finally, on the afternoon of Sunday, March 21, he appeared before reporters at the Capitol to say he would vote for the measure, putting Democrats over the majority threshold they needed to pass a bill into law. Stupak then went to the floor of the House, where he made his case; a Republican interrupted him, calling him a baby killer.[6] But the House vote passed, by a margin of 219 to 212 votes. Two days later, Obama stepped up to the podium in the White House to sign the Affordable Care Act. The president looked relieved, and for good reason.

Some of his allies were not so relieved—quite the opposite. Obama's decision to include in the bill two elements he had specifically campaigned against—Hillary's mandate and McCain's tax credit—had even his closest allies shaking their heads in dismay. Some saw the individual mandate as inconsistent with Obama's overall message of individual empowerment. "You can think of this in a lowbrow way: someone should have thought about the politics of the mandate," said one former administration insider. "Or you can think about it in the highbrow way: there's a democratic legitimacy to the idea that if you campaigned on the fact that I'm not going to do [the mandate], then you shouldn't do it."[7]

More than any other battle during the first term, what the fight over health care reform taught the White House was that Washington had changed, in two key ways. First, the White House was learning that the loyal opposition had become, simply, the opposition. Earlier administrations had willing partners to work with; Bill Clinton got welfare reform through a Republican-controlled Congress, and George W. Bush worked with Ted Kennedy to pass sweeping education reform measures. But after initial flirtations with Snowe and Grassley, the White House had nowhere else to go.

Second, it had fewer tools at its disposal than ever before. The president's insistence on limiting earmarks, and his own distaste for the grip-and-grin method of influencing supporters, meant that the

White House gave up some of the time-tested methods for winning votes. No longer could the White House promise a big-ticket item—a bridge, a highway, an overpass—to a wavering member of Congress. Nor was that member of Congress likely to get a phone call or an invitation to a White House cocktail party, either. Those cocktail parties ended after just a few months, and the phone calls rarely came from the president himself. Then when the high-road team did cut a deal, as it did for Nelson and Landrieu, its hypocrisy highlighted what was once simply the cost of practicing politics.

Most of all, the yearlong fight for health care reform opened wounds that would never completely heal. Inside the White House, Obama gave credit to Nancy-Ann DeParle, the health care czar who had taken on part of the job Tom Daschle was supposed to do. That caused friction among the other nine or ten senior staffers tasked with passing reform, most of whom believed DeParle was getting credit for their work.

Exhausted, Neera Tanden left the West Wing to run the Center for American Progress, a liberal think tank. Emanuel departed before the 2010 midterm elections to begin preparing to run for mayor of Chicago, his hometown. The economic team began to turn over as well.

But they'd made their mark. The Affordable Care Act, the biggest expansion of government since the

1960s, was going to change the health care industry. The White House and its allies will acknowledge they didn't get a perfect bill, and its compromises forced Obama to stray dangerously near a line his team had always been wary of crossing. Obama's political appeal lies in the fact that he doesn't actually appear to be a politician; he says what he means and does what he says. The notion that Obama had governed as he'd promised in the 2008 campaign became a key undercurrent during his 2012 run for re-election. But that notion was dead: by adopting Clinton's mandate and McCain's tax, both of which he'd campaigned against, Obama was acting just like any other flip-flopping politician. What was worse was that the flip-flops came in such a politically inefficient manner. That is, Obama abandoned positions that were in line with public opinion in favor of positions that his policy people liked but that the average American opposed.

But, as Emanuel said, making deals comes with the territory. And Obama did in fact achieve a sweeping entitlement program that had eluded every Democratic president since Lyndon Johnson signed Medicare and Medicaid into law. Joe Biden, as usual, said it best. As he introduced Obama at the March 23 press conference, he turned to shake the president's hand while the audience applauded. Thinking that his words would be drowned out, Biden leaned toward the president's ear. "This is a big fucking deal," he said.

It was, though perhaps not in the manner Obama and his team had envisioned. Health care took up a year of the administration's time, a year in which any number of other agenda items could have made headway. White House advisors routinely blame the length of the debate for costing them chances to reform the nation's immigration system or pursue a climate change package that actually could have passed the Senate.

But Biden's comments, picked up by the surrounding microphones, would have a different resonance years later, when "Obamacare"—a term Republicans adopted early to pin the legislation on the president—was rolled out to the public. Then, too, it would be a "big fucking deal"—in the worst way.

CHAPTER FIVE

Reluctant Warrior

S ince the Vietnam War, Democrats have been
terrified that voters will see them as weak on
national defense, soft on using the military to protect America from her enemies, whether that enemy
is the Soviet Union, China, or stateless terrorism.
Jimmy Carter's short presidency didn't help the party
overcome its national security issues at all—if anything, it made things worse, thanks to the perceived
weakness of America on the world stage at that time,
particularly with regard to Iran and the hostage crisis there. The ghosts of both LBJ and Carter still
haunt Democrats to this day.

After the attacks on September 11, 2001, in the
brief run-up to war in Afghanistan against the Taliban and al Qaeda, and the longer, but rushed, run-up
to war in Iraq, Democrats who wanted a future in
national politics faced another test: should they stick
with the commander in chief, George W. Bush, and
authorize the use of force in a Middle East ground
war, or listen to the louder voices in the activist base,

who didn't believe the Bush administration's claims that Saddam Hussein was harboring weapons of mass destruction?

Moral decisions aside, the political calculus was fraught. Standing with the commander in chief, at a time when Bush's approval ratings soared to almost unprecedented heights, would be politically popular with independent voters but could hurt relations with the Democratic base, the segment of the population most opposed to war. Standing against the war in Iraq, a war the vast majority of Americans wanted to fight, would be politically damaging in the short run. But if the war went badly, as Americans grew weary of the fighting and the steep cost in blood and treasure, opposing the war early would start to look like a smart decision. If the war went well, however, it could only widen the perception gap with the public about the two parties on the issue of national security.

When the Senate voted to authorize the use of force in Iraq, shortly after midnight on October 11, 2002, the top Democrats who were considering running against Bush in the 2004 election universally opted to stick with the president. John Kerry, John Edwards, Joe Lieberman, Chris Dodd, Tom Daschle, and Hillary Clinton were among the twenty-nine Democrats who voted for the bill.[1] Dodd, Daschle, and Clinton would ultimately back away from running in 2004, but of the candidates who did make the race, only two—Howard Dean, a little-known governor of Vermont who had announced his candidacy six months earlier and who was lucky to register at all in public opinion surveys, and Dennis Kucinich, the ultraliberal congressman from Cleveland—stood against the war from the beginning. It should not go unremarked that the Democrats who apparently supported the war early on were all older Democrats, baby boomers who recalled the dark days of seeing the party painted as weak on defense. The younger, non-Vietnam-era Democrats had an easier time keeping old political analysis from creeping into their thinking.

Nine days before the Senate voted to authorize the use of force in Iraq, an Illinois state senator named Barack Obama delivered a speech in Chicago outlining his opposition to the war—a speech that, miraculously, someone recorded. Imagine the Obama candidacy without that recording. Is it possible he still would have been able to steal some of the moral high ground on the war from Clinton? Perhaps. But the recording gave the young Obama some much-needed gravitas and, frankly, evidence that he wasn't a finger-in-the-wind politician. After all, he could say that in 2002, when the war was popular, he wasn't afraid to speak out. Had there been no recording, opponents likely would have called into question his claims and, who knows, may even have succeeded in painting him as an opportunist. But the recording does exist, and it was among Obama's most important campaign trump cards in that 2008 primary battle.

"I don't oppose all wars," Obama said at the time. "What I am opposed to is a dumb war. What I am opposed to is a rash war. What I am opposed to is the cynical attempt by Richard Perle and Paul Wolfowitz and other armchair, weekend warriors in this administration to shove their own ideological agendas down our throats, irrespective of the costs in lives lost and in hardships borne."[2]

At the time, Obama's opposition made few headlines. He was a long-shot candidate running in what would certainly be a crowded field of candidates seeking the Democratic nomination to take on U.S. senator Peter Fitzgerald, a first-term Republican who had a reputation for centrism.[3] And one could easily imagine the local press, if there was any covering him at the time, glossing over this speech as simply a Democrat attempting to stand out in a crowded field, or even a Democrat trying to carve out an issue that appeals to some parts of the state's Democratic base.

Throughout his presidential campaign in 2007 and 2008, the political bet Obama had made turned out to be correct. As the war in Iraq dragged on, as the body count rose, public opinion swung heavily the other way. Americans wanted out of Iraq, a feeling magnified among Democratic voters. For Clinton and Edwards, their votes in October 2002 became weights around their necks. For Obama, his little-noticed 2002 speech became a touchstone. He would get the country out of Iraq, he promised, and he had shown the judgment to be right at a time when it was politically unpopular.

But left unspoken in that 2002 speech was the other war in which American troops were fighting and dying. If Iraq was the "dumb war," then Afghanistan must have been the "smart one," or so it seemed the young Senate candidate was implying. Obama had said he supported the Bush administration's fight against terrorism and the terrorists who had killed 3,000 Americans on September 11. In the 2002 speech, Obama had not uttered the word "Afghanistan," and that one missing word would prove, seven years later, to be the greater military challenge President Obama would face.

Obama, too, wanted to walk the fine line between being soft on defense and ending the wars in Iraq and Afghanistan. During the campaign, the way Obama's team decided to show off his hawkish side was to make it clear that as president, he would *not* hesitate to unilaterally go into, say, Pakistan to pursue a terrorist. That he wouldn't wait for diplomacy or permission but would act unilaterally as commander in chief. His pledge caused a bit of a stir at the time, but it was designed to make the case that he would not be a total dove. Still, promising to pursue terrorists in Pakistan wasn't enough. By the time he reached the general election, Obama had pledged to send two more combat brigades to Afghanistan. Iraq, he said, had become a distraction to American efforts in Afghanistan. "Our troops and our NATO allies are performing heroically in Afghanistan, but I have argued for years that we lack the resources to finish the job because of our commitment to Iraq," he said in a July 2008 speech. "That's what the Chairman of the Joint Chiefs of Staff said earlier this month. And that's why, as President, I will make the fight against al Qaeda and the Taliban the top priority that it should be. This is a war that we have to win."[4]

Later, the president would complain of being boxed in on Afghanistan by the Pentagon, but one could read that July 2008 speech and come away believing he actually had boxed himself in more than he wanted to admit.

As empires throughout the ages have proved, Afghanistan is no easy terrain on which to win a war. Between 1839 and 1842, the British Empire invaded, was repulsed, and withdrew from the country. For nine years in the 1980s, the Soviet Union fought mujahideen rebels, including many trained by the United States, to a stalemate. After billions of dollars spent and hundreds of thousands of lives lost,

Mikhail Gorbachev withdrew the last Soviet forces on February 15, 1989.

On October 7, 2001, less than a month after al Qaeda terrorists hijacked four planes and crashed three of them into buildings, the first coalition forces of Operation Enduring Freedom arrived to liberate the country from Taliban rule and hunt out the al Qaeda terrorists the Taliban had been harboring. But like the British and the Soviets before them, American forces and their coalition partners soon found that driving out one set of leaders and installing another would be complicated by realities on the ground: Afghanistan is a tribal nation, riven by sectarian violence and centuries of mistrust between warring factions. Simply installing a president—in this case, the U.S.-backed former mujahideen Hamid Karzai—wouldn't be enough to leave an Afghanistan capable of governing itself. It was a country that in many ways was still two or three centuries behind the rest of the world—a conclusion the president would come to before he ever took the oath of office, but given the pledges he had made during the campaign, he didn't know how to turn back.

By the middle of 2008, it had become clear to U.S. commanders in Afghanistan that the war was stagnating. Little progress was being made, either in rooting out the remnants of Taliban forces who still terrorized civilians throughout the country, or in setting up a democracy that could govern effectively when the last Americans flew home. While a troop surge in Iraq, first announced back in 2007, had given American forces and the Iraqi government space in which to achieve some goals, there had been no similar investment in Afghanistan. At the time of Obama's July 2008 speech, there were still five times as many U.S. forces in Iraq as there were in Afghanistan.

Bush's commanders on the ground in Afghanistan, and those at the Pentagon, were pushing to change that. Defense secretary Robert Gates, Joint Chiefs chairman Mike Mullen, and David McKiernan, the commander in charge of the International Security Assistance Force (the umbrella organization of coalition forces in Afghanistan), asked Bush to send new troops to Afghanistan — in essence, to repeat the surge strategy that had worked in Iraq.

But Bush said no. A troop surge would take up to a year to complete; he recognized that any actions he took in his final months in office would saddle the incoming president, whether it was Obama or McCain, with his policy. In a meeting in the Oval Office, Bush told Gates and Mullen that he wanted to leave it to the new president to implement his own policy, not Bush's. Privately, the Obama folks were at first glad Bush did this, but publicly, some of the Obama spinmeisters liked to use this as a way to attack Bush, saying he left them unfinished business. Eventually, the more they learned about the situation in Afghanistan, the more they came around to believing their spin—that Bush should have acted first.

After Obama won, Gates, Mullen, and many at the Pentagon wondered just how the new president would act. Here was a candidate who had built his political career by opposing the wars they had fought. The new commander in chief had never served in uniform. He had not served on the Senate Armed Services Committee. And he had developed few relations with the Pentagon brass. He had reached out to Gates to see whether Gates would stay on through the beginning of his term, but only indirectly. Mullen recalled meeting Obama only once, at one of Bush's State of the Union addresses, and then just for a moment.

Shortly after winning, Obama asked Mullen to fly to Chicago to meet in the transition team's offices.

Mullen, who was then sixty-two years old, had spent a career in the navy before being elevated to the top job at the Joint Chiefs by President Bush. Unlike David Petraeus or Stanley McChrystal, commanders who were almost household names, Mullen hadn't cultivated an image in the media. He spoke with journalists frequently, but rarely on the record. But you shouldn't be fooled by his seeming anonymity; though he was just as image conscious as the more preening Petraeus, Mullen was more subtle. When he appeared in Chicago with just a single aide in tow, the receptionist at the transition office didn't recognize him.[5]

But Obama did. He was solicitous, interested in Mullen's thoughts and advice. The president-elect made it a point to introduce Mullen to Emanuel; the very distracted incoming chief of staff said hello while, Mullen recalls, simultaneously pressing a cell phone to each ear. Halfway through their meeting, Michelle Obama poked her head into the room; the president-elect introduced her to Mullen as well.

Obama told Mullen he needed a better understanding of the situation on the ground in Afghanistan. One of the first decisions he would have to make as commander in chief would be how many additional troops were sent to Afghanistan; McKiernan, the commander on the ground at the time, had requested 10,000 additional troops. Mullen delivered his assessment: the lack of resources, caused by the war in Iraq, had put Afghanistan on America's back burner. Consequently there was no strategy, no plan to get the country back on its feet.

The two men came away impressed with each other; Obama had made his views clear — he wanted American troops to leave Iraq, and he wanted to focus more on Afghanistan — without being overly demanding. He had sent the message that his policy would guide U.S. strategy, but not without flexibility to help commanders do their job.

It was the first meeting on Afghanistan that

Obama had held with a senior military commander, but even in the midst of an economic crisis, with so many impending and barely averted disasters competing for his attention, it wouldn't be the last. The situation in Afghanistan would come to suck up more of Obama's time than he, or anyone on his team, could begin to imagine.

Obama understood that Afghanistan and Iraq were fundamentally different countries, and solving the problems that would allow American forces to leave would require different approaches. For one thing, Iraq had a natural resource—oil—that can provide its government with a significant amount of funding over the long term. And for the most part, Iraq had the infrastructure to cultivate that oil and get it to global markets. Highways, shipping ports, and pipelines crisscrossed the country. In short, Iraq had the ability to become a twenty-first-century country.

Afghanistan, on the other hand, had little that interested the global market. (A 2009 United Nations report claimed Afghanistan exported $403 million in goods. Iraq exported goods worth more than a hundred times that number, almost $42 billion.)[6]

A mountainous country without direct access to an ocean, Afghanistan offered few main roads; those that existed gave Taliban insurgents prime opportunities to target convoys and allowed warlords to set up roadblocks to extort the local population, at times under the guise of providing security.

The natural resources found in Afghanistan are rare-earth minerals and rich lodes of metal that lie deep within remote mountains. Analyses by the Pentagon indicated more than $1 trillion worth of iron, copper, cobalt, and gold,[7] but there were few mines, and any new ones would require years of development and billions in investment. The real money to be had short term was drug money—not exactly the way to build a country for the future. That left the Afghan government dependent on other countries—chiefly the United States—to give it the cash it needed to survive. Very early in his presidential term, the young chief executive was giving his unvarnished, off-the-record take on Afghanistan to a small group over lunch. He admitted that the U.S. goal wasn't democracy in Afghanistan, it was simply getting the country to some form of stability. He said the country was still stuck in the sixteenth century; with luck, he opined, perhaps the United States could leave an infrastructure that would allow the country to enter the eighteenth, maybe the nineteenth, century.

It didn't help, either, that Hamid Karzai, America's partner in Afghanistan, was increasingly viewed as entirely off his rocker—acting irrational, even suggesting in private that he might quit the government to join the Taliban. Some United Nations officials even believed Karzai might have a drug problem.[8] A key question Obama would have to answer would be whether Karzai was stable enough to run a country, even with U.S. support.

Obama's transition team, for the most part, had been thoroughly impressed by the extent to which the Bush administration had dedicated itself to a smooth transition. But with time, Obama's foreign policy advisors were deeply unhappy that Bush had decided to hold off on ordering a troop surge in Afghanistan. The delay, they believed, had allowed the situation to deteriorate even further. "The president saw it as, 'Wait a second, I have to do this [order the surge] because we have a five-alarm fire,'" recalled Ben Rhodes. But imagine the response if Obama had been stuck with a decision Bush had made and he had to finish implementing a policy he didn't agree with. Although there was no easy answer on this one for Bush, finger-pointing didn't matter now; there was a fire.

And there was little sense of how to put it out. Afghanistan's elections were just a few months away, and the new troops, the generals hoped, would provide security to ensure that one of the most critical moments in the long and arduous process of setting up a government wouldn't turn into an opportunity for the Taliban to strike back. But the details within the request for additional troops themselves kept changing. The surge that had worked in Iraq had sent an additional 30,000 American troops to key regions around the country; McKiernan had requested that an identical number be sent to Afghanistan. A later Pentagon report sent to Obama's National Security Council said they would need 13,000 troops. A few days later, they revised the number upward, to 17,000. When Obama sat down with his NSC to discuss Afghanistan for the first time, on Friday, January 23, 2009, no fewer than three different strategic reviews of the situation in Afghanistan were under way or had been recently completed. Lieutenant General Douglas Lute, who had been Bush's top NSC advisor on Afghanistan, had delivered his version of the situation three weeks after Obama had been elected. General David Petraeus, who had left Iraq to take over Central Command, had assigned a top aide, retired colonel Derek Harvey, to assess the situation as well. Mullen, as head of the Joint Chiefs of Staff, had his own review under way.[9]

Obama wanted those reviews consolidated, and he wanted one of his people to do it. At the end of January he called Bruce Riedel, a veteran of the U.S. intelligence community who had served as an advisor to the campaign, to head up a two-month review for the NSC. Riedel would report to Jim Jones, Obama's national security advisor, and to the president.[10]

The Pentagon brass came over to the White House and met again on February 13, two days after Riedel's review was announced, to present the president with options for troop deployments to Afghanistan. One would be to decide on troop levels only after Riedel's work was finished. A second would send an additional 17,000 troops immediately. A third option would send the 17,000 troops in two stages, to give the president time to change his mind if need be. A fourth option would send 27,000 troops — in effect, filling McKiernan's original request.

Withdrawal was clearly not on the table. The Pentagon wanted more troops sent to Afghanistan, and the most influential names on his national security team — Hillary Clinton, Robert Gates, Mike Mullen, and David Petraeus, even Riedel himself — agreed that those troops were needed. Obama had campaigned on a pledge to send more troops to Afghanistan, and those campaign promises, his war cabinet, and the pressure he felt from the Pentagon conspired against him. The new president felt he had no alternative than to acquiesce and send more troops.

Obama took the weekend to consider his options, or lack thereof. Not surprisingly, Obama decided on the third option — to send 17,000 troops to secure the Afghan elections. In hindsight, it was pretty obvious that Riedel was essentially leading Obama to that decision when he presented the three options in the first place. But answers to the larger questions—beyond those 17,000, how many more troops would be sent, how long would they stay there, and what, in fact, would constitute an American victory in Afghanistan?—would be delayed as Riedel and his team at the NSC conducted their review. And it was at this point that Obama started to calibrate his expectations of what success in Afghanistan would look like. It was not "democracy" that was going to define success, but simple stability. As Obama saw it, Afghanistan was a country struggling to become something other than a relic of the Middle Ages.

When it arrived, Riedel's review suggested much of the change in strategy Obama had hinted at during the campaign: the United States should shift its focus from Afghanistan to Pakistan, where terrorists had increasingly found safe haven and taken root, and America would define its goal as disrupting, dismantling, and defeating al Qaeda. To accomplish the mission, it was recommended that the U.S. military focus on growing an Afghan military by more than 130,000 troops, while increasing aid to Pakistan in order to bolster the besieged government there.

Most of the senior members of the NSC—Clinton, Gates, Mullen, Petraeus—endorsed the review. Only Biden, who had become a pessimist and fought against almost every troop increase the Pentagon proposed, wanted to add his objections. What isn't clear is whether Biden was disagreeing because that's what he believed or because he'd been encouraged to do so, because the president needed someone to take another position in order to rein in the Pentagon. As the years pass there is more circumstantial evidence suggesting that Biden was perhaps playing a version of "good cop/bad cop," if for no other reason than to force an alternative view to the table, given how much the groupthink taking place on Afghanistan was frustrating the president.

Gates and Biden disagreed on almost everything related to foreign policy. But Gates, working for his third president in twenty-five years, began to believe that the vice president wasn't fully leveraging the power he held. During his tenure in the Reagan administration, Gates had watched Vice President George H. W. Bush keep his cards much closer to the vest. Bush would be at the table during NSC briefings, but he never offered his advice, and he never voiced a preference in public for one strategy or decision over another. Bush had scheduled private time with Reagan every week; he could offer his opinion to the president, and Reagan would hear it independent of the rest of his NSC. What's more, for the purposes of an increasingly inquisitive national media, no one ever knew whether Reagan was accepting Bush's advice or rejecting it outright.

Biden was the opposite. He would offer his opinion with little prompting, holding forth for twenty minutes when he'd promised to take just two. Whether he agreed with his fellow cabinet members or not, his views were expressed publicly. Meanwhile, the press always seemed to get wind of Biden's thoughts, even when the vice president had lost the argument.

Riedel's review suggested what the NSC principals believed were two realistic options with regard to troop levels: Biden's suggestion, which would leave levels static and focus on counterterrorism in Afghanistan (this would become the shrinking footprint strategy that would eventually be rejected); and an additional 4,000 trainers aimed at bolstering the ranks of Afghanistan's army, which McKiernan, Petraeus, and Gates formally suggested. Every member of the NSC except the vice president supported sending the additional trainers.

Obama, the only vote that mattered, joined the majority. A few days later, on March 27, 2009, Obama used Riedel's words to describe the U.S. mission in Afghanistan. "I want the American people to understand that we have a clear and focused goal: to disrupt, dismantle, and defeat al Qaeda in Pakistan and Afghanistan, and to prevent their return to either country in the future," Obama said. "To achieve our goals, we need a stronger, smarter and comprehensive strategy. To focus on the greatest threat to our people, America must no longer deny resources to Afghanistan because of the war in Iraq."[11] What wasn't included in the statement was a full-throated endorsement of a free, independent, and democratic Afghanistan. There would be no pledge of nation building.

With the directional shift in the works, Gates and Mullen were slowly realizing that they had another problem in Afghanistan: their commander on the ground. McKiernan had spent his career overseeing conventional forces, and in Afghanistan the United States faced no conventional enemies. While the war in Iraq had been turned around by Petraeus, General Raymond Odierno, and others who relied more on special forces and counterinsurgency tactics, the war in Afghanistan had flagged under McKiernan.

Mullen had signed off on McKiernan's appointment to head the International Security Assistance Force in Afghanistan in 2008. As his doubts grew, he shared them with Petraeus, who agreed that McKiernan's approach wasn't working. Mullen then approached Gates, who also agreed. Gates and Mullen went to Obama; the president told them he trusted them and that McKiernan should be relieved.

In filling McKiernan's place, Gates and Mullen turned to a career special operations officer, Lieutenant General Stanley McChrystal. McChrystal had been a close aide to Mullen as director of the Joint

Chiefs of Staff. In Iraq, he had overseen the teams that had captured Saddam Hussein and killed Abu Musab al Zarqawi, among other insurgent leaders.[12] He had been a Green Beret, and he had been known to accompany his special forces teams on some of their nighttime raids in Iraq, which was unusual for such a high-ranking officer. More important, though, McChrystal had developed a reputation similar to that of Petraeus, as an unconventional thinker when it came to the battlefield. Compared to his contemporaries, McChrystal was thought of as someone who simply seemed more nimble in his thinking, and if any country needed nimble commanders, it was Afghanistan.

Any new commander in a war zone needs to conduct his own review. McChrystal was already well versed in the intricacies of the war in Afghanistan, and especially in the tremendously troubled relationship between Afghanistan and Pakistan. As director of the Joint Chiefs, McChrystal had begun a campaign to bring officers who had served in Afghanistan into the Pentagon to share their experiences and their insights.

But what McChrystal saw on the ground as he toured the war zone that was now his responsibility was beyond anything he had expected. The Afghan army was a wreck, the American strategy was still ill defined, and the United States faced a real risk of defeat. In a sixty-six-page memo to Gates, who passed it on to the White House, McChrystal said he needed more troops in Afghanistan within the next calendar year, or the entire war—an eight-year investment of American blood and treasure—"will likely result in defeat."

McChrystal's warning came on August 30, five months after Obama had approved the initial round of 17,000 new troops. By then, 68,000 American servicemen and -women were in the theater, but the new commander made clear that he would request even more, from 10,000 to as many as 45,000.[13] He later told Gates that he would request 40,000 more troops, the number he believed he needed to turn around the situation on the ground.

Obama's national security staff was frustrated. Instead of simply assessing the situation without specific recommendations, which is what the White House believed McChrystal's mandate had been, the commander had started asking for more resources—more troops, more money—even before the president had heard McCrystal's own assessment. Every White House during wartime expresses aggravation with a Pentagon that answers every question with "more troops," but in this case McChrystal had skipped to Go without fully describing the game board—and the Obama White House staff knew the American media would focus only on the troop number, not the strategy. Once a troop number gains traction, it's hard for any other part of a military debate to materialize. Even in private, the debate comes back to numbers.

What's more, the core of Riedel's report had been to refocus the American goal in Afghanistan, to essentially aim to do less, and thus complete the task with fewer resources. Did the United States, which already had 68,000 troops in Afghanistan, really need another 40,000 more to "disrupt, dismantle, and defeat al Qaeda in Pakistan and Afghanistan," as Obama had said almost five months earlier?

Obama had a habit of asking his advisors for three options, but everyone quickly figured out how to game that system, which meant in this case the president felt he had only one plausible choice. Like Riedel, McChrystal had offered two alternatives that felt implausible — sending 80,000 additional troops, which would stretch an already-exhausted military that had been engaged in two wars for most of a decade even further; and sending 10,000 to 15,000 troops to train the Afghan military. McChrystal's third option, sending 40,000 troops specifically to reinforce American forces in regions with a strong Taliban presence, was the only serious one.[14]

The White House felt that it was getting rolled by the more experienced generals across the Potomac. "What was interesting is that even as the analysis changed, the Pentagon requests never changed. It was always 40,000 troops," said Ben Rhodes. "So on the one hand you've got this whole process that is focused on trying to set resources to goals and strategy, and yet the resources never change, and they just keep coming up with a rationale for why you need 40,000 troops for this mission."

The NSC staff concluded that the military wasn't taking Obama seriously. Pentagon officials kept showing up at the White House with various charts projecting troop levels off into the future; one chart Rhodes remembers showed a projection of the 40,000 troops arriving in Afghanistan and staying for three years. Another scenario presented to Obama showed that even if he served two full terms, he would leave office with more troops on the ground than had been there when he took the oath. Had it been lost on the Pentagon that Obama had been elected while campaigning on ending the wars in Iraq and Afghanistan, even if it meant sending reinforcements to Kabul and Kandahar on a short-term basis? Finally, in one meeting Obama lost it. "You keep giving me one option," he shouted. "I'm asking for options, and every option [is] the same!"

Two weeks after McChrystal's report arrived at the Pentagon and the White House, Mullen caused a stir by agreeing with its assessments in public— even though the report was still a work in progress and hadn't even been presented publicly. During a hearing of the Senate Armed Services Committee, Mullen hinted at McChrystal's conclusions, which he and the White House had already seen. "I do believe that having heard [McChrystal's] views and having great confidence in his leadership, a properly resourced counterinsurgency probably means more forces," Mullen told the senators. He said the situation in Afghanistan would deteriorate further if left up to the Afghan army, and that McChrystal had been "alarmed" by what he found on the ground, including the strength of the insurgency opposing the American-led coalition. It was, Mullen said, "very clear we need more resources to execute the president's strategy."[15]

The White House was incensed. Mullen realized he had given one side of the Afghanistan debate—the side that wanted more troops—a huge political advantage. The only way to strain the White House's relationship with the Pentagon even further would be if McChrystal's report landed in the hands of a journalist. Lo and behold, the *Washington Post*'s Bob Woodward reported the contents of McChrystal's review on September 20, 2009.[16] The newspaper even posted a PDF of the report, with a few redactions made at the request of the Pentagon, on its website that evening.[17]

Woodward's report had come a week after Obama and his National Security Council sat down for the first of an almost unprecedented string of meetings for the president. On September 13, Obama had met with Biden, Clinton, Gates, Jones, Mullen, Mullen's vice chairman, General James "Hoss" Cartwright, and Michelle Flournoy, Gates's deputy at the Pentagon, among others, to begin to formulate a plan of action; over the next three months, the principals would meet another fourteen times, almost every session stretching over three hours or more. One cannot overstate how unprecedented it is for a senior group of leaders to meet for this long so often. The president never did so on the economy, on health care, you name it. But that's how complicated the Afghanistan debate had become. On the Friday after Thanksgiving, the meetings lasted eleven hours.[18] Once again Obama found himself contemplating whether to acquiesce—a second time—to McChrystal's request or to go the other way and take on political ownership if the situation deteriorated further.

The debate broke down along familiar lines: Gates, Clinton, and Mullen wanted to send more troops, to give the commanders what they said they needed—Clinton usually favored sending even more than Gates did. Biden steadfastly stuck to his opposition, and while he continued to make his point clear in meetings, he also took to writing private memos to Obama to lay out his case.

The review took so long, Obama's closest advisors said, because Obama simply hadn't been convinced by either side. "He really wasn't persuaded, and they had to keep going back and coming up with more information to persuade him," said Valerie Jarrett, one of his closest confidants.

For eight years under George W. Bush, the Pentagon was used to getting its way. When a president didn't agree with the generals, they could go to supporters in Congress to put the pressure on, or even use powerful pro-military lobbyists to also help. It did not go unnoticed in the White House that Mullen, unlike many of his predecessors as chairman of the Joint Chiefs, enjoyed warm relations with the media, or that Petraeus, who some of Obama's advisors secretly worried might harbor an interest in presidential politics himself in 2012, was a rock star who enjoyed almost nothing but favorable media coverage. These were men who knew the power of the media and its ability to leverage public opinion and political pressure to get what they wanted.

The one person in the equation who wasn't media savvy was the man who had, however inadvertently, caused many of the fissures that had opened between the White House and the Pentagon—Stanley McChrystal.

McChrystal had tried to keep a tight lid on the report he would send to Obama, distributing it to Gates and Mullen in person rather than electronically, and strictly limiting the number of people who had access to it before it reached Washington. Still, it had leaked. He had allowed a camera crew and CBS's David Martin to follow him around for a profile piece several months before he completed his assessment. CBS held it until September 27, a week after Woodward had reported the existence of McChrystal's review, when it ran on *60 Minutes*. Regardless of the protestations from McChrystal and the Pentagon, White House conspiracy theorists detected the beginnings of another Petraeus, a media-friendly general, one who was trying to corner them into a troop decision.

When McChrystal addressed military specialists at the Institute for Strategic Studies in London on October 1 — less than a month after the Obama-led NSC review of Afghanistan had begun — he made sure to vet his remarks through the West Wing before he delivered them. But after his speech, when an audience member asked whether he would support an exclusive focus on al Qaeda rather than the Taliban — an option Biden had been recommending in private, which had leaked in the media[19] — McChrystal wandered off his White House–approved remarks. "The short answer is no," he said. "A strategy that does not leave Afghanistan in a stable position is probably a short-sighted strategy."[20]

The White House went ballistic. McChrystal was taken aback by the fury. Senior Obama advisors began giving quotes to reporters, strictly anonymously, pushing back at what they increasingly saw as an orchestrated campaign to push Obama toward the Pentagon's view.

As the sniping across the Potomac grew worse and the tensions more fraught even as the review continued inside the White House, Gates, whose role as the civilian in charge of the Defense Department meant he straddled the two competing worlds, took the unusual step of using a speech before the Association of the United States Army in October 2009 to urge both sides to call a truce and stop fighting in public—in essence, according to a close aide, "to shut the fuck up." In his speech Gates left out the "fuck."

"I believe that the decisions that the president will make for the next stage of the Afghanistan campaign will be among the most important of his presidency," he declared. "So it is important that we take our time to do all we can to get this right. And in this process it is imperative that all of us taking part in these deliberations—civilian and military alike—provide our best advice to the president candidly but privately. And speaking for the Department of Defense, once the commander-in-chief makes his decisions, we will salute and execute those decisions faithfully and to the best of our ability."[21]

Gates's remarks were seen as a shot at some of the commanders, including McChrystal, but Gates also intended his remarks for the White House political folks as well. Bottom line: for the next two months, the intramural feuding died down. The fact of the matter was, both Gates and Mullen knew the White House was losing faith in them; and Mullen in particular, trying to see things through the West Wing's prism, saw that it looked as if the generals were trying to roll the civilians.

In the end it was Gates who brokered the compromise that ultimately underpinned the conclusions Obama reached. In a speech to cadets and the nation at the United States Military Academy at West Point on December 1, Obama said he would deploy 30,000 additional troops—not 40,000—to Afghanistan, with a goal of targeting the insurgency and securing population centers. Another 10,000 non-U.S. troops (NATO allies) were likely to be added, so technically, McChrystal got what he wanted.

But while the plan looked much more like the counterinsurgency strategy that had worked in Iraq, it came with an important caveat: a drawdown date. By July 2011, just over a year and a half from the day Obama announced the new strategy, the first U.S. forces would begin leaving Afghanistan, as part of the beginning of the end of what had already become America's longest war. "These additional American and international troops will allow us to accelerate handing over responsibility to Afghan forces, and allow us to begin the transfer of our forces out of Afghanistan in July of 2011," the president explained. "This effort must be based on performance. The days of providing a blank check are over."[22]

After nearly a year of continuous planning, review, and strategy, after sessions that lasted for hours on end, the "war of necessity," as Obama the candidate called it, he had altered the strategy and the goals, and announced the beginning of the end. It had finally become the president's own.

A President McCain would likely have sent the 40,000 troops and done it sooner. Ditto with a President Hillary Clinton. Obama essentially gave the commanders what they wanted in troops, but the difference between what McCain would have done and what Obama did do was pledge an end date. And while the ultimate result should have been viewed as something that emerged after a healthy debate, it was actually anything but. The cost to his administration, after the fights required with that other rock-solid member of the Washington establishment, the Pentagon, took a heavy toll.

One consequence of the mistrust on both sides of the Potomac was the withdrawal date. Some saw it as politically timed, coming a year before Obama faced voters one final time. But inside the White House, the drawdown date sent a clear message to the generals: there will be no blank check — not to Afghanistan, and not to the Pentagon. "It was really a policy decision," claims Rhodes, because it was the only way to convey to the Pentagon that Obama would leave office with fewer boots on the ground in Afghanistan than he had inherited when he arrived. "It was the only way to discipline the resource issue, for the president to say this is a temporary surge to achieve limited objectives. And we're going to set a timeline here so that everybody understands that this is not an open-ended commitment to remake Afghanistan."

In retrospect, there was no grand conspiracy within the Pentagon to force Obama to capitulate. If there had been, the generals involved couldn't have chosen a clumsier way to go about it—public testimony, public speeches, leaking a review that was supposed to have limited circulation, all of which would have pointed to the conspirators. If there had been an effort to force Obama into an untenable position, it would have been pretty obvious who was behind it. "These guys wouldn't know how to orchestrate a political conspiracy or pressure plan if their lives depended on it. They're not that savvy," concluded Geoff Morrell, who as Defense Department spokesman found himself in the midst of more than a few Pentagon versus White House spats. "It's too ham-handed to actually be a real conspiracy."

But conspiracy or not, the effect was the same: Obama felt boxed in by the various dribs and drabs because, well, he was. And he had a war cabinet that was sympathetic to the generals, and in particular to Gates and Clinton. Some observers might have gone too far in connecting the dots and assuming an orchestrated Pentagon campaign, but with the dots so close together, it was hard not to do a little sketching of one's own.

"It's very difficult for a president to push back [against the Pentagon] in a reasoned way," Mullen said later, reflecting on the series of events. "We did [Obama] a disservice by boxing him in, even though it was accidental. Of course, the White House thought it was on purpose. We're not that smart."

But perception can become reality, and, as Mullen told his fellow members of the Joint Chiefs along with Petraeus and McChrystal, "This is a scar that will not go away with this president," he told them. "Ever."

If there was a lesson the president took away from his experience with the Pentagon that first year of his presidency, it was the feeling that he had little influence—even as commander in chief. And he wasn't going to let that happen again. Gates had been great for sending the message that continuity and experience mattered to the new president; now his departure would send a message, too. It's no accident that with each subsequent defense secretary, the president chose someone he believed would be more of an administration team player. First came

Leon Panetta (who didn't turn out that way, at least as far as the West Wing was concerned), and then in Chuck Hagel, Obama selected someone who was decidedly more cautious in general on the use of the military and, more important to the president, pro–West Wing.

CHAPTER SIX

The Re-election Begins . . . Sort Of

A president must maintain a delicate balance between his official duties and his campaign duties. Legally speaking, presidents can use the perks of office — Air Force One to travel, the bully pulpit to command media attention, the trappings of the White House itself to reward donors — to their political benefit. His campaign, or an affiliated party apparatus, must pay for political travel, but at a laughably low rate; if he flies to a fund-raiser in Los Angeles, for example, he pays only the equivalent of first-class airfare to get there, a tiny fraction of the cost of renting the world's most advanced 747 for a transcontinental flight. He can "cut down" that cost even more if he pairs political fund-raising duties with an ostensibly official event, though in today's world of perpetual campaigning even official events can be scheduled with an eye to political benefit. Basically, if the president does a meet and greet with some tech industry leaders who are using some government grant, he can call it an official duty and defray the costs even more. This is always how presidents handle their fund-raising excursions to California. It's a very expensive trip if there are no "official" events, but add a stop in Silicon Valley to talk about the outdated energy grid, say, and voilà!—using Air Force One to raise money for the party is not only extremely economical, it's a huge advantage to the sitting president in campaign mode.

In recent decades, the way the president operates has become successively more political. Bill Clinton was the first to work on what his team openly dubbed a permanent campaign basis. George W. Bush took it a step further and kept his top political aide, Karl Rove, on the actual West Wing payroll. Few decisions in Barack Obama's White House were made without considering the politics of re-election, even within weeks of his taking the oath of office. As one former senior staffer remembers, with some disgust, "These guys poll everything." In fact, a week doesn't go by without a poll that was in some way paid for by Team Obama being perused by the key members of the West Wing political team. These were *never* national polls. These were surveys of *only* the swing states. Whether it was October 2009 or October 2012, someone in the Obama White House would have data reporting where independent voters in Colorado stood.

*   *   *

Senior members of Obama's staff were never *not* focusing on re-election and on the states he would need to win in order to stick around for a second term. In the first few months of the president's first term, his domestic travels took him almost exclusively to the narrowly divided states that would determine the outcome of the 2012 election. He signed the stimulus bill in Denver; he stopped off in North Carolina; he traveled to Virginia and Florida. Reading Obama's travel schedule in February 2009, when he and his staff were still figuring out how the phones in the White House worked, one could be excused for thinking the 2012 re-election campaign was already off the ground.

The president's staff had obvious cover for sending Obama to such key battlegrounds—he was trying to win swing voters over to his agenda, and to pressure the members of Congress whose votes he would need on later initiatives (all four of those early states also featured competitive House and Senate races in both 2010 and 2012). But at times, they allowed their political considerations to shine through; it was hard, if not impossible, to have a five-minute conversation with any member of the Obama brain trust without hearing them quote the latest poll numbers for independent voters in Colorado, Hispanic voters in Florida, or suburban mothers in the crucial northern Virginia suburbs. From

Axelrod, the architect of Obama's first victory, to Messina, who would manage his re-election effort, it was clear that Obama's most senior advisors had one eye on the 2012 campaign from the moment they set foot in the White House in January 2009.

For a staff that steeped itself in history, determined as it was to avoid the mistakes of past presidents, such concern was understandable. History does not look kindly on one-term presidents; though Obama repeatedly told interviewers he would rather be a great one-term president than a mediocre two-term chief executive, his staff had no illusions that one term would be enough. And, by the way, every president proclaims this, because it sounds good to the general public. But it is B.S., pure and simple. The last two sitting presidents to lose their re-election bids—Jimmy Carter and George H. W. Bush—missed early opportunities during their first two years in office to benefit by playing politics. Further, presidents defeated after one term give opponents a mandate to roll back parts of their agenda. So the only way to cement first-term achievements is to simply *win* a second term. As much as Obama seemed to disdain the actual work of it, his team was not going to sit on their hands. And the Obama political team rationalized this focus on re-election another way: it was about the only avenue left for Obama to have any juice inside the Washington Beltway and get his agenda through. Winning begets influence, or so Obama hoped.

Axelrod, Messina, and Emanuel were aware from the beginning that the Democratic majority Obama had helped usher into Congress would face a test in the midterm elections. Axelrod recalls thinking the majority was in trouble at the December 18, 2008, meeting in which the administration's economic advisors laid out just how bad the recession would get. Emanuel knew that any first midterm election, when turnout would be lower than for a general election, and when the president's most ardent fans wouldn't necessarily be motivated to vote if the name Barack Obama wasn't on the ballot, meant hard times for the party in power, doubly so when an economic recovery was under way.

Obama's advisors also knew that midterm elections would be an opportunity to test their campaign apparatus, and the results would give them insights into the political mood of the country, especially in key battleground states for 2012. So in 2010, the White House team didn't hide their 2012 interest. The team was especially interested in three elections. In Nevada, Harry Reid was seeking re-election. In Colorado, newly appointed senator Michael Bennet was running for his first full term in office. And in Ohio, Governor Ted Strickland was asking voters for another four years in office.

The conventional wisdom among Obama's brain trust held that if those three Democrats won their races — or even two of the three — it was a sign that the president's re-election bid would be stronger than the pundits believed, in spite of Obama's low poll numbers and the shellacking that was likely coming in many of the redder states.

Reid wasn't making it easy; he was as unpopular as almost any incumbent senator in the country. The majority leader is by definition a partisan figure, and Reid's bullheadedness hadn't helped him with voters. Nevada's economy, meanwhile, was one of the worst in the nation, given its dependence on tourism and construction, sectors that had dried up during the recession. He began the race trailing almost every potential Republican nominee he might have faced, including the wackadoodles.

Emanuel had a rule of thumb that helped determine which candidates the president would help: if the candidate was a sure loser, there was no point in sending Obama, who would then look weak for backing someone who couldn't win. No matter how bad Reid's poll numbers got, though, Obama traveled to Nevada several times, and his top strategists continually checked in. Reid's campaign, it turned out, was something of a dry run for the president's re-election bid; the majority leader's campaign built a political machine that focused on getting voters to the polls during the state's early-voting period, especially Hispanic and African American voters who traditionally turned out in lower percentages than their white counterparts. Plus, many of Reid's political problems in Nevada were caused by his devotion to enacting Obama's agenda. So Obama had no choice but to do whatever it took to help him, no matter how bleak things looked.

Reid had some unwitting assistance from Republicans, who nominated Sharron Angle, a walking disaster of a candidate. A favorite of the farthest extremes of Nevada's Republican Party, Angle beat out far more able candidates in the primary, then began a slow and torturous process of completely undermining her own campaign, making intemperate statements on rape, religion, and ethnicity within the space of a few weeks. Reid's campaign took advantage, running an almost completely negative advertising campaign—another tactic Obama advisors would duplicate a few years later against an opponent far superior to Angle—while focusing on turning out the voters most likely to back the Democrat, no matter how unpopular. Reid won by a surprisingly comfortable five-point margin, even though his approval rating never improved.

Reid's victory taught Obama's campaign that the Hispanic vote was a potent force to be harnessed. A later study by the William C. Velasquez Institute in San Antonio found that while nearly seven in ten white Americans who are eligible to vote are in fact registered, just over 60 percent of African Americans and just over half of Hispanics who meet the same eligibility requirements are registered.[1] And minorities turn out in smaller percentages than their white counterparts. Searching for new voters, and faced with polling data that showed their candidate deeply unpopular with white Americans, the strategists who would guide Obama's campaign got a clear message: Democrats were leaving hundreds of thousands, if not millions, of votes on the table, and turning out Hispanic voters in droves would be key to winning several western states.*

A few states away, in Colorado, Obama himself had created something of a political mess. After winning election in 2008, Obama wanted Ken Salazar, a freshman senator, to serve as his secretary of the interior, a post traditionally reserved for a western politician. Salazar resigned from the Senate to take the cabinet post; in his place, Democratic governor Bill Ritter could have picked any number of accomplished politicians. Instead, he turned to Michael Bennet, chief of the Denver school system, someone who had never run for office and whose patrician Washington, D.C., private-school upbringing could appear at odds with the state's frontiersman spirit.

---

* Throughout the subsequent presidential campaign, it was hard to miss the signs of the Obama campaign's interest in those voters: in briefings with reporters, Messina constantly touted the number of new voters the campaign had registered.

But Bennet wowed Ritter in a private interview, and he got the job, ahead of several more experienced candidates.

Bennet was not a natural politician, especially in the Mountain West. He looked more at home in a well-tailored suit discussing finances than he did wearing a hunting jacket and drinking a Coors with the snowcapped Rockies in the background. That made him vulnerable, not only to Republicans determined to take back control of the Senate but also to the very politicians Ritter had bypassed to select Bennet in the first place. Though Washington Democrats did all they could to keep the primary field clear for Bennet, one of those Ritter had scorned, former Colorado House Speaker Andrew Romanoff, decided to take a shot at the prize he had been denied. Messina, in a last-ditch effort to keep Romanoff out of the race, appeared to offer him a position in the administration. Their exchange earned conservative media claims that Messina had violated the Hatch Act, which prohibits such tit-for-tat offers of help. And while Messina was smart enough to not *technically* break the law, it seemed painfully obvious what he was up to. Romanoff tried to score political points by going public with his refusal to back down.[2] In the end, Bennet outlasted Romanoff in a blistering primary, winning by a little over eight percentage points.

Primaries can rip a party apart or produce a badly

damaged nominee. But in Bennet's case, the reverse happened: he had survived his trial by fire against an experienced politician such as Romanoff. More intriguing, Bennet became one of the few candidates to beat an opponent who had been endorsed by Bill Clinton. (Most of the forays Bubba made during the 2010 cycle were for candidates like Romanoff who had backed his wife two years earlier. During the later part of the cycle, Clinton would eventually travel for candidates who had supported Obama in the 2008 primaries, but only after months of begging. Bill Clinton and his closest confidants were the keepers of the unofficial grudge list for most of 2010. But after that year's pummeling of Democrats, bygones finally became bygones for the former president, and the blacklist was essentially shelved.)

Obama seemed to click on a personal level with Bennet, another young outsider who came to Washington determined to change the system. And Bennet's rise to prominence coincided with the mental image Obama had of himself: intellectual—to Obama's *Harvard Law Review,* Bennet had edited the *Yale Law Review*—and disgusted with and disdainful of the process of politics. The two got to know each other in part because Obama seemed to travel to Colorado an inordinate number of times, whether for bill signings or public events, anything to keep his name in the papers in an important battleground state.

Like Reid, Bennet benefitted from the Republican primary. Former lieutenant governor Jane Norton looked like a shoo-in, a prominent centrist who had backing from the Washington establishment. But the populist furor that inspired the Tea Party movement struck again, and Norton lost the primary to a local county attorney named Ken Buck. Like Angle, Buck was proud of his determination not to be politically correct. He made controversial comments on abortion and proposed repealing the Seventeenth Amendment, which allowed for direct election of senators.

The key to Reid's victory in Nevada was the untapped well of Hispanic voters. The key to Bennet's in Colorado was women, voters Buck seemed to offend at every turn. Overtly, the television advertising campaign Bennet ran contrasted the career politician versus the outsider; but under the radar, Bennet was communicating directly with women, particularly with social moderates in the booming Denver suburbs, about Buck's stands on abortion and contraception. Bennet won by just under 29,000 votes out of more than 1.7 million cast, or about 1.7 percentage points. It was women voters who edged him to victory—again, something Team Obama took note of. Bennet's campaign wasn't just a blueprint for Obama in 2012; it also became a blueprint for Democrats all over the country by 2014.

In Ohio, Ted Strickland was running one of the

more promising campaigns in the country, staffed by some of the most talented Democratic operatives in the country. Strickland had won election in 2006, then watched his state's auto industry slide nearly into oblivion, taking the rest of Ohio's economy with it. Now he faced John Kasich, a former congressman and Budget Committee chairman and even brief presidential candidate in 2000, who had stepped away from electoral politics a decade earlier, first to host a show on Fox News and then to make his fortune on Wall Street.

Strickland's poll numbers were dismal. But Kasich's choice of career after politics gave Democrats an opening: if they could paint him as the heartless, moneygrubbing cause of the financial collapse, the embodiment of a recession caused by greed and unchecked ambition, they had a chance to get Strickland a second term.

But Strickland couldn't make the case, or perhaps Ohio's economy hadn't recovered sufficiently. More than 120,000 Ohioans held jobs with motor vehicle companies or parts suppliers, with about one in eight Ohio jobs supported by the industry,[3] and the full effects of the stimulus package and the auto bailout wouldn't be felt for several more months. Strickland held his own and did much better than he should have in this environment, but with the enthusiasm of the Tea Party behind his rival, Kasich edged out a two-point win on November 2.

Two of the three races the White House staff viewed as most indicative of their own chances had broken their way—but could Messina, Axelrod, Plouffe, and Obama's other top strategists count on the fact that there were enough Hispanics in Nevada, suburban women in Colorado, or African Americans in key battleground states like Virginia and North Carolina? Or did Reid and Bennet survive because their opponents were laughably out of the mainstream, disasters-in-waiting who hadn't the slightest chances of winning a general election? Would Obama himself have to get involved in a Republican primary to make sure he faced an unelectable alternative in 2012?

At a national level, the atmospherics seemed to suggest the latter. Obama's victory in 2008 was total, sweeping, historic: He won states no Democrat had won in two generations, fueled by a growing coalition of minorities, single women, and the well educated. His coattails dragged nearly two dozen new Democrats into the House and another eight Democrats into the Senate. Obama won a majority of the popular vote, something no Democrat—including Bill Clinton—had achieved since Jimmy Carter in 1976. The coalition the Obama campaign stitched together looked virtually unassailable.

It wasn't. To the White House, the die had been cast against Democrats months, if not years, before voters cast their ballots in November 2010. For one

thing, there were a slew of accidental Democrats serving in Congress, candidates who essentially rode the
Obama wave in 2008. Early indications in the 2009
elections were that the Obama coalition wasn't turning out when Obama's name wasn't on the ballot.
There was also the reality of the American psyche
during midterm elections, especially during periods
of economic anxiety. Voters almost always punish
the party in the White House. It happened to Reagan and the Republicans in the 1982 midterms, and
to Carter and the Democrats in 1978, for instance.
Then add in the health care law and the fear of big
change, and the die wasn't cast only for Democratic
losses in 2010; there was a perfect storm of disaster
brewing.

Thus the president's mission, his advisors decided,
was simply to insulate himself from the damage
beforehand in order to preserve his chances for a
second term—chances that, in the depth of the
Democratic doldrums of the spring and summer of
2010, already looked perilously low.

If his survival-of-the-fittest mentality made sense,
it made sense to him alone. And that mind-set only
added to the increasing frustration of Democrats on
Capitol Hill, in the corridors of K Street, and in
campaign offices across the country. The president
and his White House seemed disconnected, resigned
to a fate other Democrats believed was not yet sealed.
And—perhaps most enraging—these Washington

Democrats hated the White House for believing that the Obama brand and the Democratic Party brand were distinct, and that one was paramount over the other. The White House did little to dispel the notion that Obama came first, over and above the party. After all, for the first time ever, a new president came in and, instead of using the official party headquarters as his political base of operations, he and his team decided to start up a competitor of sorts— they called it Organizing for America, the OFA a play off the campaign initials Obama for America. After his second-term win, this decision to keep the Obama campaign apparatus separate from the party would continue, and "Organizing for America" would morph into "Organizing for Action." At the time, it was designed to be the political apparatus that would help sell the president's agenda. But despite modest fund-raising success, this group has had little impact. And the political legacy the president is leaving the Democratic Party is that of a bankrupted Democratic National Committee. For the first time in history, the official national arm of the Democratic Party would maintain a debt for more than two straight years. Political party committees regularly take on debt late in a campaign cycle but almost always pay it back before the end of the next calendar year. That is not the case with the DNC, circa 2014. In many ways, the president's campaign team has used the DNC the exact same way the Obama campaign accused Romney's Bain Capital of using distressed companies—load them up with debt and bankrupt them. Late in 2013, the Obama political team finally decided it had to start fixing the DNC, but the damage was done. It's not clear the DNC will be a meaningful player for the next few years beyond being a vehicle to move money around. Many non-Obama Democrats have openly wondered just how powerful the DNC would be today if the 2008 Obama brain trust had truly taken it over and turned it into a similar campaign juggernaut that Obama's 2012 re-elect turned out to be.

This mind-set of distancing Obama from the Democratic Party brand began the day he decided to run and thus challenge the person and family that controlled the party—Hillary Clinton. After all, when he entered the presidential contest in 2007, he was decidedly outside the Democratic establishment. Few believed that this interloper, this freshman senator without a gray hair on his head, could defeat the former First Lady of the United States, a two-term senator with such an overwhelming fundraising advantage that any bid against her was seen as quixotic at best. Obama's top strategists were outsiders, too; Axelrod maintained an office in Chicago rather than in Washington. Obama's best moments on the trail and in debates came when he ran against Washington, the poisonous partisan swamp that had become so loathed by the average

American. Even after he took over the White House, he continued, to his party's chagrin, to set up Congress as his straw man opponent rather than singling out Republicans in Congress for criticism. But more than rhetoric was involved. After the president beat the establishment, he and his advisors had in their heads that they should *not* become the establishment. And so they tried to start their own party apparatus, of sorts. It took them a while to accept the fact that once they were in the White House, they would become the "new" establishment.

But running against Washington, standing against incumbency, can't work when one's own party controls Congress—being the outsider works only when one is truly outside. The image Obama crafted ended up working at cross-purposes with the party that needed him. That played out in the worst possible way for Democrats in 2010.

The seeds of their defeat were sown even before Obama won office. Pushed through by the Bush administration, the Troubled Asset Relief Program, which made $700 billion available to big banks on the brink of collapse, spurred conservative anger. For years, the grumbling on the right was muted by the Bush-Cheney clan, essentially out of political necessity. Winning and holding the White House trumped all, so the conservative populist wing of the party accepted the largest expansion of government in generations by Bush, on things like national security and even the Medicare prescription drug benefit, because it was deemed good politics at the moment. Bush won re-election in 2004 and Republicans controlled both the House and Senate, so why mess with success?

But with Republicans in the minority across the board by 2009, the conservative natives weren't just restless, they decided to start flexing their muscles about the size of government again. This is actually an inevitable reaction to losing. A party in regrouping mode usually tries to go back to its core principles. The Democrats did that post-2004, and it proved successful in 2006 and 2008. Republicans were now going through a similar soul-searching, and the more conservative elements were calling the shots. And so just a month after Obama accepted victory in Grant Park, the degree to which the economy was suffering became apparent to his advisors, and they could picture how a party out of power could take advantage of this anxiety.

The political landscape only got worse. In 2008, the economy lost about 2.6 million jobs. In January 2009, as Obama prepared to take the oath of office, another 800,000 jobs disappeared—in a month! Obama's approval ratings, which started in the mid-60s, followed close behind. By the end of his first year in office, Obama's rating was below 50 percent. At the same time, nearly 60 percent of Americans believed the country was headed in the wrong direction. "It was mind-boggling how bad things were. And it was also frightening to think about the things we were going to have to do to save the country from a depression. Midterm elections are always tough, but this one we knew was going to be really, really hard because of the things that we were going to have to do," Axelrod said later.

The signs of an impending Republican wave were everywhere. In 2009, Bob McDonnell trounced his Democratic opponent in the race to become governor of Virginia, running up larger margins than Obama had in the critical Washington, D.C., suburbs. Chris Christie, the bombastic former U.S. attorney, ousted a scandal-plagued Democratic governor in deep-blue New Jersey. The Tea Party movement had scared every Republican, and even some Democrats, away from working with the White House. And of course there was Massachusetts. Was that race a referendum on the president's health care bill, as Republicans interpreted it? Was it simply a case of a better candidate, Republican nominee Scott Brown, beating an inferior campaigner, as the White House would spin it?

As hard as it might have been for Obama aides to imagine, things were about to get worse.

The life of a White House staffer, several of Obama's senior advisors had come to realize, is not driven by carefully laid plans and a consistent agenda. Instead, life in the White House is driven by a series of crises, all of which have far-reaching consequences. After all, if it were a small problem, someone else would have handled it before it reached 1600 Pennsylvania Avenue, or so the president would say over and over again when talking publicly about his troubled political situation. And in the spring and summer of 2010, any of the crises that faced Obama and his team—Emanuel referred to the "G-Force," for Greece, Germany, Gaza, the Gulf, gas prices, and stock market gyrations—could have irreparably derailed a presidency.

The economy remained so stagnant that the word "recovery" hardly applied. Nervousness on Wall Street contributed to wild swings back and forth. Hundreds of billions of dollars in net worth had already been wiped out of 401(k)'s and retirement accounts, and every sign of hope was seemingly offset by a negative that might have signaled the beginning of another downward spiral. If the economy wasn't irrefutably on the way to recovery by the time Obama was running for re-election two years later, his chances would be grievously imperiled.

And in an interconnected world, the American recovery depended in large part on the European economy. Greece's government, forced to take severe austerity measures by European creditors as they struggled to curb their own budget crises, inspired a wave of protests from civil servants. On May 5, 100,000 Greeks marched through the streets of

Athens as part of a general strike; three protesters were killed. If Greece defaulted on its debts or refused to meet the conditions for loans laid out by its creditors, led by French president Nicolas Sarkozy and German chancellor Angela Merkel, the ripple effect would cascade across the Atlantic and threaten the fledgling recovery in America. For a president whose agenda had already been entirely consumed by an economic disaster, the prospect of a renewed depression spelled almost certain defeat. So that was G-Force 1.

G2 was in the Middle East. Ever since Hamas had won control of the Gaza Strip, in 2006, the already-stalled peace process had threatened to degenerate into armed conflict. Back home, that posed a challenge for the administration, which, despite rhetoric to the contrary, hadn't yet taken grand steps toward a peace deal. And the situation grew more tense by late May, when a flotilla of six ships sailed from Cyprus in an effort to break an Israeli blockade of the Gaza Strip. On May 31, Israeli naval commandos boarded the ships in an effort to force them into an Israeli port. Nine activists were killed, including an American citizen. And while this Gaza mess may seem like a typical Middle Eastern event, it was the timing that was a problem for the president. Israeli issues are one of the few foreign policy areas that can impact domestic politics. And the president was already perceived as not as "pro-Israel" as the rest of his party. And whenever so-called pro-Israel Republicans could highlight that perceived split, they did.

To compound the problem for the president, Turkish citizens had been killed, and for much of his first three years in office, the president was trying desperately to woo Turkey diplomatically. He viewed Turkey as an important intermediary between the Western and Arab worlds. Turkey was one of Israel's few Arab allies, so this incident threatened to derail whatever remote hope the president had of jump-starting the Israeli-Palestinian peace process.

But no crisis inspired more fear in the White House than the oil pouring into the Gulf of Mexico. On April 20, a methane bubble traveled up a drill column on an offshore oil rig called the Deepwater Horizon, causing a massive explosion that killed eleven men and sent as much as five million barrels of oil spewing into the Gulf. Occurring just five years after Hurricane Katrina devastated New Orleans and the coasts of Louisiana and Mississippi, the spill represented not just an environmental but a serious political threat. Obama aides remembered well that George W. Bush's lack of a fast, efficient Katrina response had effectively doomed him to the dustbin of irrelevancy, and they were determined not to repeat his mistakes.

Carol Browner, the former head of Bill Clinton's Environmental Protection Agency who had agreed to serve as Obama's energy czar, briefed Obama within twelve hours of the explosion. Energy secretary Stephen Chu visited the White House frequently, often with massive PowerPoint presentations that went into excessive detail. Browner, Chu, interior secretary Ken Salazar, EPA administrator Lisa Jackson, transportation secretary Ray LaHood, and housing and urban development secretary Shaun Donovan, who were already meeting regularly on environmental issues as part of what they dubbed the Green Cabinet, held daily conference calls to coordinate a response.[4] Obama visited the Gulf Coast five times between May and August, including a quick weekend vacation with his family in Panama City, Florida, where he waded into the ocean to send a signal to Americans that it was safe to go back to the region to vacation and swim.

The effort to fix the gusher and skim the oil was one of the largest operations the federal government had ever run, larger even than the D-day invasion of Normandy. Eighty-five days after the initial explosion, the leak was plugged. Technically, what the government pulled off was quite the impressive feat. But politically, this took a big toll on the Obama White House, and eventually they'd get no benefit for solving this problem.

It completely consumed the Obama presidency for those eighty-five days. And in hindsight, it was one of the president's success stories, if success is measured by mitigating a potential political disaster. From helping to shake down BP for a massive multibillon-dollar recovery fund to the near sole focus of the entire federal government on the cleanup, the White House didn't seem to let a single ball drop on this operation.

That said, there were plenty of times during this lengthy crisis when folks in the White House thought things looked bleak. Some of it was simply bad luck, including the ability to get a video camera at the site of the leak. While it was an incredible help to the team trying to plug the leak, the footage became a regular feature on every cable TV news outlet, almost as common as the news tickers. What this televised portion of the leak meant was that there were no "down" days for the White House during this crisis. As long as the oil was spewing out of the seabed and the country could see this every single day, the White House and the entire federal government had to be focused on plugging it.

Then there was the president's slow initial reaction, which is actually typical. The president's best asset is his even temperament, but politically, his coolness can come across as aloofness, or uncaring—when, for instance, in the case of an oil company responsible for a massive oil leak, he doesn't publicly get mad.

Robert Gibbs remembers going into the Oval Office in the early days of the leak and begging the president to show some anger. The president replied logically, "And how much oil is that going to clean up?" Gibbs said, "It'll buy you time and space politically." The president reluctantly went out that day and showed some anger. But for those who knew him and covered him closely, it was clear he was going through the motions. It's not that he wasn't upset, it's just not how he naturally reacts. Sometimes, we observers forget that the president was raised to be cool under pressure, to never flash anger, to always keep his emotions in check if he wanted to avoid ever being labeled as "angry," a dangerous description for an African American politician.

In fact, the oil spill cleanup is a fascinating lesson in what Obama is and isn't as a leader. He had a "whatever it takes" mind-set to get the job done, and that led to people like Stephen Chu working closely with BP management and others to figure out a solution. But politically, while he certainly prevented this spill from becoming a Katrina rerun for the Gulf Coast, the president somehow never looked comfortable running this successful operation. Even his Oval Office address, a speech that the president's longtime speechwriting partner Jon Favreau calls the worst of the Obama presidency, didn't exactly send the message to the public that he had this. And yet he and the government did. Of course, that Oval Office address had the unfortunate aspect of a picture-in-picture video of the spewing oil, perhaps making it impossible for anything from the president's lips to penetrate the public's consciousness.

And so went the summer of 2010 in a White House distracted by the cumulative effect of so many crises. The staff simply didn't have the bandwidth to start dealing with the political disaster that was headed their way. In fact, many of the president's best-laid plans for 2010 got derailed by this G-Force of crises. The president was getting close to hammering out a major energy deal with key Republicans. It was going to include expanded offshore drilling and new nuclear reactors, but the spill put offshore oil drilling on the back burner. And of course less than a year later, the Japanese nuclear power leak ended whatever bipartisan support there was left on the nuke issue. That's why a major energy deal never happened, and probably won't for a while.

The G-Force of crises also had a major impact on the political landscape that summer. The oil spill took the president off the fund-raising circuit, but it also paralyzed the party in many ways beyond the issue of money: the president and his party were wholly knocked off message at one of the most critical periods of the 2010 campaign. The spill meant no White House messaging on health care, which was being used as a sledgehammer against Democrats across the country. And that's only one issue.

The health care debate had come and gone without anything resembling a public option, a key staple of the liberal push for reform; the prison at Guantánamo Bay, which Obama had promised to close, remained open; and Obama had sent tens of thousands of new troops to Afghanistan, into a war he had promised to end. Worse, Obama had opened parts of the country's coastline to new oil exploration and drilling only weeks before the Deepwater Horizon rig exploded, giving environmentalists— who had become an increasingly large part of the Democratic financial base—a major reason to be unhappy with the White House.

By July, it was clear the White House was focused solely on saving the Senate, convinced that the House would fall into Republican hands. On July 11, Gibbs admitted on NBC's *Meet the Press* that Democrats could lose the House.[5] That enraged Nancy Pelosi, who was working hard to save her speakership. "How could he know what is going on in our districts?" Pelosi fumed at a meeting of the House Democratic Caucus attended by the White House's top liaison to the House, Dan Turton. "Some may weigh his words more than others. We have made our disagreement known to the White House."[6] Of course, all Gibbs had done was acknowledge the obvious political circumstances.

Gibbs pushed back at the notion that Obama wasn't helping House Democrats, authorizing the leaking of a memo to reporter Jonathan Martin that highlighted the 227 events White House officials— including Obama—had participated in or were on the calendar. The Democratic National Committee, which had by then become the chief fund-raising and political vehicle for the White House, had pledged $50 million to help Democrats up and down the ballot.

Still, some of those events weren't done willingly. Emanuel had promised Representative Allen Boyd, a conservative Democrat facing a primary challenge in Florida's Panhandle, that he would get a visit from First Lady Michelle Obama in 2009, in order to secure Boyd's vote on energy legislation. But he neglected to check with the First Lady's office first. Michelle had little interest in campaigning, but she was more in demand than the president; she was the Obama with personal ratings above 50 percent at the time. In this case, she acquiesced and reluctantly headlined an event with Boyd, though she wasn't happy when she found out his primary challenger was African American. Her anger grew when Boyd voted against one of the early iterations of the health care bill, though he voted for the final package. Boyd survived his primary challenge, but he lost to Republican Steve Southerland in the general election.[7]

"Every president has been accused by their party

of never doing enough," argues Emanuel in hindsight. "We weren't distracted, but nothing we were
going to be able to do was going to change the dynamics of the race. The biggest dynamic you needed to
change was a surging economy and dropping unemployment. We were coming out of a very deep recession that everybody acknowledges always historically
takes longer to recoup from. Could we have done
one extra fund-raiser here, or an additional this or
additional that? Yes. The question though is would
that change the fundamentals of the race? No."

No one felt the pressure about keeping the House
in Democratic hands more than Rahm Emanuel.
The chief of staff, a former chairman of the Democratic Congressional Campaign Committee himself,
had poured countless hours of effort into electing a
Democratic majority. In many cases, he had recruited
the candidates, raised their money, held their hands
through difficult times, berated them to do more to
help themselves. Now, his candidates were on the
front lines of a beating that he was powerless to stop.
He saw every poll, he communicated constantly with
the candidates, and he commiserated with his friends
on Capitol Hill.

But still he argued against sending Obama to
help. After all, he worked for the man in the Oval
Office, not for Hill Democrats, and his view of politics held that associating with a loser, no matter
how close a friend, still makes one a loser. "Rahm's

theory on politics is like a pyramid of strength," one former coworker said. "Strength begets strength begets strength. So at a certain point when you become weak politically, you can't get out there and put something on the line because if you lose, that's weakness."

And as Election Day crept nearer, every candidate with a *D* after his or her name started looking like a loser. The fights inside the White House intensified. Emanuel wanted to keep Obama away from candidates who would lose. Gibbs and others believed that the White House had to stand with its allies, especially those who had knowingly taken tough votes that would likely cost them their seats.

And no one had taken tougher votes than Virginia representative Tom Perriello. Perriello owed his seat to Obama and to the thousands of new voters Obama's campaign had turned out in Charlottesville, Virginia. He had beaten Virgil Goode, the incumbent Republican, by just 727 votes in 2008, thus guaranteeing he would be a top Republican target two years down the road. But he didn't shy away from tough votes. He voted for the stimulus bill, cap-and-trade legislation, and the health care bill. While other vulnerable Democrats strategically opposed their party on certain issues to craft an independent image, Perriello was a reliable partner when Pelosi whipped her conference toward Obama's objectives.

So when Perriello asked Obama to come to Charlottesville to rally the voters he had turned out two years before, it should have been an easy request to fulfill. Few other Democrats wanted Obama at their side in the race's waning days, and while Perriello was almost certain to lose, he had been a good soldier.

Rahm Emanuel didn't see it that way. Appearing with a loser, he again argued in meetings, only made Obama look weak. Given Perriello's dismal poll numbers, even a visit from a president who was slightly more popular than the congressman wouldn't be enough, so why waste the political capital?

Gibbs argued the opposite — loyalty demanded that Obama travel to Virginia for his soon-to-be-fallen comrade. "Tom Perriello has decided he would like this, and we're going to tell him no, after all the shit he went through?" Gibbs thought. "Don't we have to be loyal to our friends?"

Gibbs won the argument, and Obama went to Charlottesville on Friday, October 29, where a crowd of 12,000 packed the house.[8] But Emanuel was right — four days later, Perriello lost to Republican Robert Hurt by four points.

He wasn't the only one to lose on November 2. The Republicans won an astounding sixty-three seats in the House, including defeating a record fifty-two incumbents. Republicans won the popular vote for control of the House of Representatives by almost seven points. They won more than seven hundred seats in state legislatures, giving the GOP control over a 2011 redistricting process that would shape the House for a decade to come, and governorships in blue states such as Michigan and Wisconsin. Axelrod admitted that even he, the White House's senior political strategist, with access to every poll conducted for his party's candidates, didn't see the totality of the Republican wave until it was too late.

"I can tell you that some election nights are more fun than others. Some are exhilarating; some are humbling," a clearly humbled Obama told the press at a postelection news conference. "There is not only sadness about seeing them go, but there's also a lot of questioning on my part in terms of could I have done something differently or done something more so that those folks would still be here. It's hard. And I take responsibility for it in a lot of ways."

Two years after a historic victory, the success of the Obama brand, which provided a boost for Democrats from Alaska to Virginia and back, had turned into an albatross for his party. The excitement those first-time voters felt in 2008 had tempered, dampened by a struggling economy and by Obama's inability to deliver either hope or change. In 2010, Democrats experienced all the downsides of running under an unpopular incumbent president, with none of the upsides of running with an African American named Barack Obama.

"We've never figured out how to transfer the passion for him to others, and I'm not sure it's possible," Gibbs says. "If it is possible, then you have to nationalize an election almost at the very beginning. You have to make the stakes big at the very beginning. We didn't do that in [2009], and by the time we tried to do that in 2010 it was simply too late."

Five weeks after Democrats lost their majority in the House of Representatives, Joe Biden went to Capitol Hill to commiserate. The vice president knew what it was like to see colleagues lose, knew what it was like when the committee chairmanships, the curtain-draped offices with expansive views of the National Mall, and the power that came with being in the majority were about to fade away. During his time in the Senate, thirty-six long years, he had seen friends and colleagues come and go, win elections and lose. He had been chairman of the powerful and influential Judiciary Committee when Democrats controlled the Senate; after the 1994 midterm elections, when Republicans swept to power, he handed the gavel to Orrin Hatch, the Utah Republican.

Barack Obama hadn't shared the joys of victory or the agony of defeat with his colleagues in Congress. In fact, few Democrats in Congress even thought of Obama, who stayed in the Senate for only four years, as one of them. He was the outsider, too cool and aloof and unwilling to play the game when he was on

Capitol Hill, too disinterested, as the complaints among House Democrats went, to engage once he was in the White House. All Obama knew of his time in Washington, both personally and professionally, was surprisingly easy success. He won his Senate seat in 2004, Democrats swept control of the House and Senate in 2006, and then he won the presidency in 2008. The 2010 midterms were his first real electoral setback while in Washington.

So when those House Democrats, serving in the final days of the 111th Congress, wanted to talk to the White House about a deal over extending tax cuts first enacted under George W. Bush, they sent for Biden, not Obama. They wanted someone who might actually understand their frustrations.

After all, it was Biden's deal that had House Democrats upset. After the Republican trouncing that had shunted the Democrats into the minority in the House, the White House realized it was time to deal on the Bush tax cuts. Those cuts were set to expire at the end of the year, and the vice president had spent time shuttling between the two ends of Pennsylvania Avenue working with Republicans to hammer out an extension. Biden had been negotiating directly with Mitch McConnell, bypassing both the incoming Speaker of the House, John Boehner, and the Democrats who for the next three weeks would still technically control Congress.

On December 8, a Wednesday, Biden's motorcade whisked him once again down the broad six-lane boulevard bookended by the White House and the Capitol. This time, instead of heading to McConnell's office, he went to the other side of the building, down into the basement, where House Democrats were meeting.

No one in the administration had worked as hard for Democratic candidates up and down the ballot in 2010 as Biden had. He had campaigned with eighty-five candidates from coast to coast, almost three times the number with whom Obama had appeared. At the time, because of the oil spill, Biden would regularly sub for Obama at events that were not canceled altogether. And then there was the decision to keep Obama away from the red states—the president had campaigned in only one state, Missouri, that he hadn't won in 2008, while Biden had spent time in deep-red Texas, Arkansas, Indiana, Arizona, and South Carolina.[9]

Biden spent two hours consoling his fellow Democrats. The ones who had lost were by then resigned to their fates; they knew they would soon be out of jobs. But the ones destined to spend at least the next two years wandering the wilderness of the minority berated the vice president, demanded a better deal, and insisted that Biden go back to the negotiating table. Biden explained, again and again, that his strategic advice to the president was to take the deal as written and to move on to the next fight.

The 2010 voters had sent a message, and with the expiration of the Bush tax cuts looming and only a few weeks of a lame-duck session ahead of them, Biden understood that while Democrats had little room to maneuver, there were important legislative priorities that would get much harder to accomplish once Republicans took control of Congress in January.

For his part, Obama was listening to advice from a number of Democratic quarters. Liberals wanted him to refuse a deal; they saw extending the Bush tax cuts as a way to give the wealthy a break while enforcing cuts in government programs that aimed to help the poor. Some others, like New York's Chuck Schumer, thought that the longer the administration waited to cut a deal, the more Republicans would give away in order to get their tax cuts. But Biden had an alternate strategy in mind. The START nuclear arms reduction treaty with Russia was languishing in the Senate, waiting to be ratified. A measure providing health care to first responders to the September 11, 2001, terrorist attacks also still needed passage. And gay rights advocates were still pushing to repeal "Don't Ask, Don't Tell," the Clinton-era policy that prohibited gays from serving openly in the military. Biden believed that nothing would get done as long as the tax cuts remained on the table. Make the deal early, Biden told Obama, and the politically wounded president could get the rest of the legislative checklist done with a lame-duck Congress, which would give him a surprisingly productive end to a disastrous 2010.

Biden's years in the Senate had given him an outlook on legislating—and the deal making that comes with it—that was much different from Obama's. Aides who watched the president noticed that when Obama sat down at a bargaining table, he negotiated toward a common denominator. His tendency was to strip away areas of a proposal on which the two sides differed until both sides could agree on a framework. It was an idealistic, rational sensibility that began with the premise that some area of common ground always exists in every situation, however small—and it was a very *un*-Washington way to negotiate. Again and again, he'd immediately identify the common ground as a means of showing the other person that they were on the same side, and that therefore that person's prejudices and preconceptions should be abandoned. That sensibility had been professionally reinforced during his dozen years lecturing at the University of Chicago, an institution well known for its academic study of rational equilibrium, be it in law or economics, and of the means by which individuals and institutions could be incentivized to pursue long-term benefits over short-term gains.

But rational middle ground wasn't where Washington started negotiations.

That style of negotiating was taken advantage of in Washington, especially Washington in the twenty-first century. The president regularly revealed too early what he was willing to support. And Republicans would grab it and publicize it, knowing it would become a wedge with congressional Democrats. It's actually surprising that the president enjoyed playing poker so much, because in legislative negotiations he rarely acted like a sophisticated player. He metaphorically let everyone at the table see his entire hand when it came to policy debates.

Biden took a different, more tried-and-true approach: he offered something his negotiating partner wanted in exchange for something he wanted, with the intention of aggregating mutual political satisfaction toward a bill both sides could claim as a win. One former Biden aide described his style as allowing everyone to declare victory. The resulting bill might be a Frankenstein of gimmes and earmarks and U-turns, but like that monster, it was alive.

And that, in all its inglorious chaos, was how Washington worked for most of the twentieth century and even the early part of the twenty-first. Reagan and Clinton had believed in the process, and so did Biden, almost religiously. Obama's effort to transcend the "someone has to be declared the winner and someone has to be declared the loser" mentality of Washington in the twenty-first century was admirable in the abstract, but a huge flaw in terms of getting stuff done. One man—even someone as impressive as Barack Obama, someone whose election had been predicated on change—was not going to reinvent that reality. Perhaps nothing could.

CHAPTER SEVEN

The Winter Thaw

Official Washington in the twenty-first century spends ten months of the year fighting with itself. Democrats and Republicans feud on Capitol Hill, Congress faces off against the White House, and the interest groups and lobbying firms on K Street jockey for position and fight over scarce federal dollars. There is no fighting in August, when everybody with the flimsiest excuse abandons the oppressive heat and humidity of a Washington summer. And there is no fighting in December, when, on any given night, several agencies, lobbying shops, and industry organizations throw their holiday parties, an intoxicating cheer, in its liquid form and in its glimpses of civility. Everyone just wants to get home, and deals usually get cut simply so that lawmakers will for once not abandon their families for some work-related excuse. There's no doubt that elective office is hardest on politicians' immediate families, from missed soccer games and dinner parties to canceled birthday celebrations, you name it. Family rarely comes first, especially in an election year. But December is usually a different story.

The winter of 2010 was something of an exception. The Democratic-controlled House of Representatives had just a few weeks left before Republicans, victorious in that November's midterm elections, took control. Circumstances demanded that a lame-duck session of Congress pass an extension of George W. Bush's tax cuts and a host of administration priorities, all of which would become more difficult to get through a Republican-controlled House. Among these was a repeal of "Don't Ask, Don't Tell," the Clinton-era ban on gays and lesbians serving openly in the military.

The Democratic evolution on the issue of gay rights would come to mirror the party's shift on gun control. In the early 1990s, Democratic strategists saw gay rights as a wedge issue Republicans could use to separate rural and suburban voters from their party. Clinton, along with just about every prominent Democrat in Congress, said he supported the traditional definition of marriage, a union between a man and a woman. Even the great liberal hope of 2004, former Vermont governor Howard Dean, who signed the nation's first law allowing same-sex civil unions, chose the more conservative option. In 2000, the Vermont Supreme Court ordered the state to adopt either civil unions or marriage provisions for same-sex couples, and Dean chose the former.[1]

But the Democratic coalition was changing in subtle ways. Wealthy gay donors were playing an increasingly large role in funding the party, and more liberal urban members of Congress were becoming comfortable advocating a changing of the laws — both Don't Ask, Don't Tell and the Defense of Marriage Act, another Clinton-era bill, arguably signed at the time under a bit of political duress, that defined marriage as a covenant for heterosexual couples only.

Public attitudes were shifting as well, bolstered in part by celebrities who came out of the closet — including Ellen DeGeneres, Rosie O'Donnell, and Neil Patrick Harris — and the increasingly common portrayal of gay characters on television, most notably on the sitcom *Will & Grace*. The generation that came of age in the 1990s and 2000s didn't believe that homosexuality was a sin and increasingly didn't associate gayness with the stigma it had once borne. And while the battle to legalize gay marriage had achieved little political success, it began to pick up momentum in the courts. After Vermont's top court required Dean to choose a path to legalization, the Massachusetts Supreme Judicial Court ruled in 2003 that gays had the right to marry. By the time the Senate took up Don't Ask, Don't Tell, in 2010, courts in Connecticut and Iowa had followed Massachusetts's lead, and legislatures in Vermont and New Hampshire had passed the first gay marriage bills. While anti–gay marriage initiatives passed in every state where they made the ballot, polls showed a growing acceptance of same-sex marriage, especially among younger Americans.

Gay rights advocates thought the Obama administration would be their watershed moment. A Democratic Senate, a Democratic House, and a liberal president would surely advance their cause even further.

But Obama was wary of embracing an issue that, while dear to his urban liberal base's heart, could drive a wedge between him and the working-class swing voters he believed he still needed to win. And then, of course, there were the more religious African Americans, who were an important part of the president's base but also historically against gay marriage. Obama had been shaken, during his Senate race in 2004, when Alan Keyes, his Republican opponent, had knocked him hard on the issue. In response, Obama had treaded carefully, even in a race he would win with 70 percent of the vote.

"What I believe is that marriage is between a man and a woman," Obama said in a 2004 debate with Keyes, parroting the Democratic line at the time. "What I believe, in my faith, is that a man and a woman, when they get married, are performing something before God, and it's not simply the two persons who are meeting," he went on. "We have a set of traditions in place that I think need to be preserved, but I also think that we have to make sure that gays and lesbians have the same set of basic rights that are in place."[2] Obama said he believed being gay is an innate characteristic — "for the most part." (It's truly remarkable to go back and listen to Obama circa 2004, and compare his stance with that of a decade later. It's a dramatic shift, one that does seem a lot more politically planned than spontaneous. The 2004 Obama was clearly someone who worried how his position would look on the national stage.)

Democratic leaders, collectively, were moving at about the same pace Obama was on gay issues. It's why the 2008 Democratic platform began to show signs of change, but only incrementally. Democrats, the platform said, opposed the Defense of Marriage Act — a bill 120 House Democrats[3] and 32 Senate Democrats[4] supported in 1996 — "and all attempts to use this issue to divide us." But the platform explicitly omitted mention of same-sex marriage.[5]

The immediate goal for gay rights advocates, once Obama was inaugurated, was ending Don't Ask, Don't Tell. And they had reason to hope: while Bill Clinton was the first president to hold a public meeting with gay rights leaders, the Obama White House summoned activists, including leaders of the Human Rights Campaign, to meetings on an almost weekly basis.

But there was reason for skepticism, too: Obama had invited Rick Warren, a California megachurch pastor and ardent opponent of gay marriage, to give an invocation at his first inaugural. In an editorial published in the *Washington Post,* Joe Solmonese, president of the Human Rights Campaign, excoriated the new administration. "It is difficult to comprehend how our president-elect, who has been so spot-on in nearly every political move and gesture, could fail to grasp the symbolism of inviting an anti-gay theologian to deliver his inaugural invocation," he wrote.

Later Jim Messina rebuked Solmonese at a White House meeting for the op-ed,[6] but the strain was short-lived. In early 2010, as the debate over health care legislation was wrapping up, Messina was summoned to the Oval Office. He had been running the White House's rapid response team, pushing back against critics of the health care bill; Obama told him his next task would be handling the repeal of Don't Ask, Don't Tell.

Messina was confused. He had taken meetings with gay rights activists, but in the pantheon of Democratic causes, others in the White House had much deeper connections to the gay community.

"I don't have any history with the issue, and I don't know anything about it," Messina remembers telling the president. More succinctly, he simply wondered, *Why me?*

"Because I want to win," Obama said.

Obama had told the Joint Chiefs of Staff, the

military's top commanders, that Don't Ask, Don't Tell was a policy with a shelf life, and he intended to be the president who helped it expire. But there was a tightrope to walk: Obama knew he needed to get the generals on board before he moved in order to blunt Republican criticism. Robert Gates told Obama there had to be a process, part of it public, by which the Joint Chiefs and the Pentagon changed their position — *evolved,* in modern political parlance — on an issue they had long supported.

What's more, the generational change that was inspiring the Democratic Party shift on gay marriage was starting to filter into the Republican Party, too. The White House believed it could persuade a number of moderate and younger Republicans to back the policy shift, but they needed to provide those Republicans with cover. If the Pentagon brass was buying into repeal, the legislative strategists believed, so would several Republican senators.

Gates and especially Mullen saw the writing on the wall. Mullen had put together a group of advisors to study repeal even before Obama had won election. He reached out to Sam Nunn, the former Georgia senator who had been instrumental in pushing Clinton to adopt Don't Ask, Don't Tell in the first place. And he called around to gay rights organizations, too; in an odd case of strange political bedfellows, Mullen grew close to Elizabeth Birch, the longtime gay rights activist who had run the Human Rights Campaign for almost a decade.

Nevertheless, when Obama brought up repealing the policy at his first meeting with the Joint Chiefs, Mullen gently pushed back. The nation was in the middle of two wars, he said, with a military that was already feeling the strain. Any quick action could be disruptive, and it wouldn't give military commanders the time to adapt publicly, he said. Most important, Mullen wanted his fellow Joint Chiefs to endorse the plan to give everyone involved more cover.

But Mullen also wanted to provide such cover on his own. When Carl Levin, the chairman of the Senate Armed Services Committee, asked him to testify at a hearing on Don't Ask, Don't Tell in early February 2009, the chairman of the Joint Chiefs saw it as an opportunity to put his own imprimatur on the process. Mullen wrote his testimony himself, in long form, on a yellow legal pad. He went to the White House to tell the president what he would say, with Messina, the administration's point man, in the room.

Mullen's testimony before the committee landed with a bang. "No matter how I look at the issue, I cannot escape being troubled by the fact that we have in place a policy which forces young men and women to lie about who they are in order to defend their fellow citizens," he told the panel. He could hear the murmuring behind him as he delivered his remarks. "Allowing gays and lesbians to serve openly would be the right thing to do."[7] While equal rights for gay Americans is something that's hardly controversial to a vast majority of Americans now, Mullen's testimony was a symbolic turning point. For a man of his stature, in uniform, to do what he did was a huge moment, one that will never be forgotten by many gay rights activists.

At the same hearing, Gates made clear he was pushing an initiative supported by the president. There would be a formal Pentagon process, he explained, followed by a recommendation of whether to repeal, but Obama's preference was hard to miss—he wanted repeal, and he wanted a speedy implementation process. What he didn't want was rhetorical support, followed by years of military wait-and-sees.

The official Pentagon process began with Jeh Johnson, a former federal prosecutor and longtime Democratic activist whom Obama had chosen to serve as general counsel at the Pentagon. Gates tapped Johnson to run a committee to study the possible impact of repeal. No matter what Gates and Mullen had said, the four service chiefs who served on the Joint Chiefs of Staff were against repeal at the start of the process; it would be up to Johnson to persuade them otherwise.

Throughout 2010, Johnson and his team surveyed

115,000 members of the military. Perhaps unsurprisingly, they found many of the same attitudes about homosexuality in the country at large were duplicated in the armed services. Seven in ten members of the military said they had served in a unit with a gay or lesbian member; almost all of those soldiers and sailors defined their unit cohesion as very good, good, or neither good nor poor. Nine in ten army combat units and 84 percent of marine combat units said they had good or neutral experiences serving alongside gays or lesbians. Just 30 percent said they worried about a negative reaction if Congress repealed Don't Ask, Don't Tell.[8]

John McCain, the top Republican on the Senate Armed Services Committee, was emerging as the administration's chief antagonist on Don't Ask, Don't Tell. McCain, who had once said he would back repealing the policy if top military brass told him it was no longer needed, reversed himself after Mullen's and Gates's testimony. Moving the goalposts, he now wanted to see letters from the heads of the army, navy, air force, and marines—leaders who had, at various times, stated their opposition to repeal—with their views on what repeal meant to their branches. It was an effort to create distance between Mullen and his fellow Joint Chiefs.

General James Amos, commandant of the U.S. Marine Corps, was the most reluctant member of the Joint Chiefs to support a repeal, and he wrote to

McCain that getting rid of Don't Ask, Don't Tell could disrupt unit cohesion.[9] But, he told Mullen, if the policy changed, the corps would be the first to fully implement the new rules.

Still, the slow pace of progress irritated gay activists. Obama had taken office in 2009, a year had passed, and now they saw their allies dragging their feet. In fact, many activists didn't understand why "studies" were needed. They saw the studies as nothing but glorified delay tactics in an effort to never fully repeal the law. And that anger took the form of protests against the president. At a fund-raiser in Los Angeles in April 2010, gay rights protesters repeatedly interrupted Obama's speech, demanding action.[10] In October it happened again, at a speech in Bridgeport, Connecticut.[11] The following month, thirteen gay rights activists, including former army lieutenant Dan Choi, handcuffed themselves to the gates of the White House.[12] At private fund-raisers, where Obama would routinely take questions, he would hear from gay rights supporters who had just written big checks, and who wanted to know how long the foot-dragging would last.

It wore on the president, who prided himself on his ability to communicate. He wanted the protesters and activists to understand he was working on a solution, but that the solution would take time. And he was frustrated that he, rather than Republicans on Capitol Hill, was taking the heat. The Los Angeles fund-raiser had been on behalf of Senator Barbara Boxer, one of the gay community's best allies in Congress; why not demand action from Republicans who opposed the repeal, rather than from a Democrat who pushed for it?

The activists, meanwhile, were nervous in their own right. Their fates were in the hands of a Pentagon committee — hardly the friendliest territory for gay causes — and their point person at the White House, Messina, didn't have deep connections to the community. They were worried, in short, that all their eggs were in one basket, and they didn't trust Messina, who had a reputation as a political mercenary, and who could easily trade *not* repealing DADT for something else on the Obama agenda. But Messina was more committed than that.

Messina sat down with the heads of leading gay rights organizations to explain the plan: The Pentagon report would rob Republicans of their talking points. It would even give a few moderates who personally backed repeal the excuse to vote that way. And a bill that hit the 60 votes required for passage in the Senate was sure to pass the Democratic-controlled House.

Privately, White House strategists were less than confident in their outside allies. Gay rights activists, after all, had had four years of a Democratic Congress and two years in which Democrats controlled both Congress and the White House. Democrats had gotten within a few votes of repealing the policy, but activists hadn't been able to convince enough Republicans to go along with them. Just as Obama was frustrated that activists were misdirecting their anger at him rather than at Republicans, his aides were frustrated that the gay rights community couldn't deliver any Republican votes, and the White House was taking the blame.

At one meeting on Don't Ask, Don't Tell that White House aides had convened in the Roosevelt Room, representatives from the Log Cabin Republicans, a pro–gay rights group, said they were having ongoing conversations with several Republicans. Obama wasn't impressed. "Collectively, you need one Republican," he snapped.

On Capitol Hill, Steny Hoyer was getting antsy. The Maryland Democrat and House majority leader was privy to the private polling that showed his party suffering politically. The midterms were coming, and all evidence pointed to a Republican wave that would sweep Democrats out of power. If Republicans controlled the House, Hoyer knew, there was no chance Don't Ask, Don't Tell would be repealed.

Hoyer pushed for action. He wanted to get a bill through the House while he knew he had the votes (the House had already passed a repeal bill on a nearly party-line vote in May; only 5 Republicans joined 234 Democrats in favoring repeal).[13] That would give Senate Democrats more time, he thought, to corral the 60 votes they needed.

But Messina disagreed. He believed a House-passed bill would be hopelessly stained with partisanship, and that it would stand little chance of winning 60 votes. And Messina thought repeal had a better chance of passing the Senate if it was just one part of a larger bill, rather than a stand-alone measure. Democrats thus folded the repeal into the National Defense Authorization Act, which also contained another provision the president was keen on getting passed in time for 2012. Known as the DREAM Act, it incorporated controversial language that would allow immigrants who had entered the country illegally when they were children to become citizens if they graduated from college or enlisted in the military.

But the bill still couldn't get through the Senate; in September it fell four votes short of reaching cloture, the point at which debate ends and the Senate starts considering final passage. Or to put it another way, to end a filibuster.[14] It was clear that the White House needed to persuade more Republicans to come on board. And to do so, it had an ally and advocate: the president's onetime law school pal and a former Republican Party chairman, Ken Mehlman.

When he'd been among the Republicans brought in to advise Obama on how to run a White House,

Mehlman had been uneasy. He did not want to be seen as helping the president too much, given his party affiliation, and more important, he wanted to keep his GOP credibility as he attempted to build support within his own party for same-sex marriage. It was an issue that was personal for Mehlman, who had come out publicly only a few years earlier, well after he was actively involved in Republican Party politics. In October, a month after Senate Republicans had blocked the defense bill that would repeal Don't Ask, Don't Tell, Mehlman brought a group of investors to Washington to get a read on the policy fights that were consuming the capital. They heard from, among others, Eric Cantor, the second-ranking Republican in the House, and Valerie Jarrett. When Mehlman went to the White House later to thank Jarrett, she invited him to the Oval Office to see the president.

Obama told his law school classmate that he respected the way the Republican had come out of the closet, no easy matter for one of the most powerful members of a socially conservative party. In turn, Mehlman said he might be able to help on Don't Ask, Don't Tell. For the next two months, he would concentrate on ten Republican senators he was close to, votes Democrats would need to pass a repeal.

Susan Collins was one of Mehlman's easiest targets. She had voted to repeal the policy from her perch on the Senate Armed Services Committee, and as the ranking Republican on the Senate Homeland Security and Government Affairs Committee she had worked closely with Joe Lieberman, the panel's chairman, on the defense bill. She had voted against the measure in September, though, because she didn't want to see debate cut off before Republican amendments to the larger bill had been considered. This may seem an arcane strategy, but sometimes a senator does this in order to get something else she cares about even more. If repeal had been a stand-alone deal, Collins would have voted for it, but because it was connected to larger bills that had nothing to do with DADT, some folks like Collins voted it down.

Through the fall, the number of courtroom victories gay rights activists were compiling mounted. A U.S. District Court judge in Los Angeles ruled Don't Ask, Don't Tell unconstitutional in September. A month later, she issued an injunction ordering the military to stop investigations into the personal lives of rumored gay service members. Ten days later, in order to comply with the ruling the Defense Department announced that it was accepting openly gay recruits.[15]

Then, on November 30, with a new Republican majority waiting in the wings, the Pentagon released the report Jeh Johnson had spent months on. It was exhaustive, and it concluded that little or no damage would be done to the military if Don't Ask, Don't

Tell were taken off the books. It accomplished exactly what Gates and Mullen had hoped in the beginning, giving cover to Republican moderates while stripping away any lingering arguments conservatives had. At the news conference unveiling the report, Gates, who was never enthusiastic about making this change, called repeal a "matter of urgency," because he feared the courts were going to force the change and the methodical Gates preferred to have more control of the process. The court ruling, arguably, did more to move Gates to become a supporter since he feared a haphazard implementation by the courts.[16]

Everything appeared to be moving toward a repeal in the final weeks of the lame-duck session. But on December 9, when Harry Reid tried again to end debate on the defense spending bill, he ran into another roadblock when the bill again failed to reach the 60-vote threshold. Only one Republican — Collins — voted to cut off debate. One Democrat, Joe Manchin, voted against the cloture motion, joining the Republicans. Reid was exasperated, Obama was furious, and gay rights supporters worried they had run out of options.[17]

But it was the month of December, holiday party season, and that night, just hours after the Senate had again blocked the bill, another plan to repeal Don't Ask, Don't Tell came to fruition amid the clink of champagne glasses. The Human Rights Campaign's chief legislative strategists had been talking to Joe Lieberman and Susan Collins, by then the Senate's two leading supporters of repeal, to try to find another way. Suddenly, Hoyer's idea of pushing a freestanding bill through the House looked like the only remaining avenue. That evening Allison Herwitt, the Human Rights Campaign's legislative director, just happened to be at the same holiday party Hoyer had dropped by.

They mingled at the home of Steve Elmendorf, a longtime Democratic strategist turned lobbyist who had advised the last generation of Democratic leaders, Daschle and Gephardt. Herwitt was chatting with a friend when she saw Hoyer hovering over the food table. She shot across the room: did Hoyer still have a freestanding bill waiting to be scheduled that would repeal Don't Ask, Don't Tell? The House had already proved it could repeal the policy, and the chances were good, with just a little more time, that gay rights advocates could find the two or three Senate Republican votes they would need for success.

Hoyer was standing with Alexis Covey-Brandt, his chief vote counter on the House floor. He was surprised at Herwitt's confidence in the Senate numbers, but he and Covey-Brandt knew she was right about the House votes. Still, he explained, Democrats had just lost an election in a massive landslide. "It'll be really tough, Allison, to put our guys through this again," Hoyer told her. "I'm not sure we have the vehicle to do this."

Covey-Brandt went back to her deputy, then over the next few hours surveyed by phone, e-mail, and in person some of the more conservative Democrats who might be leery of voting again to repeal Don't Ask, Don't Tell. They also chatted with Utah's Jim Matheson, the conservative Blue Dog who voted against his party's leadership more often than almost any other Democrat. And what Matheson said was a surprise: He had already voted for repeal, and the sky hadn't fallen on him. Matheson had survived yet another difficult re-election bid in 2010, one of the very few Democrats in deeply Republican territory to stave off a credible Republican challenger, yet it was probably the one controversial issue that national Republicans hadn't used against him in their television ads. The political risk of being against Don't Ask, Don't Tell, he said, was gone.

Covey-Brandt told Hoyer to put the freestanding bill on the floor. Hoyer called Reid, his counterpart in the Senate, to inform him of their plans so that Reid wouldn't be blindsided by the House maneuver. Reid was even less optimistic than Hoyer had been that the Republican votes were there in the Senate.

On Friday, December 10, the day after Elmendorf's holiday party, Hoyer called Joe Solmonese to tell him the House would proceed with a bill. But there was a catch: all the conversations the repeal's backers were having with Republicans needed to come to a conclusion over a narrow weekend stretch. They had to start working the phones, and hard.

Hoyer himself called Collins and Lisa Murkowski, who had been somewhat liberated from party leadership's control after she lost a Republican primary to a conservative activist earlier that year, only to win the November election as a write-in candidate. Mehlman called Murkowski and his other Republican targets, too. Lieberman, an orthodox Jew who observes the Sabbath, walked from his home in Georgetown to the Capitol building to help with the lobbying effort.

By Monday, December 13, Hoyer thought the votes were there, but nothing could be done because at the moment Republicans were focused on the DREAM Act, which conservative activists and immigration opponents were dubbing a "backdoor" amnesty. Two days later, the House voted in favor of the repeal by a 250–175 margin—ten Republicans who hadn't supported repeal the first time around, in May, switched their votes, as did a number of Democrats nervous about their re-election prospects in Democratic primaries should they oppose.[18]

Three days later, on Saturday, December 18, the DREAM Act fell five votes short of reaching cloture in the Senate. But the Don't Ask, Don't Tell repeal reached the 60 votes it needed—and then some. Once the bill reached the 60-vote threshold, several

Republicans, including North Carolina's Richard Burr and Nevada's John Ensign, surprisingly voted in favor, too—the old "fear of being on the wrong side of history" vote that happens on controversial bills that finally pass. The final vote count was 65 to 31[19] in favor; seven of the ten Republicans Mehlman had lobbied voted for repeal.

As the vote came in, Messina and Solmonese stood in the back of the Senate chamber. Both men were in tears. As the effort to repeal Don't Ask, Don't Tell began, the normally stoic and emotionally awkward Messina had told Solmonese that on the list of important things he would do in his lifetime, ending the discriminatory policy would be the most important. He included his next job—managing Obama's re-election campaign—on that list.

The measure required the president, the secretary of defense, and the chairman of the Joint Chiefs of Staff—Obama, Gates, and Mullen—to formally certify that the military wouldn't suffer readiness issues before Don't Ask, Don't Tell came off the books. That process would take another six months, but gay rights activists and legislative strategists at the White House (Messina) and in the House (Hoyer) and Senate (Lieberman and Collins) had gotten the bill through at the last minute. Four years later, Gates, during his book tour, would admit that the transition went without a hitch, a lot more smoothly than he'd anticipated, and more smoothly than the uniformed chiefs secretly feared.

Messina kept a copy of the bill on the wall in his Chicago office, a testament to a rare bipartisan, bicameral legislative victory. Solmonese and others in the gay rights community jokingly referred to Messina as an "honorary gay."

The most fascinating aspect about this legislative victory for the Obama White House is that it was done in a very traditional Washington way, using an old playbook. Find someone who can help corral bipartisan support; when one legislative path is blocked, another is found, good old-fashioned Washington elbow grease. It should have been seen as a potential model for how the president might be able to govern in a more polarized climate when dealing with divided government.

But it turns out this blueprint for achieving a tough bipartisan legislative victory was an outlier. The various strategies that so many lobbyists, activists, and politicians came up with to get DADT repealed were never duplicated in as effective a way on other issues. Then again, so many Republicans *wanted* to get in a better place on gay rights, and so it allowed this bipartisan compromise to become a classic "win-win" proposition.

Finding similar compromises on issues like taxes,

immigration, and entitlements just may not exist in this current political climate. But looking back, it's surprising that the Obama White House hasn't at least tried to replicate its successful DADT strategy a few more times.

The Don't Ask, Don't Tell battle was one that reflected not only society's evolution on gay rights but Barack Obama's. More evolution — on both fronts — was yet to come.

CHAPTER EIGHT

The Veep Steps Up

The Don't Ask, Don't Tell repeal wasn't the only end-of-the-year task before Democrats lost their huge advantages in the House and Senate. There was more to do. The White House couldn't ignore the fact that after Emanuel departed to run for mayor of Chicago, Biden was the administration official with the deepest ties to Capitol Hill. Nowhere had that skill been more in evidence than on START.

The Strategic Arms Reduction Treaty (START), signed by Presidents George H. W. Bush and Mikhail Gorbachev on July 31, 1991, had signaled the most significant limitation effort since the Cold War nuclear weapons race between the Soviet Union and the United States began after the end of the Second World War. It capped the number of nuclear warheads and intercontinental ballistic missiles either country could deploy, cooling, at least for the time being, one of the most dangerous threats to human life on the planet.

Obama had made nuclear nonproliferation and

containment an issue during the 2008 campaign (it was one of the few legislative efforts he made as a senator), and after START had expired, he and Russian president Dmitry Medvedev had negotiated even further cuts to both countries' arsenals. The two presidents had signed a new treaty on April 8, 2010, in Prague, but opposition from some Republicans threatened to scuttle Senate ratification.

As the lame-duck session dragged on, the White House and treaty backers grew worried. (At one point, an outside group began running television advertisements that included Lyndon Johnson's famous "Daisy" ad, complete with a cute girl picking flowers, an ominous countdown, and a mushroom cloud.) A treaty requires two-thirds of the Senate to ratify; with even more Republicans headed to the Senate in January, prospects for passage looked unlikely. That meant Democrats had to strike while the iron was hot. They couldn't afford to wait, then hope to find nearly double the Republicans after January 1. It would be a near impossibility.

But the White House legislative staff didn't know whether they had the votes. They needed 11 Republicans, combined with all the Democrats, to get to the 67 required for passage. And while some Republicans were on board from the beginning—Olympia Snowe, Susan Collins, Lamar Alexander, and Dick Lugar of Indiana—the rest of the votes to get to 67 were proving elusive. By December 19, a Sunday,

Harry Reid was anxiously watching the clock. He would have to file a cloture motion, forcing a vote that would end debate on the treaty, within hours if he had any hope of getting a vote completed before the Christmas break. At the White House, staff still didn't have an accurate count of where a few critical Republicans stood. And the White House and some supportive senators preferred not to hold a vote at all if they didn't have the votes. So there was real nervousness when Reid filed that cloture motion. After all, actual defeat in this lame-duck session would mean the treaty didn't stand a chance in January. At least if the treaty wasn't *officially* voted down in December, they would have a chance in the new year even if it took a while.

The White House legislative team held a conference call that day to render their final judgment: should Reid file cloture, or should they go back to the drawing board, hoping beyond hope that there would be an appetite in the next Congress to pass one of President Obama's foreign policy goals?

Because it's the White House, where protocol still dominates, the switchboard began calling the most junior White House staffers; they would wait while operators wrangled their more senior bosses onto the line. After twenty or twenty-five more junior West Wing officials joined the call, National Security Advisor Tom Donilon came on the line. A minute later, Biden was the last to join.

"What's this call about?" an annoyed Biden wanted to know.

Donilon said they were on the line to discuss whether to advise Reid to file cloture. They didn't know, Donilon said, whether START had the votes.

"I've talked to these people," Biden barked. "It has the votes. We're doing this."

He hung up. Biden, a man not known for having so little to say, had *very* little to say on that call, and because he was so authoritative, this actually gave those staffers some confidence. Harry Reid filed the motion for cloture. Two days later, on Tuesday, December 21, the Senate voted by a 67–28 margin to cut off debate, a margin wide enough to ratify the treaty.*

That was a big moment for Biden inside the White House, impressing even some West Wing skeptics. Biden further endeared himself to Obama with his aggressive approach to just about every task he had been assigned. He threw himself into policing the stimulus and wooing Specter (virtually on his own, Biden convinced the Pennsylvania Republican to switch sides, giving Democrats 60 senate votes in 2009; of course, that didn't work out so well for

---

* In the end, treaty backers actually had a few votes to spare, in case of an emergency: Oregon's Ron Wyden was recuperating from surgery, and Evan Bayh, who had just days left in his Senate career, was in his state on a farewell tour. Both men could have been called back if their votes had turned out to have been crucial to passage.

Specter once the 2010 election came around). And on national security issues, Biden was also comfortable playing internal foil, presenting Obama with liberal alternatives to those proposed by his generals and more aggressive national security officials. He was hungry to do as much as he could and wanted more on his plate.

Like any good vice president, the assets Biden brought to the White House complemented Obama's and made up for the president's weaknesses. The irony is that Biden's strengths have aided the White House in ways that are different from those Obama's team anticipated. Biden was hired for his foreign policy experience, a serious hole in Obama's résumé, but his most valuable role has been in helping Obama navigate Washington's rocky shoals and in defending Obama when the waters get rough.

Even without a single lane to focus on, Biden needed something to do on a daily basis. He'd done much of the legwork on the economic stimulus package that passed a month into their new term, working on three Republican senators—Snowe, Collins, and Specter—who ultimately supported the bill. And after the bill passed, Biden was put in charge of overseeing the hundreds of billions of dollars that the stimulus bill would spend on infrastructure projects around the country, ensuring that the funds got where they needed to go instead of swirling down the waste, fraud, and abuse hole.

On its face, putting Biden in charge of overseeing the money had been an extension of Obama's
commitment to transparency in government. Each
stimulus project would be listed on a government
website, Recovery.gov, giving the interested public a
complete rundown of money spent and jobs created.
But if money got misspent, Biden would suddenly
find himself in the crosshairs—and with $787 bil-
lion to be spent, it was likely that something would
go to waste.

Biden spent the next year checking in constantly
with governors, county officials, even small-town
mayors, making sure the projects the stimulus bill
funded were proceeding on time and that nothing
was wasted. In the four years after the bill was passed,
government inspectors general opened 1,942 investigations[1] into complaints of wrongdoing; still, none
resulted in major news headlines that could have
further embarrassed the White House. Of course,
as with any attempt at reform, the law of unintended
consequences reared its ugly head on the stimulus
front. So focused was the administration on making sure the money was spent on time, there actually were a lot of borderline projects. Many cities
and counties paved roads that were, say, two to three
years away from needing paving instead of trying to
build a larger project, like a bridge. Why? Getting
permits and zoning for a bridge can sometimes take
years, longer than the two-year window during which

the stimulus was designed to be spent. So if the administration wanted "shovel ready," about the only thing many local leaders could come up with was paving. In the grand scheme of things, there was no graft, no boondoggles with the 2009 stimulus, and Biden got the internal credit for that, though that mattered little to the public since *not* making a mistake or *not* allowing a rip-off to take place isn't exactly something the media will report on. But in hindsight, everyone from the president on down to local mayors looks back on this stimulus and wonders what might have been on the infrastructure front if they hadn't boxed themselves in with that phrase "shovel ready." So many larger, more impactful local projects could have been started or planned and become major economic engines had there been the political patience. But this is something that has changed in the New Washington in the age of Obama; there just is no appetite or reward for long-term plans or projects.

Biden played another important role for the president, as buffer for the Clintons. Being the old pol—and the likeable guy—that he is, he had a good relationship with both Clintons, certainly a better personal rapport than the president had. And so, among Biden's unwritten duties was that of Clinton buffer.

There were few hazards Obama faced that the media loved to follow more than his relationship with Hillary Clinton. And while the affiliation was a better one than the media hoped, it was by no means as friendly as the White House liked to pretend. Clinton, in particular, knew that the appearance of a bad relationship would both anger the White House and harm her future prospects should she decide to run. Bottom line: it was in the political best interest of both Clinton and Obama to make sure their dealings stayed drama-free.

In particular, Hillary was leery of offering Obama advice about domestic matters, even though she wanted Obama's agenda to succeed. The early word on Obama that was made clear to cabinet members is that he didn't take too kindly to backseat driving and, more important, he was a "stay in your lane" kind of executive. He was very unlike Bill Clinton, who sought out advice — even bad advice — from as many folks as he could talk to. So, dealing with this kind of presidential style was a bit new to Hillary. She also didn't want to simply keep her thoughts to herself, especially on domestic policy issues such as health care. If she had policy expertise on any issue, it was on health care, and her experience was in the 1990s. But instead of speaking with the president, she would pass messages through Biden, who came to hold what his advisors jokingly called the "Hillary portfolio."

When they were both in town, Clinton and Biden would meet for breakfast at the Naval Observatory about once a week to discuss both domestic policy and any frustrations she had. One of the biggest frustrations she shared with Biden was the lack of progress the administration was making on judicial vacancies. Clinton had seen Bush appoint dozens of federal judges, but retirements meant that many seats were open again. The administration, she told Biden, needed to move quickly to fill the vacancies and shift the judiciary to the left. Clinton was actually channeling a frustration she was hearing from lawyer friends, criticism of Obama that would only grow in liberal legal circles. Finally, early in his second term the president decided to engage on the judicial front and started appointing dozens of new judges. But the confirmations were not easy to come by as Republicans did their best to rip a page from the Democratic playbook of the Bush era (and their own playbook of the late '90s in the Clinton era) and slow-walk the confirmations—filibustering when necessary. After a while, Harry Reid decided he, too, wanted to speed up the ideological shifting of the judiciary, and he changed the rules on appointments, meaning Democrats needed just 50 votes to confirm a new judge.

Increasingly, and especially after Emanuel left the White House, Biden took over a role similar to that with Hillary—as Washington therapist—in terms of members of Congress who grew frustrated with the White House. While Washington devolved into partisan inaction, with Obama and congressional leadership talking past each other, Biden began to believe that the two sides simply weren't communicating on the same plane. Biden knew Obama gave a hell of a speech to a political crowd, but he thought the president didn't know how to speak Washington's language. And elected officials were the ones who listened most closely to what Obama said.

So when a senator couldn't get time with Obama, or when he wanted to plug a project the White House should support, he called Biden. The vice president thus became, in essence, the Washington complaint department. Biden would relay the concerns to Obama while simultaneously translating the president's public declarations into congressional dialect. There was a point in the first term when one could argue that without Biden, the line of communication between the White House and Congress would have been almost entirely severed—and with it, much hope of getting things done.

Part of Biden's appeal to his former colleagues was his ability to make friends. Through nearly four decades in the Senate, he had grown close to members on both sides of the aisle. And he kept making those friendships. When Senator Saxby Chambliss, a Georgia Republican who had never been an administration ally, announced in early 2013 that he would quit the Senate, Biden asked the White House switchboard to get Chambliss on the phone so he could wish him well. The switchboard accidentally called the other Georgia Republican senator, Chambliss's junior colleague, Johnny Isakson; Biden and Isakson laughed about the mistake and chatted for a few minutes, and in typical fashion, by the end of the call Biden had invited Isakson over for breakfast. And yes, he eventually connected with Chambliss and broke bread with him, too. Such personal outreach might be seen as trivial, but these were the sorts of gestures that helped persuade the Georgians to support larger Obama-led bipartisan efforts. In fact, both ended up in the small group of about a dozen Republican senators who in 2013 would at least be open to working with the president on a few specific budget issues.

No relationship Biden forged proved more important to the White House than his connection with Mitch McConnell. The Delaware Democrat and the Kentucky Republican shared little ideological common ground, but both were brilliant transactional politicians who grasped the balance required by the need to govern on one hand and the need to win elections on the other.

With the rise of the Tea Party movement that aimed to purify the GOP, and that cost a number of moderate Republicans their seats, it was dangerous for Republicans to be seen working closely with President Obama, a figure of almost universal scorn among the ultraconservative base. It has seemed almost fanatical, the way this crowd hates the president; the rancor is perceived to be so bad at times that some Republicans have to act outraged if the president praises one of them. During the 2014 State of the Union address, the president gave a positive shout-out to Florida Republican Marco Rubio for his position on the expansion of the earned income tax credit. The day after the speech, Rubio had to go on conservative talk radio to explain why he and the president actually differ on why the expansion is necessary. Oddly perverse, yes, but welcome to the Tea Party politics of the Obama era.

While the White House believed it wouldn't be able to reach a deal with House Republicans, given their deep loathing for the president and many members' need to be seen as opposing everything he did, there was a path to get the House to hold a vote *if* a compromise deal could be struck in the Senate. McConnell held Obama in similarly low regard, but not because of Tea Party politics; it was more about the perceived lack of respect McConnell believed Obama demonstrated. He also didn't believe Obama knew how to accept a deal. But Biden and current senators trusted each other, because each knew the other could deliver. And since working with Biden didn't carry quite the same negative political cost for Republicans, that's who McConnell negotiated with.

"McConnell is the best nose counter in the business, so if he says 'I can do this,' or 'I can't do that,' he's usually right," said Bruce Reed, Biden's chief of staff. This stood in stark contrast with the attitude of the House Republican Conference, which seemingly made a point of defying its leader, Speaker John Boehner, at every turn. Especially in 2011 and 2012, Boehner could rarely deliver a vote count with the same level of certainty as McConnell.

It was with McConnell that Biden negotiated deals on the Bush tax cuts in 2010, on raising the nation's debt ceiling in 2011, and on a last-minute deal to avoid the so-called fiscal cliff, albeit only for a brief three-month period, in late 2012.*

While Biden likes to say that he can't help making new friends, with McConnell it wasn't so simple. In fact, while the two former Senate colleagues respected and trusted each other, they would never be described as friendly. Biden still harbored animosity toward McConnell for a stunt the Republican had pulled two decades prior.

In the wake of his first presidential campaign, which he dropped in September 1987 (after a top operative for Massachusetts governor Michael Dukakis revealed that Biden had plagiarized part of a speech by a British Labor Party politician), Biden had begun feeling pain in his neck and head. In

---

* Biden's staff liked to joke that the vice president was the "McConnell whisperer."

February 1988, he suffered an aneurysm; he was rushed to Walter Reed Medical Center in Washington, his situation so dire that a priest administered last rites. But he survived and returned to the Senate seven months later.

When he returned, Biden heard that McConnell had been shopping around a bill with language similar to that of a measure Biden had already drafted. When Biden called McConnell to ask him to sign on to his legislation and merge the two efforts, McConnell was defiant and instead threatened to accuse the politically wounded Biden of plagiarizing his bill, a breach of protocol that made Biden fume. Though the two men would prove the most important negotiating partners of the Obama years, Biden never forgot the insult; he'd even tell West Wing staffers the story when they were huddling about how to deal with McConnell.

Biden never pretended to anyone that he and Mitch were pals, but they had an understanding. And Biden possessed the same political forgiveness gene that made Bill Clinton so oddly popular with some of the same congressional Republicans who tried to oust him from office. Biden was never one of those absolutists whose ethics prohibited cooperation with those who were less than perfect. You may have had to grit your teeth while you did so, but you took the other guy's horse, and he took yours.

Biden's successes in helping to end these various

fiscal standoffs with Congress raises the question, why wasn't he used more? The selective use of Biden as chief congressional lobbyist is something that will be debated in hindsight for some time after the Obama presidency. Biden may get publicly ridiculed a lot on late-night talk shows or with conservative media types, but his track record speaks for itself. And it could give Biden something to run on, should he ever get another shot at the presidency— something that seems unlikely while Hillary Clinton is around. But breaking the Washington dysfunction and being almost obsessive about cutting a deal in Congress are potentially two skills the public might actually respect after watching eight years of nearly complete gridlock.

At a national level, the 2010 midterms had seemed to signal a big red warning light for the White House: it had just lost almost every referendum race in the country. But from the perspective of Obama's own campaign, the disastrous midterms indicated a path to victory. There were those glimmers of hope in Nevada, Colorado, and Ohio, where even the close-but-no-cigar effort Strickland made against Kasich, highlighting his ties to Wall Street and the financial collapse, would bear a strong resemblance to the way Obama prosecuted his case against Mitt Romney, another man of the money markets.

The sweeping Republican wins in governorships

across the nation were a cause of concern for the White House—though in truth, even those Republicans who had been most outspoken about their anger at Obama immediately began to quietly work closely with the federal government—but they weren't seen as barriers to the president's own re-election, either. Republican gains in state legislatures would hurt Democratic chances of controlling the House over the long term, but again, that didn't fatally wound Obama's chances.

Perhaps the most damaging residual effect of the midterm elections was not that Democrats had lost control of the House of Representatives, because having the other party share the burden of running Washington was actually not a bad thing for an incumbent president. In fact, it gave him an entity to run against and contrast himself with. (It had worked quite well for the previous Democratic president to be elected with a Democratic Congress and see it get trounced two years later: that was Bill Clinton.) But what made this loss more damaging for the White House than what Clinton experienced in 1994 was the particular group of Republican freshmen that was ushered in. Elected on a Tea Party wave, the freshmen would come to Washington determined to assert their power and change the way the Capitol worked. Not only were they ferociously against basically anything Obama proposed, they planned to hold their own leaders to account for even the smallest capitulations to the White House, meaning that it was unclear whether the new Speaker, John Boehner, could actually be someone the president could work with.

But even though the Tea Party–dominated House hurt Obama's ability to enact his agenda, it, too, helped pave the way to re-election two years down the road. Because Barack Obama had been handed an excuse to run against Washington once again—and run against it he would.

CHAPTER NINE

Coming Around on Clinton

On March 21, 2010, Bill Clinton gave what amounted to an encore performance in front of one of his favorite audiences, the Washington press corps. The scene was the 125th anniversary of the Gridiron Club's annual dinner, one of those rare moments when the nation's leaders and the media that covers them get together to break bread at a swank hotel in the nation's capital—and, most important, to make fun of each other. The Gridiron dinner is essentially a fancier version of the White House Correspondents' Dinner, and is considered more exclusive; it's easily one of the tougher tickets to secure, even for an average member of Congress. It may be the last dinner in Washington where it is mandatory for men to wear white tie and tails. Obama, who, as is his anti-Washington MO, was skipping the Washington ritual for the second year in a row, had asked Clinton to stand in for him after many members of the Gridiron Club berated the

White House for its lack of respect for one of the oldest media institutions in Washington.*

Most presidents hate these events but figure out a way to tolerate and even use them as persuasion tools with the Washington elite. However, these dinners, and especially those for the various other Washington clubs, made Obama's eyes roll—more than most things—and he went out of his way to avoid them. Of course, the president's inability to hide his disdain for the dinners only added to the (correct) perception of him as someone who loathed these Washington rituals. As a result, the White House was happy to facilitate Clinton's pinch hit.

The Gridiron dinner is the type of event that best suits Clinton, a master orator who delivers a punch line better than most comedians and who has no qualms about making fun of himself at the same time he skewers the media. And indeed, he gave a tour-de-force performance that evening. But the former president's appearance served as a reminder of the contrast between him and the current resident of 1600 Pennsylvania, and that meant a reminder of the contrast between that resident and Hillary.

Of all the great Washington parlor games inspired by the Obama presidency—the second president in a row, after the famously reserved George W. Bush,

---

* Full disclosure: this author is a member of the Gridiron Club.

who refused to engage in the traditional D.C. circuit of dinner parties and cocktail affairs—few generate as much intense gossip as the relationship between Barack Obama and Bill Clinton. They represent the future and past of the modern Democratic establishment: one a minority in a party increasingly reliant on minority voters, a cerebral urban liberal from a state that hasn't voted for a Republican president since 1988; the other a southern populist able to connect not only with the emerging minority base but also with the white working-class voters who sent Roosevelt, Kennedy, Johnson, and Carter to the White House.

Over the nearly six years that Bill and Hillary Clinton fought, then worked with, then worked for Barack Obama, a sort of relationship developed. After Obama beat Hillary Clinton in the 2008 primaries, the Clintons and their allies were deeply resentful, as the Bushes had been of Reagan almost three decades earlier. But as Obama has grown into the Oval Office, the two sides have learned that they have to work together, and that this work can be to their mutual benefit.

Once established in Foggy Bottom and the White House, Hillary Clinton and Barack Obama began forging an uneasy truce. They would meet weekly, in the course of national security briefings or high-level cabinet meetings, and occasionally more often than that. And it helped that the two actually kind of liked each other. They were more alike, in some ways, than either was like Bill. Obama and Hillary were both more cerebral, bookish, and organized, and both had to force themselves to be politicians. While Bill had the intelligence and curiosity that both Obama and Hillary had, he was much more of a natural at the campaign part of politics. In fact, he liked it. Neither Hillary nor Obama much liked campaigning, and the discomfort showed; both easily could have been university presidents, Supreme Court justices, or academic deans and probably have been just as happy. But they chose the world of elective politics, and while not naturals, their competitiveness drove their success. One senior White House aide recalled being startled when he walked into the Oval Office one day in the summer of 2009 to find Obama and Clinton sitting next to each other on a couch, laughing together at a private joke. One key bond the two had was the 2008 campaign, and there is a sense that some Obama staffers, even ones who still resented Clinton, thought the president felt that only Hillary actually understood the things about the White House bubble that he didn't like and wanted to vent about.

There were bumps along the way, as one would expect of any relationship between two of the nation's most powerful and popular figures. The White

House, Clinton felt, tended to micromanage American diplomacy to an extent unprecedented in previous administrations. It's one of the undertold stories of the first Obama term that at times the Obama national security team sometimes treated Clinton almost as a figurehead, and they certainly drove policy and the agenda. It was a White House decision, not Clinton's, to make jump-starting the Middle East peace process a first-year priority. Clinton approved of Obama's decision to tap former Maine senator George Mitchell, the respected international negotiator and veteran Washington insider who had helped her husband forge a lasting peace in Northern Ireland, to serve as a special envoy to the Middle East, but chafed at the fact that Mitchell reported to the White House, not the State Department. Nevertheless, she didn't complain about the arrangement, though Mitchell was unable to restart negotiations between the Palestinians and the Israelis. This was Hillary in a nutshell: even if she didn't like the decisions, she saw herself as a team player.

By and large, Clinton made certain that her State Department worked hand in glove with the White House. Despite the deep fears of Obama's most skeptical advisors, she spent her time executing administration policy rather than freelancing on her own or undermining the president. Their only clashes were over personnel, and even then they were few: Obama's aborted effort to send Greg Craig to the State Department, where he served as director of policy planning during Bill Clinton's administration, and Clinton's leaden idea of bringing longtime political aide (and hatchet man) Sidney Blumenthal to Foggy Bottom. Blumenthal was a legendary practitioner of the dark arts of opposition research, and of spilling that research into the public domain at the opportune time. During the 2008 primary fight, right-wing Internet maven Matt Drudge unloaded a series of anti-Obama attacks, much of them supplied by the Clinton campaign — by, Gibbs and Axelrod believed, Blumenthal himself. Gibbs and Axelrod held few Clinton loyalists in lower regard than Blumenthal. They took their concerns to Obama, then to Rahm Emanuel. The chief of staff talked with Clinton and explained the White House's deep reservations. Where Bill Clinton, famously loyal to a fault to some of his closest advisors, might have fought to keep Blumenthal aboard, Hillary decided her loyalty could only go so far. It wasn't worth the fight, and Sidney Blumenthal was out of a job.

Obama and Clinton would never become confidants or friends, but in the Washington sense, that didn't matter. They became close enough to share a joke, and to trust that neither was out to undermine the other.

Bill Clinton, however, took longer to win over.

Perhaps it was because the two presidents are such different kinds of people: Clinton is gregarious, having worked a million phone lines and shaken a million hands, having spent hours every day talking with senators and congressmen from both parties. He craves human contact; less charitable observers say Clinton is almost *afraid* to be alone. Obama is the opposite, a lone wolf much more at peace with himself and much more regimented in his actions and attitudes. It's not uncommon for him to spend an evening at the White House, with headphones on and reading alone after his family has hit the hay. Clinton can vacillate between red-faced rage and childlike glee in the course of a single meeting; Obama advisors have trouble remembering more than a handful of times when their boss has shown any type of extreme emotion.

As two members of the most exclusive club in the world, Clinton and Obama both thought they understood what it took to be president of the United States. But their understandings were vastly different, and when they looked at each other, they saw little beyond the other man's flaws. Clinton saw Obama as an unskilled retail, people-to-people politician who somehow got by with weak political skills, who was terrible at hand-to-hand campaigning, yet suddenly was a two-term president. Early on, Clinton felt no sympathy for Obama in spite of the loathing the right directed at him; after all, the right had so despised Clinton they had impeached him. For his part, Obama respected Clinton's remarkable talents, but he saw in the forty-second president a deeply undisciplined soul. Clinton had all the tools required of a great president, but that lack of discipline ultimately prevented him from being truly great. If there's one thing Obama has always prided himself on, it's discipline, and he is perhaps a bit judgmental about undisciplined people around him. This is arguably why he and Bill Daley just never clicked in their president–chief-of-staff relationship; Daley's management style is more Clintonesque.

With every frustrating day Obama spent in the Oval Office, stymied by reluctant or nervous Democrats, stopped in his tracks by recalcitrant Republicans, his attitude toward Clinton began to soften. And every time Republicans took what Bill Clinton believed was another unfair shot at Obama, his antipathy softened. Clinton still believed that Obama got easy treatment from the media, but he began to empathize about some of their shared experiences.

The turning point in their relationship grew out of one of those shared experiences. In 1994, riding the wave of an unpopular effort to reform the American health care system, Republicans won back control of Congress, delivering a major blow to Clinton's hopes of an ambitious domestic agenda. In 2010, riding the wave of an unpopular but ultimately successful effort to reform the American health care system, Republicans delivered an even bigger thumping to the Democratic congressional majority than the party experienced in 1994. At that moment, Clinton came to truly sympathize with Obama. And Obama and his senior White House staff recognized that someone else had been in his position before, and that they might need Bill Clinton after all.

The disastrous 2010 midterms gave Obama an opportunity to rethink the structure of the White House he had built and the relationships and staff he had relied upon since his earliest days on the national scene. An introspective and isolated man by nature, Obama decided he needed to reach beyond the walls of the White House for perspective. On his own, with no input from his most trusted advisors, Obama set about scheduling meetings with Washington wise men from both parties, among them John Podesta; Tom Daschle; Ken Duberstein, Ronald Reagan's last chief of staff and one of those Washington players who was partisan only to power and prided himself on having bipartisan relationships (he actually made it clear he wanted to replace Rahm as chief of staff); Vernon Jordan, the longtime Democratic wise man who was very tight with the Clintons but despite being an early African American power player inside the party had very little interaction with Obama; and Ken Mehlman, the Harvard Law School classmate of Obama's who had managed George W. Bush's re-election bid.

Obama's staff was largely left out of these meetings. Pete Rouse handled the logistics, but the

gatherings themselves were private, one-on-one discussions. Few knew they were taking place at all. At
one point, Dan Pfeiffer, the communications director at the time, and David Axelrod, the senior strategist, were chatting outside the Roosevelt Room,
just down the hall from the Oval Office, and were
surprised when David Gergen walked out of the
bathroom. Obama had summoned the CNN analyst and veteran bipartisan presidential advisor to
both Reagan and Clinton to give him advice, too.
And this was the puzzle that was sometimes Obama
when it came to Republican outreach. The president loved to talk to Republicans around the country or to ex–Washington Republicans, to seek their
advice and, frankly, hear them empathize with him
about the extreme nature of the Tea Party. But talking to Republicans active inside the Beltway was
another story entirely and something he seemed to
avoid, almost afraid to hear what they believed. It
was more comforting to hear from those who had
left Washington.

Another person he summoned was the one who
would turn out to give him the best advice, at least
so believed the president. He reached out to the only
other person in the world who had faced exactly the
same situation in which he now found himself—a
Democratic president forced, by dint of his own
deeply unpopular policy positions, to work with a
deeply conservative group of Republicans elected

with a mandate to block his agenda, a president scrambling to save his legacy. Barack Obama in 2010 wanted to know how Bill Clinton in 1994 had done it.

For years, those in Clinton's orbit had dropped hints that Obama needed to solicit his predecessor's opinions more often. And Clinton himself had at various times mentioned his regular phone calls with George W. Bush during Bush's presidency, a barely veiled reminder that he still had advice to give. That Obama rarely seeks advice from anyone didn't placate Clinton: he was Bill Clinton, not just anyone else!

On December 10, 2010, they met privately in the Oval Office for more than an hour. Obama had struck a deal with House Republicans on an extension of the Bush tax cuts, an acknowledgment that the GOP had thumped the Democratic majority, and he needed Clinton's help to get reluctant Democrats on board. Beyond that, though, Obama sought Clinton's advice: How should he navigate the two years ahead? How should he reorganize his White House in order to be a more effective president? Obama never told his staff what Clinton had told him. But judging by the changes the president did make, it was clear that the emphasis was on generally sticking with the folks who had gotten him there and on focusing immediately on re-election. If there was one thing Clinton supposedly regretted about some of his reorganization decisions going into 1996, it was bringing in too many new voices, including that of Dick Morris, whose occasional good advice wasn't worth all the bad mojo he brought with him.

There was one thing Clinton told Obama that the current president wanted said publicly. So, once they'd finished chatting, the two presidents meandered through the West Wing in search of a journalist with a microphone. Talk about something Obama *never* would have done on his own...

Two presidents sharing the podium in the White House briefing room would be an unprecedented event, a startling contrast of old and new. Yet uncharacteristically for Obama, the coolheaded, methodical planner, the idea of barging into the press room on a quiet Friday afternoon in December was completely spontaneous. The unplanned nature of the impulse, and the fact that Obama would be asked questions for which he hadn't prepared with his staff, would have scared the daylights out of any professional political operative. Unscripted remarks, in short, lead to mistakes.

But Obama's team wasn't worried about the president's plan to share the podium with Bill Clinton, because at that particular moment they had no idea what was happening. In another part of the building, staffers were gathering for one of the seemingly endless number of holiday parties the White House throws every year.

Outside the press briefing room, Obama tried the handle. The door was locked, something the press office does once a "lid" is called. (That's the White House code to the press indicating that no more public statements or presidential actions will be taking place; in other words, it's a signal that the folks stuck working at the White House covering the president can go home. Of course, many press folks don't leave until after 6:30 p.m., when the network newscasts begin.)

Obama and Clinton bounded up the few steps between the locked door and the press office. Most staffers were at the party; only Katie Hogan, a young assistant press secretary, had been left behind to field emergency calls. Robert Gibbs was in his office, the door closed. Suddenly Hogan had two U.S. presidents standing above her.

"Do you know how to open up the briefing room?" Obama asked.

"Yeah, can you help us unlock it?" Clinton added.

Gibbs's ears perked up. "What are you guys up to?" he asked, walking out of his office.

"We're looking for some reporters," Obama said. Obama wanted Clinton to talk about the tax compromise — the two-year extension of the Bush tax cuts. This was going to be among his first major broken promises as president, and he needed help to sell the decision and to make some Democrats believe him when he pledged to make this the last full extension of them. Watch any rerun of a 2008 Democratic presidential primary debate and you'll hear Obama along with every other candidate talk about not whether they would repeal the Bush tax cuts for the rich, but *when*. Every plan those candidates in 2008 proposed they claimed they would pay for with the money "saved" from repealing the Bush tax cuts. But with the economy still struggling and Republicans about to be in charge of the House, Obama knew he didn't have the political capital to deal with this at the time; his best option was to punt for two years and gamble that he'd win re-election, whereupon he could fulfill the repeal promise.

"Can you guys give me about five minutes?" Gibbs asked. He practically sprinted down to the briefing room, where he flipped a switch to turn on the microphone at the podium. Hogan made an announcement over the public-address system in the West Wing. Reporters, she said, should get to the briefing room right away. Many had gone for the day because of the lid, but it was not yet 6:30, which meant that reporters from the major outlets, both TV and print, were still hanging around, working on their stories. Little did they know that they were about to have a new lead story to write and run with.

Gibbs furiously pounded out an e-mail to every staffer he could think of, though he didn't have time to summon everyone. Pfeiffer was at the Christmas party; he had to leave his parents, who were in town

visiting. When Obama and Clinton entered the briefing room, some White House staffers learned what
was happening from breaking news alerts that hit
their BlackBerrys. (Yes, the White House staff still
use Blackberrys, because iPhones and other smart-
phones are not considered national security–safe.)

In the briefing room some reporters, accustomed
to long waits for the president, asked Gibbs how
long it would be. It was about 4:30 on a Friday afternoon, and they wanted to go home. "How long?"
Gibbs replied, hardly believing what he was saying.
"They're just on the other side of the door!"[1]

Obama took the podium first. The cable networks
broke into their regularly scheduled programming.
"It's a slow news day so I thought I'd bring the other
guy in," Obama said as he waltzed in, not bothering
with the pomp that dominated other interactions
with the media.[2]

"I thought, given the fact that he presided over as
good an economy as we've seen in our lifetimes, that
it might be useful for him to share some of his
thoughts," Obama announced. "I'm going to let him
speak very briefly, and then I've actually got to go
over and do some — just one more Christmas party.
So he may decide he wants to take some questions,
but I wanted to make sure that you guys heard from
him directly."

Obama's definition of "very briefly" turned out
to be about eleven minutes. When the first reporter

asked a question, Obama saw his chance to bolt. "I've been keeping the First Lady waiting for about half an hour, so I'm going to take off," Obama said, cleverly eluding having to answer an actual question.

"Well I don't want to make her mad, please go," Clinton said with a laugh.[3]

With Obama gone, one might be forgiven for thinking the 1990s had suddenly come roaring back. Clinton leaned on the podium, the White House seal in front of him, one arm resting on the other, hand on his chin, as he'd done so many times during his eight years in office. Ann Compton, George Condon, and Mark Knoller, three veteran reporters who'd had seats in the briefing room when Clinton was in office, asked questions; Clinton called on them by name. The only things that might remind viewers that Clinton was an interloper were his white hair and the large high-definition television over his left shoulder displaying the White House's web address.

Clinton's definition of "very briefly" was different from Obama's. He took almost a dozen questions, defending the Obama administration's economic record in the manner only Clinton could. (Obama advisors even came to admit that for all his flaws, Clinton knows how to spin the story of the economy better than any living political figure.) The courtship was far from complete, but advisors to both men believed it would be politically beneficial if their bosses, the two most successful Democrats since Franklin Roosevelt, maintained at least a veneer of friendliness—even if it was only in the Washington sense of friendship. Now, in the modest-sized briefing room, Bill Clinton held court. In a few years Barack Obama would cede the stage to the former president yet again—and by then, much more would be at stake.

In the fall of 2011, Obama's brain trust was busy creating a campaign plan that would put their man on a path toward re-election. Given the president's low approval ratings, theirs would be no easy task. Only two men alive had achieved what Obama was setting out to do—win a second term as president of the United States. One of them, George W. Bush, had in effect paved the way for Obama's election in the first place. Bush's second term had been mired in the mismanaged Iraq War, the slow government response to Hurricane Katrina, and a recession that so badly tarnished the Republican brand that Obama found the wind at his back when he ran in 2008 (and then found his first term consumed by that very recession).

The other was William Jefferson Clinton. In the history of the Republic, Clinton was one of just five Democrats—along with Andrew Jackson, Grover Cleveland, Woodrow Wilson, and Franklin Roosevelt—to win two presidential elections. That's some rare air. And Clinton was no ordinary politician, but the best politician of his generation; he had a feel for the national mood, a feel for legislative and electoral politics, and he's probably among the better political strategists alive. Oh, and let's not forget his ability to get out of a personal political crisis.*

Clinton thus seemed like the perfect person to give advice to Obama's team. In addition, since former presidents' approval ratings always go up, Clinton could serve as an important validator, a high-profile surrogate able to make the case for Obama's second term, especially on the economy and with some wavering older white voters.

The only trouble was that the former president felt a deep personal antipathy toward Obama's senior advisors. Four years after Obama won the White House, the current and former president had bridged some of the personal divides between them, but the scars remained, especially over the South Carolina primary. Bill Clinton, once called America's "first black president," has never gotten over what happened to him that primary week down south in early 2008. Trying to downplay Obama's win in South Carolina, Bill Clinton made an offhand remark to the press traveling with him that Jesse Jackson had won the South Carolina primary back in the 1980s, and that it had led to nothing for him. The way

---

* One thing he does not yet grasp is the faster news cycle and the hit-and-run nature of social media. Bill Clinton likes to take his time.

Clinton said it, or at least the way Team Obama decided to interpret it, gave the impression that Clinton was implying that Obama had won the primary only because he's black—after all, even Jesse Jackson won this primary; how else do you explain it? so Clinton was trying to say. While Clinton denies to this day that he was being dismissive of black voters, it certainly came across as bitter and condescending, especially to black voters in South Carolina. The incident served essentially to win over whatever chunk of the black vote Hillary had been receiving— in this case from older black voters with positive memories of the Clinton years. The way this incident with Bill blew up, it ended up serving almost as a rallying point for the Obama campaign as it marched to victory on Super Tuesday a few weeks later.

So upset was Bill Clinton at being fingered as the reason Hillary struggled during the February primaries that it took him years to get over it. He held certain folks in personal contempt, including key members of the press (whom he blamed for carrying Obama's water) and people in the Obama inner circle.

But that was then, and now Team Obama needed to do whatever it took to keep Bill happy. As they worked on their campaign plan, political decorum and common sense demanded that Obama's advisors keep Clinton in the loop and work to get him on board. To start that process, Jim Messina, Axelrod, and Patrick Gaspard, the former White House political director who headed the Democratic National Committee, took the time to fly up to New York to meet with Clinton in his Harlem office.

Axelrod was late to the meeting, the result of a delayed flight out of Washington. When he did show up, it was clear that Clinton was uncomfortable with his presence. Clinton would add the occasional reference to the unpleasantness of 2008 — "You know, I used to be able to help you with the African American vote," he told the Obama advisors. "But after South Carolina, I can't help you there anymore." What struck the two other participants most forcefully, though, was that Clinton wouldn't even make eye contact with Axelrod.

In the summer of 2011, Gaspard called Doug Band, Clinton's protective (and sometimes vindictive) right-hand man, to ask for Clinton's help. Gaspard wanted Clinton to host several fund-raisers for Obama and to campaign in key battleground states on his behalf. Band made it clear that Clinton would need a little more wooing. Why doesn't Obama take Clinton out to Andrews Air Force Base, just outside the Beltway, for a round of golf—so it was suggested. So he did. Obama called Clinton to extend the invitation the following day. On September 24, the two men hit the links;[4] the few photographs the White House released showed Clinton, glasses on, virtually lecturing Obama, who didn't exactly seem to be enjoying himself.[5] Obama grinned and bore it, but it was an outing that was not repeated — which tells you more about how forced the arrangement at the time was. And yet that day paid the necessary campaign dividends. Obama asked Clinton for help on his re-election campaign, and Clinton agreed. But Clinton had made his point; he wanted Obama to have to work for his help. Obama sought advice, and Clinton dispensed it freely.

The first joint Obama fund-raiser Clinton attended demonstrated the generational bridge the two men were forging. It was held at the home of Terry McAuliffe, one of Clinton's biggest backers, who had enthusiastically jumped on the Obama bandwagon as the president's re-election campaign began in earnest. Of course, McAuliffe had his own motives — he wanted to be governor of Virginia, something that would happen only if the Obama coalition showed up on Election Day 2013. To guarantee Obama's cooperation, he needed to be all in. McAuliffe was an old-school transactional operator who got rich in Washington the way many had, by mixing political and business connections to his own benefit.

And McAuliffe was the quintessential Washington power broker, his generation's version of Vernon Jordan for the Democrats or Haley Barbour on the Republican side. A longtime Democratic Party fund-raiser, McAuliffe was bombastic, unafraid to tout (and sometimes exaggerate) his accomplishments, and perpetually in the know. He had raised so much money for Clinton that the president helped ensure that McAuliffe would be made chairman of the Democratic National Committee as one of the last political acts of his presidency. Then McAuliffe proceeded to raise record sums at the DNC. If there could be a bridge between Clinton and the Obama campaign's top strategists, it would be McAuliffe, who put a premium on the Democratic Party's success.

Before the April 29, 2012, fund-raiser at McAuliffe's palatial home in McLean, just across the Potomac from Washington, Clinton and Obama shared a private dinner—and Obama laid it on thick, thick enough that it actually moved Clinton. At the subsequent fund-raiser attended by five hundred major donors, he ignored virtually all of his prepared remarks, which were filled with perfunctory nods to Obama, the way a generic party leader praises another generic Democrat. Clinton had been planning to merely go through the motions, as a favor to McAuliffe and, more important, Hillary. Instead, Bill Clinton gave a full-throated defense of Obama's leadership and made the case for a second term in a way that no Democrat had done to date; Obama took notice, not just of the remarks but of the reaction of those mostly Clinton partisans at the McAuliffe home.

Perhaps as tellingly, from then on, Obama began

to use Clinton in his stump speech, citing the forty-second president's record of economic growth. For Obama, validating Clinton's legacy was a political opportunity. For Clinton, it was the balm he had craved for so long. After all, Obama based most of his 2008 campaign—at least during the never-ending primary part—on not being Clinton. In 2008 the Clintons were the past, they (at least as the Obama campaign was telling it) were part of the overt politicization of Washington that was fraying the nation. In fact, the initial motivation to use the slogan "No Drama Obama" was its contrast with the Clintons, who seemed to be mired in a never-ending soap opera. But as 2012 was getting started, Obama was beginning to appreciate Clinton's political skills, and he was trying to convince voters that he was Clinton '96.

As it turned out, trying to emulate Clinton wouldn't end with the 2012 election. Over the next six months, the rapport between Clinton and the Obama team grew markedly better. Even the relationship with Axelrod thawed a little. When Clinton traveled to Chicago to meet with Obama's senior advisors and get an update on the campaign, Axelrod took the former president into a private room. He told Clinton he understood that there had been bad blood, and he apologized for the perceived slights. What kind of apology it actually was is unclear, but it was at a minimum one of those Washington apologies, meaning that Axelrod was apologizing for all the angst, for allowing things to get so personal so quickly back in 2008. Clinton is a serial forgiver, and he appreciated Axelrod's sincerity. He's one of those remarkable politicians who never forgets but can at least pretend to forgive—at the end of the day, he does view every slight as an opportunity. This can be his best and his worst quality, wrapped up in one.

As the campaign went on, Clinton's voice would become a constant presence in Jim Messina's ear. While Clinton may have harbored ill will toward Axelrod and others, Messina was different; he hadn't been involved in the primary campaign, and Clinton respected his single-minded focus on the 270 electoral votes Obama would need to win a second term. And Messina spoke one of Clinton's favorite languages: poll numbers. Clinton would frequently call with advice: he thought the campaign should be talking about Medicare and Medicaid, offering a more nuanced message on the federal budget, and campaigning in specific places in Florida. Clinton also helped persuade the Obama team to focus on the hard-line conservative positions Mitt Romney had been forced to take in the primary. It was Clinton, for instance, who steered the Obama campaign away from focusing on Romney as a flip-flopper. He thought labeling Romney a flip-flopper would only allow independents to believe Romney would take their side once in office. After all, Clinton himself was often labeled a flip-flopper by his GOP opponents in the 1990s, and it was something Clinton believed actually helped him be perceived as a moderate.

Obama had based much of his national rise on being the anti-Clinton, not just the anti-Bush. His doing something out of political necessity might be considered by some as Obama starting to change his ways. But actually, with further distance between the point the Obama-Clinton change happened in 2010 and, say, the gridlock of 2014, it's clear Obama had Clinton in a box; it's similar to what Obama does with a lot of staff and politicians in general. He puts them in boxes and rarely views them as helpful in other areas. With Clinton, it means Obama views him as simply one of the world's expert campaigners. Because while Obama wanted and needed Clinton's help for 2012, it's not like he's been as needy of Clinton when it comes to dealing with Congress. It also exposes another truth about Obama: candidate Obama is more nimble and accommodating than President Obama. There's something about a campaign that seems to bring out the best in Obama's instincts, both internally on decisions and externally on the trail. But he has struggled to channel that same drive to win on the trail back in Washington. Bill Clinton had both ambitions.

Another key difference between the two: Obama

is someone who seems to accept his station with folks who don't like him. Perhaps living life in two worlds, black and white, has convinced him that there will always be folks who hate him and there isn't anything he can do about it. But he seems to, too easily, accept the fact that he can't work with someone who he believes is intransigent.

Bill Clinton has always believed there isn't a hater he can't turn into a lover. The more someone hates him or trashes him, the more focused he is on finding some way to accommodate the hater. Or flip the hater. It's that drive that kept Clinton focused on trying to work with Republicans in Congress who were trying to throw him out of office because of his undisciplined sexual appetite.

The story of Obama and the Clintons is a study in accommodating big personalities. There are few bigger personalities, and even fewer who are so stubbornly confident in their positions in American life, than Bill Clinton and Barack Obama. Seldom in American history have two such prominent political figures sought to share the spotlight atop the same political party. Imagine Ronald Reagan being present and active during the two terms of George W. Bush—alpha dog overload. Not since Ted Kennedy and Jimmy Carter fought for supremacy over the party have Democrats had two polestars like Bill and Obama to follow. But then there is Hillary; and that was the political brilliance of bringing her into the Obama tent. It kept Bill on the sidelines, and after a rough couple of years finding his place, Bill found a relatively productive place in Obama's universe. And while Obama had pledged to change the transactional politics of Washington, it's the one area where Obama has learned from the ultimate transactional politicians—and profited from it. Of course, why Obama hasn't applied his Clinton triangulation strategy to the rest of Washington is something many in the party have been scratching their heads about for years, and that lack of vision has only made it difficult for Obama to succeed in Washington. He's got the ballot box down; it's navigating America's most famous swamp (D.C.) that's been elusive.

CHAPTER TEN

The Hunt Begins

The president's address to the White House Correspondents' Dinner is hardly the most consequential speech he will give each year, and yet given how social media has opened it up to instantaneous analysis, criticism, and, yes, laughter, its significance has grown exponentially. It's not going to change any votes or sway any policy discussions, but in an era of wall-to-wall cable news coverage, the address has the potential to cause just as much heartburn for White House speechwriters as a State of the Union. The speech used to be relegated to C-SPAN, but as politics has become a bigger part of American pop culture, it's become Washington's Oscars. The dinner is awash with celebrities and has spawned competitive after-parties — a far cry from the days when the dinner was simply a chance for reporters to source build, meaning that invitations went to people you needed in order to do your job as a reporter. Given all the attention this dinner gets now, it's become imperative for the leader of the free world to be funny at this event. NBC's Brian Williams has called it the toughest room in show business.

Thus it made some White House staffers scratch their heads when Barack Obama tried to make his 2011 speech less funny.

On April 30, 2011, Obama and his speechwriters were reviewing the jokes he would tell that night. David Axelrod, back as full-time campaign advisor, had wandered into the room that Saturday afternoon to offer his help. One of the speechwriters had suggested a joke about Tim Pawlenty, the former Minnesota governor who had decided to run for the Republican nomination. "Poor Tim Pawlenty," one of the early drafts of the speech said. "He could be a great candidate but for that unfortunate middle name: bin Laden."

Obama, who had been laughing, scoffed. An Osama bin Laden joke? "That seems so yesterday," he said.

What Axelrod and the writers and political advisors goofing off in the White House on a warm spring day didn't know was that a team of commandos a world away were at that very moment preparing to launch an assault on a compound in Abbottabad, Pakistan, where intelligence analysts believed bin Laden might be hiding.

It had been almost ten years since the September 11 attacks on New York and Washington. During the years that followed, bin Laden's trail had gone cold. The wars in Iraq and Afghanistan had stretched the intelligence community's resources to a breaking point, and though George W. Bush had talked big about finding the mastermind behind the attacks, they were no closer to—in fact they were probably farther away from—actually finding bin Laden.

That fact had sunk into Obama's consciousness three years earlier, just after he won the presidency but before he actually had taken the oath of office. In his first meeting with Michael McConnell, director of national intelligence, and Michael Hayden, director of the CIA, Obama had learned of the various international threats and issues that made the world a very dangerous place. But he noticed that the briefers had skipped one topic: bin Laden's whereabouts.

Obama, still the president-elect, asked the CIA for everything it had on bin Laden. As they left the room, Obama and Emanuel shared a look. They were surprised at how little focus there had been in the intel world on locating bin Laden. They would have to force the intelligence community to make the hunt for the world's most wanted criminal a higher priority.

A few months later, when Obama's National Security Council met for the first time, the president brought up bin Laden again. Hillary Clinton was convinced bin Laden was in Pakistan. Obama made clear to Leon Panetta, who had taken over from

Hayden as director of the CIA, that he wanted bin Laden caught and that he expected the CIA to make this more of a priority than it had been.

For the next two years the CIA hunted, with few results. Panetta occasionally called Mike Mullen with an update, and every month, at the request of the president, Panetta would travel to the White House to brief Obama specifically on the hunt. Sometimes there were hopeful nuggets, other times there was nothing new at all. But Emanuel made sure Obama had forty-five minutes blocked out every month for a meeting about bin Laden—a further sign to the intelligence community, as if one were needed, of the president's priorities.

In August 2010, the CIA got its first inkling that something suspicious existed in Abbottabad. A recently built compound in a middle-class neighborhood had high walls, unlike other nearby homes. It had no connection to the outside world—no phone, no Internet access. Its occupants burned their trash and kept to themselves. The next month, at their monthly meeting, Panetta told Obama about the compound.

Over the course of the next several months, CIA analysts put together a better case. The home, it turned out, was connected to a Pakistani courier, someone who brought messages from bin Laden to the outside world. By January 2011, Panetta had shared with Mullen and Robert Gates the CIA's growing suspicion that something was afoot in Abbottabad. The circle of White House advisors who knew about the possible link was still small, and intentionally so: bin Laden had slipped through the United States' grasp before, and he couldn't be allowed to again.

As the president was juggling a set of thorny national security challenges, including targeting bin Laden, surging troops into Afghanistan, and the Arab Spring, he also juggled his team. While the first national security advisor, Jim Jones, spent his time globe-trotting, Tom Donilon was becoming more powerful. Donilon, another veteran of Clinton's State Department in the 1990s, had been Jones's deputy from the beginning. But he was briefing the president more often, offering his take when his boss wasn't around. When Obama had a follow-up question, he would frequently go to Donilon, not Jones.[1]

Jones felt put out about the fact that Obama had started going around him. He didn't think he had connected with Obama, whose notoriously tight inner circle was nearly impossible to penetrate. His lack of a connection with the man he was supposedly advising grated on him, especially as his deputy appeared to be getting closer to the president. But Jones did himself no favors with his own bureaucratic maneuvering. Though he had encouraged his staffers to interact with the president, he was also wary of the long-term relationships McDonough and Lippert had with Obama. Both men technically reported to Jones, but in reality neither treated Jones that way; Jones eventually fired Lippert, Obama's longest-serving White House aide, in a play for power. Eventually, Obama would right what he believed was a wrong done to Lippert by appointing him ambassador to South Korea—no throwaway post; in fact, one where a premium is put on expertise, not dollars one gave to the campaign.

By the summer of 2009, just a few months after he took office, detractors in the White House were already whispering that Jones didn't have the work ethic to hold the position, and that as Donilon took on more responsibility he was out of the loop on key issues. To hammer home the work ethic issue, some aides were free with anecdotes about how Jones never, ever, stayed at the White House past 7 p.m., which these days is quitting time only on a Friday, not during the week. The whisper campaign inspired Gates, a Jones ally, to reach out to the *Washington Post*'s David Ignatius for a rare, unsolicited interview.[2]

The tensions between Jones and Donilon, Jones and the younger NSC staffers, and Jones and the rest of the White House came to a head in the summer of 2010, when Bob Woodward published *Obama's Wars,* his first book on the new administration. The book offered a flattering portrait of Jones, written in such a way that one could easily surmise that the national security advisor was one of Woodward's major sources. While other White House staffers either refused to cooperate with Woodward or met with him briefly, much of the book was written from Jones's perspective. Woodward even painted an unflattering picture of Donilon — Gates, Woodward wrote, told Jones that Donilon succeeding him as national security advisor would be a "disaster"[3] — and of several other officials with whom Jones had clashed. Woodward's courtship was done out in the open; he even traveled with Jones to war zones, which at the time had many in the White House and in the press corps assuming that Jones was being "assigned" the task of spinning Woodward for Obama.

Jones's talking to Woodward had the opposite effect: his obvious participation gave the White House the excuse it had been searching for to confront the awkwardness at the National Security Council. The book exposed ferment in the White House — something the famously drama-averse Obama didn't want made public. Jones had planned to leave by the end of 2010, but he hastened his departure and left in October. Donilon took his place.

On February 1, 2011, Barack Obama sat in his customary seat in the Situation Room in the White House basement. It was here that the president and his national security team gathered in moments of crisis, when disaster struck at home or abroad and the United States had either to react or monitor what could become a bigger problem down the road. Ultrasecure, with numerous video monitors capable of streaming satellite images or feeds from cameras in combat zones, the Situation Room is where the president can make rapid decisions to deploy deadly weapons or heavily armed combat battalions. Many of the debates about what to do in Afghanistan had been held there, as had been discussions about the mysterious compound in Abbottabad. But that day, as Obama sat with cabinet-level officials and the advisors who had helped shape his worldview and perceptions of foreign relations since his days as a young senator, the television sets were tuned to the Qatar-based Arab news channel Al Jazeera.

A week earlier, 50,000 Egyptians had entered Tahrir Square to participate in a "day of rage," partially in solidarity with protests that had erupted in Tunisia, a few hundred miles to the west, but mostly to complain about the authoritarian rule of Egypt's longtime president, Hosni Mubarak.

Mubarak's government tightly controlled the media, the political process, and most aspects of Egyptian life. Only the military, which had a vested financial interest in stability, was as powerful as Mubarak. Wary of being seen as more heavy-handed than usual and so further enraging protesters, government security forces had shown restraint on that first day of protests. The government cut some cell phone coverage, but they believed that the demonstrations, like so many that had come during Mubarak's three decades in power, would eventually peter out on their own.

The crowds came back a second day, then a third. They grew in size, started building encampments, and began insisting they wouldn't leave until the government changed its ways. The patience Mubarak's security apparatus had shown in the beginning was wearing thin; the government imposed a curfew, which protesters ignored. On January 29, Egyptian fighter jets flew low over the square, an unprecedented show of force aimed at intimidating those who now called the square home. But the protesters smelled blood; angry street mobs that had formed in Tunisia just six weeks beforehand had succeeded, overthrowing an authoritarian government there, and Egyptians wanted their own toppling.

Mubarak didn't wait long before taking steps he hoped would alleviate the tension and assuage the anger. On January 30, as the crowd in Tahrir swelled to more than 100,000 people, he fired his deeply unpopular interior minister, Habib al-Adly, and appointed a new prime minister.[4] That wasn't going to be enough for the protesters—they wanted Mubarak himself to step aside. The next day, January 31, Al Jazeera estimated that nearly a quarter-million people had packed the square.[5] Mubarak sent his prime minister to start negotiations.

Obama's presidency had begun with the promise of a new approach to foreign policy, one that reversed the go-it-alone aggression of the George W. Bush administration and strove to work in conjunction with allies around the world toward mutual goals. After almost a decade of war in Iraq and Afghanistan, one critical element of Obama's agenda would be repairing relations with the Muslim world.

He had taken big steps toward that goal. On June 4, 2009, Obama had visited Cairo University to offer the most significant olive branch any president ever had to the Arab world. Obama told the gathering the United States wasn't out to attack Islam, and that American troops would soon leave Iraq and Afghanistan.

But Obama had another message, one that proved oddly prescient about the Arab Spring that would loom a year and a half in the future. At the university, which sits just four miles from Tahrir Square, Obama said Arab governments needed to do a better job reflecting the assent of the governed.

"I do have an unyielding belief that all people yearn for certain things: the ability to speak your mind and have a say in how you are governed; confidence in the rule of law and the equal administration of justice; government that is transparent and doesn't steal from the people; the freedom to live as you choose," Obama said. "Governments that protect these rights are ultimately more stable, success-

While Barack Obama and Bill Clinton would eventually build a decent working relationship in time for the 2012 campaign, this picture of the two of them smiling and embracing in late 2008 was only for the cameras. Clinton still harbored ill will toward Obama's campaign team, who he believes to this day unfairly portrayed him as racist during the heated primary battle between his wife and Obama. *(Bloomberg/Getty Images)*

When Obama nominated Hillary Clinton to be secretary of state, the two were not close; it was a marriage of political convenience for both of them. Obama thought it was better for the party to have her in the tent, and Clinton agreed because she didn't see a great future in the Senate. While the distrust between aides to both de-escalated but never really went away, the two former rivals themselves developed a fairly substantial bond and mutual respect, even if they never truly became friends. *(Jim Watson/Getty Images)*

President Obama made history when he became the first president ever to ask a sitting defense secretary from another party's administration to stay in office. Robert Gates (shown here in Afghanistan in July 2009) would seem to indicate he was a fish out of water during his two years of serving in the Obama administration. In his later memoir, Gates pulled few punches about his relationship with the Obama White House. As was the case with Hillary Clinton, Gates got along a lot better with Obama personally than he did with his staff, who Gates believed were way too political and intrusive in the affairs of the Pentagon. *(Pool/Getty Images)*

Politically, there may not have been a more important symbolic move by the president than his decision to appoint Sonia Sotomayor (left) to the Supreme Court. One thing that was lost on many in the English-language media was just how important her appointment was to Hispanic Americans. While most Americans are unfamiliar with Supreme Court justices, Sotomayor's personal story really resonated with Hispanic voters, and its impact on Obama's impressive ability to win over Hispanic voters in 2012 can't be discounted. *(Paul J. Richards/Getty Images)*

There's an old adage for anyone in the public square: always assume the mic is on. On the day President Obama signed the Affordable Care Act into law, as Vice President Biden introduced him at what was a sort of pep rally for the Washington Democrats, he whispered to the president, "This is a big fucking deal," and it was picked up by the microphone. To this day, "big f-ing deal" shows up every once in a while on social media. *(Chip Somodevilla/Getty Images)*

Democratic leaders were in a euphoric mood when President Obama finally was able to deliver on a promise Democrats had been making since the days of Harry Truman. But the image that day of a celebratory White House and Democratic Washington probably looked odd to a majority of the country, who, by that time, was decidedly against the president's idea of health care reform. As hard as it was for Obama and the Democrats to get the law passed, it turns out it was nothing compared to the struggles they would have implementing it. *(Chip Somodevilla/Getty Images)*

While not an official political party, the so-called Tea Party first began speaking with one voice in response to the expensive government bailouts of Wall Street and the housing and auto industries. Sparked initially by a well-received rant from CNBC commentator Rick Santelli, the Tea Party would morph into a full-fledged anti-Obama, anti-Washington movement by the fall of 2010. The Tea Party would prove to be both an asset and a liability for the GOP. In 2010, the Tea Party's enthusiasm would help fuel a takeover of the House, but some of the extreme actions by Tea Party members in Congress as well as some Tea Party groups would give Democrats and Obama the opportunity to paint the entire Republican Party as beholden to them, turning off swing voters in key states. *(Bill Pugliano/Getty Images)*

One of a president's more enduring legacies can be in his appointments to the Supreme Court. With the confirmation of Elena Kagan in August 2010, President Obama could boast that he already was responsible for more than 20 percent of the Supreme Court and he hadn't even finished his second year in office. *(Chip Somodevilla/Getty Images)*

Rahm Emanuel (left) announcing his resignation as chief of staff so he could pursue a bid to become mayor of Chicago. The president's first chief of staff was a force of nature in the first eighteen months of the Obama presidency. He believed he could do everyone's job, from fielding press calls to negotiating with senators to worrying about staffing at arcane agencies. It was a frenzied White House under Rahm's leadership, which inevitably had a short shelf life; many staffers loved working for him and yet were ready for a new style when left. His obsessive tendencies might have made him a better chief of staff *after* Republicans took the House, as his Capitol Hill experience as a congressman would have come in handy when dealing with the new GOP leadership of 2011. Rahm Emanuel was replaced temporarily by President Obama's very first chief of staff when he served in the Senate: Pete Rouse. *(Yuri Gripas/Getty Images)*

The Republican success in gaining House seats in 2010 was of historic proportions. No sitting president in the modern era had ever seen his party lose so many House seats in one election. A humbled President Obama faced the press the next day and admitted the election was a "shellacking" for him and his party. In some ways, as far as the president's domestic agenda was concerned, he would never fully recover from this electoral beatdown. *(Alex Wong/Getty Images)*

Before eventually passing the Affordable Care Act on a strict party-line vote in both the House and Senate, the White House for months courted Republican senator Olympia Snowe from Maine to help champion the bill. Snowe was a constant presence at the White House in the summer of 2009, in one of the rare times Obama personally reached out to a sitting senator. She would vote with the president on his health care bill out of committee, but she eventually became a "no" vote. She would later tell me that Obama wasn't the problem, instead blaming Senate Democratic leader Harry Reid for altering every side deal she had verbally agreed to with the president. *(Tom Williams/Getty Images)*

Republicans ride a wave of anti–big government sentiment to grab back the majority in the House. Speaker John Boehner, among the most affable, slick politicians of the modern era, ends up becoming a surprisingly enigmatic figure to the president. The two so desperately acted as if they wanted to cut deals and become the reincarnation of Tip O'Neill and Ronald Reagan, but somehow neither could ever sign on the dotted line. The real issue: neither of their political party's internal political goals were ever aligned at the right time so they actually could claim a "win-win" agreement. *(Chip Somodevilla/Getty Images)*

The Republican leader of the Senate gave the president and Democrats their favorite talking point during the 2012 campaign when Mitch McConnell implied that his top political goal as Republican leader was to make sure Obama was a one-term president. Democrats and Obama seized on the comment to paint the entire GOP as unserious about governing and more focused on their dislike of Obama. The obstruction strategy did work to stymie a lot of Obama's agenda even as, politically, it was akin to murder-suicide. While slowing Obama made him unpopular, Congressional Republicans became even more unpopular, with McConnell forced into his toughest battle for re-election in his thirty-year career. *(Chip Somodevilla/Getty Images)*

In January 2011, the entire world, not just America, was consumed with the protests taking place in its cradle of civilization, Cairo, Egypt (shown here). The push for democracy by oppressed Middle Eastern and North African populations at first seemed like one of the more amazing stories of the twenty-first century. And it all seemed so organic that the president believed he shouldn't intervene to slow it down; instead, the administration decided to weigh in on the side of the protesters. In the case of Egypt, that meant the president very publicly calling for the resignation and ouster of longtime autocrat Hosni Mubarak. Then protesters in other countries expected similar American support. For Libya, that support did come. But for Syria, it never went beyond words. To this day, it's still not clear, not even among some Obama supporters, whether pushing Mubarak out was the right call. Did it start a domino effect that just wasn't manageable? Decades from now, that may be one of the most debated foreign policy decisions of the Obama presidency. *(Peter Macdiarmid/Getty Images)*

President Obama bids farewell to one of his longest-serving political aides, White House press secretary Robert Gibbs. While Gibbs left with his ties to the president intact, many in the West Wing weren't as sad as the president to see him go. President Obama still hasn't found anyone to be as brutally honest with him as Robert Gibbs was. *(Mark Wilson/Getty Images)*

In what may have been a presidential first, President Obama was on foreign soil when the first air strikes in Libya were launched, in March 2011. Although it seemed at first like a successful strategy of "leading from behind," the president would later admit that the handling of post-Khaddafi Libya was one of his bigger mistakes. President Obama is shown here with (left to right) Chief of Staff Bill Daley, National Security Advisor Tom Donilon, and Deputy National Security Advisor Ben Rhodes, March 19, 2011, Brasilia, Brazil. *(The White House/Getty Images)*

The president's late Sunday night announcement came at the end of one of the most bizarre weeks of the entire Obama presidency. The week began with the president deciding to answer Donald Trump's questions about his place of birth by releasing his long-form Hawaii birth certificate to the nation on Tuesday, which was one of the weirder political circuses, even by Trump standards. The week ended with the singular foreign policy achievement of Obama's presidency: the capture and killing of Osama bin Laden. *(Pool/Getty Images)*

The president signs the Budget Control Act in August 2011 after a months-long standoff between House Republicans and the White House, with Republicans trying to use the issue of raising the debt ceiling as leverage to thwart Obama's budget and health care priorities and force him into more drastic deficit reduction. The deadlock would serve as a tipping point with the American public as both the president and congressional Republicans saw their poll ratings plummet. The rise of cynicism in the American public about the entire political system can be traced directly to this moment—one Washington has yet to fully recover from. *(The White House/Getty Images)*

Even though the president didn't *officially* kick off his campaign for re-election until May 2012, his December 2011 speech in Osawatomie, Kansas, would serve as the blueprint for his eventual re-election-year message: Give all Americans a "fair shot" by asking yourself whose policies will make you better off "four years from now." Osawatomie was chosen as the setting because it's where Teddy Roosevelt gave his famous "new nationalism" speech, a precursor to his Bull Moose run for president in 1912. *(Mandel Ngan/Getty Images)*

The vice president went on *Meet the Press* in May 2012 to coincide with the president's official re-election announcement in Ohio and Virginia. But Biden ended up stepping on his boss and making bigger news: coming out in support of gay marriage after persistent questioning from NBC's David Gregory. Within days of Biden's going public, the president scrambled to do the same in a hastily arranged interview with ABC's Robin Roberts. The first week of the re-election campaign became about gay marriage instead of "four more years." Obama would forgive Biden for trumping him on this issue, as Biden swore it was unintentional. But some Obama aides, including campaign manager Jim Messina, to this day believe Biden did it on purpose to score points with the left for his own potential presidential bid in 2016. *(NBC NewsWire/Getty Images)*

Perhaps no cabinet member under Obama enhanced his political résumé more than Leon Panetta. As CIA director, he oversaw the operation that got bin Laden. As Bob Gates's handpicked successor at the Pentagon, Panetta continued to transform the U.S. military to be more nimble and special forces/drone–focused. Whether this proves to be the right shift is something we won't fully know for years, but Panetta, more than any other Obama appointee to any post, left Washington with an enhanced legacy and perhaps viewed as the Democratic Party's most trusted "wise man." U.S. Secretary of Defense Leon Panetta (left) and Chairman of the Joint Chiefs of Staff, General Martin Dempsey, participate in a news briefing June 29, 2012, at the Pentagon in Arlington, Virginia. *(Alex Wong/Getty Images)*

The highlight of the 2012 Democratic Convention was not Obama's Thursday night acceptance speech but Bill Clinton's speech the night before. As is typical of Clinton speeches, it was not fully written out; just a robust outline was in the teleprompter. The speech went about twenty or thirty minutes longer than planned, and it ended up being an important moment in the general election. Clinton made the case that Obama's economic policies were starting to work; it was a message that swing voters believed. It was viewed as such a powerful help to Obama that he decided to give Clinton a new nickname when talking with close aides: "the Secretary of Explaining Shit." Of course, for the public, he simply changed "shit" to "stuff." *(Stan Honda/Getty Images)*

After a disastrous first debate in Denver, the president got his campaign groove back with a feistier performance in the second debate. Obama got a big assist from moderator Candy Crowley when, during a back-and-forth on the Benghazi attack, where Romney accused Obama of *not* calling it a terrorist attack, Crowley corrected Romney and noted that the president did call the attack an "act of terror." Of course, the reality was that, despite the phraseology, the White House was hesitant for days to actually refer to the attack as "terrorism." But Romney was caught flat-footed by the moderator's correction, and it became his low debate moment of the campaign. *(Spencer Platt/Getty Images)*

The Obamas celebrate in Chicago on Election Night 2012. No president can ever be considered successful if he doesn't win a second term. And history may some-day judge Obama's re-election as more remarkable than his 2008 win, given the state of the economy and the level of Washington dysfunction during his watch. Winning once can be a fluke, but winning a second time cements a president as consequential and potentially successful. It's easy to overturn policies put in place by a one-term president; much harder to do it after a two-term president. *(Spencer Platt/Getty Images)*

President Obama got about an hour to savor his second-term victory, immediately finding himself in yet another budget debate with House Republicans, this one tied to the expiring Bush tax cuts. The standoff would end up costing most of Congress its end-of-year vacation, with President Obama and Democrats getting their way to roll back those tax cuts for everyone making over $400,000 a year. *(Mark Wilson/Getty Images)*

President Obama showing rare public emotion after the Newtown shootings. (The only other time he cried in public was when he announced the death of his grandmother the day before his victory in 2008.) After a slew of mass shootings during the president's term, Newtown was the first to motivate him to tackle gun control. He would ultimately fail in his efforts but become more defiant about the issue. *(Mandel Ngan/Getty Images)*

As if to make it clear he was forever grateful to the Clintons for their surprising loyalty during the 2012 campaign, President Obama thought the best way to thank Hillary was to participate in an unprecedented joint exit interview on *60 Minutes*. While the Obama White House tried desperately to dissuade folks that this was Obama's way of acknowledging Hillary as his choice as heir apparent, the symbolism was not lost on many Democrats. About the only Democrat unhappy about the very public appearance was Joe Biden. *(CBS News/AP Images)*

President Obama and Health and Human Services Secretary Kathleen Sebelius walk out of the Oval Office to formally launch the start of health care enrollment on October 1, 2013. It would turn out to be a false start, as healthcare.gov was nowhere near ready for launch. This failure would turn out to be the start of a disastrous period in Obama's second term, when he was bogged down almost weekly by crisis after crisis, some of his own making, like the ACA, and some out

of his control (like Russia's decision to meddle in Ukraine). Eventually, the president would send in a fix-it team, and the website was repaired enough for over 8 million folks to sign up, more than was originally estimated by both independent analysts and the White House. But the political damage was never completely undone: a seed of doubt about the Obama administration's competency was planted in the minds of Americans that would sprout after debacles at the Department of Veterans Affairs, overseas in Iraq, and on the border of Mexico, all seeming to catch the Obama White House off guard. *(Saul Loeb/AFP/Getty Images)*

Of all the problems and crises the president faced in 2013, nothing was arguably harder for him to get his arms around or more politically debilitating than NSA leaks by Edward Snowden. It served to hurt the president on two fronts: it harmed his credibility and standing with younger, idealistic supporters, and it caused international embarrassments with key allies that the United States is still paying a price for today. If the entire Obama second term is dubbed a failure, the Snowden leaks will be viewed by many as the tipping point. *(AFPTV/AFP/Getty Images)*

When asked about Syria in private settings, the president regularly uses four-letter words to describe his dilemma: "It's a bunch of shitty options," he's fond of saying. The president has never conceded publicly that his rhetoric on Syria—from drawing a red line on chemical weapons to unequivocally calling for the ouster of Bashar al-Assad—was a mistake. But given that he hasn't followed through with any major action to back up his proclamations, the subtle signal seems clear. As much as he would *like* to see Assad go, everyone in the region and the American intelligence community are fearful of who or what would replace him. The rise of ISIS, the Islamist group with ties to al Qaeda, threatens to turn Syria into a more dangerous place today than Afghanistan was before 9/11. *(Anadolu Agency/Getty Images)*

Elected on the promise to get America out of Iraq, Obama ended up becoming the fourth straight U.S. president to order air strikes in Iraq. The threat of the new militant group ISIS has become a major concern for the president and his team in year six of his presidency, with questions about whether taking action in Syria a year earlier would have mitigated this new threat to Iraq. *(Mike Theiler via UPI / Getty Images)*

ful and secure. Suppressing ideas never succeeds in making them go away."[6]

Obama's national security team had met to discuss Egypt and the larger wave of protests sweeping across the Arab world on January 28. Mubarak, after all, had been a steadfast ally of the United States ever since he had taken over for the assassinated Anwar Sadat back in 1981. He was also the closest thing Israel had to a friend in the region; he had always been pragmatic enough to see the inevitability of the Jewish state's existence, and had dealt with Israel, albeit quietly, for years. He was a rare pillar of stability in an unforgiving, unstable region that could otherwise be hostile to American interests.

The advisors who discussed the growing tension on the streets of Cairo that day had relations with Mubarak that spanned their decades in government service. Clinton and Gates had met with Mubarak repeatedly over the years; Biden, who had served two different tenures as chairman of the Senate Foreign Relations Committee, had probably met Mubarak a dozen times or more. All three believed Mubarak would survive the protests; all were hoping, frankly, he would survive. The fear with Egypt and many Middle Eastern authoritarian regimes for the foreign policy realist crowd, of which Gates, Clinton, and Biden were all members, was always "what came next."

The president, who had been in college when Sadat

was assassinated and Mubarak took over, thought differently. He had seen what had happened in Tunisia, and he believed something had fundamentally changed. Maybe it was the proliferation of social media, which allowed protesters to organize much more quickly and spread information faster. Perhaps it was the Internet itself, or Al Jazeera, which had given Egyptians and other Arabs a real-time look at what had happened on the streets of Tunis. Or maybe it was even Obama's own experience; he had bucked the old system and defeated the old Washington guard thanks to new media (or at least he told himself this). Whatever the cause, the protests were bigger than they had been in years, even decades, and Obama began to suspect Mubarak wouldn't be able to survive. Of course, Obama, ever the idealist, also believed Mubarak had not earned the right to survive as leader. The real fear all of them had was that the aging Egyptian president might decide to try to fight his way out of the mess, which would put the United States in the worst possible situation—caught between defending one of the country's most important allies and upholding deeply held American principles of freedom. Oh, how the president hoped Mubarak wouldn't try to fight.

Obama decided to say something, in hopes of averting bloodshed. The statement needed to thread a very thin needle: Mubarak had been an ally, and he might still survive if he made the right reforms.

Gauging the temperature, the president had already asked the State Department to send a seasoned diplomat — Frank Wisner Jr. — to Cairo in an attempt to counsel Mubarak on how to depart peacefully. Obama couldn't throw Mubarak under the bus yet, but he needed to get his message across.

"I want to be very clear in calling upon the Egyptian authorities to refrain from any violence against peaceful protesters," the president told reporters in the White House's State Dining Room that night. "The people of Egypt have rights that are universal. That includes the right to peaceful assembly and association, the right to free speech, and the ability to determine their own destiny. These are human rights. And the United States will stand up for them everywhere."

Obama urged the Egyptian government to end its restrictions on Internet and cell phone networks, and he reiterated in public what he and Wisner had been telling Mubarak in private: There had to be serious "political, social, and economic reforms that meet the aspirations of the Egyptian people. In the absence of these reforms, grievances have built up over time."[7]

Obama's goal had been to avert a humanitarian disaster without jettisoning a close ally. But there was another, more carefully laid element of his plan: Obama's statement had called for reform, for rights for the protesters and for the end of restrictions on the communication tools they used to organize in the first place. He had put the United States more squarely on the side of the protesters than on Mubarak's—the message was hardly subtle. Some even suggested that Obama's statement served as an endorsement of more protests.

Now, on Wednesday, February 1, with at least a quarter-million people still making their presence felt in Tahrir Square, the senior national security principals returned to the Situation Room, revisiting the deteriorating stalemate in Egypt. The military, still maintaining its independence from Mubarak as much as possible, had refused orders to fire live ammunition at protesters over the previous weekend, but violence between the protesters and the police, who were still under his control, seemed imminent. Wisner had coached Mubarak on a series of statements he needed to make—increased reforms, new elections, all leading up to an announcement that Mubarak wouldn't seek re-election when his current term expired. Now Biden, Clinton, Gates, Mullen, and Donilon, Obama's national security advisor since Jones's departure, were meeting to discuss whether to push Mubarak even more firmly toward the exit.

Half an hour into the meeting Obama walked in, although he hadn't been scheduled to participate. The generational divide that occasionally made its presence felt in the Obama White House, where many of the principals were ten or fifteen years older than the president, emerged again: Obama and his younger advisors, including Denis McDonough, Susan Rice, Samantha Power, and Ben Rhodes, wanted more robust American support for street protests they believed would inevitably be successful; Biden, Clinton, Gates, and the older principals wanted to stand with an American ally they still believed could ride out the storm.

Halfway into the meeting, an aide handed a note to Donilon: Mubarak was addressing his people on television. The banks of TV sets clicked on, then over to Al Jazeera, which was carrying Mubarak's speech live.

"The country is passing through difficult times and tough experiences which began with noble youths and citizens who practice their rights to peaceful demonstrations and protests, expressing their concerns and aspirations but they were quickly exploited by those who sought to spread chaos and violence, confrontation and to violate the constitutional legitimacy and to attack it," Mubarak began. He followed by placing the blame on "political forces that wanted to escalate and worsen the situation," targeting "the nation's security and stability through acts of provocation, theft and looting and setting fires and blocking roads and attacking vital installations and public and private properties and storming some diplomatic missions."

He then turned to his own role: "My primary responsibility now is security and independence of the nation to ensure a peaceful transfer of power in circumstances that protect Egypt and the Egyptians and allow handing over responsibility to whoever the people choose in the coming presidential election. I say in all honesty and regardless of the current situation that I did not intend to nominate myself for a new presidential term," Mubarak said. He called on the parliament to set up a method of electing a president and the eligibility requirements that would need to be met, and he demanded the power to hunt down and prosecute the "outlaws" who were causing trouble.[8]

Back in the Situation Room, Obama wasn't impressed. The message that Mubarak would step down at the end of his term had been drowned out by the overall tone—indeed, the tone the Egyptian leader had taken since the crisis had begun a week before. Mubarak had always been combative, and in the end he had only promised first steps toward an election that wasn't even on the schedule.

"That's not going to cut it," Obama said to the room.[9]

The principals continued to debate, with Biden, Clinton, and Gates arguing that forcing Mubarak out of the picture would leave Egypt, a country huge in both size and importance, spiraling into the unknown. What if the rulers who came to power next were hard-line Islamists, suddenly eager to help Israel's enemies like Hamas, which controlled the Gaza Strip? At the very least, Clinton said, the United States should be working with Mubarak on a transition, perhaps to Omar Suleiman, his vice president, who also had close ties to American officials.

Obama cut off the debate, siding with his younger staff over the more seasoned principals. He didn't believe that Clinton, Gates, and Biden were wrong to advocate for a more orderly transition period, but Obama was certain that the writing was on the wall and that the protesters in Tahrir Square would settle for nothing less than immediate change. Mubarak, Obama believed, had already lost the battle. If the United States continued to back a lame duck, especially one who no longer had a governing mandate from his citizens, it would risk being relegated to the outside and losing influence when a new government came to power. And worse, Obama would be playing into a Middle East stereotype of the United States, that it believed in freedom only for Americans, not for all, and that its only concern in the Middle East was to protect its own narrow interests.

And so Obama did something that perhaps a President Hillary Clinton or a President John McCain would not have done at this moment: he called Mubarak and told him to step down. But Obama's decision to push Mubarak out sent a regional message: if you want to overthrow your autocratic leader, the United States will stand by you — a perceived promise that, as Syrians learned, Obama was not prepared to deliver on.

Mubarak was spitting fire. "You don't understand this part of the world," he said angrily, even before Obama's words had been translated for him. Mubarak made the same point Obama's senior advisors had just made: he repeated, over and over, that without a managed transition to a safe replacement, the alternative would be terrible.[10] Obama advisors who listened in on the call say Mubarak wasn't begging the president to stand with him; he was furious at the young upstart for forcing him aside. Obama had first met Mubarak back in 2009, when the president traveled to Cairo to give his famous speech to the Muslim world. During that meeting, the president had found himself treated like a student by Professor Mubarak. As plenty of folks around Obama, including Biden and Hillary, had learned, the president was not someone who appreciated being lectured to or treated as if he were intellectually inferior. So while Obama had been polite and had done what he had to do that day with Mubarak, the two hardly forged a personal relationship. This perhaps made it easier for Obama to make his "it's time to go" phone call, and why it was so easy for Mubarak to fire back.

It was the final time Mubarak and Obama spoke.

Obama hung up the phone and went to the White House's Grand Foyer to address the world. At 6:44 p.m., he put an important nail in the Mubarak administration's coffin. "What is clear—and what I indicated tonight to President Mubarak—is my belief that an orderly transition must be meaningful, it must be peaceful, and it must begin now," Obama said.*[11]

A little more than a week later, on February 10, Mubarak made his last speech to the nation he had ruled for thirty years. He ceded some of his power to Suleiman; the White House again issued a statement saying that intermediate step wasn't enough. The following day, Mubarak surfaced in Sharm el-Sheikh, the resort town in the Sinai Peninsula, and announced his resignation. It was a remarkable use of American influence; Mubarak never would have left office if Obama hadn't made it clear he would not enjoy U.S. support, which was what had been keeping him in power. There's probably no greater example of what kind of change Obama brought to the presidency than this decision at this

---

* Biden had been counseling Suleiman to get out ahead of what was beginning to look inevitable. He had told Suleiman to call on Mubarak to quit, and to use his meetings with protesters to build his own relationships. But Suleiman wouldn't do it. In his statement that Wednesday night, Obama praised the Egyptian army for its restraint, but he didn't mention Egypt's vice president.

moment in history. It put every authoritarian American ally on notice, from Jordan to Saudi Arabia, and every Gulf state in between.

Throughout the crisis in Egypt, Obama's advisors were still quietly debating the merits and methods of attacking the Abbottabad compound. In a March 14 meeting, Panetta laid out the viable military scenarios developed by Admiral William McRaven, commander of the Joint Special Operations Command. Option one was sending a squadron of B-2 stealth bombers, which would drop 2,000-pound bombs to flatten the compound. Option two was a commando raid, in which McRaven's troops would helicopter into Pakistani airspace to breach the compound. Option three was a joint operation between American and Pakistani forces; Pakistan wouldn't be informed of the mission's target until just before the raid, to limit the possibility of a leak.

Obama didn't like the idea of a bombing strike because it risked killing innocent bystanders.[12] The United States already had trouble with Pakistan over drone strikes that had killed hundreds of civilians along with the terrorists the missiles had been intended to hit. He also didn't like the bombing idea because it would make identifying bin Laden's body more difficult. McRaven, worried about the second issue in particular, advocated sending his own men.

Others, like Gates, recalled the disastrous rescue attempt Jimmy Carter had approved in 1980, after Iranian revolutionaries had taken hostages at the U.S. embassy in Tehran. Those who remembered the political damage done by that failed operation preferred to limit the risk to American lives and level the building with bunker-buster bombs.

Obama opted for a raid. While an air strike would have put fewer lives at risk, the United States would never know if the U.S. attack had actually killed bin Laden or someone else. It would never know, in fact, if bin Laden had ever been there in the first place, never mind the missed opportunity to gather important intelligence about al Qaeda; Pakistan wasn't going to allow an American team to investigate a bombing site inside its borders, after all. Bringing back bin Laden's body would give the United States the evidence it needed, both for peace of mind and to quell any disbelief around the globe. Special operations forces began training at Area 51, in the Nevada desert, without knowing the identity of their target, while Pentagon officials assessed what types of ordnance they would need to pull off this operation.

The underlying question remained: was Osama bin Laden actually living with his courier in Abbottabad? At the White House, Obama and his staff pushed the intelligence community to come up with something—anything—that could provide more confidence that bin Laden was present. Intelligence

analysts were developing theories using every scrap
of information they could find: How many children were playing in the yard? How many women
were in or around the house? How long were the
shadows cast by a man who occasionally paced the
grounds? (The National Geospatial Intelligence
Agency not-so-helpfully estimated that the man was
between five foot eight and six foot eight; bin Laden
fell at the taller end of that range, but then again, so
did millions of Pakistanis and Afghans.)

A week before the attack was planned to take
place, the circle of bin Laden hunters widened a little more. National Security Council staffers and several deputies to those meeting in the Situation Room
began holding separate sessions to make plans for
various outcomes. What would the United States
do if one of the helicopters it planned to use went
out of service? The compound was within a few miles
of a Pakistani military academy; what if troops
showed up, angry about the violation of Pakistan's
airspace? The contingency plans mounted quickly,
collected in a binder they called the playbook.

The plans extended far beyond Abbottabad itself.
If the raid went bad and civilians died, the United
States needed a way to get Americans out of diplo-
matic facilities in Lahore, Peshawar, Karachi, and
Islamabad, in the event they were overrun by mobs
of angry Pakistanis. But telling diplomats in those

facilities that a raid on Abbottabad was coming—broadening the circle to low-level personnel on the ground—would risk giving the Pakistani military a heads-up. In a perverse way, it was fortunate that Pakistan was such a hotbed of terrorist activity. "We couldn't tell the embassies [to] go to ground, because they wouldn't know why," Ben Rhodes said later. Instead, they would just concoct an excuse using the dangerous conditions that already existed: "You can always find a reason or a threat on a facility in Karachi or Peshawar." An alert of that sort wouldn't seem exceptional at all, just another day in the life in that tumultuous part of the world.

Perhaps the most sensitive long-term question had to do with the Pakistani government: how would the United States tell its ostensible ally that it had violated Pakistani airspace for a raid against the world's most infamous terrorist? There was never any debate over whether to give Pakistan a heads-up; too many elements of Inter-Services Intelligence, Pakistan's spy agency, were too close to al Qaeda members and the Taliban to risk spreading the word. Panetta certainly wasn't particularly tight with anyone in Pakistani leadership, nor was Clinton. Obama wasn't going to make the call, either. That job would fall to Mullen, who had a long-standing relationship with General Ashfaq Parvez Kayani, Pakistan's army chief of staff and chief spymaster.

*　　*　　*

The situation in Egypt wasn't the only one that had Washington increasingly nervous about the president's foreign policy record. And how could that record be judged? Obama saw the world in shades of gray rather than the stark black-and-white view the Bush administration had taken. His was a nuanced assessment of America's strengths and weaknesses in the world, especially when it came to the ever-changing fallout from the Arab Spring, and Obama was reluctant to place American lives in harm's way in yet another conflict in the Arab world, especially when, as was the case in Libya, two of the country's strongest allies—Great Britain and France—were willing to take a leading role. That conflict, and Obama's approach to it, would reveal yet another facet of his struggle to find foreign policy balance. Writing about the ultimately successful NATO operation to remove Libyan dictator Muammar Gaddafi, the *New Yorker*'s Ryan Lizza quoted an unnamed Obama advisor as saying that the United States would keep a low profile in French- and British-led military intervention in Libya because America was "leading from behind." The phrase, used by a few national security staffers, may have been a fancier way of emphasizing a sort of sophisticated "push" over a more muscular "pull," but it turned out to be politically toxic, especially as Republican presidential candidates, including Mitt Romney, were trying to flex their own foreign policy muscles and accusing the president of not believing in that most American of ideals — the idea of American exceptionalism. In their view, no American exceptionalist would ever "lead from behind."

Despite the Bush years, Democrats remembered the advantage Republicans held in voters' minds on national security issues. Being strong on the war on terror had helped George W. Bush expand Republican majorities in the 2002 midterm elections and win a second term in the White House. The last thing Democrats wanted was to rebuild the Republican advantage on the issue, a holdover from Vietnam-era protests that undermined voters' views of the party's national security credentials. But in the phrase "leading from behind," Obama's opponents heard another presidential apology for America's actions that they viewed as typical of his liberal, America-last outlook. The expression — which had been used by at least two members of the National Security Council, both of whom denied being the source in Lizza's piece — became an easy, if grossly out-of-context, slam against the president.

So it was that Rhodes and Jeremy Bash, Leon Panetta's chief of staff at the CIA, found themselves at the Center for American Progress, the liberal think tank, in the days before the Abbottabad raid was to take place, surrounded by antsy Democratic foreign policy strategists from Capitol Hill and the think tank world. The White House looked weak, the gathered Democrats said, and Obama had the potential to take the party in a direction they didn't want to go.

Rhodes caught Bash's eye. "If these guys knew what we knew," Rhodes was thinking. "The president's about to whack bin Laden."

CHAPTER ELEVEN

Trump, bin Laden, and the Craziest Week of the Presidency

In the midst of the president's planning the bin Laden raid and juggling the Arab Spring, another distraction that was making some Democrats nervous was coming to a bombastic conclusion. For years, almost since the moment Barack Obama appeared on the national stage, rumors had swirled in the ugly corners of the Internet that he wasn't who he said he was. A virtual cottage industry of right-wing conspiracy theorists, led by Glenn Beck and Alex Jones, their followers hanging on their every word, had spread rumors that Obama had in fact been born outside the United States and that he was doing all he could to cover up the circumstances of his birth.

The level of detail these so-called birthers fabricated was elaborate: Obama's paternal stepgrandmother had let slip that the president had been born in Kenya, some said. (The tape of the interview is cut off before Sarah Obama is able to clarify that her stepgrandson was born in Hawaii.) Others believed he had taken Indonesian citizenship when he lived there with his mother and stepfather as a child (an easily debunked claim), or that the birth announcements, published nine and ten days after his birth in the *Honolulu Advertiser* and the *Honolulu Star-Bulletin,* had been planted there so that he would have a credible claim of citizenship when, decades later, he ran for president. It didn't strike any of the conspiracy theorists as odd, however, that the supposed originators of the grand plan to plant some kind of Manchurian candidate bent on destroying America didn't bother to give Barack Hussein Obama a less conspicuous name. But then, consistency had gone out the window along with rationality.*

Regrettably, some Republicans were all too willing to play along with their rabidly anti-Obama base. Beck and Jones successfully fed the conspiracies to their audiences, who then recycled them in town hall meetings and one-on-one interactions with their elected officials. John McCain, Obama's opponent in 2008, had famously disabused a woman of this notion at a town hall meeting, assuring her that

---

* Maybe if the infant had been named "George Lincoln Washington," the whole "planting" theory might have attracted more believers.

Obama wasn't the pretender the Internet rumors had made him seem, but he was distinctly in the minority of those in attendance.

At first the White House found the questions a minor irritation that they actually used for political gain. In fact, when fringe politicians like Michele Bachmann, Maricopa County sheriff Joe Arpaio, or Sarah Palin repeated some debunked rumor, they provided Democrats with a means of painting their Republican rivals with the crazy brush. In one interview in 2010, Robert Gibbs laid into former House Speaker Newt Gingrich for a comment Gingrich had made — Obama, Gingrich had declared, displayed "Kenyan, anti-colonial behavior."

"You would normally expect better of somebody who held the position of Speaker of the House, but look, it's political season, and most people will say anything. And Newt Gingrich does that on a genuinely, on a regular basis," Gibbs said.[1] "Birtherism," as the conspiracy theory had been labeled, could be a cudgel used to marginalize Obama's opponents.

But the White House started to take notice when more serious Republicans — actual legislators, interested in passing actual legislation — started dipping their toes in the birther waters. A small Alabama newspaper reported that Richard Shelby, who was first elected to the Senate as a Democrat and now was the top Republican on the Senate Banking

Committee, had commented that he hadn't seen a birth certificate from the commander in chief. Roy Blunt, the Missouri Republican who had served in House leadership and was running for a Senate seat, said he didn't understand why Obama couldn't produce a birth certificate. "I don't know anybody else that can't produce one," Blunt told a conservative writer.[2] Perhaps most worrying to the commander in chief, at least one army officer, a lieutenant colonel based at Fort Belvoir in Virginia, refused to deploy to Afghanistan because he didn't believe Obama had the authority to order him to go. Birtherism had slowly crept from the dark recesses of Internet conspiracy theorists to the fringes of the mainstream.

But no one did more to vault the false issue to the cable news echo chamber than Donald Trump, the wealthy, eccentric Manhattan real estate mogul. Few have the raw need for attention that Trump exhibits on a regular basis. His bombastic displays regularly grab headlines, and his rises and falls from grace have been chronicled in gossipy New York tabloids and respectable business publications for three decades.

Trump had publicly flirted with a run for president in 2012, and he was stung when few respected political analysts took him seriously. Trump took to calling reporters to convince them he was serious, even offering at least one of them a well-staked bet that he would run.*

But the real bet Trump made was that birtherism would be good publicity. Beginning with a March 2011 appearance on *Good Morning America,* Trump questioned Obama's birthplace. Early the next month, he said on the *Today* show that he had sent investigators to Hawaii to track down the birth certificate. "I have people that have been studying it and they cannot believe what they're finding," he said.[3]

Trump's outlandish claims, never backed up by any evidence, were nonetheless great for television ratings; no matter how often the fact-checkers debunked the outlandish assertions, no matter how often journalists laced their reporting with caveats and their own debunking, the media couldn't stop itself from interviewing yet another birther. Trump's ridiculous declarations were great for his publicity-hungry ego, but they were beginning to worry the White House, which believed they were doing real damage. A *Time* magazine survey conducted as early as August 2010 showed that 46 percent of Republicans believed Obama was a Muslim. A Pew Forum on Religion and Public Life survey around the same time showed that 31 percent of Republicans thought the same thing.[4] A February 2011 poll conducted by

---

* This author, perhaps regrettably, declined the wager.

Public Policy Polling, the Democratic-leaning firm, showed 51 percent of voters who planned to cast a ballot in the Republican primaries believed Obama had not been born in the United States. The president's chief political strategist, David Plouffe, monitored polls religiously, and the results worried him: the extreme fringe of the conservative movement had infected mainstream Republicans. And this was creating a serious governing problem: Plouffe truly worried that some Republicans would find themselves unable to work with the president if this conspiracy theory wasn't debunked once and for all. After all, with re-election on the horizon, Plouffe needed *some* points on the scoreboard with Congress, and if the country thought this president couldn't work with the other side, it might actually punish him and not the GOP.

In an era of constant, debilitating partisanship, it is hardly surprising that the Republican base would see a Democratic president in a harshly unfavorable light. But the depth of the Republican base's hatred for Obama had begun to have a severe impact in Washington and back home. A Republican politician who negotiated a deal with the president would have to answer to an increasingly radicalized base; even working across the aisle on a health care bill that never came to a vote had cost Utah senator Bob Bennett his seat in the 2010 elections. It was no coincidence that Senator Mitch McConnell, who viewed the Tea Party movement as a potential threat to his own re-election bid in 2014—he didn't want to have to face a challenge from the right—would only be seen dealing with Vice President Joe Biden, the lesser evil in the mind of the Republican base.

The birther question only made things worse. If Republicans would refuse to work with Obama because any compromise would be detrimental to their own political well-being, then Obama was going to have a tough time getting anything done in his remaining years in office. And if military officers were actually questioning the authority of their commander in chief, the damage to the constitutional fabric of the nation could extend long past his own presidency.

In early April, Plouffe called Bob Bauer, the White House counsel, to figure out exactly how they could go about obtaining a certified copy of Obama's long-form birth certificate. Bauer told Plouffe to go to Judith Corley, Obama's personal attorney, who could formally request a copy from Hawaii's department of health. The department of health had a long-standing policy of providing only the so-called short-form, or abbreviated, birth certificate, but in this case Corley asked for the full document. Corley's letter was accompanied by a two-paragraph letter from the president authorizing Corley to accept the certified copies on his behalf.

Loretta Fuddy, head of the health department,

had been besieged by requests for the birth certificate from conspiracy theorists (and presumably
Trump's "investigators") for years. Only too glad to
comply, in a letter dated April 25, 2011, she wrote to
Obama: "I have the legal authority to approve the
process by which copies of such records are made.
Through that authority, in recognition of your status as President of the United States, I am making
an exception to current departmental policy which
is to issue a computer-generated certified copy." Then,
in a fit of bureaucratic frustration, Fuddy added, "We
hope that issuing you these copies of your original
Certificate of Live Birth will end the numerous inquiries received by the Hawaii Department of Health
to produce this document. Such inquiries have been
disruptive to staff operations and have strained State
resources."[5]

Two days later, on April 27, just four days before
he would announce to the world the capture and
killing of Osama bin Laden, Obama entered the
White House briefing room at 9:48 a.m., not to
hold a planned press conference or officially announce
Panetta as his new defense secretary (which was
among the items the reporters assumed the president was going to address). No way was he going to
add to the public spectacle of birtherism—so thought
just about everyone in that room. But Obama strolled
in with the confidence of a man who has the truth
on his side. He even made a joke at a television report-

er's expense, but inside he was irritated by what he had to do. And while Obama never liked to say publicly that race was driving birtherism, he couldn't help wondering whether a white president would have to go through this demeaning spectacle.

"Over the last two and a half years I have watched with bemusement. I've been puzzled at the degree to which this thing just kept on going," he said. "We've had every official in Hawaii, Democrat and Republican, every news outlet that has investigated this confirm that, yes, in fact, I was born in Hawaii, August 4, 1961, in Kapiolani Hospital.

"Now, normally I would not comment on something like this, because obviously there's a lot of stuff swirling in the press on any given day and I've got other things to do," Obama went on. "But two weeks ago, when the Republican House had put forward a budget that will have huge consequences potentially to the country, and when I gave a speech about my budget and how I felt that we needed to invest in education and infrastructure and making sure that we had a strong safety net for our seniors even as we were closing the deficit, during that entire week the dominant news story wasn't about these huge, monumental choices that we're going to have to make as a nation. It was about my birth certificate. And that was true on most of the news outlets that are represented here.

"I know that there's going to be a segment of

people for which, no matter what we put out, this issue will not be put to rest. But I'm speaking to the vast majority of the American people, as well as to the press. We do not have time for this kind of silliness. We've got better stuff to do. I've got better stuff to do. We've got big problems to solve. And I'm confident we can solve them, but we're going to have to focus on them — not on this."[6]

The decision to track down and release Obama's long-form birth certificate, in response to what had begun as the maniacal rantings of a few wing nuts, was not one the White House made lightly. His advisors didn't want to give legitimacy to the fringe, which they worried might set a dangerous precedent for future presidents. But it had become necessary, aides explained later, simply to get the issue out of the way. And they knew that while the vast majority of Americans believed the truth, even releasing the actual birth certificate wouldn't completely assuage the conspiracy theorists.*

The absurdity of the situation was clear, both to the White House and to the reporters who covered it. The president of the United States had been forced to release a document no other president had been

---

* The Obama campaign made as light of the situation as it could. Donors were soon bombarded with solicitations from the campaign that promised goods — a $25 T-shirt with a copy of the birth certificate on the back, a $15 mug with the same image — in exchange for donations. "We sold a hell of a lot of merchandise," Plouffe said.

asked for, all because of the rantings of a few conspiracy theorists and one of the country's biggest blowhards. That absurdity must have been doubled for Obama, because as this was going on, he was engaging in a much more important attempt to match a place with a face: the next day he gathered his advisors in the Situation Room for a final review of military options aimed at that compound in Abbottabad a mere three days later. The meeting dragged on for hours as Obama went around the table, asking every member of the team for his or her opinion. After all, Panetta's analysts at the CIA had estimated that there was only a 60 to 80 percent chance that bin Laden was at the compound.

Clinton, Mullen, Panetta, and John Brennan, Obama's chief counterterrorism advisor, favored hitting the compound. Biden was against it—"Don't go," he told Obama.[7] James "Hoss" Cartwright, Mullen's vice chairman at the Joint Chiefs of Staff and a four-star marine general who was personally close to Obama, argued once again for his own version of an air strike—a small missile fired from a drone, aimed at the tall man pacing in the yard—rather than putting boots on the ground. Gates and Mike Leiter, director of the National Counterterrorism Center, came to agree with Cartwright.

Obama left the room leaning toward ordering the strike to proceed, but he told his team he wouldn't make a decision until he had thought more. The failed Iranian operation still weighed heavily on Gates; the loss of a Black Hawk helicopter in Mogadishu, Somalia, in 1993 was weighing on Obama.

The next morning, Obama summoned Tom Donilon, his national security advisor, along with Donilon's deputy, Denis McDonough, Brennan, and Bill Daley to the Diplomatic Room. He had made his call: "It's a go."

The strike team had a window of the next three days—when the moon was new enough to provide cover of darkness—in which to conduct the raid. If the weather didn't cooperate, they would have to wait another month.

The president and his advisors went to great lengths to avoid letting anyone know that something was afoot. Obama kept his scheduled meetings with the speechwriting staff, who were still trying to come up with jokes that wouldn't bomb at the correspondents' dinner (which as it turned out would take place just twelve hours before the bin Laden raid). Obama had all but guaranteed that his birth certificate and Trump would be the dinner's dominant theme, especially since Trump was going to attend.

Gates, who would be leaving the Pentagon later that year, had agreed to attend his first and only correspondents' dinner as a guest of CBS reporter Bob Schieffer. That Saturday, with the commando team grounded in Afghanistan by bad weather in Abbottabad, Gates had invited Geoff Morrell to his home for a predinner cocktail. Although the two men traded gossip about Pentagon personnel and other classified missions, Gates never let Morrell in on the secret operation to come. At the correspondents' dinner, Morrell watched Gates chatting with Leon Panetta backstage, the two veteran Washington hands sharing a laugh without hinting that something larger was weighing on their minds—a reminder in hindsight that, yes, folks in Washington can keep a secret.

Obama's speech went fine, beginning with the president's entrance music: Bruce Springsteen's "Born in the USA,"* and then his various shots at Trump, who was there as a guest of the *Washington Post,* over his birtherism obsession, which brought down the house. The next morning, Obama kept up appearances. He left the White House at 9:42, bound for the golf course at Andrews Air Force Base, his fifth round of golf in as many weeks. It was a somewhat familiar foursome on this Sunday, two close aides who were both scratch golfers, including junior White House official Ben Finkenbinder and the president's chief personal aide, Marvin Nicholson, as well as Energy Department staffer David Katz. They played

---

* After the president had nixed the joke about Tim Pawlenty's middle name being "bin Laden," one of his young speechwriters had suggested substituting "Hosni," a reference to the recently deposed Egyptian president. Yeah, Obama had said, that works. Axelrod didn't think it was terribly funny, but it went over well enough at the dinner.

nine holes—an unseasonably cold day and a few sprinkles of rain cut short their round, the press pool report said—and arrived back home at 2:04, about two hours before the raid was set to begin.[8]

As the helicopters took off from their base in Afghanistan, two of them bound across the border to Abbottabad and another three carrying a rapid reaction force that could rescue the assault team if anything went wrong, Obama's national security advisors gathered in the Situation Room. The name is a bit misleading—there's actually more than one room. Most of Obama's team was huddled in the larger space, a conference room with television screens on every wall. At the moment, the screens showed only someone in another room, monitoring a second feed, a grainy black-and-white overhead shot from a drone. Obama's team couldn't hear the troops in the field; they heard only from McRaven, who was overseeing the mission from Afghanistan, and Panetta, who was narrating from his office at CIA headquarters in Langley.

Biden, Gates, and General Brad Webb were in the second, smaller conference room, monitoring the overhead feed. They could see the helicopters enter the visual field, but other than that, details were scarce. They couldn't even tell that one of the helicopters had gone down. One of the common assumptions based on the famous Situation Room photo of the president and the entire national security team was that their startled looks (particularly Hillary's) must have been in response to the chopper going down. That was not the case. McRaven's voice was the only indication they had that something had gone wrong. Sitting beside the president, Gates, who had watched the 1980 hostage rescue attempt in Tehran go so wrong, felt a sickening sense of déjà vu. But half a minute later, McRaven relieved the tension: the troops were okay, and the mission would continue. McRaven ordered one of the three backup Chinook helicopters to fly to Abbottabad, to scoop up the SEALs who had flown in on the downed chopper.

Donilon had suggested that the president watch the raid, as it were, through Panetta, who was connected to the Situation Room by video link. Panetta was at Langley helping to facilitate the images for everyone back in the room, including the president. After the helicopter went down, Obama got up and walked into the smaller conference room, joining his vice president.

One by one, those in the larger conference room followed Obama so they could watch the overhead feed, anything to get closer to the action. The second room, a fraction the size of the larger space, was crammed. Biden and Gates watched from opposite sides of a table. Clinton sat next to Gates, a binder and a notebook on her lap. Next to her sat McDonough, arms folded and ramrod straight. Daley, Donilon, Brennan, Mullen, and James Clapper, director of national intelligence, stood. Obama, in a white polo shirt and a light black coat, sat in a corner, leaning forward, tense.

With only a high-altitude view of events, the tension soon returned. In between the scenes of the commandos breaching walls and encountering hostile combatants there were "these periods of silence where you're like, what the fuck is going on?" remembered one person in the room. Brennan said later that "the minutes passed like days."[9]

The audio feed crackled to life again. "Visual on Geronimo," a voice said.[10] The code word confirmed that the CIA analysts had been correct — bin Laden was in Abbottabad and at that compound. A few minutes later, they confirmed that Geronimo was dead.

"Looks like we got him," Obama said.[11]

The main goal of the mission had been achieved. While the official mission was "capture or kill" Geronimo, there weren't many U.S. officials, the president included, who wanted to deal with an alive bin Laden. Just what would his rights be at that point? Where would he be housed? It's more than a decade since 9/11, and the U.S. government is still trying to figure out how to even try Khalid Sheik

Mohammed, the mastermind behind those attacks. So while nobody will ever claim that the president, McRaven, Panetta, or anyone else ordered that bin Laden be taken dead, it was the preferred outcome. Of all the contingency plans the SEALs had prepared, the one that many hoped they wouldn't have to use was the one for taking bin Laden alive. But a secondary mission was only beginning: the SEALs feverishly shoveled every bit of data they could find — files, papers, computers — into bags they had brought along. The documents would be used against others in bin Laden's network, critical intelligence that would deal what those in Washington hoped would be a decisive blow against al Qaeda.

That bagging dragged on, seemingly for an eternity. "The post–bin Laden piece of the operation took a lot longer than the pre–bin Laden piece of the operation," recalls one official who was in the room. "You're just sitting there waiting for them to get the hell out of there."

And then it was time to go. As the helicopters departed Pakistani airspace, Mullen called the head of Pakistan's powerful intelligence network, Kayani, to inform him of the incursion, and a few hours later Obama called Asif Ali Zardari, Pakistan's president — a couple of phone calls that did not go well. It was with a combination of insult and embarrassment that the Pakistanis received the news. They were insulted that the United States would invade their airspace and not inform them until after the fact, a harsh reminder of just how little trust there was in Washington among the Pakistani leadership. And, of course, there was embarrassment that bin Laden was not merely in Pakistan but hiding in plain sight in a city that essentially was that country's West Point.

Rhodes stepped out of the Situation Room and e-mailed Plouffe, Pfeiffer, and the fairly new press secretary, Jay Carney, none of whom had been included in the planning phases. It was a Sunday afternoon, but Rhodes explained to them that they had to immediately come to the White House, though he couldn't tell them why. The three advisors showed up as quickly as they could and waited in Carney's office, where they tried to guess at the reason for the late summons. Rhodes walked in, a smile on his face. "Hey guys, guess what?" he said.

In and around Washington, rumors began swirling. Christopher Isham, CBS's Washington bureau chief, and David Martin, a CBS correspondent, called Geoff Morrell, the Pentagon spokesman, around 6:30 p.m. They had a single source, they said, who was telling them bin Laden was dead, but they couldn't find a second source. Another insider reached out to NBC, simply saying, "It's somebody we've been looking for, for a long time." That comment helped torpedo the other rumor that had suddenly engulfed Washington, that somehow Libya's strongman, Muammar Gaddafi, had been killed. After all, the only "new" military exercise that Washington knew about that May evening was the no-fly zone in Libya.*

The calls kept coming. Morrell told everyone who rang that it should be obvious that he couldn't confirm anything; after all, he wouldn't be answering his phone if he *did* know something. In between the calls, he dialed his direct superior, the Pentagon's chief of staff. Morrell was told that an announcement was coming, but it wouldn't be coming from a Pentagon spokesman.

At 11:35 p.m., Obama walked down a long red carpet to a podium in the East Room of the White House. He had no staff or supporters following him. It was just the president, and a long empty hall behind him.

"Tonight, I can report to the American people and to the world that the United States has conducted an operation that killed Osama bin Laden, the leader of al Qaeda, and a terrorist who's responsible for the murder of thousands of innocent men, women, and children," Obama said. "Today, at my direction, the United States launched a targeted operation against that compound in Abbottabad,

---

* The source called this author not only to offer an early alert but to encourage the network to get wheels in motion for what was sure to be a major special report.

Pakistan. A small team of Americans carried out the operation with extraordinary courage and capability. No Americans were harmed. They took care to avoid civilian casualties. After a firefight, they killed Osama bin Laden and took custody of his body."[12]

In ordering the assault, the option that put the largest number of American lives at risk, Obama had taken a huge gamble, one that could have dealt a fatal blow to his presidency if something had gone wrong. The failed rescue mission in 1980 had further damaged Jimmy Carter at a crucial moment. Now, the Obama team was going to make sure they took advantage of the political payoffs.

The following morning, operating on little sleep and still buzzing with excitement over the enormity of the achievement, many of the same people who had crammed into the small conference room to watch the grainy feed met again, this time to plot how they would tell their story. The White House felt an intense pressure from a media ravenous for even the slightest detail about the raid, and the Obama team felt it had to get in front of the story— in the words of one defense community observer, "feed the beast."

As the White House officials debated their communications strategy, Gates piped up. "I have [a communications strategy]," he said. "It's called shut the fuck up."

The White House and some national security officials disagreed. Nevertheless, Gates and Mullen were flabbergasted when Brennan joined Carney at his daily press briefing to give details of the raid, details that were still unconfirmed and that would later inevitably change simply due to the fog of war. Brennan dished out nuggets of operational detail, including the fact that they hadn't contacted the Pakistanis until American troops were back in Afghanistan's airspace. Brennan also announced that the commandos had acquired actionable intelligence, a hint to remaining al Qaeda leaders that their security had been further breached.

"We have released a tremendous amount of information to date," Brennan said at one point in the briefing. "At the same time, we don't want to do anything that's going to compromise our ability to be as successful the next time we get one of these guys and take them off the battlefield."[13]

Gates and Mullen thought Brennan had already crossed that line, and in pursuit of something that had already been achieved. "The conventional view is somehow they needed to further enhance the President's bona fides," Mullen said later. "And my view is, you just killed the number one enemy in the world, [who] killed more Americans than anybody else. What else—you don't need it! That's it! You got him! And that just never penetrated."

"The world wanted to know how we did this, and they went out to talk about it before they had the full story," said one administration official who sympathized with Gates and Mullen. The observer saw "an erosion of the secrecy around operational tactics and procedures. How we do things is such a part of what distinguishes us from everybody else." But the race to disclose details reflected the mind-set of the White House at that period, when Obama's approval ratings were middling at best and his prospects for re-election looked shaky.

Four days later, on Thursday, Gates, Morrell, and Gates's top military assistant took a Pentagon Gulfstream to the special forces base in Virginia Beach to meet the team of heroic SEALs. Gates had heard the classified after-action report that had been delivered at the White House, but he wanted to hear it from the SEALs themselves.

What stood out to Morrell was their demeanor. Here was a team of men who had just risked their lives to take down the most wanted man in the world, and had flown through another not-so-friendly country's sovereign airspace to do so. They were home, safe and successful. They should be thrilled, joyous and jubilant. Instead, Morrell said, it was as if there was no adrenaline pumping through their veins. "It was much more clinical than I expected," he said, even "sterile."

The next day, Obama flew to Fort Campbell, Kentucky, where the SEAL team gathered once again in a drab classroom. Obama, too, was struck by their appearance — they didn't look like action stars. McRaven had told Obama they would answer every question he had, except which of them had pulled the final trigger. Obama didn't ask; instead, he wanted to know about the helicopter pilot who had maneuvered a crashing aircraft into a safe landing. He wanted to know about the translator who had helped turn neighborhood residents away, to minimize potential civilian casualties. The team used a model of bin Laden's compound to show the president, in detail, what they had done.

Obama also wanted to know about Cairo, the dog the team had with them. "I would like to meet that dog," he said.

"Mr. President, then I would advise you to bring treats," one of the SEALs replied.[14]

From Donald Trump on a Tuesday to Osama bin Laden on a Sunday, it would be hard to find a weirder week for the Obama presidency. Yet in many ways, that week sums it up about as well as any seven-day period: major high, frustrating low, bizarre twenty-first-century media firestorms that the White House decided to both feed and put out, leaving supporters relieved, opponents frustrated, and observers at times confused. This was Barack Obama's White House life, especially in the first term, trying to do great big things while simultaneously having to deal with some of the smallest of small politics of Washington and the media, successful in killing one of the world's greatest villains and yet unable to vanquish ferocious, sometimes lunatic, distraction and obstruction at home.

And it's also why no normal American ever seeks the presidency or fully appreciates the need for a president to be such a compartmentalizer. A week before meeting the SEALs who killed bin Laden, the president was calling a hasty press conference to answer a false charge from one of the great self-promoters of the modern era. As he was busy telling jokes to a crowd of Washington press and VIPs, he was overseeing what was likely the most daring American military operation in decades. He was also still trying to feel his way with regard to the Arab Spring, including at this moment trying to help Libyan protesters topple their longtime authoritarian leader, Muammar Gaddafi. During this period of the presidency, Obama was starting to relish opportunities to deal with national security challenges because he could avoid Congress.

If one looked closely, there was a pattern that would only grow: when he had to work with other elected officials, Obama found himself hitting wall after wall. When he didn't, when his team was small and the line of command clear, he achieved much of what he set out to accomplish. Of course, later he could come to learn that some of his successful small, defined operations internationally didn't always end cleanly. From Ukraine to Syria and even Egypt, the president would come to view many of his national security challenges as being as difficult as dealing with the House Republicans. There was no doubt that Republicans in Congress were doing everything they could to destroy the president's agenda, but if Barack Obama wanted to glimpse the other great obstruction, he needed only to look into the mirror. Because while he didn't have a willing dance partner, he seemed completely flummoxed by how to navigate these political waters and ask for a dance.

CHAPTER TWELVE

The Chief Executive Learns to Manage

M ike Strautmanis has a long pedigree as a Washington hand. He had been chief of staff to the general counsel at the United States Agency for International Development during the Clinton years, then served as legislative director to Representative Rod Blagojevich. During law school, he had worked at the legal firm Sidley Austin, where he met Michelle Obama and eventually her husband, Barack. Because of that friendship, in November 2004 he had been tasked with showing the senator-elect from Illinois around Capitol Hill.

At one point, the two men paused in the Hart Senate Office Building to take a break. "So, Mike," Obama said, "what do you want to do in my Senate office?"

Strautmanis thought about it. He had been around Washington long enough to want a shot at the chief of staff's job. He'd never run a Senate office before, but he had seen how a good office operates, and he thought he was up to it.

But Obama had a different idea. After all, he asked Strautmanis, did he really think both the senator and the chief of staff should be learning the ropes of their new jobs at the same time? For his part, Obama didn't have any experience running such a big office. His budget, provided by the Senate, would be about $3.5 million a year, and he would have to use that money to set up field offices, then divide salaries among senior, legislative, and constituent service staffs. And for all the attention Obama drew to his healthy ego, he acknowledged his shortcomings. In fact, he had already approached the man he wanted to run his Senate office — Pete Rouse.

What Barack Obama was good at was oratory, as he had demonstrated during his Senate campaign and the convention speech on John Kerry's behalf that vaulted him into the national political spotlight in 2004. What he was not good at was organizing and managing a staff. Even before Rouse had come on board, Obama had hired Robert Gibbs, his campaign spokesman, and then a scheduler; Rouse told him to build an organizational chart, making decisions about how many Illinois-based staffers and Washington-based staffers he wanted first and filling in the names later.

Gibbs and David Axelrod had wanted Obama to

move quickly to open offices downstate, to increase his visibility in the most Republican parts of Illinois. They wanted to open nine or ten offices throughout the state, which would eat up a big part of his budget. But Rouse talked them out of this; if they decided to shuffle priorities later and to hire more legislative staffers in Washington, it would generate bad press in downstate newspapers if doing so meant shuttering an office in a smaller community. Wait until the office is established and priorities are set, Rouse counseled, before you commit to opening too many outposts back home.

Those were the sorts of decisions that counted as important before Barack Obama ran for president. And even the decisions he had to make as a candidate were relatively straightforward, since he had Axelrod and Plouffe organizing the ground game and fund-raising sides of things. They established and fixed the primary schedule; mapped out the appearances with intent; and timed the debates so that he could practice in advance. Running for president is hard until you actually get elected, and then you miss the predictability of it.

That simplicity ended the moment Obama's mailing address changed to 1600 Pennsylvania Avenue. The man who had never led a group of employees larger than the *Harvard Law Review* staff, a statewide campaign, the resulting Senate office, and a small circle of presidential campaign advisors would now head the four-million-employee executive branch. He would be learning to manage on the fly, and it wouldn't always be pretty.

To a degree, every president faces the same challenge: no other organization in the world completely changes its top leadership — in essence, its entire headquarters staff — every four or eight years. Furthermore, every White House organizational chart is different: the way Bill Clinton set up his staff was completely different from the way George W. Bush did. And while every new White House tries to learn from the mistakes of its predecessors, there is no better reminder that the presidency of the United States is the most difficult job in the world than the length of time it takes a new White House to figure out exactly how to operate.

Even before he was elected, Obama let it be known that he had been influenced by the last president from Illinois, Abraham Lincoln. He frequently mentioned historian Doris Kearns Goodwin's book on Lincoln's cabinet, *Team of Rivals,* and hinted that he wanted to model his own cabinet in the same fashion. Some of his choices reflected that wish: Clinton, Gates, Tom Vilsack.

Obama, many of his advisors and close associates say, wanted the best available staff for any given role, and he pursued those individuals with little regard for the way they would interact. One advisor compared Obama's staffing decisions to those of a

basketball coach who pursues LeBron James, Kobe
Bryant, Kevin Durant, Carmelo Anthony, and Chris
Paul—the five best players in the NBA—rather than
a team composed of players who would work well
together. Superstars bring with them heavy egos; so
did Obama's initial staff. The good news for Obama
in that early period is that everyone wanted to work
for him, and many were willing to take lesser titles
if they had real portfolios. But the importance of
teamwork was one of the big lessons he'd learn before
his first Fourth of July in the White House.

In most White Houses, the chief of staff is a gate-
keeper of sorts, controlling the volume and flow of
paper that would cross the president's desk and the
advisors who would walk into the Oval Office. While
each chief of staff serves his purpose, the general
authority of the position rarely fluctuates. But to
Obama, a famously introverted person who trusted
the counsel of only a few close advisors, the chief of
staff became but one leg of the stool supporting the
president. There were four centers of power in
Obama's White House—the chief of staff; the senior
political advisor (first David Axelrod, then David
Plouffe); Pete Rouse, who had virtually unlimited
access to the president; and Valerie Jarrett, Obama's
longest-serving and most trusted personal counselor.
Of these four power centers, Jarrett's was the most
controversial internally. She was, essentially, the "first
friend," not an unimportant position in any White

House. She was the one person who knew Obama before he was Obama, and although having that perspective is important to most presidents it can chafe on the professional staff, who can quickly grow resentful if the friend gets the last word on big decisions. Jarrett was not well thought of by many of the president's new West Wing team, especially Rahm and Gibbs but even Axelrod, though Axelrod could hide his annoyance a lot better than his more hotheaded colleagues.

Gibbs, Axelrod, and Plouffe all had run-ins with Jarrett, and their negative feelings toward her probably influenced Rahm's opinion more than he will admit. But Jarrett had a trump card that none of the other senior advisors had, a close relationship with the First Lady, which is why every attempt Rahm, Gibbs, Plouffe, and others made at convincing the president to push Jarrett aside never came to fruition. Their issues with Jarrett were substantive: in particular her portfolio was building relationships with the business community, an effort that many in the West Wing believe she failed at. And yet they didn't get why she didn't pay a price — in a nutshell, that's where the resentment came from.

Advisors come and go, but for the president, Valerie was someone who was around before the presidency, and she'll be someone who will be there after it. Most important, as a few of these aggrieved senior staffers would come to learn and in fact appreciate,

Jarrett kept the "East Wing" in check. Michelle Obama is not a shrinking violet, but she understood that politically she couldn't be another Hillary Clinton as First Lady, even if she wanted to. Michelle trusts and knows Valerie, and the same cannot be said for any other senior advisor to her husband. One advisor remembers the president sympathizing with a particular critique of Jarrett, but he made it clear that it was important that she be in the room, because it was important to Michelle that Valerie be in the room.

To Rahm Emanuel, the fact that he was but one of four power centers chafed. Emanuel had held virtually every job in Washington—a member of Congress, a member of Democratic leadership, a top staffer at the Democratic Congressional Campaign Committee, and a staffer in Bill Clinton's White House. That's what had attracted Obama in the first place: Rahm had been there and done that, and Obama needed someone to help him navigate the rocky shoals of governing.*

But what Emanuel saw was a president trying to be his own chief of staff. Rahm, upon reflection, drew parallels between Obama and John F. Kennedy. In his *Portrait of Camelot,* the historian Richard Reeves wrote that Kennedy had realized he was

---

* A testament to Emanuel's reach and grasp in Washington: when he got to the White House, he tried to import his contact list, all 6,000 names, onto his computer. The software crashed under the burden.

trying to play that same role. It was no small thing, Emanuel believed, that Obama and Kennedy had been senators. In that role, it was possible to be both the elected official and the chief of staff—to make sure the mail got out, the trains ran on time, the legislation was filed when it needed to be, and that he was on time to get to a speech. Famously frenetic himself, Emanuel had done the same thing when he was in Congress. But you just couldn't do that as president.

Not so secretly, Rahm hated his job. He felt Obama had regularly encouraged others to go around the chief of staff. Even when Emanuel got results—passing cap-and-trade legislation through the House, or getting a health care bill—he didn't see his sphere of influence within the White House expanding. It became immensely frustrating. So when the longtime mayor of Chicago, Richard M. Daley, announced that he wouldn't run for re-election, it took Emanuel about a minute to decide to leave the White House, return home to Chicago, and run for one of the two offices he had long coveted. Emanuel had given up his hopes of becoming Speaker of the House when his president had called him to service; realizing he was nearing the "sell-by" date of most chiefs of staff, Emanuel had decided he wouldn't pass up another opportunity to achieve one of his life's goals.

Emanuel's departure coincided with another

change in Washington. As the man brought in to work with the Democratic Congress, many of whom he had helped elect during his time in House leadership, Emanuel had watched in agony as Republicans had taken back 63 House seats—and the Speaker's gavel—in the 2010 midterm elections. So to work with the new Republican majority, and to bring more order to the White House than Rahm had, Emanuel and Axelrod told Obama to reach out to another Chicago ally, Bill Daley.

On paper, Daley was an excellent choice: he had served in Bill Clinton's administration during an era of divided government, and he had deep connections within the business community, which could serve the administration well as it tried to pressure Republicans on Capitol Hill.

But almost from the beginning, Daley proved a poor fit. Though he was from Chicago and knew Obama socially, the two had little real rapport. (In their first meeting, Obama told Daley he liked to be out of the office and back home for dinner by 6:30 so he could spend time with his daughters. Daley admired Obama's commitment to his young family, but it served as an early indicator for the new chief of staff that Obama, unlike Clinton, had little patience for politics as usual.) And Washington itself had changed in the decade since Daley had last worked inside the Beltway. Gone were the politicians—Democrats and Republicans—whom Daley had worked with.

Almost immediately, Daley wondered just how much power he would have over a staff someone else had built. When chiefs of staff had rolled over in the past, some senior staffers would go with them. "What Bill Daley remembers was that the first day Erskine Bowles became chief of staff [for Bill Clinton], he fired Harold Ickes, who was a twenty-year personal friend of the Clintons and a key person who got Bill Clinton elected in 1992," recalled Ron Klain, Joe Biden's chief of staff.

But Obama liked his crop of advisors, and he wouldn't let Daley bring in his own people. Daley was allowed to bring a single staffer, David Lane, to the White House with him. Less than a month into the job, Daley went to Obama with a plan for a dramatic shake-up, mostly in the communications department; about the only person Daley didn't want to at least think about replacing was Plouffe, who had just assumed Axelrod's job (and actual office) in the West Wing. By spring Daley would still be pushing for big changes, and even suggested firing himself. Obama didn't think that necessary, even as his poll numbers sank.

Obama had introduced Daley to the White House press corps on Thursday, January 6, 2011. Two days later, a deranged gunman shot nineteen people, including Arizona representative Gabrielle Giffords, in a supermarket parking lot in Tucson, killing six. Daley didn't yet have his security clearance when he was called to the Situation Room. In February, a massive earthquake off the coast of Japan sent a tsunami roaring onto the coast, badly damaging a nuclear power plant at Fukushima and setting off the most dangerous nuclear disaster since Chernobyl—never mind the Arab Spring and the bin Laden raid, which all came in the first five months of Daley's tenure. But chaotic external events are actually expected; it was the clash with Republicans in Congress, a slow-motion train wreck that everyone saw coming, that would turn into Daley's greatest challenge.

It had been routine in years past for Congress to simply automatically raise the country's credit card spending limit, known as the debt ceiling, but Plouffe began to worry almost immediately after Republicans won back control of the House that this time would be different. Republicans believed they had won a mandate to cut spending and shrink government, and they viewed the debt ceiling as a way to extract concessions from the White House. The more extreme faction of the House Republican Conference didn't believe the debt ceiling should be raised at all, making the politics—both for the White House and for House Speaker John Boehner—even more complicated.

Beyond the external crises, Daley got off to a rocky start with the staff he inherited. He saw no point in continuing the daily 8:30 a.m. meeting that included dozens of lower-ranking staffers; everyone who came, Daley thought, reported to someone who attended the 7:30 a.m. senior staff meeting, which drew about twenty people. Staff who were used to attending the later gathering valued it as a way to get a little face time with the boss; they griped later that Daley was cold and corporate.

Daley also cut out some senior advisors. His morning meeting became a very tight circle, just Pete Rouse, Valerie Jarrett, David Plouffe, and Bob Bauer, the White House counsel; once a week Daley would convene a broader meeting with about thirty-five attendees, more for show than to actually decide policy or politics — a decision that chafed many in the White House communications shop in particular, but also many in the policy offices that littered the second and third floors of the West Wing.

Daley wasn't making any friends outside the building, either. He had been brought in specifically to work with Boehner; the deal they came up with to fund the government, which made deep cuts to social spending programs, was what voters wanted to see, according to the polling Plouffe was reading. But when the deal was announced, Democrats on Capitol Hill were apoplectic. Harry Reid and his chief of staff, David Krone, believed Daley had given away the store and gotten little in return. Nancy Pelosi, now House minority leader, was incensed that her caucus had been cut out of the negotiations. That was Daley's biggest mistake: he did a terrible job of communicating to congressional Democrats what exactly he was doing with the House Republicans.

As the year progressed, Daley's relationship with Reid's office deteriorated. In an interview with the journalist Roger Simon, Daley made the mistake of saying, "On the domestic side, both Democrats and Republicans have really made it very difficult for the president to be anything like a chief executive."[1] The comment so angered Reid that he called Nancy-Ann DeParle, by then Daley's deputy chief of staff, and Obama himself to complain. (It didn't help Daley's cause that he hadn't bothered informing the White House press shop before he gave the interview. But at that point, Daley had little regard for the press shop.)

And there was no evidence that Daley's relationship with Boehner had helped the White House. The two men spoke frequently, and Boehner tried to convey the difficult political position he faced. His conference wanted to slash any spending they could, and the typical deal making that had defined Washington for generations would be much harder to do; it certainly was going to take a lot more elbow grease on the White House's part, which may or may not have succeeded anyway given the "don't give in to anything" strategy that the rank-and-file House Republicans demanded of their Speaker. Looking back, Daley would admit that he hadn't fully appreciated the position Boehner was in. But blaming House Republican intransigence was seen by some as a cop-out. While Daley counts himself among those ex–West Wingers who have come to believe House Republicans were impossible to negotiate with, there was never a "get caught trying" attitude. Of course, it's an attitude that comes from the top. Obama is someone who is comfortable accepting a station in life and working around it. So rather than try four straight months of daily one-on-one meetings with Republican senators trying to hammer out, say, a deal on immigration, the president would prefer the executive action route. The president's thinking: he assumes he'll get nowhere, so why waste the time; do what you can and move on. It's a perfectly rational way to look at things, but in Washington it's seen as giving up.

It was obvious early on that Boehner didn't have full control of his conference the way previous Speakers had, but the White House never attempted much of an alternate outreach strategy to woo some of the really powerful conservative players. Instead it kept going back to establishment standbys like the Chamber of Commerce and other business leaders, entities that the conservative base had given up on. In hindsight, there are some who do wish the White

House had tried to find its own working caucus of conservatives to at least talk with in the House, similar to the strategy Ronald Reagan used in the early 1980s with conservative Democrats. It may not have worked, but it would have been better to try. Whether fair or not, Daley was going to be judged on how well he made things work between the White House and House Republicans, and by the summer, many of the president's close aides had begun to question the Daley hire altogether.

At one point, after the debt ceiling negotiations had sent his approval rating plunging to dangerous new lows, Obama wanted to reset the conversation and return the White House's focus to jobs and the economy. On August 31, Daley called Boehner to ask that the president be allowed to address a joint session of Congress the following Wednesday, September 7. He thought Boehner had given him the okay; White House aides tweeted the news about an hour and a half after Daley hung up the phone.[2] But at the Capitol, Boehner denied he had agreed to anything—he'd heard Daley, he said, but that didn't mean he had agreed to call a joint session and it certainly didn't mean he had agreed to a date. After all, Republican presidential candidates were scheduled to debate the night of September 7, and an address to the nation would step on the GOP's moment in the spotlight. By afternoon the snafu had been fixed when the White House agreed to give the speech the following day, September 8 — an hour and a half before the Green Bay Packers kicked off the NFL season against the New Orleans Saints, and well before prime-time viewers were glued to their televisions. It was a minor mistake, but with Daley's standing inside the West Wing and among congressional Democrats, a costly one for him, given the appearance of the president "stepping to the side," and a bit of amateurism from a chief of staff who was supposed to bring precision and order.

The end of summer 2011 could not have come soon enough for the Obama White House, and for the fledgling campaign building its foundations in Chicago. They were fighting wars on two fronts — one against the Republican House of Representatives in Washington, the other against a loud and raucous field of Republican presidential candidates traveling in Iowa and New Hampshire who were united only by their deep loathing for the man in the White House.

One war had been fought to a stalemate; the White House had tried, and failed, to reach a grand bargain with Speaker John Boehner. The potential disaster of smashing through the debt ceiling had been averted, but at what cost? Congress's approval ratings were in shambles, which was a positive for a president who still valued his image as an outsider come to change the nation's capital. But Obama's ratings sank as well, not as low as Congress's, but to the low 40s, the nadir of his first term. The entire political system in Washington never fully recovered from the debt ceiling debacle, and to this day, both the president and Congress have seen their approval ratings essentially stuck in this spot.

In early September, as they were digging out of the debt ceiling mess, Messina and Plouffe, the two men who would have the largest share in crafting Obama's re-election efforts, discussed whether the race was still winnable. It was the first moment in which Messina had contemplated the prospect that Barack Obama might be a one-term president. It was amazing to Plouffe, who had spent the first two years of Obama's presidency outside the White House bubble, how oblivious many in the West Wing were to the president's precarious political position. It was so bad at the start of 2011, when Plouffe became a full-time West Winger, that he decided to give a presentation at a staff retreat organized by Daley at Fort McNair, just across the Potomac in Arlington, Virginia, to walk everyone through how easily the president could lose. The presentation was classic Plouffe, not very emotional and filled with data, including a reminder of how Republicans had just won key races in 2010 in a slew of states the president had carried in 2008, including Florida, Wisconsin, Ohio, and Iowa; toss in Virginia's slight move to the right in both 2009 and 2010, and the path to defeat for the president was fairly obvious to Plouffe. And now it was to the rest of the folks stuck in the bubble. As one senior official remembers, "Most people were walking around here for a long period of time blithely unaware of how hard our election would be. It ended up being easier than we thought and less painful than we thought, for a whole host of reasons having to do with Mitt Romney."

But it was amazing how difficult it was for Plouffe and others to convince the West Wing elite that they could lose. There were two main reasons why Democratic elites were so cocky about 2012, 2010 notwithstanding. One was demographics, the assumption that the minority vote (both black and Hispanic) was only going to grow and it wasn't going to the Republicans. The second reason was the unimpressive Republican presidential field; these folks couldn't imagine even a candidate like Romney beating Obama. The only senior official who did drink that bitter anti–Kool-Aid was communications director Dan Pfeiffer, but others dismissed Pfeiffer's daily "we're going to lose" fears as simply "Dan being Dan."

As for Messina, he was more of a realistic optimist. Messina's résumé was chockablock with prestigious jobs that screamed Washington insider—stints as a top aide to Max Baucus, the senator from Messina's adopted home state, Montana, and with a dozen campaigns around the country. His boyish face complemented the impression of him as soft-spoken, a trait that belied his penchant for swearing up a storm at the slightest provocation. He was another of those Obama White House oddities, a creature of Washington who now worked to change it.

After the 2008 primaries had concluded, Plouffe, whose people skills are one of his weak points, had threatened to quit; he wanted to focus more on strategy, not on being a manager. But Obama wanted to find a compromise, so the decision was made to hire a deputy to help Plouffe but not give him a title that included the word "deputy" (titles always matter with Beltway types). Messina had a mind for organization thanks to the battles he had fought in other campaigns, so the Obama team brought him in with the goal of orchestrating the meteoric staffer growth that happens when a primary campaign begins focusing on a general election.

Messina would take the original Obama for America from a 550-person organization focused on primary states to a 3,000-person group with outposts in nearly every city and town of any size in a battleground state. He was the chief operating officer, and it became clear that he would be the campaign-manager-in-waiting when 2012 rolled around—essentially the same role he played in 2008, but with more authority.

Months before the midterm elections, when it had become clear that Democrats would lose the House and when Messina and others were focusing on key

Senate races they believed would preserve the Democratic majority, he and the president spoke briefly about the campaign to come. How, Obama wanted to know, would Messina organize a re-election campaign? At this point, Plouffe had already made the decision that the headquarters should remain in Chicago, unlike the re-election efforts of Bush and Clinton, who both chose the Washington area for their re-election headquarters instead of going back to Austin and Little Rock, respectively. So Messina started to outline an organization that was similar to 2008's, but with an obvious acknowledgment that the campaign still had to be run out of the White House, simply for continuity purposes. But that was the extent of what they mapped out; Plouffe was still the chief architect and ultimately would be the campaign CEO. Messina and Obama held off on any more discussions until after the midterm elections; in Hawaii that winter, during Obama's annual family vacation and after another exhausting session of a lame-duck Congress, Obama formally offered Messina the job.

Among those who had been welcomed to the White House to offer Obama advice had been Ken Mehlman. Like some of the other informal advisors (such as Ken Duberstein, who had intimated his interest in joining the White House staff), he was a Republican, but he had been in a position similar to Messina's just a few years earlier. As George W. Bush's campaign manager in 2004, Mehlman had steered his candidate to a second term despite weak poll numbers and what looked like a strong opponent—coincidentally, also from Massachusetts. What's more, Mehlman had managed a race that included a big-thinking überstrategist, Karl Rove, who would guide the campaign from a 30,000-foot level. Their relationship would be roughly equivalent to the way Messina and Plouffe, who would handle Obama's overarching strategy, would interact.

After a post-2004 stint as chairman of the RNC, Mehlman had publicly retired from politics to take a lucrative job with a Wall Street firm. But he had that personal connection with Obama that few in Washington shared: they were law school buddies. And while not close friends, the two men had a very good "professional" relationship. Such relationships, born of tangential histories and convenience, usually qualify as friendships in Washington, and were precisely the type Obama was not keen on establishing or maintaining. He made an exception for Mehlman, perhaps out of loyalty or for that political convenience he generally recoiled from. Indeed, Team Obama loved leaking anecdotes about this "personal friendship" with Mehlman, especially during times when official Washington was being extra-critical of the president for what appeared to be a lack of outreach to Republicans.

From Mehlman and the Bush 2004 campaign, Messina took a few key lessons: Mehlman and Rove had disagreed frequently, occasionally sharply, giving rise to various factions within the campaign and, from time to time, inconvenient media stories about internal feuds. Messina and Plouffe wanted desperately to avoid that; they agreed early on they would have a daily phone call, just between the two of them, to hash out any disagreements they might have. The conclusion they came to would be the united front they presented to the world, and they would never take their disputes public, even with other senior staffers on the campaign.

Mehlman also warned Messina about the dangers of allowing conclusion by committee. Decision making must be controlled by just a few top aides, he advised; the tighter the circle, the fewer details would leak to the media. That was music to Plouffe's ears and potentially uncomfortable for Messina, who never enjoyed being on the "losing" side of a debate; he cherished political cover and consensus. Plouffe was a different cat, comfortable ruling with an iron fist even if uncomfortable sending the message campaignwide.

Finally, Mehlman advised, make sure the mechanics of communications are correct. The White House is used to controlling everything about the president, from his schedule to his message. But the campaign would increasingly drive those decisions, and eventually, by virtue of the demands of the calendar, it would become the dominant player in the president's life. Communicating between the White House and Chicago, and establishing processes to do so, would be critical to keeping the president and his campaign on message.

Plouffe had always been one to hold decisions and deliberations close to the vest. He believed in keeping the circle of decision makers small and tight, to avoid both public sniping and leaks to the media. In that regard, it was easy to see why Obama trusted Plouffe so much; Plouffe was so similar to Obama, in the eyes of many West Wingers, that they referred to him as a white clone. But at the beginning of the president's re-election campaign, Obama and his senior aides tried to be inclusive. This was in response to the growing narrative in Democratic Party circles that Obama was *only* about Obama, Team Obama was *only* about Obama, and oh, by the way, we're not that interested in the advice of folks who were involved in *losing* campaigns (read: Hillary and Kerry).

One strategy session, in the fall of 2011, included so many people that the meeting had to be held in the State Dining Room, a 1,700-square-foot venue that can accommodate up to 140 guests.[3] Messina, who didn't like unnecessarily large meetings any more than Plouffe did, couldn't believe who had been included: two members of the First Lady's staff, three from Biden's, and even, for some reason, Rob Nabors from the Office of Congressional Liaison, who at the time was supposed to be all about legislation and had little experience outside Washington. These folks were in addition to dozens of senior aides and a few outside consultants—all in all, the size of a meeting that should have been called only to rally troops and fire them up, not to share strategy, let alone elicit ideas. The only thing missing was a podium and a line of cameras. It appeared to be an "event" that the press should cover, not some secret strategy meeting.

After formalities and a presentation by Messina, the president himself took control of the gathering. He dropped his guard—something even close aides had seen him do only a handful of times—and offered frank assessments of his performance. He talked about what had worked in the first three years and what hadn't, about how he wanted the campaign to play out. Most strikingly, he talked about his own flaws and shortcomings, offering the audience a glimpse into his famously private thinking. Then he made a special point of asking his staff not to repeat what he had said. It represented, Obama said, his raw, unfiltered feelings, which he had shared only because he trusted his staff so much.

A few weeks later, reporter John Heilemann called Messina. The coauthor of the wildly popular book

Game Change, about the 2008 election, was in the process of reporting a sequel about the 2012 campaign. Heilemann, along with coauthor Mark Halperin, were desperate to source build at the highest levels of the re-election effort, and in an apparent attempt to coerce Messina to play ball, Heilemann proceeded to read Messina a recap of what Obama had said at the supposedly private meeting, in startling detail. Obama's words would become public.

Messina was shaken. If deliberations that should have been secret were leaking out this early and quickly, the campaign had a problem — doubly so, given that Obama had made a point of asking for confidentiality.

Before the next meeting, which included most of the same people, Messina and Obama had lunch on the White House veranda. Messina had asked for the lunch, and Obama was immediately suspicious. "Plouffe says you have something to tell me," Obama began. Messina related what had happened: a senior staffer had betrayed the president's trust. Messina had been fingered, many times unfairly, as a frequent leaker in the first term of the Obama presidency, and he didn't want that reputation for the campaign, which served as a motivator for him to make sure his boss knew about what had happened.

Obama was furious. In the strategy meeting that followed about a week later, Messina opened with his usual presentation, to get the White House and

Chicago on the same page. Obama stopped him and took the floor. He railed against the leak and the leaker, making clear how wounded he was that one of his own would relate such sensitive information. He said he would be in the Oval Office if the leaker wanted to confess without retribution. Then he stormed out and waited. And waited some more.

With Obama stewing in the Oval Office, Biden was the next one to take the floor. For forty minutes the vice president—the man who had run against Obama in 2008—laid into the staff. For Joseph R. Biden there was no deeper insult, no greater betrayal, than a breach of trust like that. What makes every one of his gaffes forgivable in Obama's eyes is Biden's loyalty. "How could you do this?" Biden yelled, red-faced. "You know I ran against him. Name one time I've been disloyal to him."

After Biden was done, the next yeller in the room was Robert Gibbs, who was known to be friendly with the media but was always considered loyal, some-times to a fault. That Gibbs was yelling was noth-ing new to that crowd—the Alabama transplant had a quick temper, as everyone who had ever worked with him knew, usually firsthand. Others chimed in as well, including David Axelrod and Anita Dunn, less in an attempt to shame the leaker into coming forward than to remind the assembled that some-one might have leaked this by accident. Some in that room interpreted the remarks by Dunn and

Axelrod as potential confessions. Perhaps they had told a friend what the president said, and that person then told Heilemann or Halperin.

Despite all the pleas, all the yelling, all the guilt, the leaker never came forward. There was finger-pointing, but some of it seemed to be about airing a grievance against someone that one member of the team didn't like. For instance, there isn't a lot of love lost between Dunn and Gibbs. Meanwhile, Obama sat alone in the Oval Office. It was the last time so many people were included in a strategy meeting. No serious campaign meeting, held every Sunday until Election Day, included more than a handful of close aides, the small cabal that Obama felt could be trusted: Plouffe, Messina, Axelrod, hard-charging communications expert Stephanie Cutter, Larry Grisolano, who oversaw the campaign's advertising, Rouse, Jarrett, new chief of staff Jack Lew, and Pfeiffer. And the happiest person in that room: Plouffe.

Obama had initially offered Daley the chief of staff job with the understanding that he would stay through the 2012 re-election. But again, Daley was disappointed; by the summer of 2011, it became clear that he wouldn't have a major role in crafting the campaign, a role he coveted. Plouffe, along with Messina in Chicago, would control the campaign's message and strategy. Meanwhile, the campaign wanted little to do with Democrats on Capitol Hill or the fights they were having with Republicans. Daley said later he had never met a group of people more disdainful of Congress than the White House staff he worked with—an irony, given that so many of them had gone to work for Obama after long careers on the Hill. In fact, this had infuriated many Washington veterans: not that Obama was dismissive of them; they could accept that, it was who he was. What really chafed some of the Beltway crowd about the insular White House was that these same people worked on Capitol Hill in the 1990s, and they all used to complain about how insular the Clinton White House was. Plouffe was a Gephardt guy back in the day, and yet he would hold the same contempt for Congress that the president did.

That created, in Daley's mind, two universes—one based in Chicago, dedicated to campaign politics, and the other based on Capitol Hill, dedicated to Washington politics. And he wasn't involved in either one.

During a weeklong vacation over the December holidays, Daley decided he wanted to return home to Chicago. He told Obama shortly after New Year's, just a few days before his first anniversary on the job and only ten months before Obama would face voters. Obama asked him to reconsider, not because he was thrilled with the job Daley had been doing but because of the upheaval a new chief of staff at the start of an election year could cause; a day later, Daley hadn't changed his mind.[4]

A week later, when Obama thanked Daley for his service, he introduced his third chief of staff, a policy wonk named Jack Lew, who had run the Office of Management and Budget. White House staffers, and Capitol Hill, breathed a collective sigh of relief. Lew was a Washington veteran who was leading the one part of the executive branch that actually has its fingers in every part of the government. There really isn't a better position to be in if you want to truly understand how the entire government works, but more important in this age of budget fights, his appointment meant there was no need for on-the-job training for the biggest battles the chief might have to face.

Leading OMB is a job that's nearly as stressful as running the White House. It requires a breadth and depth of knowledge about the machinations of government and policy unlike almost any other, so perhaps it's not a surprise that Obama's two predecessors had also turned to their OMB directors when the chief of staff job opened up — George W. Bush had plucked Josh Bolten out of OMB, and Bill Clinton had elevated Leon Panetta.

Lew was in many ways the antithesis of Obama's first two chiefs of staff. Where Emanuel and Daley were bombastic, possessed of big personalities, and prone to snapping at staff, Lew was calm and collected. Where Emanuel was a master of politics and Daley a networker extraordinaire, Lew was a career manager—he had run OMB under Bill Clinton, then managed operations for New York University before serving as chief operating officer for a branch of Citigroup. John Podesta had pushed Hillary Clinton to hire him at the State Department; Lew's first job in the Obama administration was deputy secretary of state for management and resources.

An observant Jew who took his devotion to the Sabbath seriously, Lew brought his discipline as well as organizational and supervisory skills to a White House badly in need of staff leadership and a morale boost. For the first time since Obama took office, staffers started to recognize *process;* a policy idea ran through channels, from a low-level policy advisor to his or her supervisor, and on up the chain. Only those issues that demanded a presidential decision landed on Obama's desk.

Perhaps most crucially, where Emanuel feuded with his old colleagues on Capitol Hill and then mourned with them after their defeats, and Daley couldn't speak to Harry Reid without one of them throwing something, Lew enjoyed good relations with Congress. Like most of Obama's senior advisors, he had come from the Hill, working for Tip O'Neill in the 1980s before taking a series of administration jobs. But unlike those who felt disgust and disdain for members of the opposing congressional party, Lew had worked and negotiated with Democrats and Republicans for years.

Emanuel served at a time when managing Hill Democrats was crucial to Obama's agenda; Daley's purpose had been to reach out to the business community. Lew would fill two roles—he would put together a management structure, and he would negotiate with Hill Republicans over the budget cuts and debt limit expansion that had dominated 2011, issues that sat comfortably in his wheelhouse.

But even though Lew was a better fit with Obama's developing sense of a chief of staff's role, he, too, clashed with his negotiating partners. Members of Congress felt he talked down to them, using his mastery of the federal budget and its intricacies to bludgeon them into submission. It got so bad during the debt ceiling negotiations that Boehner and Eric Cantor asked the White House to send Gene Sperling, head of the National Economic Council, to negotiate instead of Lew.[5]

While Lew brought veteran experience to the running of the White House, Robert Gates, a veteran of four previous administrations, was noticing a profound generational change elsewhere. As he'd sat around the Situation Room or in the Oval Office when George H. W. Bush had been president, the decision-makers in the room influencing the president were few in number and senior in rank. Usually only the president, the vice president, and the national security advisor were involved.

But now, Gates was sitting in meetings with Ben

Rhodes, who was half his age, and Samantha Power, who had returned to the White House in a post at the NSC, among other more junior staffers. And everyone, he noticed, was taking notes. ("Everybody's a note-taker," Gates bemoaned to one top aide.) Gates was exasperated; in Bush's administration, that sort of thing would have invited a presidential rebuke

Those younger foreign policy aides were the ones who more accurately reflected Obama's worldview. But Obama was letting more voices into the room than previous presidents, older advisors complained. And those voices were winning the argument, because they were playing Obama's tune. The younger aides were "total idealists," said one Gates advisor. "It's honorable that they have these positions and they believe so much in the president's policy and the power of communications in this world, but you've also got guys who are much more experienced foreign policy–wise who . . . were trumped." Regardless of political positions, this addition of more and more voices was emblematic of Obama's management style — for better and for worse.

There was one thing the no-drama Obama had never been good at — firing someone. During his Senate career, during his campaigns for federal office, no one had really been fired. People were simply layered or worked around. Daley made his own decision to quit. Daley's brother, the mayor of Chicago, gave Rahm Emanuel incentive to quit by saying he wouldn't run again. Jim Jones had opened the door on his own.

But if people didn't volunteer to depart, they usually stayed, further complicating the White House dynamic. Where there should have been a clear chain of command, there were official and unofficial hierarchies. Sometimes this meant that voices that would have been excluded were heard, to positive effect. But it also meant a lack of focus and follow-up, with inadequate clarity on who was ultimately responsible—themselves or the other people who seemed to be taking ownership of a decision.

Instead of giving someone a pink slip, Obama tended to promote them to another position somewhere else in government. Folks were shuffled, escorted out of the way, but not fired. A rare exception began to unfold on June 21, 2010, when a young press aide named Tommy Vietor walked into Robert Gibbs's office.

Vietor had in his hands a story that would run in the next month's issue of *Rolling Stone,* due to hit newsstands three days later. It was a piece about Stanley McChrystal, the army general who headed U.S. and NATO forces in Afghanistan. Already, McChrystal had gotten in trouble with the White House for publicly pooh-poohing Vice President Joe Biden's position that American troops should pull out of Afghanistan. And the White House still suspected that McChrystal had leaked his own strategy review, which called for an additional 40,000 troops to surge into Afghanistan, to the media in order to box the president in.

But the article, written by the late Michael Hastings,[6] went a lot farther. In the piece, Hastings quoted McChrystal's aides mocking Biden, Richard Holbrooke (at the time Obama's envoy to Afghanistan), and Ken Eikenberry, the U.S. ambassador. It portrayed a commander whose advisors openly questioned the president's interest in military affairs and who did little to stop such inappropriate chatter.

Gibbs barely finished reading the piece before he went to Rahm Emanuel's office. Emanuel told him to call Obama, who had returned to the residence to have dinner with his family. Gibbs met Obama in a walk-through that connects the residence and the Oval Office; after he'd read three paragraphs, Obama's normally cool demeanor began to crack. "I'll be in the Oval [Office] in ten minutes," the president told Gibbs. "Go get whoever's left in the building."

Hours beforehand, McChrystal had called Biden[7] while the vice president was flying between Illinois and Washington, aboard Air Force Two. Over a line crackling with static, McChrystal offered his apology for the remarks attributed to his staff but that would also be interpreted as opinions he shared. It was all news to Biden because the article had not yet gone public. Biden said he was sure nothing would come of it and rang off. Puzzled, the vice president called Obama to check in.[8]

At the Pentagon, alarm bells were ringing. But while both Robert Gates and Mike Mullen had spoken with McChrystal before about his hard edge, they believed in his strategy; what's more, he had only been on the job for a year, and both Gates and Mullen thought changing commanders in the middle of a war a second time, especially after just a few months on the job, could destabilize the situation on the ground.

Gates called the White House. He wanted an OK to put out a statement saying that nothing would happen to McChrystal, who was sure to be contrite. Losing McChrystal at that moment, Gates worried, would sap the momentum the United States had begun to build in Afghanistan.

But Obama was furious. "Tell him not to put out the statement," Obama told Gibbs. Obama summoned the general to the White House for a meeting.

As the Pentagon scrambled to save its general, McChrystal was strangely silent. He was an old-school soldier, someone who believed in owning up to his mistakes. He didn't offer excuses or shift the blame; indeed, it had been his officers who made the disparaging comments, not the general. But in taking the fall, McChrystal seemed to be giving his allies in the Pentagon no room to defend him.

Gibbs, who had defended the president since his days in the Senate, took particular offense at McChrystal's comments. At his press briefing on June 22, Gibbs refused repeatedly to say that McChrystal's job was safe. In the story, McChrystal's aides had told Hastings that Obama appeared disengaged and distracted during meetings on Afghanistan war strategy. "[McChrystal] will have [Obama's] undivided attention tomorrow," Gibbs shot back.

There was another question, one asked by the press but also foremost on Gates's mind: did the president still have faith in McChrystal's ability to run the war in Afghanistan? "We should wait and see what the outcome of that meeting is," Gibbs replied.[9]

Geoff Morrell, watching from his desk at the Pentagon, thought the answer sounded like nails being enthusiastically driven into a coffin. Morrell even told a reporter that he thought the press secretary was enjoying taking McChrystal to the woodshed. (He later called Gibbs to apologize for the cheap shot.) But the fact of the matter was, the president had no choice but to fire McChrystal if he was going to assert himself as commander in chief.

McChrystal knew it, too. And yet he found a strange sense of peace aboard the airplane that flew him from Kabul to Washington. He had "hours for reflection, free from the cacophony of opinions," he wrote later. McChrystal realized he was about to lose his job, yet he still didn't seek advice from any mentors.[10]

While McChrystal was still in the air, the conversation in Washington began about who would take over for him. The war was at a turning point, and both the White House and the Pentagon thought they needed a commander of stature to guide it if McChrystal was forced out.

Gibbs, who was as worried about the politics of the moment as anything else, floated the name of David Petraeus. McChrystal had become something of a minor celebrity as he ran the war effort in Afghanistan, but Petraeus was practically a legend since his counterinsurgency strategy had helped turn around the war in Iraq. He had cultivated relations with the press, whose glowing profiles never failed to mention his torturous jogging regimen, his tireless work habits, and his muscular physique; more than a few articles included anecdotes about the push-up contests he won against much younger soldiers serving in the field. He was so popular that some Republicans were talking about him as a future presidential candidate. (Adding fuel to the fire, albeit unintentionally, Petraeus's status as a native of New Hampshire meant that he'd show up in that first-in-the-nation primary state from time to time.)

At that moment, Petraeus was leading U.S. Central Command. Located in Tampa, CentCom (as it is known in military shorthand) is the site from which most modern wars, including Persian Gulf Wars I and II, are actually directed. Obama liked the idea of tapping a known quantity like Petraeus, and he took Gibbs's suggestion to Gates. The defense secretary had already thought of Petraeus, but he hadn't brought it to the White House because he thought Obama wouldn't go for it, given concerns about Petraeus's close relations with the media. Hearing this idea from the president actually made Gates more comfortable with the idea of relieving McChrystal of his duties.

Hours before Obama was to sit down with McChrystal, Petraeus's name came up again, at a White House senior staff meeting. Again, Gibbs spoke up in favor of the idea. But the senior advisors were less certain about whether Obama should give McChrystal the boot. Donilon, who had just assumed the title of national security advisor, couldn't seem to make up his mind.

"Tom," Pete Rouse injected, "you're going to see the president in an hour. He wants a recommendation on whether to fire General McChrystal. Now, the press secretary has a recommendation. And a replacement," Rouse continued, suggesting that if Gibbs's lack of national security experience didn't mean he couldn't come up with an idea, surely the in-house national security expert could. "I'd suggest that you, as the national security advisor, get one or two of those before you go see the president," lectured Rouse. It was a rare moment when Rouse publicly let loose against a peer.

And yet even in the Oval Office, Donilon seemed to argue both sides of the question. It was a habit of his that frustrated the other members of the president's inner circle no end. Donilon was known as well organized, a great person to execute someone else's decision and even pretty good at running meetings designed to share information. But as a decision-maker he was notoriously ineffective. The consummate staffer, he was smart as a whip, but his fear of being on the wrong side of a presidential decision would get the best of him. Ultimately that indecisiveness would be why the president went in the opposite direction when selecting Donilon's replacement; Susan Rice would not be afraid to disagree with the president, and in fact sometimes had the ability to change his mind, something Donilon wouldn't even try to do.

While the senior staff was, sort of, making the case for Petraeus to the president, McChrystal was meeting with Gates and Mullen at the Pentagon. Both the secretary and the chairman of the Joint Chiefs were working behind the scenes to convince Obama to stick with McChrystal, but the general was resigned to his likely fate.

As Obama contemplated the situation overnight, he decided that he couldn't tolerate the public expression of discontent from a military officer. If the military respects anything, it's the chain of command, and the president concluded that if he allowed McChrystal to dishonor that chain, he'd be setting the wrong example for the rest of the uniformed. He called Petraeus to offer him the job. (Of course, Petraeus himself would fall victim to controversy a little over two years later, after a year in command and then a year as director of the CIA. Citing an extramarital affair, he handed his own resignation in to the president.)

McChrystal's meeting in the Oval Office was short, he wrote later, and professional.[11] In the Rose Garden not long thereafter, Obama announced that he had accepted McChrystal's resignation.

"I don't make this decision based on any difference in policy with General McChrystal, as we are in full agreement about our strategy. Nor do I make this decision out of any sense of personal insult. Stan McChrystal has always shown great courtesy and carried out my orders faithfully," Obama said. "But war is bigger than any one man or woman, whether a private, a general, or a president. And as difficult as it is to lose General McChrystal, I believe that it is the right decision for our national security. The conduct represented in the recently published article does not meet the standard that should be set by a commanding general. It undermines the civilian control of the military that is at the core of our democratic system. And it erodes the trust that's necessary for our team to work together to achieve our objectives in Afghanistan."[12]

The executive who had built a reputation for keeping a small team of loyalists around him had demonstrated what happens when that loyalty is broken. McChrystal returned to his home at Fort McNair, where his wife, Annie, was waiting. He told her that their life in the army was over.[13]

For the president, it was a critical moment in his professional career, the first person of significance he had ever fired, not just as president but in his entire political life. It wasn't easy to get fired in the Obama White House, a fact that frustrated even some loyalists.

Many hoped that this McChrystal incident would stiffen the president's spine; down the road, arguably bigger mistakes would be made on the domestic side and would call for some equally decisive executive action. But as even the new team of advisors would find out early in the second term, Obama doesn't easily get talked into firing anyone.

CHAPTER THIRTEEN

A Challenger Emerges

I nside the White House, Biden's relationship with Obama only grew. The two men frequently had lunch, and Obama came to value Biden's advice, especially in areas of foreign policy. Biden had argued strenuously against a troop surge in Afghanistan, staking out the most liberal position among Obama's foreign policy advisors—in part out of principle, but also to provide the president with a real alternative to Clinton, Gates, and the hawks among Obama's counselors.

But Biden's relationship with Obama's chief political aides wasn't as smooth. He had not gotten along well with David Plouffe, which actually was a real point of personal frustration for the vice president. So after Plouffe didn't come to the White House at the start of the term, Biden ingratiated himself with the other David, Axelrod. He was much closer to Biden's age than was Obama, and he respected one aspect of Biden's talents. While Axelrod loved Obama's ability to wow a crowd, he thought of Biden as one of the more gifted person-to-person politicians he had ever seen.

Still, Biden's political instincts were decidedly old-school. At one point, in the months leading up to the midterm elections, Biden and Bill Clinton had persuaded each other that the White House's political troubles were exacerbated by its inability to convince the American public of the value of health care reform. The two men sketched plans—going so far as to write the text—for a brochure they wanted the Democratic National Committee to print. Tens of millions of copies would be dropped off at voters' homes, and the communications problem would be solved. Axelrod, Obama's political advisors, and even some of Biden's top aides thought the idea was decades out-of-date in an age of e-mail; the brochures were never printed.

The transition to full-on campaign mode meant West Wing staff changes, the two biggest being the departures of David Axelrod and Robert Gibbs. Although the Axelrod exit was part of a larger plan to prep for the re-election effort, Gibbs's decision to leave was a bit more sudden. While he had helped feed the chatter that he would like a break from serving as the president's chief spokesman (it entailed lots of time behind a podium answering reporters' questions), Gibbs didn't necessarily want to exit the White House altogether. Ideally, he was hoping to stay on in a more behind-the-scenes role as a senior advisor, even sharing some of the political duties with Plouffe. But Gibbs had clashed with a few key White House insiders, including Jarrett. And those clashes with Jarrett usually had something to do with the First Lady.

Gibbs was not always very diplomatic when talking to or about Jarrett, and he didn't do his best to hide his disdain for her. It was a tension that was tolerated for a while, even by the president. Gibbs was among the "guy's guys" the president liked to surround himself with, especially when on the road. But Gibbs also had a habit of being too cold and calculating about what he thought. When the First Lady was planning a girls' vacation in Spain while the president was leading a country that still felt it was in a recession, it fell to Gibbs to beg the president to talk her out of the trip. Obama understood how bad the jaunt would look politically, but he was not about to tell the First Lady no. Whatever deal the First Couple had cut—which essentially meant prioritizing Obama's career over Michelle's—was tough enough that the president didn't think he should ask her to cancel. Gibbs's playing bad guy got back to the First Lady, and she in turn would vent her displeasure with him to Jarrett. With no obvious other place for Gibbs in the West Wing, he chose not to push to stay. He could have, but there wasn't a lot of enthusiasm for it, and he didn't need to stay *that* badly. Thus he began to play a different role in the campaign.

Axelrod's exit was less abrupt. For one thing he was tired of living in an apartment in Washington, and with the campaign gearing up in Chicago he had more than the excuse of his family to move back.

When Axelrod left the White House after the midterm elections, he had been replaced by Plouffe. On the face of it, the newcomer (so to speak) and Biden should have had plenty to talk about; both came from Delaware, both had graduated from the University of Delaware, and both were fiercely loyal to and protective of Barack Obama. But the two men clashed. Plouffe saw Biden as a dinosaur, a generation sure to be the last of its political kind. For his part, the vice president saw disloyalty in Plouffe; here, after all, was a Delaware native who chose to work for Obama, and everyone in Delaware Democratic politics was a Biden guy. Except David Plouffe. The tension went back further: in 1988, when Biden ran for president the first time, Plouffe was working for a rival campaign, for Dick Gephardt, the Missouri Democrat.

Biden's relationship with Axelrod was much better, partly because they had similar outlooks on politics, and partly because their personalities matched—both were outgoing, prone to chatter in the cloakroom and newsroom, respectively. Privately,

Biden compared Plouffe with Obama: both are cool under fire to the point of being cold, both loathe to be ruffled, both prefer the counsel of a handful of allies and friends.

Still, Plouffe needed Biden. The assets the vice president brought to the White House—foreign policy expertise, deep relations with Congress—were great from a policy perspective, but Plouffe's single-minded focus, almost from the day he moved into his West Wing office, was to re-elect Barack Obama. And Biden had credibility with some voters that Obama did not, particularly seniors in the Rust Belt and Florida.

Plouffe, Axelrod, and Obama's political advisors understood that the electorate that had voted Obama into office had fundamentally changed. Minorities had become such a significant proportion of the electorate that Democrats (whose coalition is much more racially diverse than Republicans') could rely on them to offset the white voters who more reliably voted for the GOP candidate. Jimmy Carter needed 47 percent of the white vote to beat Gerald Ford in 1976; Bill Clinton and Ross Perot together accounted for 59 percent of the white vote in 1992, when Clinton won the White House. Democrats lost in 2000 and 2004, when they received 42 percent and 41 percent of the white vote, respectively. But, underscoring the rapid growth of minority voters since then, Obama had won decisively in 2008 when he took just 43 percent of the white vote. And while Plouffe thought they could win in 2012 with less than 40 percent of that vote, he didn't believe he had much margin for error.

There wasn't enough minority support to allow the White House to give up on white voters entirely. And as Obama's approval ratings fell, it was those former fans—whites, both men and women, usually with less education, living in the industrial Midwest (or former midwesterners living in Florida)—whose attitudes soured most.

Biden was part of the answer, a surrogate who could help slow the bleeding of white votes, or so he hoped.[1] He had an ability to connect with white working-class voters that Obama simply lacked. So in November 2011, a year before Election Day, the Obama campaign announced that it would dispatch Biden to several key states—Pennsylvania and Ohio, where salvaging as many of those white votes as possible was key to victory, and Florida, where Jewish voters held the secret to improving the president's white support. Biden would also make it a point to connect with union officials in key states, in hopes of maximizing votes from a traditional Democratic power base. Republican analyst Dan Schnur put it best in a comment to USA Today: "Obama provides the speeches, and Biden provides the blue-collar subtitles."[2]

As the fall of 2011 wore on and Messina and

Plouffe were openly nervous about Obama's chances, the man they considered his likely opponent was struggling.

The Republican Party has something of a tradition of nominating presidential candidates who have run before—in fact, whoever came in second last time around. John McCain, Bob Dole, George Herbert Walker Bush, even Ronald Reagan had all run and lost before they came back to win their party's nomination the next time they had a clean shot. After 2008, when McCain had outlasted a better-funded, better-staffed Mitt Romney, it became clear that Romney was next in line.

If they had placed bets, even as early as 2008, Obama's advisors would have staked their fortunes on facing Romney four years down the road. And it was obvious that they had a wary eye on the likely Republican nominee even before Obama took the oath of office in 2009.

Given the small circle of elite politicians, it is not uncommon for candidates to have relationships with their future opponents. In a quirk that demonstrated just how unusual both Obama's and Romney's journeys had been, before Obama's inauguration the two had spoken directly to each other only a few times, and those exchanges had usually been a matter of seconds, done for cameras and not as camaraderie. The first time was in 2004, before Obama was even sworn in as a senator, when he and Romney were

guest speakers at the Gridiron dinner (the same dinner he would shirk a few years later). Most of his
and Romney's barbs were aimed at the same person,
the fast-rising star, Obama. Obama was all self-
deprecation: "It's like I was shot out of a cannon. I
am so overexposed, I make Paris Hilton look like a
recluse. After all the attention—*People* magazine,
GQ, Vanity Fair, Letterman—I figure there's
nowhere to go from here but down. So tonight, I
announce my retirement from the United States Senate. I had a good run."

Romney's poke at Obama was on the same topic.
He said Obama was "not seeking the limelight and
he's said that again and again and again on Letterman, on Leno, on *Meet the Press*..." And so it went.[3]

Their second ever conversation came in December 2008, when the president-elect called Romney
after Romney's wife had been diagnosed with breast
cancer. Obama asked Romney to convey his best
wishes for Ann's speedy recovery.[4] Otherwise their
interactions had been the standard pre- and postde-
bate handshakes.

One of those handshakes had been during the
2008 campaign, at a joint Democratic-Republican
debate, so Plouffe and the others had seen the potential Republican nominee onstage with their guy, holding his own. The Romney of 2008 was a very
aggressive debater, even more so than he would eventually be in 2012. In a sign of respect for, even trepi-

dation about, a future rival, the Obama White House would let slip more than a few times that they had Romney on the brain. Obama mentioned Romney at a ceremony awarding Edward Brooke, the last Republican senator from Massachusetts, a Congressional Gold Medal, in October 2009.[5] And press secretary Robert Gibbs brought up Romney's name for the first time in a daily briefing in March 2010, more than a year before Romney officially kicked off his presidential campaign.[6]

Perhaps most conveniently, the White House went to great lengths to compare its signature first-term accomplishment—reforming the nation's health care system—to Romney's greatest legislative accomplishment as Massachusetts governor, especially once the White House decided to go the mandate route. It even used some of the same advisors who had helped craft "RomneyCare" to come up with a version that would fit on the national stage—a fact the Obama White House enjoyed leaking and then touting.

Indeed, the image of Romney signing into law a bill actually known as Commonwealth Care at Boston's famed Faneuil Hall, with Ted Kennedy beaming as he looked over Romney's shoulder, gave the Obama White House a shield, an opportunity to point to a Republican governor's signature as evidence that its law would work on a national level and that it wasn't some wacky left-wing, socialistic idea. The image gave the Romney campaign constant headaches; as health care reform took on new and sinister meanings for Republican primary voters in 2012, Romney's rivals used the White House's association with Commonwealth Care to bludgeon the front-runner from the moment he jumped into the race. Before dropping out, Tim Pawlenty dubbed health care reform "ObomneyCare." It was a ham-handed and clunky phrase, but in some GOP corners, it stuck.

If Obama's opponents would fault him for turning his eyes to the White House mere months after arriving in the Senate, Romney's rivals would note the same single-minded focus. Elected as a moderate governor of bright-blue Massachusetts in 2002, Romney had once declared himself to the left of Ted Kennedy on gay rights issues. But since 2005, with an uphill re-election fight looming, Romney had carefully laid the groundwork for his evolution from Massachusetts moderate to mainstream national conservative. He opted against running for a second term, which he might have lost, thereby jeopardizing his presidential prospects; he became chairman of the Republican Governors Association, which gave him access to big donors who could fund his national ambitions; and he took a series of stands decidedly to the right of his previous positions. In a dramatic editorial published in the *Boston Globe,* Romney declared himself opposed to abortion, a conclusion he said he'd come to after conversations with religious figures.[7]

Romney had bragged about his accomplishments on health care during his 2008 campaign for president. But in the intervening years, the GOP's base had become ideologically more rigid, not just anti-Obama but, in the inarticulate words Romney once awkwardly used, "severely conservative." The Republican primary electorate had always been conservative, but now the establishment in Washington was feeling the need to appease this more vocal wing of the party. A fast-growing conservative news media was demanding strict adherence to a more conservative ideology, and they were leery of conservative newcomers. And although Romney veered to the right before there was a Tea Party, it wasn't soon enough for many. And then there was health care. Congressional Republicans, talk radio hosts, and tens of thousands of sign-waving, red-faced conservative activists denounced Obama's health care plan as government run amok, radical overreach that threatened their economic well-being, their way of life, and the Republic itself. Suddenly, the story went, Obama was forcing his will on millions of Americans with something called a mandate—a mandate that also happened to be at the heart of Romney's health care plan from a few years earlier.

The mandate was a requirement that everyone

buy some kind of insurance, or pay a penalty. It had its roots circa 1993 at the Heritage Foundation, a conservative Washington think tank where a top health care policy expert had crafted a requirement that individuals take responsibility for their own well-being rather than foist the costs of emergency room visits on the taxpayer. That mandate became a central tenet in the health care plan that Senate Republicans, led by Rhode Island's John Chafee, had offered as an alternative to Hillary Clinton's reform efforts in 1993 and 1994. In hindsight, one wonders whether the GOP's decision to rally around this mandate alternative to "HillaryCare" in the 1990s was a genuine effort, or simply the easiest way at the time to combat Clinton. Still, Romney had adopted that conservative position of the 1990s into his own plan in 2005 and then boasted of his achievements. But the Republican messaging of the intervening years put Romney, and some of his biggest supporters, in a difficult spot. In a sign of just how much things had changed, Jim DeMint, the conservative Republican from South Carolina who became a vanguard of the Tea Party movement, backed Romney in 2008 in part because of his health care plan. In 2012, DeMint held back on endorsing Romney, citing concerns over the same health care plan. The positive that once spoke to Romney's bipartisan, solutions-oriented approach to governing had turned into an albatross.

Romney's team was so concerned about the prospect that their candidate's record on health care could derail his presidential ambitions that they sent their man into early damage control mode. A few weeks before formally announcing his candidacy, Romney gave a detailed presentation on health care at the University of Michigan. In an attempt to thread a delicate needle, Romney, using the sort of Power-Point slides that had been a staple of his presentations as a business consultant, made clear he would not disown Commonwealth Care as a whole, though conservatives were begging him to do so. But he drew a crucial distinction: although Commonwealth Care had been right for Massachusetts at the time, he said, it shouldn't be used as a national model. It was a potentially clever appeal to states' rights, the last resort every Republican who is at odds with the national party uses to defend certain un-conservative positions. But it wasn't an easy argument to make, and it wasn't one that any of his opponents—or primary voters—ever let go.

Throughout the yearlong primary process, Romney remained a sort of fragile front-runner. The prepri-mary, the months before any actual votes were cast, became a sort of whack-a-mole game for the Romney campaign. With the conservative electorate con-stantly in search of an alternative to the man they saw as a Massachusetts moderate, a rival would have a strong debate, or deliver a well-received speech, or win a straw poll, and suddenly his numbers would soar. Some would gain traction in the polls without even announcing, including Donald Trump. The metrics—the amount of money Romney had, the number of top-tier endorsers and surrogates, the quality and volume of campaign strategists—suggested that Romney was unbeatable in the primary. But polling data disagreed; throughout 2011, he consistently found himself running behind other candidates. On any given day during the Republican primaries, it was easy to think that both of the following sentences were true: it's impossible to see how Romney isn't the nominee, and it's nearly impossible to see how he gets it.

But the anti-Romneys peaked and failed with incredible regularity, a host of Icaruses flying too close to the sun before plunging into political oblivion. Trump was the first to fall, after he went on his bizarre birtherism wild-goose chase. Herman Cain, the radio host and eccentric former head of Godfather's Pizza, enjoyed a moment at the top after his simple tax plan (9-9-9, short for a 9 percent flat income tax, 9 percent flat corporate tax, and 9 percent national sales tax) and inspiring story captured conservative imaginations. But reports that Cain had been accused of improper behavior toward a number of women while serving as head of the National Restaurant Association, although endearing him to some conservatives who suddenly had another reason to hate the liberal media, effectively ended his campaign. Michele Bachmann, the out-landishly overstated congresswoman whose conservatism made even her Republican-heavy Minnesota district vulnerable to Democratic takeover, became the first woman to win a straw poll held by the Iowa Republican Party, a touchstone event that serves as an early indicator of a candidate's organizational skills. Her repeated gaffes, however, including one confusing Concord, Massachusetts, where the first shots of the Revolutionary War were fired, with Concord, New Hampshire, helped bring her campaign to an early conclusion.*

Tim Pawlenty, who had hired top-tier advisors and introduced himself to primary voters with splashy videos that would have made over-the-top action director Michael Bay envious, had been the anti-Romney who looked best on paper, but he fared worst on the trail. He never caught fire with the grass roots, perhaps because Minnesota Nice—his worst affliction—didn't appeal either to Republican primary voters desperate for blood or archconservatives looking for someone capable of taking Romney down a peg or two. (Pawlenty dropped out a day after Bachmann, his fellow Minnesotan, beat him in the Iowa straw poll.) Later, many Republican operatives (including Romney's folks) would

---

* Among Bachmann's other blunders was mistaking the hometown of serial murderer John Wayne Gacy with that of actor John Wayne.

wonder what might have happened had Pawlenty stayed in for a while, languished, and taken off at a later date, say closer to Iowa.

Rick Perry, the governor of Texas, vaulted highest and fell fastest. There could be no questioning Perry's conservative values; he had been an early champion of Tea Party activists who invoked the Tenth Amendment guaranteeing states' rights, and he even hinted that secession was a possibility if health care reform were forced upon unwilling outposts like the Lone Star State.

Perry, unlike other understaffed Republican candidates, quickly assembled an A-list staff and big-name backers, giving those looking for a Romney alternative hope that one had finally emerged. He raised $17 million[8] in his first few weeks in the race, easily outpacing Romney and threatening to take control of the contest. But Perry had been reluctant to enter the race in the first place, at least until he had surgery on his back, which had plagued him for years. He had the surgery in July 2011, a month before jumping in, but the pain persisted; in debates, other candidates proved to be faster on their feet, and Perry's advisors privately conceded that he was in too much agony to be in top form.

If health care was a political hot potato, Perry grabbed hold of a virtual molten rock: illegal immigration — the lone issue on which he diverged from 2012 conservative orthodoxy. And thereafter his poll numbers began to fall. At one debate, he defended a Texas law that allowed the sons and daughters of illegal immigrants to attend state universities at in-state costs. Romney pounced—a decision some in Boston knew he'd regret if he became the nominee, but (one campaign at a time) he had to find a way to outflank Perry. In fact, immigration was the one issue on which Romney had been more conservative than McCain in 2008 (and it nearly allowed him to upset the Arizonan then), and it was the only issue on which he was more conservative than Perry. And Romney went at the issue—hard. The Texan never really recovered from the onslaught. A few weeks later, at a make-or-break debate in Michigan, he famously pledged to shut down three executive branch departments, then forgot the name of the third department, and his chances to consolidate the anti-Romney forces had all but collapsed.

Two other whack-a-moles remained: Rick Santorum, the former Pennsylvania senator and Christian conservative icon who had lost his seat in the 2006 Democratic wave, and Newt Gingrich, the former House Speaker who had essentially been forced to resign after his party failed to pick up seats in the 1998 midterm elections.

Both seemed long shots for the anti-Romney mantle. Santorum had been walloped in a swing state by Democrat Bob Casey, hardly the résumé of someone claiming viability in a general election against a sitting president. Santorum had little money, and on virtually every debate stage he had been relegated to the wings, a position reserved for the candidate with the lowest support in the polls. (Throughout the fall of 2011, he would be lucky if a survey showed him winning more than 1 percent of likely Republican primary voters.) But he persisted nonetheless, motivated more by the idea of redemption for 2006 than by actually winning.

Gingrich had the loyal backing of established, skilled operatives that Santorum lacked, but those operatives had spent the better parts of their careers deeply involved in Newt, Inc., the series of nonprofit groups and think tanks Gingrich used to churn out his policy positions. If Santorum wanted to be the heart of the conservative movement, Gingrich wanted to be its brain. His past included two messy divorces and enough political baggage to weigh on the minds of primary voters; an advertisement run by a Super PAC (a PAC being a political action committee, an organization that pools donor funds to support or attack candidates, legislation, and policies) backing Romney's candidacy showed actual baggage, labeled with Gingrich's flubs over the years, tumbling down an airport carousel. The simple message it conveyed: nominating Newt would be political suicide for the GOP in a general election.

As September turned to October, November, and

December, and as the days counted down to the Iowa caucuses, Romney's struggles to overcome these minor candidates fascinated the media. Every new debate seemed to give someone else the chance to be the front-runner. And while the Democratic National Committee would dutifully attack whichever candidate happened to be leading the polls at the time, Obama's senior advisors never wavered in their belief that Romney would be the eventual nominee.

Although the media outlets that hosted debates would order podium positions onstage based on polls of national primary voters—front-runners at the center, also-rans to the side—the real race for a presidential nomination is determined by the delegates needed at a convention. Cain, Bachmann, and Perry, even Gingrich from time to time, might lead a national poll, but Romney was besting everyone in surveys of Iowa and New Hampshire voters.

The Obama team, which prided itself on being steeped in the history of politics, knew the Republican trend: no candidate who had won either Iowa or New Hampshire, and then coupled it with victory in South Carolina, had failed to secure the GOP nod. Romney was leading in Iowa by a small margin, and he was miles ahead in New Hampshire. If he won both of the first two races, donations—the mother's milk of presidential campaigns—to any other contender would evaporate (how things worked before one person could fund one Super PAC), and Romney could lock up the party's nomination by mid-January.

The possibility that they would have an all-but-official opponent by mid-January gave the Obama team reason to worry. They knew they would likely be able to raise more money under existing campaign finance laws than any other presidential candidate in the country's history; Obama, after all, had broken all the records in 2008, raising and spending almost $800 million. But campaign finance laws were changing, fast, and the new rules would give Romney an advantage Obama could never overcome.

It was a fear born of Obama's firsthand experience in 2010, when he watched his party drown in a sea of outside money. A 2009 Supreme Court decision, *Citizens United v. Federal Election Commission*, had struck down a key provision of the Bipartisan Campaign Reform Act, better known as McCain-Feingold, and opened the door for unlimited political contributions by labor unions and corporations. Organized labor had already found ways around the prohibitions on political spending, so the decision was a much bigger benefit to Republican-backing corporations, which could suddenly funnel money to outside groups in larger amounts than ever before.

Another decision made in the Washington, D.C., circuit court, known as *SpeechNow.org v. Federal Election Commission*, allowed those independent groups to raise and spend unlimited sums of money on advertisements that directly endorsed a candidate.* The two decisions served as a reminder to individuals of their own unlimited donation rights, and they made the idea of giving money to a Super PAC rather than to, say, the Republican or Democratic National Committee much more appealing. Thanks to McCain-Feingold, a donor can give a certain regulated amount—currently about $32,500—to the national parties. Of that money, between 30 and 40 percent is spent on operations, staff, security, and maintenance of the two parties' national headquarters buildings just a few blocks from the Capitol. But Super PAC donations are not capped, and the relatively low overheard required by a nearly anonymous (or in some cases entirely anonymous) outside group means that only the tiniest fraction of a big donor's check, 2 or 3 percent in some cases, will go toward operations costs. The other 97 or 98 percent will go directly into advertising attacking a foe or supporting an ally. The courts' decisions, in effect, made investing in outside groups rather than a national party a much more attractive prospect for a wealthy individual.

Obama hated what the Supreme Court had done,

---

* After losing in the D.C. circuit court, the Federal Election Commission's lawyers read the writing on the wall and dropped any appeal to the Supreme Court, which would have almost certainly been doomed to failure.

and not just because it neutralized his advantages. It struck at the core of what the former community organizer believed campaigns should represent: the collective will of thousands or hundreds of thousands. *Organizing* should be rewarded, not the wealth of one extremely affluent individual.

While a president usually offers little more than pro forma public disagreement with the Supreme Court—an equal branch of government, after all—Obama was so personally offended by the Court's action that, less than a week after it issued its ruling, he used the biggest platform a sitting president has at his disposal, the State of the Union address, to publicly lambast the *Citizens United* decision: "With all due deference to separation of powers, last week the Supreme Court reversed a century of law that I believe will open the floodgates for special interests— including foreign corporations—to spend without limit in our elections. I don't think American elections should be bankrolled by America's most powerful interests, or worse, by foreign entities. They should be decided by the American people."*

---

* The "foreign" money claim may have been one of the weaker arguments against the *Citizens United* decision, and it certainly was an ironic one, given that Republican conspiracy theorists openly questioned whether Obama's own campaign was receiving foreign money in both 2008 and 2012. In any case, Justice Samuel Alito, a George W. Bush appointee who had written the *Citizens United* decision and who had attended the State of the Union that year, was caught on camera mouthing the words "not true."

While Democrats had understood campaign finance regulations better in the early part of the decade, and accordingly built outside groups under sections of the Internal Revenue Code that allowed them to spend freely on campaigns and elections, Republicans were readier to take advantage of the new court decisions the second time around. Just after those 2009 decisions, Karl Rove and Mike Duncan, a former chairman of the Republican National Committee, had jumped at the opportunity to solicit money from wealthy donors and to spend it directly on candidates they backed. Democrats from across the country were inundated with negative advertising, and of course for Republicans, having an unpopular health care law and a high unemployment rate to run against helped.

In addition to American Crossroads and Crossroads Grassroots Policy Strategies, the twin organizations founded by Rove and Duncan and funded by the biggest donors within the Republican Party, other Super PACs quickly sprang up: Americans for Prosperity, the political arm of David and Charles Koch, two wealthy libertarian political activists from Kansas; the American Action Network, which eventually became the Super PAC wing of John Boehner's political organization; the Congressional Leadership Fund, run by former top staffers to House Republican Eric Cantor, Boehner's second in command and archrival until mid-2014, when he lost a primary for his House seat; and a host of other innocuous-sounding groups that could suddenly spend millions of dollars attacking Obama or any Democrat on the ballot.

Campaign finance debates are almost never successful ways to convert voters and win an election, and 2010 proved this again, but Obama's focus on outside groups foreshadowed his fear that he would be their next victim. Every speech Obama gave in the run-up to the 2010 elections mentioned Rove or the Koch brothers or Super PACs and the corrupting influence of money in politics.

As Obama complained publicly about new sources of money in politics, hoping his holier-than-thou lectures would penetrate an electorate already saturated by Super PAC television advertising, anger among Democrats on Capitol Hill grew. They shared Obama's outrage over the new money, but they faced the political reality that that new money was aimed at robbing them of their jobs; and they were the ones who had to win re-election now, in 2010. Obama was railing against the presence of outside money at exactly the time when House and Senate Democrats needed to build their own sources of outside money.

Obama's opposition to outside groups had in effect frozen the Democratic donor community in 2010. Obama was signaling that the big donors who forked over their cash wouldn't be rewarded with the traditional perks they had come to expect, and while

Republican businessmen and megadonors were writing checks with abandon, Democrats were wondering why they should shell out big bucks for organizations that flew in the face of the way their president promised to do business. In 2010, Rove's groups smashed through their fund-raising goals; their Democratic counterparts raised some money, but they almost struggled to keep the lights on. Democratic-leaning Super PAC television ads in 2010 were almost nonexistent.

Among the mantras that Rahm Emanuel preached as chief of staff was that political fund-raising should be kept as far away from the White House as possible. This reflected the political damage the Clintons had suffered when the public learned that major donors had been invited to stay overnight in the White House's Lincoln Bedroom. Emanuel had even made clear that at least one top staffer in Obama's 2008 campaign wouldn't be welcome in his White House: Julianna Smoot, the campaign's chief fund-raiser, was supposed to become head of White House personnel, but Emanuel vetoed her appointment, simply to eliminate even the illusion of fund-raising taking place on the White House grounds.

Emanuel's position was in large part Obama's position, too: unlike Bill Clinton, this president didn't like socializing with donors, begging for another check by leveraging the trappings of the nation's highest office. This was a case in which

Obama's personal loathing of political schmoozing fit his principles.

To many large donors and bundlers, those were clear signs that the unspoken tit-for-tat of political fund-raising was different in the Obama administration than it had been with the Clintons. Democrats who signed over big checks, or got their friends to do so, wouldn't reap the traditional rewards of access and influence that they had come to expect. There would be no Lincoln Bedroom stays, no intimate cocktail parties with the president, no appointments to key or prestigious positions. And if writing a large check to a Democratic outside group wasn't going to gain them access, or at least the thanks of a grateful president, why bother?

After the drubbing Democrats took in the midterm elections, the fear that Super PACs would play a significant role in 2012 took on new urgency. But then Team Obama caught a break. While Romney swatted away Bachmann and Cain and Perry, the Republican primaries had begun to resemble a playground for the rich and powerful. Santorum had surged at the right time, late in December. He and Romney had finished in a dead heat in Iowa; a recount of the delegates elected on Caucus Night showed the former Pennsylvania senator had actually eked out a victory over the once-unbeatable front-runner. Romney won New Hampshire, virtually his home state, but Gingrich charged to a surprising come-back and crushed the field in South Carolina.

The Obama team's fear that their opponent would emerge unscathed in January after trouncing a field of nobodies evaporated. But their apprehension that a giant onslaught of money waited to bury them in a torrent of negative advertising built steadily, and for good reason: Santorum and Gingrich, it turned out, had some wealthy friends, and what both these candidates lacked in traditional campaign infrastructure, they made up for in überdonations.

For all his prominent staff and longtime associates, Gingrich had very few traditional resources with which to run a campaign. He had raised far less traditional money (in increments of $2,500 or less) than Romney, the barometer by which previously successful candidates can be measured. But when Gingrich finished a distant fourth in the Iowa caucuses, a lackluster performance that would have killed a campaign in any previous year, he wasn't forced out of the race. Instead, his friend Sheldon Adelson, a billionaire whose fortune had been made and broken and made again as stock from his Las Vegas Sands Corporation bounced around in the volatile market, invested enough in a Super PAC to keep Gingrich alive. Adelson and his wife donated $10 million to a pro-Gingrich Super PAC run by a former Newt, Inc., staffer, and when part of that money flooded the South Carolina airwaves it handed Gingrich his bigger-than-expected victory.*

After Gingrich's Super PAC bought the South Carolina primary win (helped by a stirring debate performance in which Gingrich attacked the moderator over a question about his personal life, thereby gaining the loyalty of conservatives who loathe the so-called mainstream media), it was on to Florida. Back in 2008, the Sunshine State had been the last stand for Rudy Giuliani, the candidate who was supposed to stop John McCain in his tracks. This time, Gingrich was all that stood in Romney's way.

Anyone familiar with the rhythms of Las Vegas business was familiar with the Sheldon Adelson brand, but few had ever heard of Foster Friess, the wildly successful investment banker whose antipathy toward Romney would become yet another stumbling block to the nomination. Friess, who lived in the Wyoming woods, had helped Santorum build off his surprising Iowa upset, bankrolling another Super PAC that, although ostensibly independent from the Pennsylvania Republican's presidential campaign, ended up carrying his message from coast to coast when the campaign itself ran out of money. Friess's appearance in the late winter

---

* To put Adelson's primary help in perspective, realize that Joe Biden, during his run for the presidency in 2008, raised $17 million from thousands of donors. Gingrich's Super PAC raised more than half of that from one household.

of 2011 created a strange cocktail of political players: an outside group backing Gingrich, bankrolled
by a fantastically wealthy casino operator from Las
Vegas, and an outside group backing Santorum,
funded by an eccentric entrepreneur turned billionaire from the Wyoming wilderness. Those efforts
kept two broke candidates in the game as another
Super PAC, aided by less wealthy but equally determined Republicans for Romney, dumped their
opposition research and their still considerable afflu-
ence not on Obama, but on Santorum and Gingrich. Plouffe and Messina could not have devised a
better plan, and it was buying Obama precious time
and wasting GOP resources.

The pro-Romney Super PAC demonstrated the
ridiculousness of the new rules. Outside groups were
ostensibly supposed to be run independently of a
campaign, but the pro-Romney group was run by a
prominent Republican operative, Carl Forti, who had
been the Romney campaign's political director in
2008. Forti shared office space with Alex Gage, one
of the Republican Party's top microtargeting operatives, whose wife happened to be employed as a top
staffer on the Romney campaign. Forti was also the
political director of Rove's group, American Crossroads, which had declared neutrality in the primary
process despite the fact that Rove, Duncan, and others involved in the Crossroads high command were
all private fans of Romney and all but openly rooting

for the former Massachusetts governor. Meanwhile Gingrich met frequently with the top donor to his supposedly independent Super PAC, and Santorum's top benefactor was so closely linked to the campaign that Friess began appearing in the same sorts of sweater vests as Santorum.

To Obama's senior advisors, the irony must have been immense: Romney could not become the nominee until he bested the Super PACs run by other Republican candidates. But once a nominee emerged, the onslaught of Super PAC advertising, from the pro-Romney group to Foster Friess to Sheldon Adelson (who voiced, and delivered on, a promise that he would spend $100 million to beat Obama), would turn exclusively toward the president. Speaking at the 2013 White House Correspondents' Dinner, Obama told Adelson, who was not present, that the billionaire would have been better off simply offering him $100 million not to run. He would have turned him down, Obama joked, but he might have thought about it.

As the Obama team watched the ugly, heated Republican primary, they began agitating for a solution to a problem they could see coming: they needed a Super PAC of their own. Once again it fell to Jim Messina to fight the battle inside the White House. He took it upon himself to begin the lobbying on behalf of what would prove to be a major flip-flop by a politician who prided himself on not changing his mind. In order to survive in this new landscape, the president now needed to signal to major Democratic donors that donating to Super PACs would be acceptable.

With other issues on which Obama had flip-flopped—the health care mandate and expanded use of drones, among others—the president had been persuaded by data, or at least he needed the data to justify the flip-flop. So Messina used data to make his case. On a whiteboard in his office, the campaign manager began doing the math. Showing what Republican Super PACs had raised during the 2010 elections, incorporating what Romney's Super PAC had already raised from the former Massachusetts governor's rich private sector friends, and including a few extrapolations based on public declarations by the outside groups that backed Gingrich and Santorum, and the ones funded by the Koch brothers, he estimated that the Obama campaign would face about $660 million in outside spending alone over the coming months. And that didn't include the $600 million to $1 billion Messina estimated that Romney would raise for his own campaign once he was the official nominee.

Messina asked Axelrod to a meeting in his new office in Chicago. Axelrod, who had been involved in every Obama campaign since the 2004 Senate race, had never seen Obama outspent. As both men knew, one of the secrets of Obama's success had been his ability to do what many Democrats rarely do: raise and spend more than his opponents. When he launched his campaign in 2007, Obama had pledged to abide by rules that restricted how and where a presidential candidate could spend his or her money; he quickly broke those rules when his campaign raised more than it had ever anticipated. In doing so, Obama became the first candidate in the post-Watergate era to abandon voluntary fund-raising guidelines, because his campaign could then attract more than it could sticking to the rules for general election matching funds. But given the Republican outside groups, Rove's organization, and Romney's fund-raising prowess, Obama's financial acumen wasn't going to be a given advantage this time around.

Who could establish the Democratic alternative to Karl Rove? Rove was a known quantity, one of the Republican Party's best fund-raisers, given his strong ties to the big-donor community. Crossroads had proved itself calculating and influential in 2010, when it helped Republicans take back the House and win back seats in the Senate. Since Obama's 2012 campaign was going to retain the brain trust — Plouffe, Axelrod, and Messina — who would serve as the surrogate, the Obama insider able to convince donors who had already given the campaign the maximum allowed by law to pledge even more money to an outside group?

Besides Robert Gibbs, perhaps no one else had

spoken more on Barack Obama's behalf, either as a candidate or as president of the United States, than Bill Burton. Though he was much younger than others who might have run an outside group and didn't seem to be someone you could picture wooing some of the wealthiest people in the country, people who might be inclined to fork over a seven-figure check, Burton had an impressive enough résumé. He had run communications for the Democratic Congressional Campaign Committee when Rahm Emanuel had been its chairman, and he had worked in the press shops for Dick Gephardt, John Kerry, and Tom Harkin at various points during his time in Washington. He'd even done some time in Iowa in 2004 for Gephardt's unsuccessful presidential campaign.

Burton had signed on to Obama's campaign almost from the beginning. He had been through the pressure cooker of the 2008 primaries and survived most of the first term even as Gibbs had become an increasingly controversial presence in the West Wing. When Gibbs made official his decision to leave in late 2010, Burton was an obvious candidate to take over the press room podium, perhaps the most prominent job in his profession.

But Burton wasn't the only candidate, and eventually he fell victim to the "deputy" syndrome that happens in any organization when the boss simply can't envision the number two as the chief. Going outside the West Wing altogether, Obama tapped Jay Carney, the former *Time* magazine correspondent and spokesman for Vice President Joe Biden. The same day Carney took over the podium from Gibbs, on February 16, 2011, Burton announced that he would leave the White House, the barest hint of internal strife peeking out.

When it became clear to Burton that he wouldn't be getting the podium, his friend Sean Sweeney, a top Emanuel aide, suggested that the two form a consulting firm.[9] After all, two top advisors to a sitting president could leverage their relationships in Washington in lucrative ways. Plus, neither wanted to go to Chicago to work on the campaign; Burton's wife, Laura, was pregnant with the couple's first child, and moving halfway across the country to work twenty-hour days didn't much appeal to Burton.

At the same time, Karl Rove and the Koch brothers were making their plans known. Rove's Crossroads organization announced that it would spend $120 million on Republican causes. Americans for Prosperity, the Koch brothers' outside vehicle, said its goal would be to raise $88 million to defeat the president. Sweeney broached an idea with Burton: with all the outside money aimed in Obama's direction, why don't we found a group that can fight back?

In 2010, the White House had shouted down efforts to found, and properly fund, a real Super PAC to help congressional Democrats. In doing so, it had ensured that its own party would be bringing a knife to a gunfight. Now, Burton and Sweeney— former aides who would avoid tainting the White House with the stain of outside cash but were close enough that they could give donors the impression they were speaking for the White House—would help their old colleagues fire back with equal force.

Burton and Sweeney signed up some of the best Democratic strategists in the business, many of whom had long histories in Bill Clinton's White House. Harold Ickes, in 2008 a fierce Hillary Clinton defender, became the group's president; Paul Begala, the strategist who had helped guide Clinton's 1992 campaign and remained close to the Clinton family, would serve on its board of directors. Hiring the former was somewhat tricky. There had been rumors for months that Ickes, still fuming at having a donation he made to Obama and the DNC rejected because he was a registered lobbyist, had been shopping around for someone to challenge Obama in a primary. This never got anywhere, a pipe dream of the formerly well-connected Democrat who believed—like many a Washington Democrat over the age of fifty—that he'd never gotten the respect he deserved from the Obama White House. But Ickes had big-time labor connections, something this new Super PAC needed; and whether Ickes liked it or not, Obama was the party's guy, and Ickes was a party guy at the end of the day.

Priorities USA filed its papers with the Federal Election Commission a few days later, on April 29, 2011. The first check came from Jeffrey Katzenberg, CEO of the movie studio DreamWorks, in the amount of $2 million. The Service Employees International Union, which had spent the past two decades building its prominence as a first-among-equals partner of the labor coalition, pledged $1.5 million. Those donations turned the lights on, in Burton's words, and allowed the group to begin hiring staff and renting office space.

But they would be frugal, and they saved money in every way possible. They could find office space only through October 31, so instead of spending another several thousand dollars on rent for November, the Super PAC would end up homeless on Election Day, using laptops from home or coffee-shop WiFi to tie up any loose ends. Of course, a Super PAC's real work is all done a week out from the election.

Katzenberg and SEIU had been quick with their checkbooks, but their generosity didn't translate to more contributions. Donors told Burton and Sweeney they were leery of getting involved in a Super PAC after the president had spent so much time recounting the evils of outside money. After the initial elation at raising $3.5 million from exactly two donors, the money slowed to a trickle, and it became clear the operatives would have to spend much more time convincing and cajoling than they would scripting and filming advertisements. It didn't help that the *New York Times* ran a front-page story featuring photographs of Burton and Katzenberg; the next day the paper, famously opposed to money in politics in any form, wrote a scathing op-ed taking both men to task. "A lot of donors that we went to, that was their top concern," Burton said. Conservative donors laugh at a *New York Times* editorial about big money; liberal donors feel shame. Translation: the Republican Super PACs were having no such trouble raising their own money. In fact, in September 2011, the Crossroads organizations said they would double their fund-raising goal, to $240 million.*

In 2011, the monthly Super PAC reports comparing Republican donations to Democratic ones were embarrassing for Burton's group. The low point for Burton and Priorities was their February 2012 Federal Election Commission report: that month they'd raised less than $60,000 *total* while Mitt Romney's Super PAC had pulled in more than a hundred times what Burton had—over $6.6 million, to be exact. In fact, the *average* donation to Romney's Super PAC in January (which the February report reflected) was just under $48,000, within striking distance of what the president's unofficial Super PAC raised for

---

* They made the announcement, perhaps tauntingly, by talking to a reporter from the Center for Public Integrity.

the entire month, period. And this was just one pro-Romney Super PAC—what Rove's Crossroads and the Koch brothers' Americans for Prosperity were raising and spending was equally intimidating to the Democrats.

Burton needed help, and he needed the president to bless the Super PAC; until and unless the president did that publicly, they were going to struggle to raise money.

But within twenty-four hours of finding out just how poorly his fund-raising was going, the president gave Burton a thumbs-up. Obama himself didn't announce the reversal. It was done via conference call by campaign officials, who asked that the exchange be kept on background—a signal that the president wasn't exactly proud of this decision. It was clearly not something they were excited about doing, but something they felt they had to do. It was going to fall to Plouffe and a few other prominent Obama surrogates to actually show up and raise money for this Super PAC the president never wanted. Obama himself stayed away from Super PAC fund-raising in 2012, but by 2014, he started helping personally. And he rarely spoke out about campaign finance issues after 2012.

While hanging on, Santorum and Gingrich toyed with the idea of running as a ticket in their stop-Romney efforts, but those talks died when neither candidate could agree on who was top dog. So knowing how important it was to knock Santorum out for good, as the April 3 Wisconsin primary approached, Romney courted one last Republican establishment figure with his finger on the pulse of the new conservative movement: Wisconsin's own Paul Ryan, who had stayed silent on the presidential race for months.

Ryan had long been a Romney admirer, though he saw no political advantage in endorsing a candidate early. And since Ryan himself had toyed with a 2012 bid (even discussing running as late as August 2011 while vacationing with his family in Colorado), he figured he might as well wait until his endorsement mattered. He went for Romney just before the Cheesehead primary, and to his surprise, once he hit the trail, he discovered a rapport with the former Massachusetts governor. They geeked out together on budget wonkery and developed a real intellectual bond. And while few people could make the normally stiff and reserved Romney crack a smile, Ryan got the candidate laughing. Romney advisors took notice.

Following his victory in Wisconsin, Romney ran off wins in every subsequent primary, and as the end of April approached, the Republican National Committee formally declared Romney the presumptive nominee (in fact the RNC had been working closely with Romney's campaign for almost a month beforehand, though privately, in order to avoid a backlash from conservatives committed to Gingrich or Santorum).[10] With that, the general election began.*

Obama faced two opponents as the general election loomed: Romney, who though his campaign appeared hapless at times was still the formidable opponent Obama's team had worried about since 2008, and the economy, which appeared to be slowing precisely at the most inopportune time for the president. The nation's unemployment rate stood at 8.2 percent, well off its highest figure but still in dreadful territory. Perhaps more frightening, the pace of job creation had slowed markedly; after a robust 275,000 new jobs in January 2012, the Bureau of Labor Statistics reported the economy had added just 120,000 new jobs in March. The unemployment rate fell to 8.1 percent in April, but the economy added an even more anemic 115,000 jobs. The grim truth was that the unemployment rate had fallen only because more Americans had stopped looking for work, and thus weren't counted as part of the workforce. And then there was an unpredictable decision on the legality of the president's health care plan that the Supreme Court was due to hand down in

---

* An ambitious effort to launch a third-party Unity ticket fizzled out. Even with their low poll numbers, all of the potential Unity candidates ended up drawing more support away from Romney than from the president. If anything, a third-party candidacy meant that Obama would have an easier path to re-election.

June—a lot of unknowns out of the campaign's control, and a scary proposition for Plouffe and Messina.

Most polling in April showed Obama's approval rating hovering in the mid–40 percent range. Less than a third of voters believed the country was headed in the right direction, and almost two-thirds thought America was on the wrong track. Public surveys showed him barely ahead of, if not tied with, Romney, who hadn't yet had a chance to make his case directly to the electorate; Republican-leaning pollsters even showed Romney ahead.

The advertisements blasting Romney as an out-of-touch businessman bent on protecting the rich were written and waiting to be produced and aired in key swing states. But there was no way to advertise against the economy or to tout Obama's record as good enough in an atmosphere in which Americans clearly didn't believe things were headed in the right direction. By 2012, Americans did not believe they were better off than they had been when Obama assumed office, and the track record on this issue was pretty clear: If Americans believed they *were* better off, they usually rewarded the incumbent or his party. If they didn't think so, electoral upheaval was imminent.

On the other hand, the Obama team could try to change the discussion to something more forward-looking that would help them avoid the uncomfortable truth that Americans didn't feel terribly happy with the results, or lack thereof, of the president's performance. Plus they did have one thing going for them when it came to the economy: voters did not blame Obama for the economy, they blamed Bush, even as late as 2012. And so the Obama campaign took on the unprecedented task of persuading voters to ask themselves a different question: will you be better off in four years under Barack Obama than you would be under Mitt Romney?

This wasn't an original strategy. John Kerry's advisors had believed in their hearts that 2004 would be a referendum on Bush. The Bush team feared that, and instead sought to change it from a "referendum" to a "choice" concept. It had worked for Bush, and now Team Obama was adopting the same strategy.

Throughout the summer of 2011, when most of Washington was obsessed with negotiations over raising the debt ceiling, a small team inside the White House set to work on the American Jobs Act, a largely symbolic piece of legislation that would serve primarily as a messaging vehicle for the beginning of the campaign. Plouffe, Stephanie Cutter, Bill Daley, Tim Geithner, and Gene Sperling spent hours designing the bill, which they would pitch as a solution to the stagnant recovery.

In part, this was an exercise in team building. The White House couldn't simply ask for more tax cuts, because it needed Democrats not only to support the bill but to show a unified front. The point was to design a bill that would mobilize a variety of constituencies that wouldn't get off the bench without an incentive to do so. What it was *not* designed to do was to be passed by Congress. This was about giving the president something to run on — and, when summarily rejected by the GOP, something to run against.

Obama introduced the plan in an address to a joint session of Congress on September 8, 2011. The American Jobs Act would cut taxes on businesses that hired workers or raised salaries; spend money repairing infrastructure and upgrading roads, bridges, and even the nation's air traffic control system; and modernize 35,000 schools, another infusion of infrastructure funds that would put people to work quickly. It would appropriate money to hire new teachers and to provide summer jobs for young people; it even specifically incentivized hiring workers who had been out of work for more than six months. At every turn Obama emphasized the bipartisan elements of the bill, and yet it was hardly a plan the White House thought had much of a chance to be enacted — which was just fine with Plouffe.

The speech was aimed directly at the middle of America, the swath of voters who would make the choice the Obama team was trying to set up. The media, Obama told the gathered members of Congress, had been asking, " 'What will this speech mean for the President? What will it mean for Congress? How will it affect their polls, and the next election?'

"But," he explained, "the millions of Americans who are watching right now, they don't care about politics. They have real-life concerns." It was a nice thought, though the speech, and the bill itself, had been written with exactly those very political questions in mind.

Three months later, Obama gave a second speech aimed at framing the same choice. This one came in Osawatomie, Kansas, a town of just 4,447 people that lies an hour south of Kansas City. Obama's trip to a deep-red part of a deep-red state—he ended up losing Miami County, where Osawatomie is located, by a 66 to 32 percent margin in November[11]— wasn't aimed at winning those specific electoral votes in Kansas. Instead, he hoped to draw a clear comparison to one of his predecessors, one who had drawn a similar contrast in his own election campaign: Theodore Roosevelt.

Nothing irks Obama more than the idea that he's somehow a leftist or liberal; he believes that most of his ideas are old Republican ideas from another era. That last phrase is the key—these are almost always ideas that would fail on the runway with today's GOP. And it isn't clear that his support of them has done much to change existing Republican minds, either, just as Republican claims that JFK was a tax cutter rarely persuaded Democrats to jump the fence.

But policy specifics aside, Obama's big speeches on the campaign trail weren't so much about doing something new as about finding a historical hook to justify his position, so it was to the history books that his speechwriters turned.

On August 31, 1910, Roosevelt stopped in Osawatomie to call for what he dubbed the "New Nationalism." He argued that only the federal government had a reach broad enough to provide for human welfare; he called for a national income tax, national laws to protect the rights of children and women in the workplace, and more oversight of the nation's banking system. "I do not ask for the over centralization; but I do ask that we work in a spirit of broad and far-reaching nationalism where we work for what concerns our people as a whole. We are all Americans. Our common interests are as broad as the continent," Roosevelt said.[12]

Obama's team didn't want to draw too direct a comparison to the New Nationalism — Roosevelt had given the address almost two years after leaving the White House, just before he ran for a third term on the Bull Moose ticket, and he lost the 1912 election badly. Instead, Obama used the address to call his proposal for an extension of a middle-class tax cut a "square deal," the phrase Roosevelt had used to describe his program of domestic initiatives. And much of his speech would have sounded familiar to Teddy himself.

"For most Americans, the basic bargain that made this country great has eroded. Long before the recession hit, hard work stopped paying off for too many people," Obama said. "This is not just another political debate. This is the defining issue of our time. This is a make-or-break moment for the middle class, and for all those who are fighting to get into the middle class. Because what's at stake is whether this will be a country where working people can earn enough to raise a family, build a modest savings, own a home, secure their retirement."[13]

Obama's position thus defined, he set up the choice his campaign wanted Americans to face: "In the midst of this debate, there are some who seem to be suffering from a kind of collective amnesia. After all that's happened, after the worst economic crisis, the worst financial crisis since the Great Depression, they want to return to the same practices that got us into this mess. In fact, they want to go back to the same policies that stacked the deck against middle-class Americans for way too many years. And their philosophy is simple: We are better off when everybody is left to fend for themselves and play by their own rules," Obama said.

He went on: "I am here to say they are wrong. I'm here in Kansas to reaffirm my deep conviction that we're greater together than we are on our own. I believe that this country succeeds when everyone gets a fair shot, when everyone does their fair share, when everyone plays by the same rules. These aren't

Democratic values or Republican values. These aren't 1 percent values or 99 percent values. They're American values. And we have to reclaim them."[14]

"Osawatomie really framed the campaign," Valerie Jarrett would say later. "The thought that went into that speech was, 'What's going to be our theory of the case for re-election? What's going to distinguish the president from whoever ultimately wins the [Republican] primary?'" For Plouffe, the speech was the beginning of a simpler mission: "We're just going to repeat the same thing, over and over again: Fair shot, fair shake."*

Obama's team had already planned its main lines of attack: Romney's business record and his penchant for flip-flopping as he'd disavowed position after position when moving to the right. Gingrich, Santorum, Perry, and the other anti-Romney candidates running in the primaries had seen some success doing the same thing but focusing on his past preferences as opposed to his current beliefs, but Obama's labeling Romney a flip-flopper might cause him trouble with a Republican base already skeptical of the president's record.

---

* The speech actually wasn't really that well received in the moment, partly because the president looked like he was in the basement of some old school building with a few makeshift American flags. This was yet another staple of the Obama presidential years—some awful, very plain backdrops or wildly overcompensating sets clogged with American flags and imperial columns.

Thus the campaign slowly moved away from the flip-flopper label. Messina, Axelrod, and Plouffe began to have doubts that the strategy would work in a general election—doubts echoed by Bill Clinton, still one of the best political strategists in the country, who ultimately was the one who convinced them to give it up entirely. Clinton told Messina to step away from the flip-flopper line of attack. Clinton, himself accused of being a flip-flopper, knew that this could actually be a strength, a coded message to suburban voters that Romney would take the centrist position and was secretly a moderate.

The most promising angle for contrasting Romney and Obama was the very strength that made Romney a viable candidate in Massachusetts and the front-runner for the Republican nomination: his background as a successful businessman and turnaround artist.

Romney was the classic example of an overachiever. Married to his high school sweetheart, possessed of a top-notch mind for business, generous with his ample wealth, and, thanks to his strict observance of his Mormon faith, unblemished by personal skeletons anywhere near his closet, Romney seemed to offer nothing to an opposition researcher looking for juicy tidbits. His greatest scandal, it seemed, was that he had once lost his temper with a police officer in the early 1980s and was briefly detained. Compared with recent presidents—an impeached philanderer, a recovering alcoholic, and Obama, who went so far as to detail some of his hard drug use in his memoir—Romney was untouchable on the personal front.

Romney's wealth came from the world of private equity, a cutthroat line of work in which businesses leverage their access to huge amounts of wealth to buy other businesses and make them profitable. Romney often touted his work with companies such as Sports Authority and Staples to show he had spent his time in the private sector turning failing companies around and saving jobs in the process. At a moment when the U.S. economy needed its own turnaround artist, that sounded like a winning biography. Simply being described as a "businessman" invariably had what political strategists call a "halo effect" with voters, for any candidate during any period. So imagine how well a candidate who was described as a "successful" businessman would be received in the midst of a recession.

Yet for every Sports Authority or Staples, there were companies like Holson Burnes Group, Cambridge Industries, and GS Industries. All three of those smaller firms shared common themes: they had once employed hundreds of workers in skilled manufacturing jobs. Holson Burnes made photo albums and picture frames in Gaffney, South Carolina.[15] Cambridge made plastic parts for automobiles in Michigan. GS Industries was a Kansas

City–based steel manufacturer. In each case, Bain Capital, under Romney's management, had purchased the firm and then charged it eye-popping management fees while loading the company with debt. For example, Bain would borrow against the assets of a troubled company and use the cash for new investments, including the purchase of other companies. This was a way to leverage an investor's money; instead of relying on one turnaround, the assets of one troubled company could be used to buy a new one without asking for more new cash from the investor, thus giving an investor two separate shots at making money with the same dollar. In each case, the debt proved too much for the small company to handle: factories were closed, workers were laid off, jobs either disappeared or moved overseas — and Bain still raked in millions, because bankruptcy didn't cost Bain's investors anything. Bain had more successes than failures, and with the failures it did have, it was able to keep its eventual losses to a minimum, since it stripped those companies of all their assets before bankrupting them. This is a crude shorthand description, but it represented capitalism in its purest survival-of-the-fittest mode.

During the fifteen years Romney ran the company, Bain bought controlling stakes in more than forty businesses. At least seven, including Holson Burns, Cambridge, and GS Industries, filed for bankruptcy while Bain held a controlling stake, according to a review by two *New York Times* reporters.

For a private equity firm, more than thirty successes compared with just seven failures is an outstanding record, one with which most blue-chip firms can't hope to compete. But the seven failures meant hundreds, if not thousands, of jobs lost; couple those with the big profits Bain made while the companies were failing—$10 million from Cambridge alone[16]—and the negative advertisements virtually wrote themselves. All the Obama campaign had to do was find a former employee of one of these companies and invite him or her to talk about the experience of getting laid off by a company Romney controlled.

Romney had a habit of exacerbating his greatest weakness. He would occasionally make offhand references to his personal wealth or to his wealthy friends. In February 2012, when he was asked during a visit to Daytona, one of NASCAR's holy sites, whether he followed auto racing, Romney replied that he didn't follow the sport closely. But, he said, "I have some friends who are NASCAR team owners."[17] Two weeks later, while appearing on a radio program in Alabama, Romney was asked where he thought Indianapolis Colts quarterback Peyton Manning, who was looking around for a new team, should go. Romney said he didn't want Manning playing anywhere near New England, then added, apropos of nothing at all: "I have a lot of good friends, the owners of the Miami Dolphins and the New York Jets—both owners are friends of mine. But let's keep away from New England so that Tom Brady has a better of shot of picking up a championship for us."[18] The one sport he was very familiar with was something only the wealthy could afford: an equestrian sport called dressage.

The sports references were easy to make fun of and made stereotyping him as a rich guy easy, but one comment stuck in the Obama team's mind: in August 2011, when a protester at the Iowa State Fair yelled at Romney to raise taxes on corporations, Romney had put the man in his place. "Corporations are people, my friend," Romney had retorted. "Everything corporations earn ultimately goes to people. Where do you think it goes?"[19] That gem got its own special place in Obama campaign talking points.

Obama's travel schedule during his first three years in office already resembled a campaign flight plan. He stopped much more frequently in swing states than he did in run-of-the-mill noncompetitive states. So traveling back to Columbus, Ohio, and Richmond, Virginia, to campaign was no different from the schedule for any other week. This time, however, Obama would be framing the argument against Romney himself—the first time the president had directly engaged his opponent and made the case not against a generic "them," but against a specific person. And in a thirty-five-minute stump speech at Ohio State University on May 5, 2012, he was as subtle as a hammer in framing the question that would soon be before voters.

"After a long and spirited primary, Republicans in Congress have found a nominee for president who has promised to rubber-stamp this agenda if he gets the chance," Obama said. "We cannot give him that chance."

Then came the reframe: "The other side...won't offer a better vision or a new set of ideas. But they will be spending more money than we've ever seen before on negative ads, on TV, on radio, in the mail, on the Internet—ads that exploit people's frustrations for my opponent's political gain. Over and over again, they will tell you that America is down and out, and they'll tell you who to blame, and ask if you're better off than you were before the worst crisis in our lifetime. We've seen that play before. But you know what? The real question—the question that will actually make a difference in your life and in the lives of your children—is not just about how we're doing today. It's about how we'll be doing tomorrow."[20]

As Obama looked around the arena that day, he couldn't help but notice a difference from four years before: When the Buckeyes played a basketball game, the Schottenstein Center at Ohio State University held a full capacity of 18,300 spectators. But as he kicked off his re-election bid, Obama—who in 2008 had been besieged by crowds numbering in the six figures, both at home and overseas—stared out at 4,000 empty seats. He would have to remember to speak to someone on his campaign staff about that. If, after all, there was a real enthusiasm gap, if the hundreds of thousands, if not millions, of new voters the 2008 campaign had identified, registered, and turned out simply weren't interested or inspired this time around, the campaign was going to have a real problem.

The crowd in Richmond, on the campus of Virginia Commonwealth University, was smaller, but packed in tighter. Yet for some reason no one was standing behind the president, which left him oddly alone in the camera shot. Obama's campaign, it seemed, was starting off with a few minor missteps—not so terrible that a voter would notice, but troubling nonetheless, and the kinds of mistakes Obama's campaign hadn't made four years ago. If the campaign was missing small details, when would it miss a larger one?

Obama didn't know that in fact, a larger misstep had already occurred. In an interview marking the campaign kickoff on NBC's *Meet the Press,* taped the same day Obama was speaking in Columbus and Richmond, Biden had hit all the right notes, defending the administration's record on the economic recovery while taking Romney and his business career to task. Host David Gregory then asked the vice president about same-sex marriage. Biden managed to dodge the question twice, but when Gregory asked a third time — "And you're comfortable with same-sex marriage now?" — Biden strayed from his talking points.

"I am vice president of the United States of America. The president sets the policy." (And hard stop — or so the campaign wished Biden would have done, but he didn't. He kept talking.)

"I am absolutely comfortable with the fact that men marrying men, women marrying women, and heterosexual men and women marrying each other are entitled to the same exact rights, all the civil rights, all the civil liberties. And quite frankly, I don't see much of a distinction beyond that," Biden said.

The Obama campaign had known it was going to have to deal with same-sex marriage at some point. The liberal base of the Democratic Party was simply too supportive of gay marriage to allow their platform, or their president, to stay silent. It was something the campaign was worried could become a distraction at their convention in September if they didn't do something. Still, this wasn't how they wanted to deal with it. Because now, if Obama didn't back same-sex marriage by the time the Democratic convention rolled around in September, he would face an embarrassing fight on the convention floor, something the optics-obsessed campaign wanted to avoid at all costs.

When the president himself decided to change his mind is less than clear. By 2008, it wouldn't have been a surprise for a Chicago liberal to be in favor of gay marriage. But Obama, then and earlier, had always followed the moderate Democratic candidate's playbook when it came to social issues, including abortion and gay rights, even guns; in fact, he sounded like a Southern Democrat when it came to those issues for much of his short career in the Senate. Gay rights activists then turned up the heat, big-time, starting in 2010 and continuing in 2011, interrupting Obama's large, low-dollar fund-raisers as well as more intimate high-dollar settings, demanding to know why the president was suddenly behind where every other Democrat was on the issue of marriage.

Senior White House staffers—Pfeiffer, Plouffe, Axelrod, and Cutter—had been working since the summer of 2011 on a strategy to allow Obama to come out in favor of gay marriage. They kept their deliberations muted and their group small, to prevent leaks, for fear it would look ham-handedly political, which, well, it was. And they had settled on a venue: *The View,* a daytime program that drew a sympathetic audience, had largely sympathetic hosts, and would give Obama time to explain his personal evolution on gay marriage without an interruption. The appearance was less than two weeks away when Biden stole Obama's thunder and turned the president into a follower of his own vice president.

So how did Biden so easily get pushed off message? The backstory was that a few weeks before his *Meet the Press* appearance Biden had been at a fundraiser in Hollywood, where a gay couple had opened their mansion to the campaign. There, Biden had met the couple's young son. What are we doing, Biden wondered, opposing gay marriage, when this kid has a loving home? Biden later called the moment his epiphany, a strong word for a lifelong practicing Catholic that underscored the impact he had felt.

It was classic Biden, who wore his heart and more on his sleeve. It was Biden being Biden. But he'd gotten out in front of a major policy change, and that required damage control.

Biden hadn't known the senior advisors were plotting Obama's public about-face for *The View,* and when he found out about it, he felt even worse. His advisors, always conscious of the vice president's place within the White House hierarchy, scrambled to let the president's team know just how bad he felt.

To know Biden was to know how he easily could have stumbled into this, but at least initially, some in Obama's orbit believed the vice president had pulled a fast one, zipping out in front of the president to score points with a base he would need if he wanted his own shot at the Oval Office in 2016. (Messina especially has always been skeptical of Biden's motives.) Obama never believed that Biden had jammed him intentionally. Still, it was a big stumble, more for the timing than anything else, knocking the president off message in the most important week of his re-election push: the campaign kickoff week!

Biden's flub, the empty seats in Columbus, the visuals of the stage in Richmond—these mistakes were minor, but they hinted at deeper problems. Obama came away from his first week back on the trail chastising staff, urging them to button up and get their acts together. Even Michelle Obama expressed her dissatisfaction with the little ways the campaign wasn't executing perfectly. It was particularly unnerving for Team Obama that the announcement week went as poorly as it did, since they'd had months to prepare for it. Their plan had always been to announce in either late March or early April, and they would have done it even sooner had Romney wrapped up the nomination earlier. But the longer the GOP primaries went on, the more time the campaign bought for planning the announcement. They never thought they'd get to wait until May to announce, and yet the extra time hadn't ended up in a smooth launch.

But the arc of the campaign's message had less to do with those early rallies than with the advertising it was about to launch. Anticipating the piles of secret Super PAC money that was sure to rain down on their heads at any moment, the Obama campaign had always planned to get on television first. They would be outspent, but with a little strategic think-ing they could determine the story the media would write on any given day by being first—first to run television ads, first to put the candidate on camera, and first to viciously attack the straw man they would create, the one with the Mitt Romney name tag.

As Cutter prepared to pull the trigger on the Bain attack ads, she warned her fellow senior strategists that their line of attack wasn't wholly without risk. Here was a Democratic candidate who already had a difficult time getting along with business, about to use business as an excuse to vote against the other guy; class warfare doesn't always help the side attack-ing the rich. Plenty of Democrats, Cutter predicted, especially those from the Acela Corridor (folks who live between New York City and Washington), would question their strategy: was Obama attacking busi-ness itself?

Axelrod, for one, was nervous that some of the ads would come across as too negative. But Cutter argued that the campaign couldn't flinch. "We can't do this half-assed," she told Plouffe, Axelrod, and Messina. "Either we're going to do it with gusto, or we're not going to do it." And Plouffe had an iron stomach—he wanted to hit Romney, and hard.

The first advertisements Obama's team had run, beginning way back in January, had largely been positive spots. Then, on May 14, Cutter and Larry Grisolano introduced Joe Soptic, a steelworker from

Kansas City who had lost his job when Bain Capital came to town. In a two-minute spot, Soptic, near tears at times, and several of his former coworkers castigate Bain and the men who ran it for sucking the money out of GST Steel, a part of GS Industries. "It's like a vampire. They came in and sucked the life out of us," says Jack Cobb, another former steelworker. "We view Mitt Romney as a job destroyer," says John Wiseman, a third man who lost his job.

The amount of money Obama's campaign spent on the two-minute ad was relatively small—it was a "show buy" in political parlance, aimed as much at earning media attention, and thus new eyeballs the campaign didn't have to pay for, than at actually persuading voters.

Cutter had been right to predict trouble ahead. The Sunday after launching the attacks on Bain, Cory Booker, the young mayor of Newark, New Jersey (hence resident in the Acela Corridor), who was fast becoming one of the media's favorite Obama surrogates, voiced his discomfort with the president's line of attack. "I have to just say, from a very personal level, I'm not about to sit here and indict private equity," Booker said on *Meet the Press*. "If you look at the totality of Bain Capital's record, they've done a lot to support businesses, to grow businesses. And this to me, I'm very uncomfortable with.

"This kind of stuff is nauseating to me on both

sides," Booker went on. "It's nauseating to the American public. Enough is enough. Stop attacking private equity. Stop attacking Jeremiah Wright."[21]

The Wright reference was particularly jarring. The week before, news had leaked that conservative billionaire Joe Ricketts—founder of TDAmeritrade and owner of the Chicago Cubs—was planning a major advertising campaign that would once again bring up Obama's former minister, forcing the Obama campaign to stay adept at making sure any Wright reference was viewed solely as a racial attack whether it was intended or not. It took Ricketts all of about twenty-four hours to pledge *not* to run the Wright spot after mainstream Republicans denounced the tactic.

As for the Bain attacks, Booker wasn't the lone Democrat wetting himself, as Plouffe often described squeamish Democrats. Former representative Harold Ford, another young African American leader who had decamped to New York after losing a Tennessee Senate race in 2006, and former Pennsylvania governor Ed Rendell, one of the stalwarts of the Northeast Democratic establishment, joined Booker in his complaint. The Bain ads were "very disappointing," Rendell said.[22] So the Obama campaign moved swiftly to snuff out dissent. The very afternoon Booker was on *Meet the Press,* he was deluged with attacks from the left on social media; it got so bad that he decided to film a video from his office in Newark reiterating his support for the president. Tieless, direct-to-camera, Booker completely walked back his criticism of the Bain Capital ad: "Mitt Romney has made his business record a centerpiece of his campaign. He's talked about himself as a job creator. And therefore, it is reasonable, and in fact I encourage it, for the Obama campaign to examine that record and to discuss it. I have no problem with that," Booker explained. Republicans mocked it as a hostage video. They weren't that far off: someone from Chicago had very clearly taken Booker to the woodshed. Interestingly, this was a rare instance in which the president okayed a hardball tactic like that, something that would have made LBJ or Bill Clinton proud. Oddly, the president has never had trouble playing hardball with members of his own party; it is figuring out how to play hardball against the GOP that has always eluded him.

Still, the Bain attack launch provided more evidence to the president that key surrogates were not prepped on their strategy, and that the campaign, as it kicked off, looked sloppy. A few weeks later, after one more self-inflicted wound, Obama would reach his wits' end and let his team have it.

Cutter had built a network of more than 1,000 surrogates in every state and city of significant size, and she sent one of her most prominent stand-ins, David Axelrod, to Boston. Axelrod would appear on the steps of the Massachusetts state capitol, on

Beacon Hill, to try to undermine the other foundational pillar of Romney's record—his term as governor.

Voters have an inherently positive view of governors; their executive experience lends them credibility, and their distance from Washington gives them the opportunity to run against a political culture most voters believe needs change and an outsider's perspective. (It's no coincidence that four of the last six presidents—Carter, Reagan, Clinton, and George W. Bush—had governed a state as their last elected job before being elevated.)

Romney's record, Axelrod said, was "alarmingly weak." During his tenure, Massachusetts had been forty-seventh among the states in job creation—a statistic the campaign would repeat endlessly during the following months—and that state's government had grown six times faster than the private sector had.

But holding an event in Boston came with a built-in risk: Beacon Hill was just a few miles from Romney's headquarters, where hundreds of staffers and volunteers worked feverishly for their man. The Romney campaign held a conference call the night before Axelrod's event, then mobilized what seemed like every supporter they had in the greater Boston area. By the time Axelrod showed up, he found as many Romney supporters as Obama supporters waiting for him.

In hindsight, this event was emblematic of what would become one of the more uninspiring political campaigns of the modern era. The two sides competed for attention. Obama fans screamed their man's signature chant—"Fired up, ready to go!"—while Romney supporters yelled back, "Solyndra!" "Forward!" the Obama team shouted. "Off a cliff!" the Romney partisans shot back. One Romney staffer, a member of the advance team, blew bubbles at Axelrod while the campaign's senior strategist spoke.[23]

Back in Washington, Obama was beside himself. He watched coverage of the Axelrod event in disbelief, wondering how his team could have screwed up so badly. Why not just hold the press conference inside the capitol, in a conference room, someplace where the Romney backers couldn't intervene?

Obama went looking for someone to yell at. He found Dan Pfeiffer. How could this event, he wanted to know, this *simplest* of exercises, so routine a professional political operative could have designed it in his sleep, have turned into such a mess? Obama chewed out David Plouffe in the same manner.

A few days later, Obama told his senior advisors they needed to shape up. He made clear that they had to tighten their game, that the campaign had been signaling its plays before the snap. Shape up, Obama told his team, and do it now.

From that moment on, Plouffe and Messina would work together much more closely, excluding others (including Cutter) who were filling vacuums that were being ignored by the White House, with Plouffe becoming the final word on messaging: it meant deciding what issue they would focus on, what they were going to say about that issue on a given day, and who was going to say it. To make sure the campaign's two outposts—the headquarters in Chicago and the White House—were on the same page, Pfeiffer began traveling to Chicago on a regular basis, spending a day or two a week working out of the campaign office.

"The thing that was missing," Pfeiffer said later, "was the discipline. Who's making sure the consultants don't talk to reporters on background? Who's the one who's making the decision that we're not doing every interview that everyone wants to do?" Still, the fundamental plan that Plouffe and Messina had charted from the beginning stayed intact: they would begin the campaign with a relentless focus on Romney's record. They would use the Democratic convention, in Charlotte in September, to make the positive case for a second term. And they would contrast those two visions during the home stretch, the two-month sprint between Labor Day and Election Day.

In 2004, John Kerry had accepted public matching funds, which meant he had only $75 million[24] to spend on advertising between the time he accepted the Democratic nomination, on July 29, and Election Day. George W. Bush would formally accept the Republican nomination more than a month later, on September 2, which allowed him to spend money he had raised for the primaries up until the first week of September before dipping into his own $75 million in public financing.

In 2004, $75 million was still thought of as a lot of money for a three-month campaign sprint. (By 2012, $75 million was about the average amount the campaigns and Super PACs spent on TV advertising in a given week. The acceleration of campaign spending on the presidential level is bordering on unsustainable.) To husband those resources, and because Kerry would have to spread his money over a longer period than Bush, Kerry's campaign didn't advertise during August. But the airwaves weren't completely free of political ads. One group, dubbed the Swift Boat Veterans for Truth, spent a comparatively paltry sum—about $2 million[25]—on spots that attacked Kerry's service record during the Vietnam War. The misleading ads had attacked the very foundation on which Kerry was building his campaign. He hadn't responded beyond issuing press releases, and the ads took a heavy political toll.

Messina faced the very real prospect that several groups were promising to spend hundreds of times more than the Swift Boat Veterans, and he was determined not to make the same mistake Kerry's team had made; every attack would be answered, in one form or another, even if the campaign couldn't spend as much as the outside groups. And indeed, the Obama campaign's very first advertisement, way back in January 2012, was not some glossy "why he's running again" spot; it was instead a negative ad, a response to one funded by the Koch brothers. In hindsight, this simple fact is truly symbolic of just how negative the 2012 campaign was. To think that the first TV ad aired by the sitting president of the United States running for re-election was a negative response ad to a Super PAC! When the campaign financing system someday comes completely undone (if it hasn't already), this moment will be among the seminal bullet points tracking this downward trajectory.

But spending money early also meant, if Messina's conservative estimates were right and the enthusiasm Democratic donors exhibited in 2008 never materialized in 2012, that the Obama team might wake up one morning in late September or early October and realize they were out of money. They could keep their advertising reservations until the last minute, but there might come a time when they would have to cancel them en masse simply because they could no longer afford them. Or they could limit advertising to the most competitive states, something Al Gore was forced to do in 2000 when he pulled out of Ohio — of all places — because he was out of cash.

On May 26, during a weekly senior advisors' meeting with the president, Messina laid out his plan:

take the risk and spend money early, either to paint an unflattering portrait of Romney or to defend against attacks from outside groups. Plouffe and Axelrod agreed with Messina's strategy. Obama signed off, knowing full well that there was a real danger he could find himself buried by Romney's late spending in the crucial final stretch.

"We...kind of gambled on the front end and front-loaded our media, without any guarantee that we were going to be able to make it up on the back end," Axelrod said later, at a postelection conference at Harvard University.[26] Of course, had they been out of money in October, it would have been a sign that the Obama campaign had lost the confidence of its supporters anyway.

June and July were nerve-wracking. Rove's Crossroads organization spent a few million a week across battleground states, while Koch brothers–affiliated groups occasionally dropped in their own ad buys. But the hammer never really came down as the Obama team expected. Sure, a lot of money was spent by outside groups, but it was somewhat sporadic and never carried a cohesive message—a complaint the Romney campaign would quietly be making to reporters in an effort to publicly shame the GOP outside groups into doing a better job on messaging.

What's more, Federal Communications Commission rules allow candidates to pay a lower rate for advertisements than noncandidate outside groups. That meant the campaigns would pay the lowest available rate, while outside groups, car dealerships, furniture stores—any other entity trying to purchase television time—were paying the market rate. So even though it was being outspent on the air, the Obama campaign was actually running more individual advertisements than the various Republican and conservative outside groups were. And Romney's campaign was waiting until the last minute to place their TV buys, costing them more on the front end. This was a fine way to buy ads for, say, toothpaste, since you'd be advertising toothpaste for years to come and could take full advantage of the eventual refund. But since campaigns have a specific end date, this was not the best way to husband resources. All the buys the Obama campaign made were done weeks or even months in advance, which is the cheapest way to guarantee the best time slots—a seemingly small but strategic way the Obama campaign outperformed Romney's.

The number of available ad spaces was finite, and the supply didn't increase in response to demand; people didn't go out and start new television stations just to capture the candidates' advertising dollars. About the only way new TV ad space was created was if local stations decided to shorten their newscasts from twenty-two minutes to twenty or even eighteen minutes, which gave their ad sales teams

496 • THE STRANGER

two to four more minutes to sell. Thus competition for the small number of slots was fierce, and prices kept rising. By the end of the campaign, ads in the Washington, D.C., media market, which would reach crucial swing voters in the northern Virginia suburbs, were as expensive as advertisements were in New York City, the nation's priciest media market. Demand was so great that ads that reached swing voters in markets like Las Vegas, Denver, Tampa, and Orlando ended up costing four, five, even six times the regular rate—but again, candidates are to a point exempt from this inflation, which is mostly intended for the protection of the local congressional or state senate candidates trying to get their message out, not presidential campaigns.

Despite the gamble of spending early, the Obama campaign maintained the reservations it had already made for September and October and locked in those cheaper rates. Not thinking about those rates was one of the Romney campaign's worst strategic blunders. It was as if his team was more worried about ad agency and consultant fees than about making sure they could afford to advertise, let alone reserving slots when they would most need them.

The disparity in ad buying highlights an area in which Obama's campaign excelled: planning ahead. To be sure, Team Obama made some mistakes—witness Boston. But those were exceptions. Not only was the team particularly good at preparation; Romney's campaign was fantastically bad at long-term planning. In terms of TV ad buying, Romney's team was using a playbook from the '90s, while Obama's team was writing an entirely new one.

The Obama campaign had mapped out their reactions to just about every possible contingency well in advance. While waiting for the Supreme Court's decision on the constitutionality of the individual mandate in the health care law, Stephanie Cutter and Jennifer Palmieri (a real professional and a Clinton White House veteran brought in as deputy White House communications director in 2011 in an attempt to repair relations with the White House press corps) had created so many reaction plans for the various scenarios that they ended up filling a binder. "The only thing we didn't have planned out was, like, a nuclear war," Cutter joked later. The White House even had a legislative alternative ready to go had the Court ruled against it, and a carrot to entice the states to establish health care exchanges, and a mandate, on their own.

The case before the Supreme Court was actually an argument that had begun on the fringes: that the mandate was unconstitutional because the government couldn't penalize someone for *not* participating in commerce. While the argument started on the fringes, it took off in the conservative grass roots, and many Republican attorneys general decided to sign on. There were a few other cases challenging different aspects of the law for which some judges had found in favor, so the Supreme Court consolidated all of them into one case. But the central focus was on the mandate. The Obama White House maintained that under the commerce clause, it did have the right to force people to buy a product or face a penalty. There was enough precedent for using the commerce clause that many in the legal community assumed it would win its case rather easily. Well, the White House won it, but not the way it had expected. It came as an' extraordinary relief to the West Wing when the Court, in a strange 5–4 decision authored by Chief Justice John Roberts, ruled in favor of the mandate by declaring it a tax, which was consistent with Congress's powers to levy fees, at the same time implying, however, that Congress did not have the power to do this under the commerce clause — a significant decision in its own right.

Obama had always been confident that his health care law would pass constitutional muster. Privately, he and his legal people were convinced the law would survive 6–3, believing they would win Anthony Kennedy — the usual swing vote on the Court of late — and Roberts. And if they won 5–4, they assumed it would be Kennedy who would give them their fifth vote.

What no one in the White House imagined was that John Roberts would be the swing vote, especially if it was clear that conservatives had won Kennedy over.

Just how this actually went down inside the Court is something the public won't know for sure for decades, when the internal deliberations and the papers of retired or deceased justices finally become public, which is at the discretion of each justice. (For instance, Justice Byron "Whizzer" White allowed his papers to be made public ten years after his death.) What is clear is that Roberts was inclined to strike down the law; he had assigned himself the opinion, knowing it was going to be a legacy maker for his Court no matter which side he ended up on. It was during his deliberations—which included some subtle lobbying by fellow justice Stephen Breyer—that he concluded that just because he didn't like the law didn't mean it wasn't constitutional, and that overturning it would be a form of judicial activism that Roberts was predisposed against. One thing many Court observers have learned about Roberts is that at the end of the day, he's an institutionalist, meaning he believes if you do plan to set new precedents, you should do so gradually, respecting the other two branches of government along the way—hence ruling in favor of the health care law but curbing the expansion of the commerce clause.

The decision was a massive blow to Obamacare opponents. While Team Obama is convinced that they could have survived a summer of questions surrounding the constitutionality of the health care law had it been struck down, the campaign would likely have looked a lot different. For one thing, it would have given Romney more credibility on the issue of health care when he claimed what was right for Massachusetts wasn't necessarily right for the country as a whole. And, of course, it would have meant that the health care issue, something the Obama campaign hoped to essentially ignore for the duration of the re-election phase, would have been front and center. No way could they have devoted weeks or months to discrediting Romney; instead, they would have had to spend weeks defending a new health care fix, one unlikely to ever pass muster with a Republican House. In short, John Roberts saved the Obama campaign.

And so, the last element Barack Obama needed was a case for a second term.

For a candidate who desperately needed voters to consider whether they would be better off after another four years rather than whether they were better off than they had been, Obama had been remarkably defensive about his first-term agenda. And to some degree, circumstances—like the Court's decision to take up the health care law in the first place—required such a defense. But voters still needed to hear what would come next, why they would be better off with another four years of Barack Obama.

The venue in which to make that case would be the convention, set for the first week of September in North Carolina.

Obama's team had watched with barely concealed glee as Republicans had all but wasted their own convention. A hurricane had barreled through the Caribbean and up Florida's Gulf coast, barely missing Tampa, where Republican delegates had gathered, and forcing organizers—for the second time in four years—to cancel the first day of events.

On the second day Ann Romney gave a moving, heartfelt speech that helped humanize her stiff and at times standoffish husband, but just minutes later Chris Christie, governor of New Jersey and one of the party's rising stars, delivered a keynote address focused almost entirely on himself and his own record rather than on his party or its presidential nominee. Christie and Ann were not supposed to speak on the same night, but events dictated that the two would have to share their prime-time hours. Ann's remarks ran a tad long, and to save time the Republican Party's executive producer for the convention informed Christie's folks that they would have to kill his introductory video. That did not go over well with the New Jersey governor. According to some eyewitnesses backstage, Christie used some version of the f-bomb and implied that if the video didn't play, he wouldn't speak. It was a potential disaster. In order to avoid a scene the video was aired, which created an awkward interlude between Ann and Christie. To make matters worse, and to the eternal befuddlement of Team Romney, Christie never praised or even acknowledged Ann for her remarks before jumping into his self-promotion. Christie's not mentioning Romney by name became a thing on Twitter. Finally, after about fifteen minutes into his speech, Christie did talk about Mitt, but the damage was done.

The next night (technically day three), Paul Ryan gave a speech riddled with factual inaccuracies. Day four was the Romney campaign's final opportunity to sell millions of Americans on their plan without having to deal with a media filter. The final hour, which was to include Romney's acceptance speech, was instead dominated by one of the odder moments in recent political memory: actor Clint Eastwood made a surprise appearance, and then for twelve awkward, surreal minutes he lectured an empty chair—which he said stood in for President Obama. Romney advisors were horrified. They had wasted a dozen of the most valuable minutes of the entire campaign, when the eyes of the nation were on them, and had just guaranteed that the talk of the media and the bandwidth of YouTube would make their candidate look like a fool.

The irony of all this was that two of the three broadcast networks—CBS and NBC—had asked the Romney campaign whether they wanted to play their candidate's campaign video in the 10 p.m. hour as the introduction to Romney's speech. The networks had done this for every nominee of both parties going back twenty years. But the Romney team decided instead to claim the 9 p.m. hour, when only the cable networks were airing the convention. Featuring a series of testimonials from people who had worked for Romney over the years, the video did what the campaign had failed to do for months before the convention, which was humanize the sometimes-stiff Republican nominee. It was probably the best case for Romney the person that anyone had ever seen—but alas, only those watching cable saw it, and they were the diehards of both parties, whose minds were already made up. The swing voters who would watch in the 10 p.m. hour, when every broadcast network cut in, instead saw a cranky old man yelling at an empty chair.

Marco Rubio, the popular young Florida senator who was already a rising star in the party, gave his own well-received speech after the weird Eastwood deal. But after Eastwood's rambling talk, Romney's acceptance speech ran well past the planned 11 p.m. cutoff. Most news stations delayed their local news broadcasts to continue airing the speech, but the later the hour, the more likely viewers were to turn off the set (or, in the case of some, fall asleep in their chairs).

Romney's address was surprisingly personal for a man not known for sharing his feelings. But the following day, as feared, almost every major news outlet mentioned Eastwood's bizarre speech in their coverage of Romney.

The Republican convention was the Romney campaign in a nutshell—poorly planned, too gimmicky, and off message.

The Obama team exerted much tighter control on their convention. They edited speeches line by line, strictly regulated the time each speaker was allowed at the podium, and even managed that most difficult task of convention organizers—allotting speaking time to candidates who might try to succeed Obama four years down the road, like Maryland governor Martin O'Malley and Montana governor Brian Schweitzer, in a manner that kept everyone relatively happy.

The only speech the Obama team left largely up to its author demonstrated just how far one of the most fascinating relationships in American politics had come. By now, Axelrod and Bill Clinton had grown to deeply respect each other even if there were still sore feelings. Clinton's speech-writing process had always been frenetic, marked by last-minute revisions and handwritten edits; this time around, in the days before his convention address, Clinton actually called Axelrod for help. (Even after it had been edited down to 3,000 words, Clinton added another 2,000 extemporaneously.[27] When he would go off script, the teleprompter operator would scroll up and down, frantically looking for the section Clinton was reading—or, more accurately, ad-libbing.)

Clinton's speech stood in stark contrast to Eastwood's bizarre rant the week before in Tampa. Despite some physical signs that the former president was slowing down (and close watchers of the man say they are more pronounced than casual watchers might notice), he was on his game when the lights came on. Bill Clinton demonstrated again his ability to connect national issues with an individual voter's situation, in a manner that resonates. "If you want a 'you're-on-your-own, winner-take-all' society, you should support the Republican ticket," he said. "If you want a country of shared prosperity and shared responsibility, [a] 'we're-all-in-this-together' society, you should vote for Barack Obama and Joe Biden."[28]

The former president neatly summed up the sluggish economic recovery, what Obama had accomplished in his first term, and the contrast between Obama and Romney better in a single address than Obama had been able to do in his four years in office. Clinton's speech was a much bigger hit, and arguably made a bigger postconvention splash, than the one Obama gave the next night. What really made Obama jealous was not that Clinton stole the show, it was how he did it—with an incredibly wonky, long, and sometimes rambling address. Obama so desperately wanted to wonk out more, ramble more like a professor, but when *he* did it, it didn't work. Maybe it's the southern part of Clinton, the preacherlike qualities that make his audiences more patient.

The Democratic convention was not without its

unscripted flubs. The enthusiasm gap Democrats now faced meant they wouldn't be able to re-create the high-intensity acceptance speech Obama had given four years earlier, in Denver, when his supporters had packed Mile High Stadium to cheer him on. Convention organizers had planned to duplicate that crowd in Bank of America Stadium, home of the Carolina Panthers, but they scrubbed that venue when it became clear they wouldn't be able to give away enough tickets to fill the seats. Still, they didn't want to look as if they were scrubbing the outdoor speech because of a ticket issue, so the organizers were praying for rain. And they got just enough of a storm passing through the area that they were able to make the decision seem to be due solely to the weather. There really was a storm headed to Charlotte on Thursday, but it wasn't nearly as dire as organizers pretended to fear; it was just enough for them to look overly cautious. When Obama took the stage that night, there was hardly a cloud in the Charlotte sky.

There was one other blip. Reporters scrutinizing a draft of the party platform noticed that it failed to include a reference to God, and that it eliminated language used four years earlier, when it specifically identified Jerusalem as the capital of Israel.

The White House had been asked to vet the platform before it went to the committee. Denis McDonough and Ben Rhodes, the two most political members of the national security team, had signed off on the Israel language, which they had changed to reflect current U.S. policy. Both put accuracy above what made political sense, and calling Jerusalem the capital is important to many voters, including those in the swing state of Florida. Patrick Gaspard, the former White House political director who left to become executive director of the Democratic National Committee, swears he drafted but never sent an e-mail to the platform committee reminding them to keep references to God and faith in the document. There was no overarching reason why he didn't send it; he simply forgot.

Obama blamed Gaspard for the screwup. "Patrick, I have two vulnerabilities — Israel and faith," Obama said. "And we botched both."

Gaspard moved fast to fix the problem. The platform would be amended from the floor of the convention, with the assistance of convention chairman Antonio Villaraigosa, then the mayor of Los Angeles and perhaps the highest-profile Hispanic in the Democratic Party at the time. Villaraigosa would call for a vote on the new language, then rule in favor of the changes no matter how many liberals voted no. "I got this," Villaraigosa told Gaspard. "I know how to call a vote." There were audible boos over the change, but Villaraigosa rammed it through — crisis averted, at least with the mainstream media; conservative news outlets were having a field day, but at this point in the campaign, the Obama folks didn't worry much about right-wing outrage.

Obama addressed delegates the following night, offering a delicate balance between a defense of his first term and a forward-looking vision for the future. "I won't pretend the path I'm offering is quick or easy; I never have," Obama said. "You didn't elect me to tell you what you wanted to hear. You elected me to tell you the truth. And the truth is, it will take more than a few years for us to solve challenges that have built up over decades.

"Our problems can be solved. Our challenges can be met. The path we offer may be harder, but it leads to a better place. And I'm asking you to choose that future," he said. That path included more policy in a single speech than Obama had offered during the rest of the campaign, but it wasn't anything revolutionary. Pledges included one million new manufacturing jobs and a $4 trillion cut in the deficit — the jobs number was something the economic recovery should automatically take care of; the deficit cut was a pledge Republicans were going to try to make him keep regardless of whether he pushed for it or not. But the real message Obama intended to send was that the election offered a stark choice between his plan and the conservative alternative. Gone were the references to Romney the flip-flopper; instead, Obama made clear, it was right versus left. It was time to make this a "choice" election.

As a measure of just how polarized the electorate had become, neither Romney nor Obama received much benefit from either the Tampa or Charlotte event; the proverbial convention bounce in the polls never materialized, because so many voters had already made up their minds.* Nevertheless, the lack of a bounce hurt Romney more than it did Obama. In the first surveys conducted after the conventions, every news organization in America found the same results: Obama was ahead. Even Rasmussen, the autodial polling firm whose methods had been criticized for including too many Republican voters in order to guarantee the best possible GOP spin on a matchup, showed Obama leading by five points. Polling in virtually every swing state showed the same trends: in the week following the convention, Obama led Romney in Ohio by four to seven points and in Virginia by five to eight points. Similar margins showed up in surveys conducted in Iowa, Nevada, New Hampshire—almost every swing state. Even polls in Florida, a state Republicans believed they could put away early, showed a competitive race, with results ranging from an NBC/*Wall Street Journal* poll showing Obama leading by five to a Republican firm's poll showing Romney leading by three.

Romney, it was clear, was running out of time to

---

* Gallup measured only a three-point increase in Obama's standing, one of the smaller bounces in recent history.

change the equation. He would have only three chances — the presidential debates.

Obama saw the same polls. A year earlier, after the fight over raising the debt ceiling, his job approval number had been toxically mired in the 40s. Now, as Obama retreated to a less-than-swanky resort at Lake Las Vegas, a half-hour drive from the glitz and glamour of the Strip, to spend a few days preparing for his first face-to-face encounter with Romney, his cockiness showed through even the thick veil the campaign had put between their candidate and the press. Instead of spending quiet time studying the issues and his opponent's likely positions, Obama attended a rally of Nevada supporters. A few days later, he visited the Hoover Dam. During a stop at a campaign office, where he dropped in to thank volunteers with a pile of six pizzas, he said preparing for debates "is a drag." "They're making me do my homework," he told one volunteer. "Basically, they're keeping me indoors all the time."[29] Obviously, he was trying to show that he was keeping his cool, but he was doing nothing, even halfheartedly, to frame the challenge ahead of him. The fact of the matter was, Obama didn't view Romney as a really worthy opponent. Little comments like the one to Nevada campaign workers were telling.

There is always a blurry line when candidates discuss debate prep: how much work do you want to admit having to do? After all, you've been telling the public how obviously wrong your opponent's proposals are, so why do you need to review those arguments? And it's certainly expected that you know your own positions. Yet Obama's comments carried a tone that went beyond joke or spin, and right into arrogance. His was hardly the attitude of someone throwing himself full-bore into the rigors of preparation.

Behind closed doors, Obama had been similarly dismissive. Presidents running for re-election frequently find themselves in an odd position when they debate their opponents. For several years, they have been unchallenged in person; no one is the president's equal, and the Seal of the President of the United States lends a kind of protective shield that elevates one man above all others. But when presidents land on a debate stage, they face a person who will be treated as their equal, at least by the moderators. For the first time in a very long time, someone can actually tell the president of the United States to stop talking.

In 2008, Obama may not have particularly liked John McCain, but he respected the Arizona Republican and thought him worthy of the presidency. In 2012, Obama had come to personally dislike Mitt Romney on a much deeper level. (This is apparently not an unusual occurrence for Romney; McCain and his fellow Republican candidates came to feel the same way about Romney during the 2008 primaries.) Obama's feelings toward Romney, he later acknowledged to his closest advisors, had blinded him to the former Massachusetts governor's strengths and led him to underestimate his opponent.[30]

On October 3, the two men met at the University of Denver for their first debate, and Obama's lack of preparation showed almost immediately. He missed his cues and flubbed some lines, as if he had been asked questions he didn't anticipate. But the questions that seemed to trip Obama up the most were ones his advisors had anticipated and prepared for — the health care reform law, for example.

Watching from another room, Obama's top advisors saw with a growing sense of horror their candidate flailing about. Focus groups were showing new enthusiasm for Romney; thanks to high-tech dial monitoring of undecided voters across the country, Obama advisors could feel their lead — stable but slim — slipping away in real time. The split-screen broadcast, which kept cameras focused on both candidates no matter who was answering a question, showed a shifty-eyed Obama visibly disgusted with the more poised, calm, and polished Republican. Several top advisors who had been buoyed by predebate polls felt their stomachs sink: their guy might have just blown the election.

Across the hall, in the room reserved for Romney advisors, the mood was incredulous. Here was their candidate, a stiff, distant businessman, beating up on one of the most practiced and talented politicians of his generation. In Boston, Romney's communications director, Gail Gitcho, had to warn her surrogates not to pound their chests or declare victory too loudly.[31]

As Obama walked offstage after declaring it "a terrific debate," he knew he had screwed up. Twenty years before that evening he had married Michelle Robinson, and his staff had planned an anniversary celebration at Obama's hotel later that night. But the party was subdued at best. Obama spent the rest of the evening and the following morning on the phone with his biggest supporters, apologizing for his lousy performance.

The next morning, Obama needed a pick-me-up. On debate day, the weather in Denver had been gorgeous; temperatures reached the mid-70s. But the morning after, when the campaign had scheduled a rally at the city's Sloan's Lake Park, the mercury had plummeted to the 40s.[32] Still, the park was packed, and people in the crowd started shouting when Obama got to the stage: "We got your back!"

Obama was moved, and so was his staff, even though many of that evening's newscasts ran interviews with those supporters, all of them concerned about the president's debate performance.

In the next two debates Obama was sharper. He contrasted himself with Romney at almost every turn, negotiating a delicate line between being critical and sounding mean. And even though the focus groups had rendered a terrifying verdict in Denver, one thing didn't change: the poll numbers. Obama's campaign still showed their man ahead and their coalition ready to turn out to vote.

On Monday, November 5, Barack Obama attended his last-ever campaign rally as a candidate. At two minutes to 10 p.m., Michelle Obama walked out onstage at the intersection of East Fourth and East Locust Streets in Des Moines, Iowa, in the heart of the state that had launched his presidential ambitions. The president joined her a few minutes later, at times tearing up as his campaign journey came to an end.

"I came back to ask you to help us finish what we started because this is where our movement for change began," Obama said. "To all of you who've lived and breathed the hard work of change: I want to thank you. You took this campaign and made it your own."

At 10:35, Obama asked God to bless the United States of America. Two hours and fourteen minutes later, Marine One touched down at a landing zone just a few blocks from Obama's Hyde Park home in Chicago.

On Election Day, Obama woke up in his own bed, as he had done so rarely during his first term in office. He sat for television interviews with ten local news channels that reached seven key swing states —

Iowa, Wisconsin, Ohio, Florida, Virginia, Colorado, and Nevada.

He played basketball with some of his closest friends: education secretary Arne Duncan, his body man Reggie Love, Marty Nesbitt, and Mike Ramos, a friend from Obama's high school days in Hawaii. Michelle's brother, Craig Robinson, White House chef Sam Kass, and Chicago Bulls legend Scottie Pippen were also on the court.[33]

All along, Republicans had assumed that there was no way that African American and Hispanic voters would turn out at the same levels they had in 2008, though they would certainly make up a larger part of the electorate than they had in 2010. Moreover youth turnout would be down; the trend of union households losing market share would continue; and independents would give Romney much more support than they had given McCain four years earlier.

Those assumptions flew in the face of historical precedent, which showed the share of white voters in the electorate declining every four years. But, the logic went, the Obama campaign in 2008 had expanded the electorate so much that it couldn't expand any further.

In essence, the Romney campaign was giving the 2008 Obama campaign more credit than it deserved. And they were wrong. Black voters turned out at a higher level than they had in 2008; for the first time in American history, a larger percentage of black voters cast a ballot than did white voters. Hispanic voters showed up in greater numbers, too, and more important, they actually voted for Obama in higher proportions than they had four years earlier. Self-described independents had given Romney 50 percent of the vote, compared with 45 percent for Obama, but those who called themselves moderates—a whopping 41 percent of the electorate—had given Obama a fifteen-point edge. It turns out quite a few self-described independents were ex-Republicans, right-leaning voters who did not want to identify with their former political party.

What surprised the Obama campaign most was younger voters: those between the ages of eighteen and twenty-nine, a segment that went for Obama by a 60 to 37 percent margin, made up 19 percent of the electorate, a slightly larger percentage than they had been in 2008. "No one—you, me, no one—thought we'd increase youth turnout," Messina marveled.

The 2012 campaign was a far cry from Obama's first victory, in 2008; "Hope and Change" had been replaced by "Forward." This may have been a calculated effort to change a conversation the White House would otherwise lose, but the campaign had showcased what was vintage Obama: lofty rhetoric, a populist pitch, a cocky candidate, and, as in every Obama story, at least a few moments of back-against-the-wall panic. And ultimately, on Election Day, the president displayed his trademark preternatural cool. Obama had played basketball.

That night, as polls closed across the nation, Obama and his senior advisors watched the network broadcasts on a bank of TVs at the Fairmont Hotel. Exit surveys showed Obama running away with swing state after swing state. At 11:14, NBC was the first network to call the presidency, just fourteen minutes later than it had called the election four years earlier. It was not technically a landslide re-election, but in this political environment it was about as close as one party could get.

CHAPTER FOURTEEN

If He Had a Son

In the rare moments when Barack Obama addressed the touchy subject of race in America, he did so in response to some outside event, one of the myriad of small moments when the scab was ripped off the ever-fresh wound. In such cases, the cycle seemed to repeat itself: he would respond to a race-inspired frenzy in an awkward fashion, opening himself to attacks from the right and disappointment from black leaders on the left. Then, after reflection, he would respond with a well-thought-out meditation on race relations—it would earn praise with those formerly disappointed black leaders but earn scorn again from the right.

Six months into Obama's presidency, Henry Louis Gates arrived home from a trip to China. The well-known Harvard professor of African American studies had been researching the family of the cellist Yo-Yo Ma for an upcoming series on PBS[1] when he returned home only to have the key to the front door of his Cambridge home jam. Gates and his driver were trying to pry the door open when a neighbor called police to report a possible burglary in progress. When Gates and the responding officer, Cambridge police sergeant James Crowley, argued, Crowley arrested Gates and charged him with disorderly conduct.

The incident would have been only another unfortunate occurrence, one of dozens that take place every day across America, in which a white police officer and a black man have a negative interaction. But such incidents don't happen to a well-known Harvard professor, one who has hosted several shows on public television and whose scholarship is widely respected. The story festered on cable news channels as liberals and conservatives retreated to their familiar positions: Gates had been profiled unjustly, the left screamed; the police were the ones being scapegoated, the right bemoaned.

Six days later, on July 22, 2009, at 8:01 p.m., President Obama met the press in the East Room of the White House to talk about health care at a critical juncture. With Congress scheduled to return home for the August recess just a few days later, Obama wanted to keep the momentum going. He devoted more than 7,200 words to the politics of health care, trying to clear up the misinformation he thought Republicans were pushing to try to kill the measure and reassuring the public that his bill would expand access while cutting costs. Then he called on a familiar face from his Illinois days, Lynn

Sweet of the *Chicago Sun-Times,* to ask the final question. "Recently Professor Henry Louis Gates Jr. was arrested at his home in Cambridge," Sweet began. "What does that incident say to you and what does it say about race relations in America?"

Commenting on a case in Cambridge, about which he admitted he didn't have all the facts, was not a wise move for a president who is ordinarily cautious. The day before, on July 21, the Cambridge police had dropped the case. But "Skip" Gates, as he is known, is a friend of the president's, and Obama decided to comment anyway.

"I don't know, not having been there and not seeing all the facts, what role race played in that, but I think it's fair to say, number one, any of us would be pretty angry; number two, that the Cambridge Police acted stupidly in arresting somebody when there was already proof that they were in their own home," he said. "And number three, what I think we know separate and apart from this incident is that there is a long history in this country of African Americans and Latinos being stopped by law enforcement disproportionately. That's just a fact."[2]

Instantly what had been a smoldering cable flame erupted into a full-blown national commotion. Police unions called on Obama to apologize, Cambridge's police commissioner said his department was "deeply pained," and (predictably) Fox News had a field day. An entire press conference meant to bolster the prospects of the top item on the president's first-term to-do list was nullified by a single remark. The following week, 17 percent of Americans said the controversy was the news story they were following most closely. This was only two percentage points lower than the attention the cratering economy earned, and more than half as much attention as the debate over health care reform received.[3]

The White House spent the next several days backtracking. Obama hadn't called Sergeant Crowley or the police department as a whole stupid, Gibbs insisted. Obama, he said, believed that "at a certain point the situation got far out of hand." In an interview with ABC's *Nightline,* Obama had to remind Americans that he respected police officers, "and that everybody should have just settled down and cooler heads should have prevailed. That's my suspicion." He said Crowley was an "outstanding police officer."[4]

A few days later, Obama invited Gates and Crowley to the White House for a beer. The three men, plus Joe Biden, sat on the patio of the Rose Garden on a warm July day; Obama drank a Bud Light, Gates had a Sam Adams Light, Crowley sipped a Blue Moon, and Biden, who doesn't drink, swigged a nonalcoholic Buckler. As an indication of the continued interest in the story, the Associated Press dedicated five reporters to its write-up, as many as they assign to the State of the Union.[5]

Obama said he was "fascinated by the fascination" with what the media had dubbed the Beer Summit. But he shouldn't have been. The nation that had elected the first African American president in its history encompassed numerous voters, even in the twenty-first century, who would view a black man with suspicion — especially one with a Muslim-sounding name, elected during a time when the United States was engaged in two wars in the Muslim world and constantly on the lookout for terrorists with dark skin. A white president would not have been reflexively linked to, say, Ku Klux Klan groups, but Fox News routinely ran stories about the radical antiwhite New Black Panther Party, which had allegedly intimidated voters in Philadelphia during the 2008 elections. It didn't matter that Obama had won Pennsylvania by more than 600,000 votes; the story still outraged conservative talk radio listeners. A Harvard doctoral student later calculated that Obama had lost 3 to 5 percent of the popular vote due to racial prejudice, but the study appears to have underestimated the jump in minority voters who had turned out because Obama himself was a minority figure. Still, it's clear that a generic white Democrat would have performed better with white voters.

Obama wasn't naïve. The nation's first black president would certainly have an impact on race relations in America. The question was how much, and in what context, he would address his skin color and the community that saw him as a model. Obama's goal was to set an example for young African Americans, a perpetually underserved community that could use a role model — indeed, the ultimate role model.

The African American community clearly saw the president as one of its own. Polls showed his support among black voters stayed strong, and he received more than 90 percent of their votes in both 2008 and 2012. But their support wasn't universal, and black elites in both the media and academic communities wondered aloud whether Obama was doing as much as he could to help the African American community.

Two in particular, Tavis Smiley and Cornel West, became especially tough critics. West, perhaps the nation's best-known scholar in the field of African American studies, is a frequent guest on Smiley's popular radio and PBS shows. Together, the two men spent the summer of 2011 touring eighteen cities for town hall meetings on race in America and poverty in the African American community. Along the way, both men harshly criticized the amount of attention — or lack thereof — Obama paid to the black community.

The data backed them up. The Great Recession hit African American communities harder than it did white ones. The unemployment rate among blacks topped 10 percent in July 2008, eventually peaking at 17.3 percent in January 2010. The unemployment rate for whites never reached double digits; by February 2010, 9.7 percent of whites were unemployed. Black unemployment still hasn't returned to single digits.

But while it was easy for the president (and the media) to avoid discussing the plight of the African American community, tensions between whites and blacks were never more than a small incident away from erupting anew.

On February 26, 2012, events in a gated community in the small town of Sanford, Florida, once again ripped open the old wounds. That night a young man named Trayvon Martin was returning from a store when a neighborhood watch volunteer named George Zimmerman grew suspicious. Zimmerman followed Martin, a struggle ensued, and a call to 911 recorded a gunshot being fired at 7:16 p.m. When police arrived, Martin lay dead on the street.

Police questioned Zimmerman for hours and treated his injuries. They initially declined to charge Zimmerman with a crime, but public pressure from the black community forced new investigations at the state level. As demands to charge Zimmerman heated up, Obama was once again asked to weigh in on a local investigation at the end of a press conference, this one in the Rose Garden, where Obama was nominating Dr. Jim Yong Kim to head the World Bank.

"Obviously, this is a tragedy. I can only imagine what these parents are going through. And when I think about this boy, I think about my own kids. And I think every parent in America should be able to understand why it is absolutely imperative that we investigate every aspect of this, and that everybody pulls together—federal, state and local—to figure out exactly how this tragedy happened," Obama said. "But my main message is to the parents of Trayvon Martin. If I had a son, he'd look like Trayvon. And I think they are right to expect that all of us as Americans are going to take this with the seriousness it deserves, and that we're going to get to the bottom of exactly what happened."[6]

If I had a son, he'd look like Trayvon. No other president in American history could have spoken to the raw emotions African Americans felt, and Obama had taken the opportunity to do so.

A year thereafter, late on a Saturday night, Zimmerman was acquitted by a jury of six women. An outpouring of grief and outrage surged once again through black communities; justice, they believed, hadn't been served. The White House issued only a brief statement.

But Obama wanted to say more. He waited for the end of the week, when on a hot and muggy summer Friday he appeared in the White House briefing room virtually unannounced, and gave one of the more stunning statements of his presidency. Trayvon Martin wasn't just someone who looked like his son, Obama explained. It could have been him.

"You know, when Trayvon Martin was first shot I said that this could have been my son. Another way of saying that is Trayvon Martin could have been me 35 years ago. And when you think about why, in the African American community at least, there's a lot of pain around what happened here, I think it's important to recognize that the African American community is looking at this issue through a set of experiences and a history that doesn't go away," Obama said. "There are very few African American men in this country who haven't had the experience of being followed when they were shopping in a department store. That includes me. There are very few African American men who haven't had the experience of walking across the street and hearing the locks click on the doors of cars. That happens to me — at least before I was a senator. There are very few African Americans who haven't had the experience of getting on an elevator and a woman clutching her purse nervously and holding her breath until she had a chance to get off. That happens often.

"And I don't want to exaggerate this, but those sets of experiences inform how the African American community interprets what happened one night in Florida. And it's inescapable for people to bring those experiences to bear. The African American community is also knowledgeable that there is a history of racial disparities in the application of our criminal laws—everything from the death penalty to enforcement of our drug laws. And that ends up having an impact in terms of how people interpret the case."[7]

Obama was speaking to two audiences: The African American community was deeply wounded yet again, convinced that justice in America was applied differently, based on race. Whites in America didn't view the world through the same prism. Obama's goal was to bridge the divide, to explain to blacks that justice would be served while explaining to whites why minorities felt the way they did. The anthropologist's son had evolved from observer to explainer.

That he's a person uniquely able to do this is something many black political activists have never fully understood about Obama. His black experience was a lot different from that of the vast majority of African Americans. He didn't grow up in the segregated South, nor did he really experience life in the northern inner cities. He grew up in the most diverse state in the country, where whites were *not* the majority. Indeed, a good number of the people around the president believe deep down that if Obama had grown up in a black community he might not have been able to be the country's first African American president, that one of the reasons white America accepted

Obama a lot more easily than, say, they did Jesse Jackson during Jackson's two unsuccessful presidential runs in the 1980s is that different experience growing up. He seemed more relaxed about race, less confrontational, someone who didn't come to politics with the scars of the civil rights movement. That bothered some African American political activists, but even some of them admitted privately that such status probably helped the president maneuver between white and black America.

Being a role model for young black men is an issue that has weighed on the president since before he decided to run; in fact, one of the positive impacts he thought he could have on society was simply winning and giving young black men a different perspective on what was truly possible for them. It's an issue Obama would like to spend much of his post-presidential time on, though it's an issue many African American activists wish he'd address sooner. But that's the thing with Obama: he's very careful about when he thinks the public is ready for him to be an activist for black America, indeed on any issue.

The Trayvon experience was a turning point for Obama, personally, on how he should deal with race while he was in office. It was the moment that he came to realize that if he was going to be the role model for young black men that he knew he should be, he would have to start acting, not just talking, and that he needed to do so *before* he left the White

House. He therefore launched a program aimed at helping vulnerable black men, called My Brother's Keeper, a program that advisors say will also be a big part of Obama's postpresidential life.

When Obama was inaugurated, Mitch McConnell, a month shy of his sixty-seventh birthday, had been the top Senate Republican for just two years, since Tennessee's Bill Frist had retired. McConnell was the consummate Senate leader, exceedingly deliberate with his words, fiercely defensive of his party, and in touch with each of its members. While the House Republican Conference proved unruly and nearly unmanageable after they took the majority in the 112th Congress, McConnell maintained almost total control over the Senate Republican Conference. Sometimes he twisted arms; other times he backed off. He might lose a conference member, but only when he could afford to do so, and he let his wavering charges come back to the fold on their own — which they usually did.

McConnell's ideology was subtle, but sometimes surprisingly malleable, unlike that of the House Republicans, who were a starkly conservative lot. He started his political career at a time when Kentucky was dominated by Democrats; at the University of Louisville in 1964, he had been a strong advocate for civil rights at a time when that wasn't a popular position in the Bluegrass State. That year, he advocated not for the ardently conservative Barry Goldwater, but for Henry Cabot Lodge Jr., the Republican civil rights supporter from Massachusetts.[8] He worked on Capitol Hill for John Sherman Cooper and Marlow Cook, two centrist Republicans from Kentucky.

As his career progressed, McConnell's political philosophy did, too. He was never purely conservative or purely centrist; instead, his ideology revolved around growing the number of Republicans in office. A telling moment came in a 2010 interview with *National Journal,* on the eve of a Republican electoral landslide, when McConnell was asked about his political goals. "The single most important thing we want to achieve," McConnell said, "is for President Obama to be a one-term president."[9]

McConnell played a key role in keeping Republicans cohesive during the first two years of Obama's tenure. While Democrats controlled the House by huge margins, enough to make the Republican minority virtually irrelevant, the fact that McConnell controlled a caucus of forty senators meant that he needed just one Democrat to put the brakes on any administration priority. Time and time again, McConnell used that power to slow down Obama's agenda. Delicate negotiations between bipartisan pairs of senators broke down at key moments, when Republicans either backed away or went silent. Only a trio of liberal Republicans from Maine and Pennsylvania broke with their party on the stimulus measure, and they didn't even do that until they had actually gotten some key concessions that McConnell wanted. And only the two Republicans from Maine—Arlen Specter had become a Democrat in the intervening time—voted for Dodd-Frank, the administration's signature financial reform package. In each instance, Democrats saw McConnell's hidden hand at work.

The Dodd-Frank example was very frustrating to the administration because there were a number of Senate Republicans who wanted to be a part of this bill; they knew the anti–Wall Street fervor that was running deep in the country would mean that this legislation would likely pass. But McConnell broke up every bipartisan team, including one that included Tennessee Republican Bob Corker. Corker eventually walked away, too, after he decided the White House was being too stubborn. Dodd-Frank was one of the rare times when the White House, via the Treasury Department, controlled the entire process. It wrote the legislation for Congress and then let Senator Chris Dodd and Representative Barney Frank tinker with it—essentially exactly the opposite strategy the White House used for health care. Why? The folks at Treasury, including Secretary Tim Geithner, didn't think Congress had the capacity to write the legislation. The financial industry, Geithner believed, was too complex for Congress, and there weren't enough Bob Corkers or Mark Warners in the Senate to write good legislation. But owning the legislation meant giving McConnell an even easier target for Republicans to rally against.

The growing animosity with which the Republican base viewed Obama played into McConnell's hands. Even mainstream politicians like McConnell used code words when asked about Obama's faith or his citizenship. "The president says he's a Christian. I take him at his word. I don't think that's in dispute," McConnell told NBC's David Gregory in August 2010, during one of his many appearances on *Meet the Press*.[10] It was an odd way to phrase what should have been a given.

Increasingly, the building anger Republican activists felt toward Obama meant pressure on those politicians to be seen opposing the president in ways that went far beyond simply voting against his agenda. Media coverage of town hall meetings in which Tea Party activists screamed at Democratic elected officials over health care reform overshadowed those being held by Republican members of Congress, but Republicans got just as much pressure to oppose Obama. Rallies for some Republican candidates had gotten ugly. At some, Obama was hanged in effigy; at others, activists threw around incendiary, racially tinged words. Although Republican candidates had distanced themselves from the ugliest examples—with the occasional embarrassing exception—the message from the activist class was clear: we are sending you to Washington to oppose Barack Obama and all he stands for.

The hyperpartisan America that Obama inherited meant that not only were there no Republicans to work with, there weren't even Republicans to talk to, or so he concluded. Just after his first inauguration, Obama had hosted a bipartisan gathering of lawmakers at the White House to watch the Pittsburgh Steelers play the Arizona Cardinals in the Super Bowl. After the game, which four Republicans attended, Representative Trent Franks, the conservative Cardinals fan from Arizona, said such a gathering "humanizes and personalizes opponents."[11] Four years later, when the director Steven Spielberg screened his award-winning movie *Lincoln* at the White House, Obama invited five Republicans—including both John Boehner and McConnell—to join him. None showed up.[12]

This would be a constant thorn in the side of the White House when many veteran members of the Washington political elite criticized Obama—not the Republicans—for the lack of bipartisan cooperation. Why blame Obama? Because the power of the presidency means he can command a stage anytime he wants. If Republicans weren't showing up for movie night at the White House, so what? Why wasn't the president going down to Capitol Hill more? Why weren't senators being invited for *unpublicized* one-on-one lunches with the leader of the free world? There were plenty of Republicans who wanted to help, but they wanted the White House to acknowledge the (sometimes ridiculous) political peril being seen with him might cause. And it was absurd at times.

Even associating with Obama became a liability for Republicans. Kirk Dillard, the Republican state senator who'd appeared in an Obama ad way back in 2007, lost his party's nomination for governor in 2010 amid griping that he had been involved in the campaign. Richard Lugar lost a primary two years later; his ties to Obama, helping him on START and loose nukes among other issues, made him appear to be a dreaded moderate in the eyes of Tea Party rival Richard Mourdock. (This was the same Dick Lugar who, when he served as mayor of Indianapolis, was once considered such a partisan Republican that he was dubbed Richard Nixon's favorite mayor.) When Obama hugged his pal Tom Coburn on the Senate floor, Coburn's office got fifty letters criticizing the senator.[13]

Aside from the rare moderates like Snowe and Collins, about the only Republicans to whom Obama could get through was a small contingent of governors desperate for the federal money that would turn their flagging economies around.

For example, four Republicans—Charlie Crist of Florida, Jim Douglas of Vermont, Arnold Schwarzenegger of California, and Jodi Rell of Connecticut—publicly supported the stimulus bill. When Obama traveled to Florida to tout the bill with Crist onstage, the men shared a bear hug. Crist heard about it for the next year and a half, right up until the time he had to bolt the Republican Party to run as an independent because he couldn't beat a little-known state representative named Marco Rubio in a primary. "It was the death knell for me as a Republican," Crist said of the embrace. (Crist is now a Democrat.)[14]

Beyond those state leaders, Democrats entertained particular hope in several Republicans who had once served as governors or mayors. They especially focused on those who had voted to expand the State Children's Health Insurance Program back in August 2007. The list of Republican yes votes included Lamar Alexander, former governor of Tennessee; Kit Bond, former Missouri governor; and Bob Corker, former mayor of Chattanooga and one of the GOP's key liaisons to the business community. Lisa Murkowski, the Alaska moderate, and Pat Roberts, the veteran appropriator from Kansas, had also voted for the insurance program, so they too were on the list.

But the White House failed to reach out consistently. Alexander, in particular, represented a missed opportunity. He was willing to take the president's call, but a call never came. Even when Alexander phoned the White House liaison to the Senate to ask for a meeting on appointees to the Tennessee Valley Authority, which oversees rivers and dams that provide power to his state, he never got a call back.

If Obama's first two years were a failed attempt to win over McConnell—or, really, any Senate Republican—the second two years, after the 2010 midterm elections, had been about winning over John Boehner and the House Republican Conference.

It did not start well.

As Axelrod and other senior White House aides watched the 2010 midterm returns, they realized they had a bit of a logistical problem: no one had Boehner's cell phone number. They hadn't needed to keep in touch with the leader of the small and irrelevant Republican House Conference in the preceding two years, so no one had prepared for the prospect— the likelihood—that Republicans would win and thus that Boehner would deserve a presidential phone call. They scrambled and eventually got Boehner's number, but it was an ominous sign—shouldn't they have had Boehner's number, because shouldn't they have had more than a perfunctory relationship with him? Were they *that* out of touch with the House GOP?

In the previous session, the legislative liaison's office had only needed to reach out to Nancy Pelosi, the Democratic Speaker; Democrats had enough seats that Republican members of the House were treated as an afterthought at best. But that was just one measure of the consequences of the White House's early approach to the House. When Democrats had been in the minority during George W. Bush's terms in office, Dick Gephardt, and then Pelosi, had both been included in weekly leadership meetings with the president. Obama hadn't continued those meetings, despite the advice of some of his most trusted confidants—including Tom Daschle, who had also attended Bush's meetings.

Boehner was by no means a Newt Gingrich type, a leader who charged forward, confident that his troops would be behind him. He was more like a chairman of the board, a leader by consensus. Boehner's survival as Speaker of the House depended on making his increasingly agitated and splintering conference happy—which meant that if he tried to move his team toward some sort of cooperative accommodation with the White House, he'd likely be kicked to the curb. So Boehner, too, would try to lead from behind.

Just months into Boehner's tenure, the problem with his more passive style became evident. As the White House and Boehner's office negotiated over a deal to fund the government through the rest of the fiscal year—a package known as a continuing resolution, which didn't save taxpayers much money, since continuing resolutions make long-term planning, ergo long-term purchasing, impossible—Democrats grew frustrated with the administration's proposed budget cuts. That money would come out of social programs Democrats cherished, yet these cuts didn't go far enough for Republicans, who wanted to slash even more. Republicans were also unwilling to even consider raising taxes or closing loopholes that would lead to more revenue.

In terms of public opinion, Republicans had the upper hand. The polls that David Plouffe was parsing showed a clear message: Americans wanted spending cuts, not Washington-speak about raising revenue, and they certainly weren't interested in raising taxes.

But national polls meant only so much to those whose re-election depended not on national mood so much as the sense that they were fighting for their home districts. And there were also legitimate policy questions about whether cuts without revenue increases would be adding to the deficit. Harry Reid, along with Pelosi, believed the White House's chief negotiator—Daley—was giving away the store during that first 2011 negotiation. Reid and Pelosi wanted the White House to call the Republican bluff and shut down the government. Boehner, on the other hand, couldn't appear to be getting rolled by the White House, which meant delivering on almost every demand he and his conference had made. Many Democrats believed that Rush Limbaugh spoke for the extreme conservative wing of the Republican

Party; they were slow to recognize the growing power of Glenn Beck, Mark Levin, Alex Jones, and others who have staked out territory even farther to the right than Rush. Thanks partly to their conservative media echo chamber, any concession, no matter how small, would be perceived as a loss; Boehner would hear about it for weeks on talk radio and Fox News, while his members would be pressured by conservative activists when they went back home. And yet he didn't want the government to shut down; that scene had played out in 1995, when Newt Gingrich, pouting about his seat on Air Force One, had given Bill Clinton a clear win.

Throughout the negotiations, Boehner kept trying to explain his situation to the White House. *You don't understand this conference,* Boehner told Daley. *You don't understand the new Republican members. This isn't the '90s,* referring to the first conservative revolution against a Democratic president that actually led to *some* cooperation. He sent emissaries, like Barry Jackson, his chief of staff, to try to explain his political position. The White House believed the Speaker was just playing politics, but Boehner didn't believe he had the trust of these new Tea Party members, and his staff didn't trust some other members of the GOP leadership, namely the number two, Eric Cantor. Boehner's staff was sure, at least in 2011, that Cantor was plotting against their man. And if Boehner caved too quickly, his people envisioned

Cantor using it to his advantage. That was the predicament Boehner believed the White House didn't appreciate. Did they really want to deal with a Speaker Cantor?

Finally, Boehner and Daley came up with a solution: they would jam everyone. At the eleventh hour, literally minutes before the previous stopgap measure expired, Obama and Boehner agreed on a deal that gave Republicans most of what they wanted and, more important, gave Boehner a way to save face with his conference. It was a short-term solution. Boehner wasn't making any long-term deals; he was buying time. How could you justify shutting down the government in early 2011 over a disputed budget resolution that was only going to be good for a few months?

The compromise passed, but only barely and at the last minute. It was the first time the new Republican conference had tangled with the two-year-old administration, and it was the first hint that Boehner's warning about his own precarious political situation was something more than Chicken Little pessimism. "Boehner may have known in his head that he had no choice" but to cut a deal, Daley recalled later. "If he went in early to that caucus, he was fucked." Boehner had run out the clock before kicking a field goal, but as he would learn to his dismay, his fellow House Republicans wanted touchdowns.

Late in the 2012 campaign, Obama had begun

promising supporters that his re-election would finally show Republicans that legislative logjams weren't a winning strategy; it would show them the need to help break the partisan "fever" that held Washington back from solving the nation's problems.[15] Yet Obama understood the reality of his conundrum. Almost from the moment he started promising a new direction, his public optimism was tempered by the private realization that Washington had fundamentally changed not with his re-election, but with the 2010 wave.

With nobody to work with in the Republican-controlled House, just days after Obama said the fever would break, his aides began preparing a second-term agenda that looked remarkably modest. They planned to shuffle White House leadership, moving chief of staff Jack Lew to the Treasury Department, and to work on senators who might be persuaded to cut deals on taxes and the ever-present threat of the fiscal cliff. But they devoted much less time to the sorts of ambitious legislative proposals that had dominated their first two years in office.[16]

Every now and then Obama would come across a Republican with whom he could find common ground. Weeks before the 2012 election, when Hurricane Sandy slammed into the New York and New Jersey coastlines, Obama won plaudits for showing up on the Jersey Shore to tour damaged communities with Chris Christie, the loud and state-proud governor who had contemplated running for president. The two men had spoken often by phone since the storm hit; Christie hadn't hidden his gratitude for the administration's response to the storm. During helicopter rides while they viewed the damage, the two became friendly, even jocular, gossiping about the campaign. Obama seemed to enjoy the fact that Christie didn't care—even enjoyed it—when he got under someone's skin. After their initial bonding over Hurricane Sandy, the two continued to swap political gossip.*

Obama did listen to some advisors who urged him to reach out more. In the spring of 2013, once he had been sworn for a second term, Obama arranged for a series of dinners with small groups of Senate Republicans. When Joe Biden offered to accompany the president, Obama declined; he didn't want the senators to think he was reaching out only because Biden had made him do so. Some of those dinners actually resulted in closer relationships with senators Obama hadn't connected with in his first term; for instance, Wisconsin's Ron Johnson, seen by many as a Tea Party victor in 2010, after one of those din-

---

* If the Romney team wasn't upset enough with Christie for his behavior at the Republican convention, their jaws dropped when they saw pictures of him and the president touring the Sandy wreckage together. The images were as good an endorsement as any Obama could have hoped for, and a statement by Christie that he could offer the sort of bipartisanship most Americans were hungry for.

ners followed up regularly with the White House's new chief of staff, Denis McDonough. But despite the open channels of communication with senators like Johnson, so far none have resulted in significant legislative achievement.

The story of American politics today is in part a story of two sides that fundamentally don't understand each other, and nowhere did the incomprehension between Democrats and Republicans manifest itself more clearly than on immigration reform, an issue Obama had been sure would break the fever.

Obama received 71 percent of the Hispanic vote in 2012, an even higher percentage than he'd gotten in 2008. Hispanic voters were becoming an increasingly large portion of the electorate, and they viewed Republicans as almost universally hostile. If they began voting for Democrats in percentages as high as African Americans did, the Republican Party would soon become a permanent minority. Already, California was unwinnable for a Republican presidential contender; given the rate of Hispanic growth, soon Texas and Georgia, two reliably red states, would fall into the same category if the GOP wasn't careful. It was clear, Obama thought, that Republicans were looking at the same math and drawing the same conclusions. Passing a reform plan wouldn't in and of itself fix the GOP's problem, but it would begin a conversation that Republicans could eventually use to make inroads into a crucial voting bloc.

But once again, the difference between what Democrats thought and what Republicans felt caused a comprehensive bill to fall between the cracks. Immigration reform had divided Republicans on Capitol Hill in 1986, when Ronald Reagan signed a comprehensive overhaul that led to amnesty for millions of undocumented immigrants. It had wedged conservatives away from George W. Bush's coalition in 2005, when Bush had tried to advance his own set of reforms. While Bush had received 44 percent of the Hispanic vote in 2004, a modern high for a Republican, his brethren on Capitol Hill had used inflammatory language to disparage immigrants crossing the Mexican border. The Minutemen, a group of vigilantes who took it upon themselves to police the border (and to appear on CNN while they did so), became a face of the post-Bush Republican Party.

A few Republican senators hoped that this time would be different, because they agreed with Obama's conclusion: John McCain and Jeff Flake of Arizona, Lindsey Graham of South Carolina, and, most notably, Marco Rubio, the young Florida senator of Cuban descent, joined with four Democrats to negotiate a comprehensive bill. The White House even conceded some points to its Republican negotiating partners, adding much stronger border-security language than was initially wanted but retaining the pathway to citizenship, the ultimate test of whether immigration activists would view the bill as a step forward. Reform advocates hoped that an overwhelming margin of victory in the Senate would force the more conservative House to act. Yet the margin wasn't *that* overwhelming, just 68 votes total, with barely a dozen Republican senators, not the 80-plus votes that could have provided real cover to Boehner to pursue similar reform in the Republican-controlled House.

For those who watched centrists and even conservatives lose primaries because of minor deviations from a strict ideology, adhering to party orthodoxy was critical for political survival. Voting for spending projects was one thing: Eric Cantor, for example, spent years appropriating tens of millions of dollars earmarked for his district before reinventing himself as a fiscal hawk. Constituents across the spectrum were just fine with cutting the other guy's budgets and totally comfortable justifying their own reach into the cookie jar. But no Republican worried about a challenge from the right would be stupid enough to grab on to an issue like immigration reform that has become the third rail of Republican politics.*

Most of the fourteen Republicans who voted for the bill on final passage, on June 27, 2013, did so

---

* It may be safer, in the modern GOP, to be pro-choice than to be in favor of a path to citizenship for an undocumented immigrant living in America.

out of political necessity: Senator Dean Heller of
Nevada, a heavily Hispanic state, worked behind
the scenes for months to take full advantage of his
vote for the bill. Bob Corker and John Hoeven of
North Dakota were two of the pro-business senators
(Hoeven needed agriculture workers) who'd crafted
the stronger border-security language that gave them
the cover to vote for the bill. Mark Kirk of Illinois,
another state with a growing Hispanic population,
and Democratic-leaning to boot, gave a thumbs-up.
Kirk's Senate seat being up in 2016, the fact that it
was a presidential year also mattered. And the moderate caucus — Collins, McCain, Murkowski, and
Graham among them — voted in lockstep for the
bill.

Others who at another political moment in time
might have supported the bill backed away. McConnell, the ultimate pragmatic power broker, had his
eye on his own re-election bid in 2014, and the fear
of a backlash from his conservative base in the form
of a Tea Party challenger drove many of his decisions. John Cornyn, the Senate Republican whip who
ran for office in 2002 as a centrist, felt the same
pressure, as he was also up for re-election in a midterm year, 2014. (One Austin Republican joked to
Politico that Cornyn hewed so closely to Tea Party
enthusiast Ted Cruz that Cruz was the only freshman senator with two votes.) Rob Portman, the Ohio
Republican who had come out in favor of gay mar-

riage, voted against the bill. So did Roy Blunt, another Republican pragmatist, but from a state, Missouri, that no longer rewarded moderate Republicans. Most of the no votes came from senators who didn't fear the political pressure of a growing Hispanic electorate. A handful of Republican nos—from Cornyn, Cruz, Jerry Moran and Pat Roberts of Kansas, Mike Crapo and Jim Risch of Idaho, and Mike Lee of Utah—came from states where more than 10 percent of residents were of Hispanic descent; each of those votes was really about fear of a primary challenger or a greater fear of being on the wrong side of the conservative movement.

Obama couldn't understand it: why wouldn't Republicans act in their own self-interest? But what he didn't understand was that Republicans were acting in their near-term self-interest, and in this case self-interest had become opposing him. This goes to the core of Obama's struggles trying to figure out his opponents: He doesn't understand why others don't think as logically as he does. It befuddles him that Republicans don't see their long-term self-interest on this issue. And the problem for the president is that in private, with some of these Republicans, he almost lectures them when questioning the lack of logic—and it's not well received.

To the strategists who shepherded Obama's rise to power, the changing media landscape and their candidate's raw star power meant that the rules they

had to play by were changing, too. And among the
key first-term players—Axelrod, Gibbs, Pfeiffer—
the strategy of keeping the media at arm's length, of
effectively using his popularity with his devoted base
to shield him from published criticisms, not only
dictated how they interacted with the media during
the campaign, but changed the traditional playbook
once they got into the White House.

Pfeiffer, in particular, was known for prickly relations with some members of the press corps. He was
proud of some of the hoary traditions the Obama
campaign broke—Obama spoke with Adam Nagourney, chief political correspondent for the *New York
Times,* a grand total of twice during the primary
season. (One of those sessions involved a walk from
an event to a waiting car.) Dan Balz, Nagourney's
counterpart at the *Washington Post,* was furious that
he hadn't received the sort of access routinely offered
by previous administrations. Obama became the
first major presidential candidate in a generation to
say no to a sit-down with the *Washington Post*'s editorial board. Simply put, this White House had a
different goal in mind.

The Washington media serves a political purpose,
to be certain. It allows the White House, or Congress, to inform its governing counterpart of its plans,
to posture and appear stronger than it might be, or
to float trial balloons that can lead to important agree-
ments down the road. It can be used to attack an

opponent, anonymously or publicly. It can be used
to leak embarrassing information, or to rewrite history to make one's boss look good or bad.

The new White House communications team
used the media in all of those ways, and yet they
still viewed the reporters who covered the White
House with barely veiled contempt. Just a few days
after he was inaugurated, Obama stopped by the
press room to glad-hand reporters. When one of them
asked a question about a former Raytheon lobbyist
who had been nominated for a senior Pentagon post,
the president became plainly irritated. "Ahh, see, I
came down here to visit. See, this is what happens. I
can't end up visiting with you guys and shaking hands
if I'm going to get grilled every time I come down
here," Obama said, apparently without realizing the
irony that he was standing in the middle of the White
House press quarters. There were times when it
seemed Obama didn't understand why the Washington press corps wasn't treating him the way he
had read the press corps treated Kennedy back in
his day.[17]

In addition to such general evasion, Pfeiffer relent-
lessly avoided what he called the "cocktail party interview," an interview a strategist makes his boss give
in order to placate some pestering reporter he keeps
running into at a party. "In a campaign, from the
day you start to Election Day, there's X number of
minutes. You can raise more money, you can get

more volunteers, you can never get more minutes," he said later. "And every minute should be seen through its utility for reaching your goal of 270, to win the state, whatever it is. So that's the filter through which we use the president's time, and we try to do it in as cold-blooded and rational way as you can."*

Obama's team wasn't totally immune from the pressures of the cocktail party circuit, but they weren't about to go into anything that might be a lion's den. Late in the 2012 campaign, Bret Baier, the Fox News anchor, had been pestering the Obama team to make the candidate available for an interview. Several campaign insiders began pushing to make it happen, since Baier was the one professional at the cable channel the White House loved to hate. At a meeting of senior aides, Pfeiffer lost it. "That's the craziest fucking idea I've ever heard in my life," he exploded. What could the campaign possibly get out of exposing Obama to a news outlet that had been hostile to the president since before he took office? The president agreed.

The speed of Obama's rise had played a significant role in how his relationship with the media developed. Almost immediately after his 2004 conven-

---

* Obama's media strategists had privately mocked Hillary Clinton's campaign for giving away some of the candidate's precious time to Jake Tapper, the ABC News reporter, for an interview that would run only on his podcast. No undecided voter listens to a political podcast, they joked.

tion speech, he'd faced questions about whether he would give an address at the next convention, too—not as a keynote speaker, but accepting the Democratic nomination for president. Gibbs went from fielding a few reporter calls a day to fending off big names at the networks, all of whom wanted an interview with the fresh-faced young Senate candidate. The media's relationship with Barack Obama went in a matter of days from passive and uninterested to all-consuming and obsessive.

One journalist Obama was close to, David Mendell, recalled an early moment when the Senate candidate had to give a radio interview. Sitting in the front seat of an SUV, Obama turned to Mendell apologetically: would Mendell mind stepping out of the car? Having a second reporter there would feel like "being in a hall of mirrors," Obama said.[18]

Obama was personally taken aback by the gotcha attitude of journalists, especially when it was directed at him.* In his interview with the late Tim Russert, famous for his ability to dig up the most embarrassing quote or most hypocritical line, the *Meet the Press* host had asked Obama what he'd meant when he'd told an *Atlantic Monthly* writer several months earlier that Kerry lacked the "oomph" to be president. Obama dodged artfully, but he grew

---

* His own path to stardom, however, had led straight over the fallen bodies of two contenders torn apart by a vicious and merciless Chicago media.

irritated when the *Chicago Sun-Times* put the old comment on its cover the next day. "Is that good reporting, good journalism—to take something I said months ago and print it now?" Obama asked Mendell the next day.[19]

In the intervening four years, Gibbs, Pfeiffer, and Axelrod, all veteran communicators with long histories of dealing with reporters, joined Obama in recognizing this changing media landscape. The fragmentation and proliferation of political media led to the rise of partisan cable networks that catered to specific ideologies—Fox News on the right, MSNBC on the left, CNN claiming to be presiding over a decreasing share of the viewership in the middle, though with a tendency toward the tabloid. The Internet allowed a thousand thorns to bloom. Outlets like *Politico,* the *Huffington Post,* and *Real Clear Politics* made their money by attracting eyeballs, and eyeballs wanted to see scandal, or partisan fighting, or the latest embarrassing quote—in or out of context. *Click bait,* as it is referred to these days. Those outlets amplified the cheap rhetoric in Washington and set the two parties more firmly at each other's throats. Their partisans outside the Beltway clicked along, enraged or overjoyed with each new development. And with every click, someone at one of the new fast-paced, report-first-add-context-second outlets got a little richer (or at least lost a little less money).

Like the rest of a White House that prides itself

on being steeped in history, Obama's press team spent time analyzing their predecessors and themselves. George W. Bush had a tendency to make mistakes when he was asked questions that strayed from prepared talking points. Bill Clinton got himself in trouble at the end of long days, when he was tired or when he meandered off script in a speech. Obama's team would face the media scrutiny Bush and Clinton had, multiplied by the proliferation of new outlets on the lookout for click-driving tidbits, so the message to Obama's team was clear: they had to control their most precious commodity, Obama himself, to a degree far beyond what either Clinton or Bush had to do.

Obama's communications team was quick to point out that, in his first term, Obama held 36 press conferences on his own, compared with just 17 for George W. Bush. He sat for 674 interviews, twice as many as Bush and Clinton combined. Almost 200 of those interviews were with local reporters or regional news outlets, the better to direct a specific message to a specific state or district without having to fear knowledgeable follow-up questions that might make news in the Beltway but would obscure the larger White House message. The White House believed that most of the public didn't care if the president sidestepped Washington process questions. Some thought they had used the president too much, and that offering him up for comment on the news of the day distracted from the larger message arc they had so carefully plotted.

But quantity didn't mean quality. Previous White House press officials had, of course, tried to protect their boss, but they'd understood that their relationship with the media went both ways, that — just as with legislation — the process was ultimately transactional: you give some, you get some. Team Obama's philosophy was almost entirely one of take it or leave it; and more important, they believed that nontraditional outlets were so interested in him, they could essentially control the market for his time — setting a precedent for future White Houses that someday these same White House aides will complain about. It's not hard to imagine the next Republican president granting far more access to conservative outlets to a point where they could ice out the traditional media altogether. And when they do so, these Republican administrations will be able to cite the Obama White House as precedent.

While the White House spent less time with reporters they saw as rabble-rousing, they spent a good deal more courting the biggest names in journalism and commentary. A little more than a week before he was inaugurated, Obama sat down for dinner with center-right columnists George Will, David Brooks, Charles Krauthammer, Peggy Noonan, Paul Gigot, and William Kristol, among others.[20] The following night he had dinner with E. J. Dionne,

Eugene Robinson, Gerry Seib, Ron Brownstein, Frank Rich, Maureen Dowd, Andrew Sullivan, and Rachel Maddow.[21] Such columnists and hosts served to keep Obama in touch with the opinion leaders he believed actually move the debate. Brooks, the *New York Times*'s center-right columnist, and Sullivan, the former *Atlantic* blogger (and former conservative), were particular focuses of presidential attention.

These off-the-record meetings continued once Obama moved into the White House. He sat with network anchors and White House correspondents,* newspaper and magazine editors, and columnists. The sessions gave the White House an opportunity to better explain its policies through its most effective spokesman. However, the off-the-record nature of the conversations meant that no "news" could come out of them, and when those same reporters asked questions in public, they were blown off.

On the spectrum of presidents paying attention to the coverage they receive, Obama's familiarity with what was written about him fell closer to that of Bill Clinton, a voracious reader who was quick to snap at any reporter he believed had treated him unfairly, than to George W. Bush, who left the stress of news consumption to his communications staff. The proliferation of online news organizations meant that Obama had much more to read about his presidency

---

* This author included.

than Clinton ever did. Beyond the world of print, the fragmented television landscape meant that one could likely find someone critical of one of his policies on Fox News, a supportive cheerleader on parts of MSNBC at night, and more watered-down, '90s-like pedestrian punditry on CNN. Obama himself avoided the cable TV chatter, but he certainly heard about it from his staff. He was a consumer of news, but mostly at night and online through his iPad; not much of a television watcher, he'd see clips as they were referenced on his favorite blogger sites. The constitutional law professor in Obama loved reading commentary more than news accounts so much, many close aides have mused that in another life, he'd have been an op-ed writer in the *New York Times*. In fact, some aides think he may still want to do that in his postpresidential years.

Perhaps most frustrating to Team Obama was that even their allies weren't always allies. If Clinton, who tried hard to govern from the center, irritated the left, the worst he might face was an angry quote or op-ed in the *New York Times*. In the age of Maddow, Chris Matthews, and Ed Schultz—the prime-time lineup on MSNBC—"now there's an entire industry," Pfeiffer said, of liberals who have the audience, and the television time, to assault Obama's left flank. The whole scene made Obama even less enthusiastic about reaching out to the media—after all, if your friends were betraying you, why bother with *anyone?*

There was one exception when it came to cable TV: Obama, like his predecessors, carved time out of his day for ESPN, in a probably futile effort to unwind from the stress of the presidency. Sports were an obsession for the two previous commanders in chief: Bill Clinton loved the Arkansas Razorbacks and appeared on ESPN Radio when his Hogs made a run in the 1994 NCAA tournament. George W. Bush had owned the Texas Rangers, which made him the First Fan of America's Pastime. In his own case, Obama watched, and played, basketball as much as possible. He even became the first president to fill out his NCAA tournament brackets on live television. It was coincidence, no doubt, that half of his Final Four picks during his first four years in office were teams from swing states.[22] So famous was Obama for watching ESPN that D.C. cable and satellite outlets began marketing that fact to issue groups looking to woo the president via media campaigns. Lo and behold, by the middle of his presidency, in the morning hours of *SportsCenter* reruns on ESPN, in the D.C. market, ads for climate change or gun control or whatever issue that wanted the president's attention actually popped up.

CHAPTER FIFTEEN

They Were First-Graders

The president got to work late on December 14, 2012. With just seventeen days to go until the country fell off what pundits were calling the fiscal cliff, Obama had spent the previous evening meeting with John Boehner at the White House, trying to hammer out a deal. The House Speaker had brought Mike Sommers, his chief of staff, and Brett Loper, his policy director; Obama had Tim Geithner and Rob Nabors, his top liaison to Capitol Hill, join the others for the session in the Oval Office.[1] There was a decided undertone of urgency: without an agreement, a severe combination of spending cuts and tax increases that were intended to reduce the nation's deficit were set to go into effect, and the resulting economic fallout might be devastating—even if it would radically fix the federal budget. Boehner had offered to allow an additional $800 billion in revenue—that is, tax increases—but he wanted $1 trillion in cuts to entitlement spending. Obama's revenue target was

$1.4 trillion, and he was willing to cut $600 billion from entitlement programs. Concession by concession, the two sides made progress, but Boehner was scheduled to fly home to Ohio the next day, a sign that the talks still weren't close to a final resolution. Aides to both Boehner and Obama later told reporters the meeting had been "frank," that peculiar bit of Washington-speak meaning "not very productive."

Obama, who usually arrives in his West Wing office around 9 a.m., did not show up until 10:30 the next morning for his daily briefing, the intelligence report essentially prepared nightly by the CIA that fills him in on world conditions, especially in the hot spots.[2] This particular morning, the presentation he got wasn't the one his security advisors had prepared the night before. Almost an hour before he showed up that Friday morning, at 9:35 a.m., an emergency dispatcher in Newtown, Connecticut, had answered a call from Sandy Hook Elementary School.

John Brennan, the White House counterterrorism official, was the first to notify the president, around 10:30 a.m. As reports swirled over the number of victims and the circumstances of their deaths, the White House dropped everything to monitor the situation second by second. By the time the final, horrifying details came in, the president was deeply affected. The carnage inflicted by Adam Lanza, a twenty-year-old former Sandy Hook student who had shot his way into the school, was almost incomprehensible.[3] Twenty-eight people had died, including six teachers, Lanza's mother, and the shooter himself.

What left Obama deeply shaken, though, were the other twenty victims. They were all first-grade students.

One was Noah Pozner, a smiley six-year-old with close-cropped brown hair who already knew how to read. He used words like "dynamic" and "DNA," his mother told a newspaper a few days later. He was so enamored of tacos that he told his mom he wanted to manage a taco factory when he grew up, in between stints as an astronaut and a doctor. He wanted to know whether God existed, and who had created God. Lanza had shot Noah Pozner eleven times. Noah was too young to have owned a tie; a family friend would buy a small one to put on the boy at his funeral.[4]

The unspeakable evil that tore apart Sandy Hook Elementary was even more tragic for the fact that it wasn't an isolated incident. Since he'd become president, Barack Obama had heard briefings on at least eighteen shootings that killed more than one person. Some were so shocking that they dominated headlines for weeks, even months: Jared Lee Loughner murdering six people and wounding more than a dozen, including Congresswoman Gabrielle Giffords in Tucson; medical student James Holmes, armed with multiple weapons and covered in body armor, unleashing a barrage into a movie theater in Aurora, Colorado, that killed twelve people who had stayed up late to get a sneak peek at the newest Batman movie; army major Nidal Malik Hassan, a psychiatrist who was supposed to be helping military personnel who came through Fort Hood, Texas, killing thirteen soldiers; Amy Bishop, a biology professor denied tenure at the University of Alabama in Huntsville, opening fire during a faculty meeting and killing three of her colleagues.

For every mass murder that stayed in the headlines for days on end and spurred calls for change, there were two or three that went almost completely overlooked. Two weeks after Holmes murdered moviegoers in Aurora, Wade Michael Page shot and killed six people at a Sikh temple in Oak Creek, Wisconsin. Six months before Hassan's rampage at Fort Hood, a software engineer in Santa Clara murdered his two children, their aunt and uncle, and their eleven-month-old cousin. The same day, a forty-five-year-old murdered eight people and wounded two more at a nursing home in Carthage, North Carolina, where his estranged wife worked. Those incidents occurred less than three weeks after a gunman killed ten people, among them family members and random bystanders, in a shooting spree that spanned two towns in southern Alabama.

A coffee shop in Seattle. An immigration center in Binghamton, New York. A Christian college in

Oakland, California. An IHOP in Carson City, Nevada. A beer distributorship in Manchester, Connecticut. All were scenes of mass shootings since Obama had taken office in 2009.[5] In Obama's own hometown, gun violence was becoming even worse; on December 28, 2012, an alleged gang member named Nathaniel T. Jackson became the 500th person murdered in a single calendar year.[6]

And the horror in Newtown wasn't even the first high-profile shooting that month. On December 1, 2012, a football player for the Kansas City Chiefs, Jovan Belcher, murdered his girlfriend, then shot himself, outside the team's stadium. On December 11, a twenty-two-year-old wearing a hockey mask fired a Bushmaster AR-15 semiautomatic rifle—the same brand of rifle Lanza would use three days later—to shoot innocent bystanders at the Clackamas Town Center, a mall on the outskirts of Portland, Oregon. He killed two people.

But Obama couldn't get over the children who had died in Connecticut. He couldn't get over their names, and the fact that just a few years earlier, his daughters had been in first grade.

"I know there's not a parent in America who does not feel the same overwhelming grief that I do. The majority of those who died today were children, beautiful little kids between the ages of five and ten years old," Obama said in the White House briefing room later that day. His voice nearly cracked as he raised his left hand to his eye, to wipe something away. Then he paused, for thirteen long seconds, as he tried to collect himself. "They had their entire lives ahead of them—birthdays, weddings, kids of their own."[7]

He wiped his left eye three more times, his right eye twice more in the course of a four-minute statement. He paused to collect himself three long, painful times.

It was, with the single exception of his announcement that his grandmother had died, shortly before the 2008 election, the most profoundly emotional, profoundly human moment Barack Obama had ever shared with the nation. And that emotion—outrage, anger, grief—would have an impact on Obama's legislative agenda. "We're going to have to come together and take meaningful action to prevent more tragedies like this, regardless of the politics," he said.[8]

Through the weekend that followed, the White House made its first real effort to come up with legislation that they believed would curb gun violence. It embraced a proposal from Senator Dianne Feinstein that would reinstate the assault weapons ban, the measure that had sent so many Democrats to defeat in 1994. It would support closing a loophole that allowed guns purchased at firearms shows to change hands without the background check that would otherwise be required. And it contemplated legislation that would ban high-capacity ammunition clips like the type Lanza had brandished at the elementary school.

Obama tapped Joe Biden to head the new gun control initiative. A working group Biden headed began the new year by considering expanding universal background checks for gun purchasers, tracking sales of firearms through a national database, and strengthening mental health checks that could lead to new restrictions on gun purchases. The vast majority of Americans, up to 80 or 90 percent in some cases, backed those proposals. There was no way, the White House believed, that Republicans in Congress would be able to withstand public pressure to tighten even the least controversial rules. These were little kids, after all, who were mowed down with a weapon that was simply too easy to access.

In an earlier generation, the politics of gun legislation wouldn't have worked. Forget the Republicans in the House, who would certainly have voted to block any new restrictions on guns; even the Democrats hadn't been lockstep in favor of new gun legislation.

But with Sandy Hook, something had changed, or so the White House wanted to believe. Senator Joe Manchin, a pro-gun West Virginia Democrat who had aired a television commercial that showed him literally shooting a copy of cap-and-trade legislation with a rifle, said he was open to regulating military-style rifles like the Bushmaster Lanza had used in Connecticut.[9] Fellow senator Pat Toomey of Pennsylvania, who had won election as an archconservative in the 2010 wave but who would need more moderate voters to keep his seat in 2016, joined with Manchin to come up with a bill—an almost heretical act for a Republican politician.

For the first time in two decades, the politics of gun control were working against the National Rifle Association. The pro-gun organization didn't help its cause when Wayne LaPierre, its longtime executive vice president, offered a full-throated defense of existing gun laws at a Washington press conference a week after the Newtown tragedy. LaPierre pinned the blame on violent video games, violent movies, the media, and even gun-free zones at schools, while proposing new funding to put armed police officers in every school, a program the NRA called the National School Shield Program.[10]

Gun control advocates weren't prepared for the new attention. After all, they hadn't had a real foothold in the political process since Bill Clinton's first term in office.

It's hard to understate the fear the NRA had long inspired among Democratic elected officials. In the 1994 elections, two dozen Democrats who had supported the assault weapons ban had lost their seats in Congress after the NRA spent millions attacking their votes; Bill Clinton publicly blamed the NRA (and the vote on the gun bill) for ousting so many longtime Democrats. In fact, he believed Democrats could have held Congress had it not been for the ban.

Thereafter the Democratic Party developed a serious phobia about discussing guns. Banished to the minority in the House, Democrats believed their only path back to a majority ran through places like suburban Texas and rural Washington State, places where traditionally conservative Democratic voters had begun casting Republican ballots. For these voters— white, nonurban sportsmen who hunted for sport and food—guns were a way of life, and the Democratic Party seemed precariously out of touch.

Though Clinton still touted the assault weapons ban, Democrats in the late 1990s began to change their tune. The 1996 Democratic Party platform acknowledged both the ban and its political cost, with an important caveat that would become a de facto line among even progressive Democrats: "We oppose efforts to restrict weapons used for legitimate sporting purposes, and we are proud that not one hunter or sportsman was forced to change guns because of the assault weapons ban. But we know that the military-style guns we banned have no place on America's streets, and we are proud of the courageous Democrats who defied the gun lobby and sacrificed their seats in Congress to make America safer," the platform read.[11]

The 2000 platform pledged to keep guns off streets and out of schools "in ways that respect the rights of hunters, sportsmen, and legitimate gun owners."[12] In 2004, John Kerry was photographed hunting geese in Ohio just two weeks before Election Day. He told reporters he and his three companions had each bagged a goose, with blood from one of the birds still staining his hands.[13]

The Democrats who led the Senate in the early years of the Bush administration either supported the NRA or understood the political risks of opposing it too vigorously. Tom Daschle didn't advance any gun legislation when he served as Senate majority leader; his deputy, Harry Reid, who didn't support extending the assault weapons ban in 2004, even found ways to kill gun control measures when they popped up inside his own party.*

Many politicians may have wanted stronger gun control laws, but they also wanted to keep their jobs. For almost two decades, the conventional wisdom on Capitol Hill held that the NRA's power was virtually unlimited—and so was unchallenged by gun control advocates. Gun rights groups gave more than $30 million to supportive politicians between 1989 and 2012, and spent another $41 million on independent advertisements advocating their cause,

---

* The NRA ran advertisements against Daschle that year, when he lost his re-election bid; at the same time, the gun rights group endorsed Reid.

according to data compiled by the Center for Responsive Politics. (Gun control backers gave less than $2 million to their favored candidates in the same time period.) The NRA accounted for the lion's share, $46 million, of that $71 million total,[14] and the organization became so powerful it even began playing in some Democratic primaries. The group spent money to successfully launch the career of gun control opponent Michael Michaud, a rural Democrat who won a six-way primary in Maine's Second District in 2002. It also waded into the fight between John Dingell and Lynn Rivers, a member-versus-member primary brought on when Michigan lost a congressional seat in 2002. Dingell, a longtime NRA backer and former member of its board of directors, beat Rivers, a liberal who supported gun control.

For Obama's part, ever since his "cling" comment during the 2008 primaries, he had been careful not to appear as hostile to those for whom guns were a way of life. One moment, in his second debate against Mitt Romney, stood as a clear example of his hesitancy to embrace the issue. Asked about his 2008 promise to keep assault weapons out of criminals' hands, Obama started his response by defending the Second Amendment to the Constitution: "We're a nation that believes in the Second Amendment, and I believe in the Second Amendment. We've got a long tradition of hunting and sportsmen and people who want to make sure they can protect themselves,"

Obama said, before returning to the mass shootings that had occurred during his presidency.[15] Obama was well aware, when starting off his gun answer that way, that the wrong gun answer could cause him problems in pro-gun blue states. Ironically, one thing Obama didn't tout but could have was the fact that arguably, no Democratic president had expanded gun rights more in the past fifty years than Obama had, when in 2009 he signed a key piece of legislation into law that included an amendment allowing guns to be carried in national parks. It wasn't an amendment Obama supported, but it was tacked onto a credit card bill that the president desperately wanted enacted, and so he signed it without complaining.

It was a poll-driven message: Obama's strategists, in both 2008 and 2012, were worried about alienating voters in Colorado, Iowa, Pennsylvania, and Virginia, swing states in which gun culture still reigned supreme. Even after earlier mass shootings, Obama had avoided supporting what the White House saw as an unwinnable cause. Following the shootings in Tucson, he called for civility in politics, not gun control. After the murderous rampage in Aurora, he preached healing rather than gun control.

But an elementary school in peaceful Newtown, Connecticut, was a bridge too far. A few days after the shootings, an intern working in the White House correspondence office was surprised when the president walked in unannounced. He wanted to read letters Americans had sent him about the Sandy Hook shootings. Obama spent more than an hour sitting in the White House mail room, poring over the letters, digesting the anger and anguish the shootings had inspired in his constituents.

His own pain spurred Obama to pursue an option he hadn't tried during his first term: instead of pushing modest measures he believed he could get through Congress, Obama decided to vigorously advocate for gun control, though it would be a challenge to pass a bill reflecting his concerns through a narrowly divided Senate, much less a Republican-controlled House. But the anger the public felt demanded that their leader feel the same and actually try to lead. Obama would pursue what his strategists believed would be a losing cause—this was a rare decision by Obama, and the president embraced it with gusto, as if he'd been liberated and transported back to the time when he'd been a first-time candidate and could hope for anything.

Despite the odds, through the winter and spring of 2013 Obama and his allies on Capitol Hill worked diligently to put together a package that might pass the Senate. In the end, it was far from what gun control advocates had hoped for, but suddenly they had allies in the White House, an almost historic first step. Then Manchin and Toomey crafted the bill that would have expanded background checks for gun buyers and closed the so-called gun show loophole.

At one point, Manchin believed he had convinced the National Rifle Association to stay on the sidelines; the country's largest gun rights organization wouldn't support the bill, but it wouldn't actively oppose it, either. Manchin was surprised and angry when the NRA came out against the bill. It turns out, unbeknownst to Manchin, there was a partisan struggle inside the NRA, where the more partisan board members wanted to fight Obama at every turn on this, while others on the NRA board argued that they would lose their bipartisan credentials if they didn't let pro-gun Democrats do *something* after Newtown. What gave the NRA its power was bipartisan influence; the more moderate forces inside the NRA feared that if they snubbed a longtime ally like Manchin, they could see all of the Democratic allies buck them, and suddenly the NRA would be vulnerable anytime Democrats ruled both Congress and the presidency. One reason gun control went nowhere in the first two years of the Obama presidency when Democrats controlled both houses of Congress was that the NRA had allies like Manchin and even Harry Reid.

Aides to members of Congress were frustrated, too, by the White House's lack of outreach; Obama called Manchin, often a swing vote on critical legislation, for the first time after the Newtown shootings, more than two years after he had won his Senate seat. Digest that for a minute. Two years. A Democrat. Then again, Manchin wasn't alone; Obama didn't call many senators, period.

The NRA's opposition was enough to convince members of Congress—mostly Republicans, but with a handful of red-state Democrats thrown in—to vote against the overwhelming will of the American people. On April 17, just four months after the disaster at Newtown, 46 senators voted to block the Manchin-Toomey compromise, enough to effectively kill the bill. Two women sitting in the Senate gallery, which was packed with relatives of victims of the shootings in Newtown and Tucson, couldn't contain themselves. "Shame on you!" they shouted, before being escorted from the chamber.[16]

Only two Republicans, Toomey and Mark Kirk of Illinois, voted for the measure. Four Democrats voted against the bill. (Reid was actually a fifth no vote, but as majority leader, if he hoped to bring the bill back to the floor for another vote, he had to do this as a procedural maneuver.) The bill won 54 votes—with Reid's switch, that meant it was 5 short of the 60-vote margin it needed to reach a straight up-or-down vote on the Senate floor.

At the White House, Obama was incensed. Just hours after the Senate voted, Obama joined families of victims in a Rose Garden press conference to decry the results.

"I'm going to speak plainly and honestly about what's happened here because the American people are trying to figure out how can something have 90 percent support and yet not happen," Obama said. "Even the NRA used to support expanded background checks. The current leader of the NRA used to support these background checks. So while this compromise didn't contain everything I wanted or everything that these families wanted, it did represent progress. It represented moderation and common sense. That's why 90 percent of the American people supported it.

"It came down to politics—the worry that that vocal minority of gun owners would come after them in future elections. They worried that the gun lobby would spend a lot of money and paint them as anti–Second Amendment. And obviously, a lot of Republicans had that fear, but Democrats had that fear, too. And so they caved to the pressure, and they started looking for an excuse—any excuse—to vote 'no,'" Obama went on.

The anger Obama felt boiled over. "All in all, this was a pretty shameful day for Washington," he said in the Rose Garden that day. It would become a more common refrain: the fight, he promised, "is not over."[17]

But the truth was that there had never been much hope of passing any kind of new gun laws in the first place. For one thing, Republican control of the

House of Representatives meant John Boehner would have never had to bring a bill up; discharge petitions, which require a majority of the House to force a vote on a bill, have been sidelined as a tool of legislative action.

This was one of those odder moments in Washington, when the president and senators made a huge issue of a Senate vote that wouldn't even see a vote in the Republican House. Of course, what the White House said after all this was that at least it had tried. And that is something that was different about this incident: for the first time since he took office, the president actually was willing to publicly fight a losing battle, to forcefully spend political capital, something many pols don't do. But he didn't have a very well laid-out plan as to how he was going to get this done. Basically, the strategy was to use his platform and position to focus the public guilt; but behind the scenes, there was no horse-trading, and Washington's focus moved on.

Obama himself stopped fighting for gun law changes almost completely. And when asked about it, he sounds resigned that he's powerless, as he did more than a year after his high-profile loss in the Senate. During a Q&A on Tumblr, the president went off when asked about yet another series of mass shootings post-Newtown: "The country has to do some soul-searching on this. This is becoming the norm.

Our levels of gun violence are off the charts. There's no advanced developed country on earth that would put up with this." He then pointed the finger at Congress and the NRA. "Most members of Congress are terrified of the NRA. The only thing that is going to change is public opinion. If public opinion does not demand change in Congress, it will not change.

"The United States does not have a monopoly on crazy people. It's not the only country that has psychosis," he said. "And yet we kill each other in these mass shootings at rates that are exponentially higher than anyone else. Well, what's the difference? The difference is that these guys can stack up a bunch of ammunition in their houses, and that's sort of par for the course."

But other than those comments on Tumblr, the president has not attempted to rally the country again on the gun issue; he hasn't toured his hometown of Chicago, trying to help rally that city to figure out how to quell the gang violence that has led to so many shootings in that city. These nonactions on guns, this public declaration that his presidency is powerless on this issue, are things the 2007 and 2008 version of Obama would be highly critical of. Just another indication of how Washington's scar tissue has changed him.

Chapter Sixteen

The Lost Year

At 11:55 a.m. on a clear and bitingly cold January morning in 2013, Barack Obama joined an exclusive club of just sixteen men. Obama was already one of just forty-three men to serve as president of the United States. Now he was part of an even smaller handful who had been elected to two terms. Throughout the hard-fought battle to win that second term, Obama had predicted that the Republicans who had so resisted him during his first term would wake up and, in his words, their fever would break. After so much partisan rancor, wouldn't the loyal opposition have to recognize that the American people had spoken, again, and that it was time to work together to achieve common goals, and maybe even swap a few horses to reach some more partisan goals? Not only that, the American people, in their great wisdom, re-elected *everyone,* Democrats to the presidency and the Senate, and Republicans to the House. Translation: figure it out, but figure it out together.

In his second inaugural address, Obama laid out an ambitious agenda: Climate change. Income inequality. An end to a decade of ceaseless wars. Civil rights, pointedly including gay rights by his citing the Stonewall Inn riots along with Selma and Seneca Falls as key monuments on the march to justice.

That day, a newly elected Obama with an approval rating north of 50 percent sketched out his hopes for a second term and the legacy he hoped to leave after exiting office.

A year later, in 2014, looking back on twelve more months of gridlock, mistakes, miscalculations, wasted opportunities, and poll numbers that had sunk to the low 40s, Dan Pfeiffer, Obama's senior advisor, would conclude that the White House needed to seriously revise its approach to the presidency if the president wanted to get *anything* done before he left for retirement. In a memo to the president in January, Pfeiffer concluded that the White House had failed to use the rules available to an executive to implement policy, and that Obama's team had abandoned a focus on explaining his agenda to voters. The lack of discipline, the tangles with a still-recalcitrant Congress, and a year of unforeseen crises ranging from a terrorist attack in Boston to a massive security leak, a government shutdown to a disastrously bungled rollout of a critical website, had firmly tarnished Obama's pristine reputation as a different kind of politician.

But even without those crises, Obama had already set himself on a path to failure; before he even took his second oath of office, he had chosen to focus on issues that would shorten his already-brief honeymoon.

A little more than a month before he was sworn in a second time, the massacre in Newtown, Connecticut, had shaken Obama deeply. He had spoken at memorial services for mass shooting victims before, in Tucson, Arizona, and Aurora, Colorado. Serious revisions to the nation's gun control laws hadn't emerged from either of those incidents, nor from the dozens of others that had happened under Obama's watch. But the deaths of innocent children just a few weeks away from celebrating the holidays were too much to ignore.

By pushing so hard to pass gun control legislation, the White House virtually guaranteed that it would start the first year of its second term with a loss—a loss it couldn't blame on Republicans. The sheen of a newly elected president with a bold, ambitious agenda was being tarnished by the legislative realities of dealing with Congress barely a month into his second term.

Immigration reform should have been different. While there were few political incentives to pass gun control measures, Republicans had almost every excuse in the world to make reforming the nation's immigration rules a priority in the 113th Congress.

After all, Obama had won re-election with more than 70 percent of the Hispanic vote, the fastest-growing minority population in the country. Republican political strategists worried that if the trend continued, Hispanics would become as reliably a part of the Democratic coalition as African American voters had become.

Hispanic and immigrant rights groups weren't completely happy with Obama, especially concerning the record-setting number of deportations of undocumented immigrants that had happened during his administration—but they were more willing to back a politician who gave them a seat at the table than a party whose presidential primary contenders pandered to anti-immigrant hard-liners like Iowa representative Steve King, former Colorado representative Tom Tancredo, or any of the talking heads on conservative radio stations who complained that any reform would amount to amnesty for the eleven million people in the country without proper documentation.

Recognizing these trends in electoral politics, some Republicans (including Boehner and his deputy, House majority leader Eric Cantor) did begin calling for immigration reform soon after the 2012 elections. And for Obama, reforming immigration laws could stand as a cornerstone of his second-term legacy. It was a rare moment when both parties' political interests were ostensibly in alignment. The reality is that the *only* time big compromise deals happen in Washington is when there is true political benefit for both parties.

To highlight the priority the administration placed on immigration reform, Obama dedicated the first outside-the-Beltway trip of his second term to unveiling the outlines of his plan. A little over a week after being inaugurated, Obama traveled to a Las Vegas high school to call for a quick overhaul of immigration law. The White House had contemplated releasing a full legislative version of its own proposal, but it held back as a bipartisan group of eight senators hammered out its own version.[1]

And they kept on hammering. The negotiations between the four Democrats (Chuck Schumer of New York, Dick Durbin of Illinois, Bob Menendez of New Jersey, and Michael Bennet of Colorado) and four Republicans (Jeff Flake and John McCain of Arizona, Lindsey Graham of South Carolina, and Marco Rubio of Florida) dragged on for months. Ultimately the two sides agreed on a compromise that would have created a path to citizenship for the millions of undocumented immigrants already in the United States while expanding employer verification systems and improving work visa options for low-skilled workers, including agriculture workers essential to farms in western and midwestern states.

Immigration hard-liners hated the legislation, and they promised revenge on Rubio, who very clearly had eyes on the White House in 2016. While Republicans could afford to hold unorthodox positions on some issues and still hope for a future in national politics, immigration issues, the hawks believed, were still political nonstarters with the conservative base: touch them and watch your career go up in a puff of smoke.

But Rubio held fast, and so did the other seven members, through an onslaught of proposed amendments designed to weaken or strengthen parts of the bill and upset the delicate balance the gang had struck. The Senate Judiciary Committee heard more than three hundred proposed amendments, then passed the bill by a wide 13–5 margin. Then, on the Senate floor, the gang accepted just one significant amendment — backed by Republicans Bob Corker of Tennessee and John Hoeven of North Dakota — to strengthen border protections. That single amendment brought about 10 Republican votes to the final package. On June 27, the Senate passed the compromise package by a 68–32 vote; 14 Republicans eventually supported the bill. It was a successful day on the face of things, but actually terribly disappointing to immigration reform advocates. The fact that more than half of Senate Republicans voted no meant the legislation was likely doomed in the Republican-controlled House. They needed a show of support in the 70s or even 80 to give Boehner the cover he needed. But those numbers were not enough for Boehner to sell to the 100 or so Republicans who might have been persuadable on this issue.

Still, on paper, there did seem to be a bipartisan consensus, at least when it came to some key constituency groups like business and labor.

Interest groups had played a heavy role in forcing through the legislation: labor groups joined with the Chamber of Commerce, and farmworkers joined with big agricultural interests to urge the Senate to pass a bill. McCain, Graham, and Schumer all called New Jersey governor Chris Christie, who had appointed a close political ally to temporarily fill a vacant Senate seat, to urge him to convince the temporary senator, Jeff Chiesa, to vote in favor. He did.[2]

But only hours after the Senate vote, harsh political reality brought the reform package's progress to a sharp and painful halt. Despite voicing support for the broader concept of immigration reform, Boehner had been feeling pressure for months from his more conservative members. Boehner's own 113th Congress had started out inauspiciously: he had only narrowly avoided being denied the speakership when a rump group of conservatives, who didn't see Boehner as fighting sufficiently for their cause, split apart at the last minute, ruining a planned coup. Boehner hadn't helped his own politics with conservatives when, just after the president won a second term, he said that "health care is the law of the land." While it was a statement of fact, it was viewed by some

Republicans as surrender. Couple that with Boehner's unwillingness to fight harder—at least in the eyes of conservatives—to save the Bush tax cuts, and he suddenly had problems.

So Boehner was treading lightly a few months later when immigration came to his turf, and he wasn't about to take a Rubioesque risk. "I issued a statement that I thought was pretty clear, but apparently some haven't gotten the message: the House is not going to take up and vote on whatever the Senate passes," he said the morning after the Senate vote.[3]

The political calculus had changed, largely because the two sides that wanted to get something done weren't fully considering the third faction: the House Republican rank and file.

Boehner, Cantor, and the rest of the Republican leadership had initially seen passing immigration reform as something to be done for the good of the Republican Party as a whole. It might not be popular with the outspoken base, which would label almost anything that included a path to citizenship as amnesty, but it would allow the party to begin anew and try to fix what had been a broken and harmful conversation with the Hispanic community.

The political concerns the rank and file faced, though, were less about the overall political health of the national party and more about their own survival in coming primary elections. How could they go to their voters, the most conservative activists who showed up in a primary election, and brag about voting for immigration reform in Washington? For the average Republican who turned up at a local district meeting or a county convention, the only thing worse than a member of Congress who voted for immigration reform would have been a member voting for immigration reform that Barack Obama and Chuck Schumer also backed.

And let's not forget another reality for rank-and-file House Republicans: the bizarre U.S. redistricting process has essentially segregated their districts from the rest of the multiethnic population that is growing in this country. Their districts are more homogeneous than the United States as a whole, and since they aren't dependent on Hispanics to win re-election, how was it in the rank and file's interest to pass immigration reform? Political logic may have dictated that Republicans would vote in their best interests to see that some kind of pathway to citizenship—the only provision that immigrant rights groups and the most vociferous Democrats would call real reform—made it through Congress. But this assumed that everyone in Washington faced the same math problem; they didn't, and backbench members of Congress determined to win re-election were going to save themselves before they saved their party.

That meant Boehner's calculus changed, too: he stood to gain nothing by sticking his neck out on a bill that probably wouldn't pass his House Republican Conference anyway. There was no logic in suddenly becoming a martyr. Boehner wouldn't budge, and the chairman of the House Judiciary Committee, Virginia Republican Bob Goodlatte, didn't seem any more interested in moving even piecemeal bills.

What had once looked like a sure thing, a cornerstone of Obama's second-term legacy and perhaps even the cornerstone of Boehner's speakership, ground to a halt. By mid-June, immigration was no longer dominating the White House's radar screen. Once again, instead of proactively pushing the president's legislation, the administration was thrown into crisis by outside actors — this time a twenty-nine-year-old computer programmer with sandy blond hair and the outlines of a beard.

In 2012, Edward Snowden, a contractor at the defense giant Booz Allen Hamilton, contacted the journalists Glenn Greenwald, Laura Poitras, and Barton Gellman, offering to disclose documents he had downloaded from the servers of a remote, and as it turns out not-so-secure, National Security Agency outpost in Honolulu. After communicating for months using encrypted channels, Snowden flew to Hong Kong on May 20, 2013, having received permission to leave the NSA, ostensibly for treatment of epilepsy. He was still there on June 5, when the *Guardian* newspaper published its first story under Greenwald's byline, revealing that the American telecom giant Verizon was collecting millions of phone records from its customers on a daily basis and handing them over to the NSA.[4]

A day later, the *Guardian,* under the bylines of Greenwald and Ewen MacAskill, and the *Washington Post,* under Gellman's and Poitras's names, revealed that the NSA and the FBI were tapping directly into the data servers maintained by nine top U.S. Internet companies under a program code-named PRISM.

The revelations kept coming, day after day: a presidential policy directive ordered government officials to come up with a list of targets for cyberattacks; the NSA had collected almost three billion pieces of information on U.S. citizens in a single month; U.S. and British intelligence agencies were monitoring foreign leaders and diplomats at a G20 meeting in 2009; a secret court allowed the NSA to use data collected from American citizens without obtaining a warrant. Every morning the two papers revealed new crown jewels of the American and British intelligence networks.

The NSA scrambled to answer basic questions, both to respond to the White House and for its own internal security: How did a low-level contractor collect so much information without being detected? How had he escaped to Hong Kong? Was he working for a foreign power, and how could the United States stem the bleeding?

Six weeks after the leaks first became public, Denis McDonough had Keith Alexander, the four-star army general who headed the NSA, in his office. McDonough wanted answers; Alexander still had few of them. Finally, McDonough snapped: How is it, he demanded, that you can't tell us what Snowden has stolen? You're telling me, with the great powers of the NSA, that you can't figure out what he stole? It took until February 2014 for intelligence officials to finally understand the scope of Snowden's theft: approximately 1.7 million files, according to testimony NSA officials gave to the House Intelligence Committee.[5]

Intelligence professionals marveled at the holes within their own networks. The two largest leaks of proprietary national security data had both occurred during the Obama administration, a sign of the increasingly diffuse network of U.S. intelligence outposts. In 2010, army private Bradley Manning had delivered hundreds of thousands of classified U.S. diplomatic cables and documents to the pro-transparency organization WikiLeaks. Three years later, Snowden's disclosures rocked the intelligence community anew. Both had been inside jobs; the national security apparatus was apparently expert at keeping other countries out, but their blind spot was inside their own organizations.

If 2013 was the year many Americans who liked Barack Obama began to think he was just another politician, the disclosures of covert NSA activity made 2013 the year foreign leaders began to believe that Obama represented less of a break with George W. Bush's tenure than he wanted to convey. The anger at Obama over the Snowden revelations seeped out of editorials across once-supportive European papers, while foreign diplomats and leaders voiced their own skepticism.

"Barack Obama—the man who carried so much hope and was long believed to be a very European US president—has become the butt of jokes," wrote *Der Spiegel,* the German weekly that published some of Snowden's revelations under Greenwald's byline, in a scathing editorial. "Some view [Obama] as the embodiment of the very 'Big Brother' once sketched by George Orwell, the dictator who spies on, monitors and controls every citizen without any scruples."[6]

Obama's transformation from European hero when first elected to untrustworthy ally had its deepest impact in Germany. The domestic politics both George W. Bush and Obama faced had meant that there was no way America could bail out struggling countries in Europe, even though those countries' stability would have a direct and drastic impact on the United States. That meant U.S. officials had to lobby Europe's stronger economies—particularly France and Angela Merkel's Germany—to stave off a global depression. Though Obama believed there were few world leaders of great stature serving with him—no Thatchers or Rabins, and even Nicolas Sarkozy had lost his last election—he thought highly of Merkel, the former research scientist who had served as Germany's chancellor since 2005. Thanks to her performance during the economic recession, when Germany became the saving grace of a European economy on the brink of destruction, and her stature at international meetings, Obama had an overwhelmingly positive impression of Merkel.

And Obama was scheduled to go to Berlin on an official visit, his first since his grand speech at the Brandenburg Gate during the 2008 campaign, just two weeks after the first of Snowden's stolen documents began hitting newspapers.

Ostensibly, the trip combined a meeting of the G8 economic powers in Northern Ireland with a side trip to Berlin, where Obama hoped to underscore what the White House called the "vital importance of the transatlantic alliance, the deep and enduring bonds between the United States and Germany."[7] The White House and Merkel's advisors agreed that another speech at the Brandenburg Gate would be well timed to honor the fiftieth anniversary of John F. Kennedy's famous 1963 speech, when he declared, in grammatically tortured German, that he was a Berliner.

It was also, as advisors would acknowledge later, something of an unofficial campaign swing on

Merkel's behalf: Obama did meet with Peer Steinbrück, the leader of the opposition Social Democrats, but his several appearances with Merkel lent
her some of the aura that still existed for Obama in
Europe. In federal elections held September 22,
Merkel's party won 41.5 percent of the vote, almost
16 points higher than its nearest rival, Steinbrück's
Social Democrats.

A month after Obama's visit, *Der Spiegel* reported
that Germany's intelligence agency, the BND, helped
the NSA with its data collection. A month after
Merkel's re-election, however, came the real bomb-
shell: on October 23, *Der Spiegel* revealed that
Merkel's personal cell phone number had been listed
in a special NSA catalog, and may have been monitored by American intelligence agencies, for more
than ten years.

Merkel placed an outraged phone call to Obama,
in which she told the American president she
"unequivocally disapproves of such practices and sees
them as completely unacceptable," a Merkel spokesman told reporters. Monitoring allied heads of state,
the spokesman said, "would be a grave breach of
trust."[8] A White House readout of the call painted
it in a different light: "The President assured the
Chancellor that the United States is not monitoring
and will not monitor the communications of Chancellor Merkel."[9]

The White House statement made no mention of the past tense.

For the next year, Merkel agitated for ways to avoid the NSA. Merkel and French president François Hollande began preliminary discussions about building a European communications network to circumvent the NSA's reach into U.S. data centers.[10] The new proposal, and other closed networks that countries might build to avoid sending their data through the United States and into the NSA's net, would cost U.S. technology companies billions of dollars, given the hardware investments they would have to make in new networks built away from American shores.

Merkel's outrage was personal: While Deutschland was split into a free West Germany and a Soviet satellite, Merkel grew up in East Germany and saw firsthand the dangers of surveillance. "Privacy" is the freedom Germans, especially East Germans, value perhaps above all other freedoms. While many countries, which of course do their own spying, expressed faux outrage at the NSA disclosures, Merkel's anger was rooted in something real.

The rift between Germany and the United States over NSA surveillance mirrors the growing divide between Europe, where Obama's approval ratings once topped every other politician's and institution's, and a president five years into the new reality of international politics. When he arrived in Berlin in 2008, he was hailed as a hero, a new kind of American ready to repair the United States' image abroad. "In Europe, the view that America is part of what has gone wrong in our world, rather than a force to help make it right, has become all too common," Obama the candidate told 200,000 screaming fans in 2008. "True partnership and true progress require constant work and sustained sacrifice. They require sharing the burdens of development and diplomacy; of progress and peace. They require allies who will listen to each other, learn from each other, and, most of all, trust each other."

Two weeks after Snowden's revelations began leaking out, Obama went to Berlin again, this time to the Brandenburg Gate. Five thousand invited guests—one-fortieth the size of his initial crowd—showed up.[11]

By 2013, revelations of NSA spying were but the straw on an overloaded camel's back. Obama had failed Europeans on so many levels. He failed to close the prison facility at Guantánamo Bay in Cuba, something European diplomats had pushed the United States to do for years. Drone strikes were killing more terrorists than ever—and a significant number of civilians—in countries from Yemen to Pakistan. And the Snowden files confirmed every European stereotype about America, the overbearing superpower that spies on its friends and covertly attempts to influence outcomes for the good only of America, and American industry.

The political damage caused by Snowden's disclosures is deep and lasting—and not just overseas. Domestically, the revelations contributed to a growing disillusionment with the president, both among his politically active young liberal base and among a burgeoning libertarian strain that is beginning to influence both parties. For the most part, Americans have been accepting of government surveillance under the guise of national security; they are less accepting of surveillance writ large, regardless of which president first gave the okay.

The months of embarrassing revelations that endangered American relations with countries the NSA had spied upon continued. Brazil's new president, Dilma Rousseff, upset at the agency's eavesdropping over her country's communications network, became the first foreign leader to refuse a state dinner that had been planned on her behalf at the White House.[12] To avoid future uncomfortable moments, the White House quietly began telling its allies what they expected would leak out, desperately trying to get ahead of the sensitive information before it could further damage relations.

Obama has taken heat for failing to engage in foreign policy and its outcomes during his administration, but for misguided reasons. Although the perception is that Obama isn't engaged, White House advisors say he is actually more engaged in foreign policy debates than in domestic policy debates, especially as a recalcitrant Congress blocks his agenda.

And yet critics, both at home and abroad, maintain that Obama has not done enough to break with Bush's administration. While the American commitment to Afghanistan is winding down, it and Iraq remain troubled, and the totality of America's position in the world over the six years of Obama's presidency is nowhere near as materially different from the Bush-era image as Obama once pledged it would be.

Instead, the changing world order is threatening America's place, and there isn't much Obama or any other president can do about it. Rising economic powers like Brazil and China are amassing power, though they aren't ready to become major diplomatic players and start actually influencing outcomes à la the Western powers. Something Obama has attempted—a pivot to Asia, aimed at confronting China's growing power—has run into problems as traditional American allies Japan and South Korea feud over century-old issues.

The European Union, rather than assisting in hot spots like northern Africa and the Middle East, is still dealing with economic challenges in its own backyard, from countries like Italy, Portugal, and Greece. And Russia is reasserting itself as America's main rival even while the United States tries to keep the relationship friendly. On virtually every major foreign crisis, whether it's Iran's nuclear program or North Korea or Syria, even the recent tug and pull between pro-European and pro-Kremlin politicians in Ukraine, Russia has set itself on the side opposite the United States. Where Obama once had a good working relationship with President Dmitry Medvedev, Medvedev's patron, predecessor, and successor, Vladimir Putin, has seemingly taken it upon himself to score points by antagonizing, and in some cases besting, the United States.

Obama has had trouble, he has told advisors, understanding why world leaders like Putin in Russia, or Benjamin Netanyahu in Israel, or Recep Tayyip Erdoğan in Turkey, won't engage, while he remains willing to negotiate. It mirrors the frustration Obama has felt among Republicans on Capitol Hill: Obama believes that both his domestic opponents and his global negotiating partners are too reactive to immediate domestic politics. More of his initiatives have been stopped in their tracks, the White House believes, because other world leaders are too concerned with the short run. But despite his frustration, one thing he seems incapable of doing internationally is playing true hardball. Obama argues there is only a certain amount of cajoling that can be done with some allies and countries like Russia, which are more rivals than straight-out adversaries. But it does seem as if, as is the case with Congress, there is only a certain amount of elbow grease the White House is willing to apply.

Back in Washington, Obama wasn't the only one having a difficult year in 2013. Republicans on Capitol Hill, eager to bog down the administration under a flurry of subpoenas amid aggressive oversight, began to see two possible opportunities to go much further and label Obama as more than ineffective, as somehow corrupt: investigations into the murder of U.S. ambassador Christopher Stevens in Benghazi, Libya, in the early fall of 2012 and the Internal Revenue Service's close scrutiny of conservative groups held the potential to bring down senior administration officials.

But in both cases, House Oversight and Government Reform Committee chairman Darrell Issa, the aggressive California Republican, faced a choice: On one hand, he could build a case demonstrating that the Obama administration had a competence problem, exemplified by insufficiently protecting diplomats in dangerous places and by allowing a government agency to go rogue by inappropriately targeting groups with a specific political ideology. On the other, he could try to make the larger case that the administration had actually covered up what it knew and when it knew it — and in Washington, the cover-up is always worse than the crime. His choice, in essence, lay between settling for a single or swinging for the fences.

Issa swung away, and instead of winding up on base, Republicans missed an opportunity to undermine Obama's credibility to a far greater degree than it had been undermined to date.

The events in Benghazi, on September 11, 2012, are well documented. A group of militants launched an assault on two U.S. diplomatic outposts, one of which was actually a covert CIA outpost. Four Americans, including Stevens, were killed. But back in the White House, seven hours behind local time in Libya, the facts on the ground were far from clear.

In advance of major events like the anniversary of the 2001 terror attacks, the Super Bowl, or a presidential inauguration—anything that might present terrorists with an attractive target—national security staffers run through a meeting known as the threat assessment. In the Obama White House, John Brennan, then the president's counterterrorism advisor, led the meeting earlier that week. Threat assessments are designed to explore all potential threats, which by their very nature makes them frightening. But September 11, 2012, was a bright and, by all indications, quiet day. Tommy Vietor, then the NSC spokesman, met his girlfriend for lunch, something he had never had time to do before.

A few hours later, the mood changed. A diplomatic

outpost half a world away had been attacked. The State Department knew that Stevens had been in Benghazi, but the White House doesn't track the movements of individual ambassadors on a daily basis; the problem was that State didn't know for sure where Stevens was after the attack.

The NSC staff, meeting in the Situation Room, patched in the State Department's Sensitive Compartmented Information Facility, or SCIF, the room designed to allow video communications without risk of interception. Cheryl Mills, Hillary Clinton's chief of staff, was sitting before the camera as both the White House and the State Department struggled to wade through the rumors flying through the intelligence community. One rumor held that an American was alive at a hospital; they worked to get video or photo confirmation. Another source heard that the hospital could be a trap, and that any State Department or CIA personnel who went to find the American would become the next victim.

One person in the Situation Room that afternoon realized how serious it was when he heard the loud, distinctive clack of the SCIF's big metal door. Over the video link he could see Mills look at the off-screen door, then get up to make room for the person who had walked in: Hillary Clinton.

Clinton didn't deal with many ambassadors individually; that was left to one of her deputies. But Stevens was no ordinary ambassador. He had been on the front lines in post–civil war Libya, the latest hot spot in the Arab Spring, which meant that he and Clinton had communicated more than usual. Clinton was clearly worried for the safety of her personnel. "This wasn't some ambassador that people didn't really know," the person present in the Situation Room said later. "This was the guy who led the charge in Libya."

Upstairs in the Oval Office, Thomas Donilon, the national security advisor, had informed Obama. As late night turned to early morning in Libya, Donilon, who had moved to the Situation Room, kept the president updated on the search for Stevens. Obama had ordered Martin Dempsey, chairman of the Joint Chiefs of Staff, to get military units into the area as fast as possible. There weren't many assets close by, even though it hadn't been that long since U.S. military assets had been used to help topple the Libyan regime. But Libya was one of those rare U.S. interventions where, after the success, zero military presence was left to deal with the likely fallout—a policy decision by the Obama administration that will be debated by some for years.

In those early hours there was little evidence that the assault was premeditated—there still isn't. It appears now that it was an opportunistic attack, something planned in theory but timed for that day simply due to the unrest taking place in other capitals in the region. The raw intelligence flooding into the CIA pointed to a spontaneous attack; the agency's assessment made that point.

The next morning, in the Rose Garden, Obama condemned the "outrageous and shocking attack." "No acts of terror will ever shake the resolve of this great nation, alter that character, or eclipse the light of the values that we stand for," he said.[13]

To some Republicans, the attack on the diplomatic consulate proved an opportunity to take on one of Obama's greatest strengths as a president: the fact that he had ordered the raid that killed Osama bin Laden. Here, finally, was proof that Obama's counterterrorism strategy was flawed, the first terrorist attack on U.S. soil—technically the consulate, a diplomatic property, was part of the United States—in eleven years. The conservative media, hypersensitive to Obama's perceived lack of interest in condemning everything in the Islamic world in the harshest terms, leapt on Obama's choice of language and the relatively few times Obama used the word "terror" or "terrorism."

Mitt Romney's campaign decided to try to use the attack to undercut Obama's credentials on national security. The campaign seized on a statement, issued by the U.S. embassy in Egypt hours before the attack in neighboring Libya began, that was critical of an offensive video about the prophet Muhammad that had touched off riots in Cairo and other cities.

"I'm outraged by the attacks on American diplomatic missions in Libya and Egypt and by the death of an American consulate worker in Benghazi. It's disgraceful that the Obama administration's first response was not to condemn attacks on our diplomatic missions, but to sympathize with those who waged the attacks," Romney said in a statement provided to the *New York Times* two minutes after Clinton confirmed the death of one American—unnamed—on September 11.

The White House was surprised by Romney's statement, and it wasted no time in swinging back. "We are shocked that, at a time when the United States of America is confronting the tragic death of one of our diplomatic officers in Libya, Governor Romney would choose to launch a political attack," the Obama campaign's Ben LaBolt said.[14]

The mainstream media scrambled to get an administration official on the following Sunday morning's talk shows. Clinton, who hates doing weekend television shows, refused. Donilon, who might have been the logical choice, was so risk averse that he made for bad television, and hesitancy on TV would have made the administration look worse. The White House tapped Susan Rice, then the ambassador to the United Nations, thinking she would be able to convey in human terms the cost of losing a fellow ambassador.

Rice used talking points that had been approved

by both the State Department and the Central Intelligence Agency. But the intelligence community had stuck to one particular assessment that would eventually help bring down Rice's bid to follow Clinton: she insisted, repeatedly, that the attack was the result of a protest that had boiled over into violence. That, the White House would privately admit later, had never been the case: the intelligence community was wrong.

The conservative media continued to bang the drum, insisting that the administration had covered up a terrorist attack in the heat of a presidential campaign, and it became certain that Obama would have to answer questions about Benghazi again, in the second presidential debate, which was to focus on foreign policy.

Obama couldn't understand the logic: Republicans were criticizing him for refusing to admit, in their minds, that al Qaeda was responsible for the attack. Never mind that Obama's intelligence advisors at the CIA and other intelligence agencies didn't find a link to any known al Qaeda operative; Obama didn't see the logic in giving al Qaeda credit, what amounted to a public relations win, at all.

Still, the team practiced their answers on Benghazi time and again leading up to the foreign policy debate with Romney. The night before, after a particularly arduous preparation session, Obama got frustrated. "I called it terrorism," he said of the Benghazi attack.

Ben Rhodes stopped him. "No sir, you didn't. You called it an act of terror."

The following night, Rhodes's reminder served Obama well. Romney criticized the president for continuing with campaign events after the tragedy. Obama fired back: "The day after the attack, Governor, I stood in the Rose Garden, and I told the American people and the world that we are going to find out exactly what happened, that this was an act of terror. And I also said that we're going to hunt down those who committed this crime. And then a few days later, I was there greeting the caskets coming into Andrews [actually Dover] Air Force Base and grieving with the families. And the suggestion that anybody in my team, whether the secretary of state, our U.N. ambassador, anybody on my team would play politics or mislead when we've lost four of our own, Governor, is offensive. That's not what we do. That's not what I do as president. That's not what I do as commander in chief."[15]

Romney tried to push back on the "terrorism" point again during the back-and-forth and got caught in that "act of terror" choice of words when even the moderator of the debate jumped in to Obama's defense and told Romney he was wrong that the president had used the term "terrorism." Of course, the White House in those few days after the attack *was* hesitant to use the word "terrorism." It wasn't until a hearing a week later on Capitol Hill that they fully embraced the idea that the Benghazi attack was indeed a planned act of "terrorism." Still, Romney looked shallow in that moment when he went after Obama on the use of the word "terror" or "terrorism," rather than hitting him on having a security issue in the country or questioning the entire "leading from behind" policy. Yet another instance of the Romney campaign trying too hard to win a news cycle and missing the bigger picture.

Even after Obama beat Romney, Republicans continued to insist that a cover-up had taken place. Fox News ran frequent reports, and in an interview taped before the Super Bowl in 2014, Bill O'Reilly used one of his questions to press the president. Issa and Representative Jason Chaffetz, a Utah Republican who served on his committee, maintained that the party would continue its investigations into the midterm years.

But report after report concluded the same thing: The State Department could have done more to protect its diplomats. There were no smoking guns, no explicit efforts to cover up any information. Instead, there were only botched assessments that led to incorrect talking points. The House Armed Services Committee, run by Republicans, took the White House and the State Department to task for failing to account for serious security risks, though it couldn't make broader conclusions even after reviewing thousands of pages of documents.[16] The Republicans swung, but they missed: Benghazi remains a cause célèbre on the right, and it is likely to come up again if Clinton runs for president, though few in the mainstream media take the incident, and the administration's response, seriously as a scandal. A botched policy? Perhaps, but a cover-up? There's just no evidence. Everyone was playing politics at the margins of the event itself, from Romney to Obama, but the politics being played was the predictable image kind of the moment, not something as salacious as the right has tried to claim.

Issa's committee, and Republicans across the country, got another chance to paint the administration as either incompetent or corrupt in the spring of 2013, when an inspector general at the IRS revealed that the agency had used improper criteria for determining which nonprofit groups deserved special attention. Some auditors in the agency's Cincinnati office and two other regions had singled out groups with names that included words like "Tea Party" or "patriot," or that focused on opposition to the Affordable Care Act.

Once they got their hands on the report, Republicans on Capitol Hill erupted. It was, in their telling, nothing less than a government assault on a particular political ideology, one that just so happened to stand against the president. Fox News, once again carrying the conservatives' banner, painted the still-unfolding scandal as directed from the administration's highest levels—made clear, they believed, by the fact that the head of the IRS had been cleared for entry into the White House more than one hundred times. (Doug Shulman, the IRS chief, had been cleared in for meetings on how to implement the Affordable Care Act, though he attended those meetings only a handful of times, preferring instead to send a deputy. It is standard practice to be cleared for White House access even if you never end up going. For instance, many news organizations clear backup correspondents and reporters for White House press access every working day for months even if that person never actually enters. It's done in case the person decides to show or needs to be there.)

On May 14, the day the report was formally released and two days after Republicans began clamoring for an investigation, the White House issued a statement from the president. "The report's findings are intolerable and inexcusable. The federal government must conduct itself in a way that's worthy of the public's trust, and that's especially true for the IRS. The IRS must apply the law in a fair and impartial way, and its employees must act with utmost integrity. This report shows that some of its employees failed that test," Obama said.[17]

The statement hardly expressed the outrage so

many felt. The IRS had erected certain walls to ensure that the agency would not be used for political purposes after Richard Nixon had his enemies audited and harassed; now it appeared that the IRS had waded into politics. If nothing else, the White House should have recognized the impending danger of allowing that impression to linger.

The White House believed the facts were on its side: there was no proof, it insisted, that the administration had anything to do with the actions of agency auditors hundreds of miles from the Beltway. Indeed, no proof has ever emerged that the White House was involved at all. The press shop insisted that it would wait for the proper investigations, by treasury secretary Jack Lew and Attorney General Eric Holder, to play out and vindicate their position.

But the reliance on rationality and logic that so defines Obama and his White House ignores the irrationality of politics. The scandal wasn't about the misguided actions of bureaucrats in some little-known agency; it was the IRS, the most hated institution in government. It reeked of the kinds of awful politics that had brought down the Nixon administration; the burden of proof, in the irrational world of politics, lay with the Obama administration, not with its critics. The idea that the president's team didn't see the pitfalls in this story is implausible; it's as if not a single person in the West Wing had paid attention to the power of the conservative media complex, from talk radio to Drudge to Fox and the blogs. Did they have amnesia during the birther mess?

Issa launched more investigations. Lois Lerner, a top-ranking IRS official who had tried to apologize for the agency's actions before the results came out, invoked her Fifth Amendment right to avoid self-incrimination. Shulman testified that he had visited the White House, but not to discuss targeting conservative groups. The Treasury Department asked for and accepted the resignation of the IRS's acting commissioner; the new commissioner, Danny Werfel, asked for Lerner's resignation, then put her on administrative leave after she refused. She retired a few months later.

In January 2014, the FBI said it would not file any criminal charges relating to the investigation. But like Benghazi, the story lives at the margins of conservative media because no smoking gun was ever found.

Republicans had spent 2013 hunting for a scandal that would kill the Obama administration. While doing so, they missed the opportunity to portray the administration as incompetent, either because it hadn't stopped the IRS's scrutiny of conservative groups, because it hadn't protected diplomats in a dangerous situation, because it hadn't stopped the largest leak of classified documents in U.S. history, or even because it couldn't build a functioning website for its signature domestic achievement. It was a missed opportunity for a party so desperate to oust a president that it overreached, again and again, when all it had to do was chip away.

Ironically, by the summer of 2014, after yet another scandal of incompetence, this time at the Veterans Administration regarding how it handled—or mishandled—veterans' waiting times for medical care, the public's outrage caught up with the irrational exuberance of the right. The weight of the seemingly unmanageable bureaucracies of the federal government was too much for the public, and as bad as 2013 was for the president politically, the summer of 2014 was even worse on this front. His approval ratings began dipping below 40 percent; a majority of the country believed Obama was no more or less competent at running the federal government than Bush was post-Katrina. It was a dip in his sixth year that many a two-term president had experienced before him, from Nixon and Reagan to Clinton and Bush. Two recovered (Reagan and Clinton) and two didn't (Nixon and Bush).

CHAPTER SEVENTEEN

A Thick Red Line

The language of diplomacy is precise to a fault. Diplomats negotiate for days over the placement of commas, parse every word, and speak slowly and carefully in measured tones. The slightest misstatement or ill-considered word can lead to an international incident. Throughout the Arab Spring, as governments rose and fell and protests turned violent, even deadly, the Obama administration and the State Department had been careful to tread lightly. In a changing region, one that has led to more wars than any other in the world, the United States, stuck between ruthless dictators and unpredictable opposition groups, some of whom had close ties to terrorists, saw only a minefield. "Caution" was the word of the day.

But one country, the most deadly and most dangerous of those swept up into the Arab Spring, stood out: Syria. And in one of the most crucial battlefields of the Arab Spring, the United States was caught off guard and hamstrung by the off-the-cuff comments of its own leaders, Barack Obama and John Kerry, Hillary Clinton's successor as secretary of state. For all the caution the White House and the State Department had exercised, buzzwords and flippant remarks—unforced diplomatic errors—gave America's geopolitical rivals an opening.

Syria plays an important role in the puzzle that makes up the Middle East. Egypt's military has always had a good relationship with the United States—and thus we could tolerate military control. Libya and Tunisia, farther to the west, are more traditionally influenced by the European powers that once colonized them. Yemen, a haven for a potent branch of al Qaeda, had a government so weak that it became a charity case of the U.S. military and the Central Intelligence Agency.

But Syria stood at a crossroads, both geopolitically and strategically. Geographically, Syria served as a buffer between its patron state, Iran; Iraq, where thousands of militants streamed across borders to join the fighting; and West-friendly Lebanon, Jordan, and, most important, Israel. The Israeli military had already destroyed a site purported to be the beginnings of a nuclear power plant inside Syria, and America's most important ally in the Middle East wouldn't stand for a neighbor run by Islamic militants.

Complicating matters was Russia's involvement. Russia, and before it the Soviet Union, has cultivated its relationship with Syria for decades. The two countries do billions of dollars in business annually, and Syria's president, Bashar al-Assad, allows the Russian navy to maintain a base at Tartus, the country's only military outpost in the Mediterranean.

U.S. relations with Syria have been tricky; it's a country that the United States has at times had strategic relationships with, even if neither country trusted the other. Assad's father and the first Bush administration had famously "okay" relations. And at the start of the Obama presidency, there was talk of a reset in Syrian relations; to back up the intention, the president even named an ambassador in February 2010, Robert Ford. But his nomination was held up by the Senate, and by the time he was confirmed, via recess appointment at the end of 2010, Syria was just weeks away from the start of a civil war, and the very idea of diplomatic relations between the two countries became remote in a hurry.

The president officially recalled Ford from his Syria post in October 2011 — a diplomatic message a country sends when it makes it clear that it no longer condones any of the actions of that government or even recognizes its legitimacy. In this case, President Obama was on the record as saying Assad had to go.

Like other countries involved in the Arab Spring, Assad's government began facing local protests in March 2011. By the following month, they had escalated to national outpourings of anger. Violent clashes soon followed, and over the next two years more than 140,000 Syrians, most of them civilians, had lost their lives. The powder keg, fueled by ethnic and religious differences that have existed just beneath the surface since World War I, had finally exploded. And like the Syrian dilemma itself, the debates within the halls of American government were equally complex; as America looked on, then slowly began to get sucked into the most complicated civil war of the Arab Spring, the familiar battle lines began forming inside the White House, between those who saw the civil war in humanitarian terms and those who wanted desperately to avoid another military crusade into the Middle East—all while Republican critics on Capitol Hill, perpetually dissatisfied with the administration's actions, pushed for an undefined resolution.

Interestingly, there was no clear indication of whose side Israel was on. Israelis weren't fans of Assad, since he was viewed as somewhat of a puppet of Iran; Assad also allowed leaders of Hamas and Hezbollah, two militant anti-Israel organizations, sanctuary in Damascus. But Netanyahu preferred the devil he knew (Assad) to the devil he feared (the al Qaeda–supported insurgents). Israel already saw the downside of democracy in the Muslim world take place on two of its borders, in Gaza when Hamas took over by democratic means and in Egypt when, following the initial ousting of Mubarak, the country elected a Muslim Brotherhood sympathizer, Mohammed Morsi. Neither outcome made Israel feel safer. Needless to say, Israel expected no less from any supposed democracy play in Syria.

And Israel's fears were those of the United States. Consequently there was a passive stance about the standoff in Syria for quite some time. But there were certain lines Obama couldn't allow Assad to cross, and that became clear as the war wore on. After all, if he could call Mubarak out for his actions in Egypt, there was no way he could not decry the same actions by Assad. Of course, the differences between U.S. relationships with the two countries were stark. For one thing, the United States actually had influence over Egypt and leverage to wield. With Syria, it had nothing, unless it somehow got drawn in—something that a bipartisan group of old-fashioned foreign policy interventionists led by John McCain and Lindsey Graham hoped would happen.

They got their potential wish one afternoon in August during the 2012 presidential campaign.

Looking back, it's a day some may come to view as the time Obama inadvertently got in his own way, thanks to his re-election campaign wanting to score a political point, and it came from an unlikely source.

*　　*　　*

In Todd Akin, running against Missouri senator Claire McCaskill, Democrats had a straw man brought to life, a candidate who embodied every point Obama's campaign was trying to drive home about its opponents. Democrats were seeking to exploit their advantages with women voters, and they had no shortage of policy differences with which to contrast themselves with Republicans— especially after an interview with a local Fox affiliate in which Akin had seemingly drawn a distinction between different kinds of rape.

"First of all, from what I understand from doctors, that's extremely rare," Akin said when asked whether women should be able to terminate pregnancies resulting from rapes. "If it's a legitimate rape, the female body has ways to try to shut that whole thing down. But let's assume that maybe that didn't work or something. I think there should be some punishment, but the punishment ought to be on the rapist and not attacking the child."[1]

Akin had demonstrated a shocking lack of scientific knowledge, and of political acumen. He had also handed Democrats a cudgel with which to beat every one of his fellow Republicans, from the presidential ticket of Mitt Romney and Paul Ryan down to candidates running for Congress in far-flung states. In the course of the next three months, Akin would be featured in more Democratic attack ads than anyone other than Romney (the Romney team immediately recognized the danger in being associated with Akin and distanced itself even before Obama's campaign began firing back).

Obama's campaign team had to figure out how to take advantage of, and amplify, Akin's comments. Rushing to make a statement could look crass and unpresidential, but waiting for others to pick up the story could be missing an opportunity. Obama's advisors decided to let the question come naturally, and to let the president swing away at the big fat pitch he would certainly get. So on Monday, August 20, 2012, when Jay Carney entered the press briefing room at the White House, he had a special guest: Obama himself.

"Jay tells me that you guys have been missing me," Obama began. "So I thought I'd come by and say hello." Ostensibly, Obama was there to tout billions of dollars in savings on prescription drugs, thanks to the Affordable Care Act. But his real purpose was hardly opaque. Obama called on Jim Kuhnhenn, the veteran Associated Press reporter, for the first question. The AP plays the role of asking the "news of the day" question, and Akin was that day's "news."

"You're no doubt aware of the comments that the Missouri Senate candidate, Republican Todd Akin, made on rape and abortion," Kuhnhenn said. "I wondered if you think those views represent the views of the Republican Party in general."

Obama had his whack, lambasting Akin, Romney, and the entire Republican Party. "Rape is rape. And the idea that we should be parsing and qualifying and slicing what types of rape we're talking about doesn't make sense to the American people and it certainly doesn't make sense to me," he said. The campaign team got exactly what it wanted out of the press conference.

Obama took a few more questions. Eventually he called on this author, who asked for the president's latest thoughts on the civil war in Syria. Syria had a well-known stockpile of chemical weapons; would the United States ever consider sending in the military in order to secure those weapons and to make sure they didn't fall into the hands of terrorist organizations? There was no prodding about a line in the sand.

The president repeated his talking points: Bashar al-Assad had lost his legitimacy as ruler of the Syrian people and needed to step down. The United States would bolster humanitarian aid and provide limited help to some of the more moderate opposition groups. Then he went further than he had before.

"I have, at this point, not ordered military engagement in the situation. But the point that you made about chemical and biological weapons is critical. That's an issue that doesn't just concern Syria; it concerns our close allies in the region, including Israel. It concerns us. We cannot have a situation where chemical or biological weapons are falling into the hands of the wrong people," Obama said. "We have been very clear to the Assad regime, but also to other players on the ground, that a red line for us is we start seeing a whole bunch of chemical weapons moving around or being utilized. That would change my calculus. That would change my equation."[2]

"Red line," in diplomatic-speak, is a heavily loaded word. Red lines are not to be crossed, lest military action follow. Obama's predecessors have used the phrase only sparingly, and always at moments of extreme tension.

Obama's choice of language was no accident. In fact, he repeated it just a moment later, in response to a follow-up question: "We have communicated in no uncertain terms with every player in the region that [using chemical weapons] is a red line for us and that there would be enormous consequences if we start seeing movement on the chemical weapons front or the use of chemical weapons."

Obama wrapped up and walked out, twenty-two minutes after taking the stage. The news of the moment from that press conference was Akin and the president's "rape is rape" retort. Akin would lose badly to McCaskill, and women chose Obama over Romney by an eleven-point margin. But the bigger impact of the press conference came with those two little words, "red line," that set the White House on record for the next year to come.

The White House decided that using such strong diplomatic language would send a clear message to Assad, who at the time appeared increasingly desperate as rebels advanced. Obama didn't want to get the military involved, given how significant an intervention in Syria would be; in a slide show presentation in early 2012, Joint Chiefs of Staff chairman Martin Dempsey said that imposing a no-fly zone across Syria would require up to 70,000 troops.[3] Those were troops Obama didn't want to send into harm's way in yet another Middle Eastern country.

For the next several months, the tough talk appeared to work. But with Assad's back to the wall, signs of trouble began to emerge. Intelligence agencies started seeing evidence that Assad's military was moving chemical weapons around, perhaps even preparing them for use. In January 2013, a State Department cable from Istanbul, where U.S. intelligence agencies were closely monitoring the situation across the border in Syria, cited "compelling evidence" that Assad's forces had used a "poisonous gas" in Homs, one of the rebel strongholds. The assessment was based on seven dead bodies U.S. intelligence forces had analyzed.

The red line, it appeared, had been crossed, and Obama's calculus would have to change. But the White House wasn't so sure, and they pushed back on the State Department report, denying that any chemical weapons had been used. The report was "inconsistent" with what the White House knew about Assad's weapons program, said Tommy Vietor, the spokesman for the National Security Council. The White House didn't want the red line dabbled with; it wanted proof Assad had blown through the line before acting. It was clear that this president was extremely reluctant to use any force in Syria.

CIA director David Petraeus offered a plan to arm and train groups of rebel fighters at bases in Jordan. Secretary of State Hillary Clinton, who would stay on at Foggy Bottom another four or five months, supported the plan. So did Dempsey and defense secretary Leon Panetta.

But Susan Rice, then the U.S. ambassador to the United Nations and soon to become Obama's national security advisor, stood in the way. A few days after Obama drew his red line, Rice warned that arming rebel groups would make the United States more involved than it wanted to be. At that meeting, Obama seemed hesitant to make a quick decision and skeptical of the plan to arm rebels.[4]

Rice was aligned with Denis McDonough, then the deputy national security advisor and soon to replace Jack Lew as chief of staff. McDonough was worried about the possibility of the United States being bogged down in another long war. But Samantha Power, who had been aligned with Rice and

McDonough in earlier debates over the moral obligation to use force, now found herself allied with Clinton, Panetta, and Petraeus, members of the old guard who had feuded with the more idealistic younger set in debates over Libya.

Obama began to fear that anything he did in Syria would go wrong. Stay out, and countless innocent lives could be lost. Get involved, and the lives lost might be American. He began telling advisors that he saw too many risks, and he started using a phrase that became an off-the-record commonplace for him: "Syria was a series of shitty options."

The allegations of chemical weapons use continued pouring in: Two months later, the Assad regime claimed that the opposition had used chemical weapons. The opposition claimed that Assad's forces were still using the banned weapons. The White House didn't buy it; in fact, some on the NSC were concerned that the opposition was making up—or maybe even staging—chemical weapons attacks in an effort to lure the United States into the conflict on their side.

The third allegation against Assad came in April. Obama and his team remained skeptical that these weapons had been used, and with the red line hanging out there, the White House wanted to be certain that Assad had crossed it, clearly and obviously. For six weeks, Western intelligence agencies from France to Israel to the United Kingdom concluded the same thing: that Assad's forces had used chemical weapons in a small, almost surgical strike. Obama, not eager to enforce his red line without absolute proof, needed more convincing, though he did authorize a CIA plan to ship arms to Syrian rebels.

From the outside, it looked as if the White House was in denial about the intelligence America's Western allies had collected. National security advisors used what they privately called the "Iraq defense," contrasting Obama's slow and steady approach with George W. Bush's rush to war over weapons of mass destruction that didn't exist. The White House made the case that after Bush, American credibility within the intelligence community wasn't as high as it had been, especially when it involved the existence or use of chemical weapons or other weapons of mass destruction.

But behind the scenes, while making sure that the intelligence was credible was a priority, Obama's advisors were busy trying to figure out just how to enforce the president's red line. That was the real delay. Obama's own diplomatic credibility was on the line—worse, Russia's president, Vladimir Putin, was on the opposing side, waiting for a slipup. How could they credibly say Obama was standing by his ultimatum if the response amounted to nothing more than increasing American support for the moderate opposition? John Kerry, the secretary of state, warned that inaction would give Assad the "green light" to continue using chemical weapons.[5]

Obama was getting pressure from overseas, too. Israel wasn't heavily invested in the success of one side or the other; after all, the Assad regime's troubles were dragging down Israel's primary enemy, Iran, and Iran's terrorist surrogate, Hezbollah. But during a trip to Israel, Obama was lobbied hard by Prime Minister Benjamin Netanyahu, who feared that Syria's chemical weapons could find their way into Hezbollah's arms. Then, instead of raining down on the suburbs of Damascus, chemical weapons would be falling on Tel Aviv.[6]

Jordan's King Abdullah II told Obama the following night that he would let the CIA use his country as a base for drone strikes, an escalation far beyond what anyone in the White House had considered. And King Abdullah of Saudi Arabia was urging the Americans to get more involved, too. Assad's actions had shocked Abdullah, who felt personally attacked when Sunni civilians were killed. And Saudi Arabia and Israel shared a joint interest in seeing the Iranians kept otherwise occupied.

Tom Donilon, the outgoing national security advisor, began to think the United States should arm the rebels. So, too, did Rice, the early opponent. But McDonough, who had a close personal relationship with the president, remained a skeptic. Obama eventually signed a secret finding allowing the CIA to operate training camps in Jordan, thereby giving the White House plausible deniability as more and more extreme militant groups joined the fight against the Assad regime. The CIA had to be doubly careful that it was training the right rebel groups.

On June 13, the White House issued its verdict on the April attack: it was confirmed; the red line had been crossed. But it did so in surprisingly muted fashion, instead of using a presidential address or a dramatic appearance like Colin Powell had made at the United Nations during Bush's tenure. Now the administration simply declared that it, too, had concluded that Assad had used chemical weapons in a statement issued by Ben Rhodes, deputy national security advisor for strategic communications.

"Following a deliberative review, our intelligence community assesses that the Assad regime has used chemical weapons, including the nerve agent sarin, on a small scale against the opposition multiple times in the last year," Rhodes's statement said. "We believe that the Assad regime maintains control of these weapons. We have no reliable, corroborated reporting to indicate that the opposition in Syria has acquired or used chemical weapons.

"The President has said that the use of chemical weapons would change his calculus, and it has," Rhodes went on. But Obama wasn't about to commit troops to the region. Instead, Obama said, the United States would boost its nonlethal aid to the Syrian opposition and to the Supreme Military Council, which was already receiving military aid from some neighboring Middle Eastern countries that wanted Assad gone.

"Put simply, the Assad regime should know that its actions have led us to increase the scope and scale of assistance that we provide to the opposition, including direct support to the SMC. These efforts will increase going forward," Rhodes said.[7]

The statement was remarkable, especially given that it hadn't come from the president's mouth directly. That was a conscious decision on the White House's part; given the weakness of the statement, why have the president deliver it?

But others in the White House thought Obama's initial statement, that crossing the red line would force him to change his calculus, gave them enough wiggle room. After all, there were other responses available to a president than lobbing a cruise missile at the presidential palace. "Military action is not the only response to a crossed red line," a former senior foreign policy advisor said. "We'd put out before where [Assad] had minor incidents, and we took additional steps," like arming key rebel groups or beginning training at the facility in Jordan.

Despite his words, Obama simply didn't believe that committing troops to Syria was in America's best interest, or that his critics in Congress who wanted military involvement understood the scope of the problem ahead.

Kerry began lobbying members of Congress, including in closed-door briefings to the House and Senate Intelligence Committees, to allow the CIA to train rebels. Members of Congress wanted to know how he could be certain that American money wouldn't be going to train al Qaeda rebels, though they eventually signed off on the plans.

The fact was, though, that Obama had few options, and not much room to maneuver. America's intervention in Libya's civil war, limited in scope and successful without costing a single American life, was unpopular with Republicans and Democrats in Congress who thought they should have been consulted, and with a war-weary public. The thought of another attack on a Middle Eastern country, especially one that posed no obvious threat to U.S. national security, was unpalatable after a decade of war, no matter how awful the atrocities broadcast on the nightly news.

So the White House hoped, perhaps naïvely, that Assad would take notice and stop using chemical weapons before something bigger happened — something that would necessitate actual military involvement.

Then someone in Assad's regime clearly stepped

across the red line. On August 21, 2013—a year and a day after Obama had drawn his public red line—Assad's forces launched a large-scale attack in a suburb of Damascus that left hundreds, including children, writhing horribly before they died. It wasn't clear exactly who had ordered the strike; Germany's intelligence agency captured radio traffic that suggested Assad himself may not have given permission for it. Some in the U.S. intelligence community believed it was Assad's brother who had ordered the attack. Regardless of who had given the order, the pictures and video that flooded the Internet put pressure on the United States to respond, and forcefully. Some 1,429 men, women, and children had died gruesome deaths.

This time, the White House wouldn't drag its feet. Obama would begin building both a coalition of the willing and a legal case for a strike.

The most obvious body that would lend international credibility, the United Nations, was a nonstarter. Russia's position on the Security Council, where it was one of five permanent members with veto power, made that certain. And Putin was still miffed at what he thought was an abuse of a UN resolution on the Libya intervention—a decision made by Putin's Russian predecessor, Dmitry Medvedev.

Enough treaties existed, and a sufficient number of other countries had expressed concern over Syria, that the lawyers could search for diplomatic cover while the diplomats began courting potential coalition partners.

Five days after the attack, Secretary of State John Kerry became the highest-ranking U.S. official to indict Assad's regime. Kerry said at a press briefing that the information that intelligence agencies had obtained, from the reports of the number of victims to their symptoms and firsthand accounts from humanitarian organizations, strongly indicated that chemical weapons had been used. Kerry also accused the Assad regime of trying to cover up the attack.

Part of that cover-up attempt, he argued, included stopping international inspectors from reaching the site of the attack. In Syria, a convoy transporting a team of UN inspectors was attacked by snipers on the very day that Kerry held his press conference. No inspectors were injured, but they were unable to reach their target site, which was proof as far as the United States was concerned of a cover-up.

Two days later, on August 28, Obama sat for an interview on PBS, where for the first time the president of the United States accused the Assad regime of conducting chemical weapons attacks against civilians. Obama used the interview to begin making the case to the American public that military action would be necessary.

"What I ... said was that if the Assad regime used

chemical weapons on his own people, that that would
change some of our calculations. And the reason
has to do with not only international norms but also
America's core self-interest. We've got a situation in
which you've got a well-established international
norm against the use of chemical weapons," Obama
said. "We cannot see a breach of the nonproliferation norm that allows, potentially, chemical weapons to fall into the hands of all kinds of folks. So
what I've said is that we have not yet made a decision, but the international norm against the use of
chemical weapons needs to be kept in place. And
nobody disputes—or hardly anybody disputes that
chemical weapons were used on a large scale in Syria
against civilian populations.

"We have looked at all the evidence, and we do
not believe the opposition possessed...chemical
weapons of that sort. We do not believe that, given
the delivery systems, using rockets, that the opposition could have carried out these attacks. We have
concluded that the Syrian government in fact carried these out. And if that's so, then there need to be
international consequences," he said.[8]

But internationally, the coalition of the willing
wasn't proving to be very cohesive. A day after
Obama's remarks, and after British intelligence issued
a report adding to the credibility of the charges against
Assad, the British Parliament issued a stinging defeat

to Prime Minister David Cameron by voting against a resolution supporting military action in Syria. Cameron's coalition government, which had supported the resolution, was taken by surprise. The White House was not happy with their partners across the pond, especially given the number of high-ranking officials within Cameron's coalition government who either didn't show up for the vote or voted against Cameron. It turns out that Cameron had called for the vote too quickly and hadn't given his supporters in Parliament enough time to come back to London from their August holidays. Cameron's government, though, was a bit peeved at the United States for dragging its feet for weeks and then suddenly hoping everyone could turn on a dime. Still, Cameron was blindsided by local politics, most notably on the part of the Labor Party, Tony Blair's political party, which was desperately trying to distance itself from Blair and Iraq. As in the United States, "Iraq Syndrome" had consumed the UK Parliament.

Despite what looked like an important setback, the White House continued pursuing its case and did extract a pledge from the French to get on board. On August 30, the United States released an intelligence community assessment accusing Assad of using chemical weapons multiple times over the previous year. Kerry said, for the first time, that discussions on possible military action were under way.

So certain was the prospect of a military strike

that the White House press office advised correspondents to work through the weekend. Speculation in official Washington wasn't circulating around whether the United States would strike, but when, and how. Saturday night, August 31, or Sunday, September 1, seemed the most likely windows, just hours after the UN inspectors, who were still in Syria, were scheduled to leave. Warships were in place, armed and ready for the order from the commander in chief.

While those discussions played out on the international stage and in the salons of greater Washington, at the White House they involved a surprisingly small number of people. Obama had had enough of Assad's recalcitrance, and he was leaning toward ordering an attack on key parts of Syria's military infrastructure. The president knew he had the evidence to back up a strike; he had sent Kerry out to make the case that Assad — whom Kerry had called "a thug and a murderer" — needed to be reprimanded, through military strikes, for the attack. Kerry's speech appeared to be one of his finest hours as an orator. He met the moment and seemed to prepare the country for war; he was compared favorably to Winston Churchill by supporters of the action and compared to Colin Powell at the UN by detractors. As political theater, it was a huge moment for Kerry.

But hours after Kerry's speech, on a sunny summer afternoon, Obama and his new chief of staff,

Denis McDonough, took a walk around the South Lawn. McDonough has a reputation for being chronically unable to sit still, and the stroll was a habit; this time, he had company. Obama told McDonough he had had a change of heart: he wanted Congress to approve any potential strikes on Syria, ostensibly to provide political accountability but in reality to provide political cover to both parties. And unlike its military action in Libya, the United States didn't have the same international support for an attack on Syria, making bipartisan buy-in all the more essential. What was really nagging at Obama was the rejection by the British Parliament. Even Bush had the British on his side for Iraq; Obama wouldn't have that. He knew he couldn't go it alone. Talk about undermining then candidate Obama's entire foreign policy modus operandi.

Returning from the walk, Obama called his top foreign policy advisors into the Oval Office, including national security advisor Susan Rice and others. He told them of his new plan to consult Congress and seek approval before ordering strikes on Syria.

There have been few times when Obama's advisors have so quickly and vociferously disagreed with their boss, but this was one of them. Obama's plan was completely unexpected, in part because no key leaders in Congress had actually requested a specific vote on military intervention. Even Republican leaders were largely in lockstep with the plans to hold Syria accountable. The last thing John Boehner or Nancy Pelosi, Harry Reid or Mitch McConnell, wanted was a vote. They knew many of their members supported the action but had no stomach for having to publicly admit that.

Obama's advisors, who just hours before had listened to Kerry lay out the U.S. case for military action, felt whiplashed. The NSC staff had believed since the prior weekend that asking Congress for approval wasn't even an option; they believed they would consult Congress, in the form of private briefings and conversations, rather than actually formally seek legislation. After national security staffers had briefed Obama on the available evidence, they believed he was leaning toward a military strike.

But by the end of the week a growing number of members of Congress had begun to question the administration's strategy. And surveys showed that the public was decidedly against an attack: an NBC News poll released the morning of Kerry's speech (and Obama's decision) showed that 80 percent of Americans believed that Obama should seek Congress's approval before ordering strikes.

Obama didn't want to face the backlash of a military strike when the public so clearly opposed one, but his advisors on Friday made the case that Cameron's defeat could soon foreshadow his own. The vote in Parliament was a preview of the dangers of appealing to Congress, not a warning to seek political cover, they said. Obama countered that the vote in Parliament showed exactly why he needed to seek approval. What's more, going to Congress would be consistent with what Obama saw as his own governing philosophy.

The advisors tried to talk Obama out of his position late into the night that Friday. But by the morning, they had acquiesced.

On August 31, a Saturday, Obama addressed the nation and declared that he would seek approval from Congress before the strikes. Obama said he was "mindful that I'm the president of the world's oldest constitutional democracy. I've long believed that our power is rooted not just in our military might, but in our example as a government of the people, by the people and for the people.

"While I believe I have the authority to carry out this military action without specific congressional authorization, I know that the country will be stronger if we take this course, and our actions will be even more effective," Obama said.

The senior aides who had tried to talk Obama out of seeking congressional approval believed nonetheless that they would be able to convince Congress to grant that approval. They told reporters that Obama would be acting within his constitutional authority if he decided to strike Syria even if Congress said no.

Congress wasn't scheduled to return until the following week. The intervening Labor Day and the Jewish holidays made an early return unlikely. The Pentagon conveyed to the White House that a delay wouldn't diminish the country's military capabilities in the Middle East, and the White House hoped it would give them a chance to continue winning over allies in Congress and internationally.

In the meantime, Obama actually had a prime opportunity to build an international coalition that week. The G20 countries, representing the largest economies in the world, were scheduled to meet in St. Petersburg, Russia, a gathering that would include a working dinner on Syria. There, Obama could buttonhole G20 nations and rally them to his cause. This was the trip that was supposed to include a stop in Moscow for a one-on-one with Putin, but Obama had canceled, ostensibly as a public snub over Russia's decision to give asylum to NSA leaker Edward Snowden.

The dispute was not an insignificant part of the backdrop of the group dynamics at the G20 meeting.

The leader dinner, a ritual at these summits, lasted much longer than anticipated. Normally a cocktail party/salon-style dinner for the world's most powerful, this one was very different. It was completely dominated by Obama, who argued for a robust response to Syria's use of chemical weapons, and Putin, who maintained, without much evidence, that the attacks a few weeks before had been orchestrated by rebels. Heads of state from seventeen other countries and one foreign minister—Australia's prime minister, Kevin Rudd, had sent a deputy in his place because of that country's elections—barely spoke as the two Cold War powerhouses, no longer openly hostile but barely concealing their distrust of each other, debated military strikes. France, Turkey, Canada, Saudi Arabia, and Britain's David Cameron sided with Obama. China, India, Indonesia, Argentina, Brazil, South Africa, and Italy sided with Putin.[9]

Notably silent was Angela Merkel. Throughout the economic recession, Merkel's Germany had been the backstop, helping fellow European Union members avoid bankruptcy or default, and the German economy was recovering faster than its neighbors'. Merkel's support was something the White House had counted upon. Without it, and thanks to Putin's pushback, no clear consensus emerged from the G20 summit.

The White House was desperate to unite more than half of the G20 nations around a Syria policy of some kind. In the end, they passed around a heavily watered-down joint statement condemning the August 21 attack, agreeing that evidence pointed to Syria's culpability, and calling for an undefined international response. But even that milquetoast response persuaded only ten other nations to sign on: France, Britain, Australia, Canada, Japan, South Korea, Turkey, Saudi Arabia, Spain, and Italy. Merkel's signature wasn't on the document.[10]

Syria, too, expected that an attack would come. In an interview with Charlie Rose on September 9 in Damascus, Assad accused the United States of lying about the chemical weapons attack and of violating international law. "As long as the United States doesn't obey the international law and tramples over the charter of the United Nations, we have to worry that any administration, not only this one, would do anything. But, according to the lies that we've been hearing for the last two weeks from high-ranking officials in this administration, we have to expect the worst," Assad said.

Kerry had had an exhausting few weeks. Just a few months before his seventieth birthday, Kerry had maintained a breakneck travel schedule. He was reaching out to members of Congress and the international community, while his State Department jet zipped from Washington to Lithuania to Paris to London, where he pressed the flesh with foes and allies alike. Finally, on Monday, September 9, the day Congress was supposed to return, Kerry met with William Hague, the British foreign secretary, and was asked by a CBS reporter whether there was anything Syria could do to avoid an attack.

"Sure," a weary Kerry said. "He could turn over every single bit of his chemical weapons to the international community in the next week. Turn it over, all of it, without delay, and allow a full and total accounting for that. But he isn't about to do it, and it can't be done, obviously."[11]

This was decidedly undiplomatic language for a secretary of state, words that sounded more like Kerry the senator than Kerry the diplomat. But they also represented an opportunity for one side that desperately wanted to avoid an American strike—Russia.

If the United States had gotten involved in a military push against Syria, it is unlikely that Assad's regime would have survived. Without Assad in power, Russia's toehold in the Mediterranean would have been jeopardized. And Russia was desperate to keep its influence in the Middle East—for some in Moscow, the Cold War had never really ended.

After Kerry's comments, Sergey Lavrov, Russia's long-serving foreign minister, pounced. Kerry didn't seem to believe that Syria could get rid of its chemical weapons in a week, but what about giving them up altogether? Russia proposed requiring Syria to place its chemical weapons under international control, to be removed from the country and dismantled, in exchange for avoiding a military strike. Syria was one of a handful of countries that had never joined the Chemical Weapons Convention; it would do so under Lavrov's proposal.

Obama, whose chances of getting a resolution through Congress looked less likely, suddenly had an out, an opportunity to extract his administration from a one-way street. He said he would consider Lavrov's proposal; the following day, Obama discussed it with Cameron and French president François Hollande, another early advocate of military action. France began to draft a resolution that could pass the UN Security Council with Russia's cooperation, but one that authorized the use of force if Assad failed or refused to hand over his weapons.

That night, for the second time in two weeks, Obama addressed the nation to explain his thinking on Syria, and to hit the Pause button on congressional action. "Over the last few days, we've seen some encouraging signs. In part because of the credible threat of U.S. military action, as well as constructive talks that I had with President Putin, the Russian government has indicated a willingness to join with the international community in pushing Assad to give up his chemical weapons. The Assad regime has now admitted that it has these weapons," Obama said. "It's too early to tell whether this offer will succeed, and any agreement must verify that the Assad regime keeps its commitments. But this initiative has the potential to remove the threat of chemical weapons without the use of force, particularly because Russia is one of Assad's strongest allies.

"I have, therefore, asked the leaders of Congress to postpone a vote to authorize the use of force while we pursue this diplomatic path," he said.

The move infuriated those on Capitol Hill who had backed Obama on Syria. Senator Bob Corker, the Tennessee Republican whom the White House saw as one of the few reasonable and pragmatic members of his party, summed up what many came to believe about Obama: "The president just seems to be very uncomfortable being commander in chief of this nation," Corker told CNN the day after Obama's second address to the nation.[12] Earlier that day, Corker had sent an e-mail to McDonough at the White House. "You guys are really hard to help," he wrote.

Nonetheless, Obama dispatched Kerry on one more foreign trip, to Geneva, to meet with Lavrov to hammer out the details. The eventual final product required Syria not to rid itself of chemical weapons within a week, but to declare its stockpile in that time frame. The UN and the Organization for the Prevention of Chemical Weapons would have access to all chemical weapons facilities, and most of the weapons would be destroyed by the middle of 2014, with the most lethal being the very last Assad would turn over, leading to concerns by some in the United States that he would never give up his most lethal cache.

Still, in the moment, the agreement was a minor, and in some ways insufficient, response to a clear violation of a red line posited by the president of the United States. Even if Assad wasn't the one who had given the order, his regime had used chemical weapons on multiple occasions against his own people. Obama didn't explicitly promise a military attack when laying out that red line, but it's hard to see how changing the calculus led only to an offhand remark from Kerry and a helping hand from Russia's foreign minister.

The on-again, off-again nature of the debate surrounding Syria was not the image of strength and decisiveness a president wants to convey. Obama got a big part of the outcome he desired—an end to Syria's use of chemical weapons—but the White House didn't handle the situation as well as it could have. "We won't get style points for the way we made this decision," Obama said later, both privately and publicly.

In the Obama era and for the presidents after him, style points would take on greater weight than ever, both at home and abroad.

Despite his stated and evident obsession with pragmatism—the very thing that had helped get him elected, as a referendum against Bush—Obama himself appeared to be worried that his stature on the national and international stage was shrinking.

In many ways, it was. Where Bush's actions generally diminished America's image abroad, Obama's inaction may have diminished the country's stature among some of its closest foreign partners. Where Bush rushed to war, Obama waited, and in the eyes even of some of his advisors, he hesitated too long. Where Bush overreacted, Obama underreacted. And where Bush called out his political opponents, questioning their patriotism in the run-up to the war in Iraq, Obama called out his political opponents in hopes of winning their votes—even though ultimately, on this and so many other issues, he couldn't seem to do so.

Within eight months of Obama's decision to pull back on a military strike against Assad, the civil war in Syria was as messy as ever and has since spilled over into Iraq, foreshadowing the real possibility that the entire region could end up in a Sunni-Shia hot war. Iraq's future, as of this writing, is truly in doubt; the likelihood of the country self-partitioning is very real. Meanwhile, a vicious al Qaeda–like group has risen up. They are the most radical fighters against Assad and are seen by the United States as so dangerous that they could aspire to be as lethal and dangerous as al Qaeda in the '90s pre-9/11. In fact, one U.S. official described the situation in Syria to be more chaotic and unstable than the situation in Afghanistan before 9/11.

Could the rise of this vicious terrorist group,

called ISIS (the Islamic State of Iraq and Syria), have been avoided had the United States and its allies acted faster in supporting a moderate opposition to Assad? If Obama had gone through with the military strike, would the fallout have knocked Assad completely out of power, leaving a more civil fight to see who will lead Syria? Would a strike have quickened the speed with which more extreme elements took over?

Or did the Obama administration bungle the entire Arab Spring from the start? One prominent Democratic senator who recently retired believes the fundamental policy mistake was getting involved in Egypt, which led to Libya then Syria. This senator believes that the Obama administration, when it pushed Mubarak out, got so involved in the propping up of a new and real democracy (which was basically short-lived), whether it realizes it or not, that it sent a signal to the oppressed in Syria and elsewhere that the United States would stand by to help any opposition against any authoritarian Mideast ruler. But the politics of engagement overseas is now fraught with peril in the United States, and post-Egypt each subsequent engagement by the United States is more limited. It gives an appearance of weakness around the world and indecision at home, a perilous place for any president. Then again, in the words of the president, it's a bunch of "shitty options"—which may best sum up the Middle East for the next decade. In fact, early on in the second term, as Syria was becoming messier and messier and the umpteenth attempt to broker peace between the Israelis and the Palestinians was coming to an abrupt end, Joe Biden went to his boss with a simple piece of advice: Just manage the chaos in the Middle East. Don't make big commitments; nothing will work, it's that messy. Instead, protect U.S. interests, keep the focus on rooting out terrorism, and then pivot to Asia and Latin America, where, economically, the future of the United States might be more promising. It's advice the president has been trying to take, but so many Mideast fires erupt, it's been difficult for him to fully pivot.

Chapter Eighteen

Control-Alt-Delete

The evening of March 21, 2010, had been unseasonably warm. It was a Sunday, and the mercury hit 75 degrees in Washington. On Capitol Hill, Democrats scrambled to count votes on what would become the single biggest achievement of Nancy Pelosi's tenure as Speaker of the House of Representatives: after months of difficult negotiations, failed entreaties even to moderate Republicans, loud protests, and the almost constant drumbeat of declining poll numbers, the House was in the home stretch of passing the Affordable Care Act.

Pelosi and her top deputy, House majority whip Steny Hoyer, worked the phones, scrupulously counting every last vote. They knew that Republicans would make the unpopular bill a centerpiece of their campaign to retake Congress later that year. They also knew they wouldn't be able to persuade Blue Dog Democrats, members who represented conservative districts in the South or Mountain West who had to be against Obamacare (a term the White

House decided to start embracing as an attempt to make the derisive use of it by the right less effective), and they wanted to reassure those on the fence that they wouldn't be the last vote in favor—all too many Democrats remembered Marjorie Margolies-Mezvinsky, the Pennsylvania Democrat who had cast the deciding 218th vote in favor of Bill Clinton's 1993 budget proposal. As Margolies-Mezvinsky walked onto the House floor to cast her vote, Republicans taunted her: "Hey, hey, hey, goodbye!"

No Democrat wanted to be the 218th vote in favor of health care reform, so Pelosi and Hoyer twisted arms, begged, pleaded, promised help in the coming midterm elections, hoping to get to 219. Finally, a little after 10 p.m., they opened the roll call vote. Kathleen Sebelius, the health and human services secretary who had spent her entire tenure promoting the health care law, watched from Pelosi's box above the floor.

At the White House, secretaries were calling senior advisors at home: the president wanted company. Valerie Jarrett was in her pajamas, she later recalled, when she heard from Obama's personal assistant.[1] Nancy-Ann DeParle ignored the fact that the next day was a school day; she brought her son into the office.[2] As the vote tally clicked toward the magic number, at 10:45 Obama's friends, watching on television sixteen blocks up Pennsylvania Avenue, let out a cheer. On the House floor, Democrats broke into a familiar chant: "Yes we can! Yes we can!"[3]

The party moved onto the White House's Truman Balcony. The champagne started flowing. The guests stayed late into the night. About 2 a.m., Jarrett asked Obama how that day compared with Election Day a year and a half earlier. "There's no comparison," Jarrett remembered the president saying. "Election night was simply the means to get us to this night."[4]

But Obama didn't let his team savor the moment very long that night, three and a half years before Americans without health insurance would be required to sign up for it. The bill was so complicated, with so many interlocking pieces, with regulations to write and rules to implement, that the team that had just engineered passage of one of the largest social programs in American history would have to begin the very next day to make sure it was implemented correctly.[5]

One of the questions that will plague historians looking back on the presidency of Barack Obama will revolve around this fundamental disconnect: how could a president so powerfully make a law so central to his legacy and then fail so miserably to make it real?

Obama, elected by voters tired of seeing government so badly mismanaged under George W. Bush, had an opportunity before him that liberals hadn't had since Lyndon Johnson's presidency: the chance to show voters that government could function properly in an effort to make their lives better. Bill Clinton declared the era of big government over; now Barack Obama could declare the era of smarter, more effective government under way. Instead, the rollout of the health insurance website — rocky, to put it charitably; disastrous, to be more realistic — threatened to undermine Obama's central promise and the governing philosophy that underpinned his party.

Other Democrats had seen this problem coming.

The first to raise concerns over getting implementation right was Bob Menendez, the highly (some would say overly) political New Jersey Democrat who sat on the Senate Finance Committee and who was tasked with heading up the Senate Democrats' campaign arm. As early as the summer of 2009, a year and a half before Democratic senators would face voters, Menendez joined a series of meetings with DeParle and Jeanne Lambrew, then a high-ranking official at the Health and Human Services Department. Democrats were riding high; with big majorities in the House and Senate, the party could force through almost any legislation they wished. Early that summer, House Democratic strategists believed that included the health care law. The most optimistic members believed they could pass the entire bill before Congress broke for recess in October. Some planners thought the measure could even be fully implemented by 2010, before members of Congress would next face voters. Seems absurd to ponder now, but policy planners were that optimistic.

The White House was skeptical. After all, the model for the Affordable Care Act, Massachusetts's version, had taken more than a year to implement, and legislators had made significant changes two, three, even six years later. Commonwealth Care covered just one state; it wasn't likely that a program aimed at insuring tens of millions of people across the nation could be operational in a similar time frame.

White House policy aides were thinking 2012 at the earliest to get everything up and running, with a goal of trying to move things up to 2011. As Senate Democrats were putting together the framework, they debated the sign-up date, and the working assumption was that something akin to HealthCare.gov would be working by October 1, 2012, a full two and a half years after passage; it seemed like a perfectly reasonable amount of time.

That's when Menendez shook his head and put the final kibosh on the time frame. Menendez didn't want the Democrats he was responsible for protecting to be swept away if some bureaucrat couldn't get the job done. "If [implementation] goes well, great," said one White House advisor, summing up the message Menendez sent the White House. "If it doesn't, there could be problems with it."

The White House came to agree. Just as Menendez wanted to protect the electoral interests of Democratic senators, so Obama's top advisors wanted to protect the president. What if problems arose? Obama's advisors remembered what had happened when George W. Bush had pushed a prescription drug benefit through Congress: early in the implementation process, glitches prevented some seniors from getting the benefits they were due, and the negative publicity hurt Bush's approval rating. With their own re-election bid just a few years down the road, why take the risk of similar implementation snafus hurting Obama during the 2012 campaign?

Given what *actually* happened with the rollout of HealthCare.gov, it's not hyperbole to say that Bob Menendez saved the presidency for Democrats in 2012 simply by being the political realist in the room.

Political considerations came to define the three-and-a-half-year march from passage to implementation. In fact, the White House was so anxious to avoid political risks that it delayed issuing regulations that would have allowed states and the federal government to make needed progress. In an effort to avoid short-term pain, it made the long-term injury even worse.

Obama's advisors saw the effort to provide tens

of millions of Americans with health insurance as consisting of two key elements, neither of which would work without the other: On one hand, they had to get people to sign up, enrolling either in Medicaid, which would be expanded to include more Americans living just slightly over the poverty line, or in private plans. On the other, they would have to build from scratch a system that allowed those people to sign up—the website, HealthCare. gov. The White House viewed enrollment volume almost as a campaign, one in which it could utilize the vaunted infrastructure built during 2008 and 2012 to push uninsured Americans into health care plans. They viewed the technological side as something that could be run out of the bureaucracy of the Health and Human Services Department.

After that night on the Truman Balcony, Obama would occasionally sit in on meetings dedicated to implementation. Whatever the focus of a given meeting, he would warn: "All of that is well and good, but if the website doesn't work, nothing else matters."

Although the two aspects that would make the law a success couldn't operate without each other, and in spite of the president's warnings, no one took direct responsibility for building the website. It's quite mind-boggling that an administration run by the most technologically savvy campaign team in American history botched a website, but the failure really had to do with the fact that, like some of the administration's other missteps, it was rooted in poor management, in this case not designating someone, *anyone,* to own implementation — a CEO of sorts.

For three years, even as outside consultants and advisors warned of a problem, there was no single person whose sole job description was responsibility for creating the online portal millions of Americans would need to sign up for insurance. Specific warnings began early. Just two months after the Affordable Care Act passed, David Cutler, a Harvard professor who had advised the White House on health policy, warned in a memo to Larry Summers, then director of the White House's National Economic Council, and Office of Management and Budget chief Peter Orszag that the administration was hopelessly underqualified to implement the law.

"My general view is that the early implementation efforts are far short of what it will take to implement reform successfully," Cutler wrote in the memo, obtained later by the *Washington Post.* "For health reform to be successful, the relevant people need a vision about health system transformation and the managerial ability to carry out that vision. The President has sketched out such a vision. However, I do not believe the relevant members of the Administration understand the President's vision or have the capability to carry it out."

He wrote the last sentence in boldface.

In the weeks after the bill's passage, the White House was consumed with the question of who would be in charge of implementation. Members of the economic team, like Summers and Orszag, and health care advisor Zeke Emanuel, Rahm's brother, urged Obama to appoint a "czar," whose sole responsibility would be implementation. But the health care aides who helped pass the bill made the case that they could do the job. Obama sided with the aides and tapped Nancy-Ann DeParle, head of the Office of Health Reform, to manage the process.[6]

DeParle asked for a spreadsheet listing every provision in the law from Health and Human Services, the agency responsible for its implementation and its current status. The spreadsheet ran for hundreds of pages, underscoring just how complicated implementation would be. Agencies ranging from the Food and Drug Administration to the Government Accountability Office and the Internal Revenue Service held responsibilities; some, like the GAO, operated quickly, and others, like the FDA, dragged their feet.

To facilitate the complex process, DeParle began holding regular meetings in the Old Executive Office Building. Three times a week, then later twice a week, agencies would send top officials to give updates on the progress of their piece of the pie. The meetings lasted for hours. At the beginning, top officials showed up; later, they sent their deputies. DeParle also held monthly meetings with more senior-level officials, aimed at hashing out the most controversial regulations. Sebelius, treasury secretary Timothy Geithner, Emanuel, and domestic policy advisor Melody Barnes began attending. But the meetings quickly flagged; soon Sebelius was the only principal in the room.

DeParle, who had spent most of her career on health policy and was not fully confident of the team at Health and Human Services, knew she needed help. She reached out to the one man with experience in building something similar: Jon Kingsdale, who had put together the Massachusetts health insurance exchange. Once, while trying to persuade him, DeParle broke White House protocol and took Kingsdale by the Oval Office while Obama was there working. She wanted to impress on Kingsdale the magnitude of the work they needed.

At HHS, Sebelius hired her own czar, a former Missouri insurance commissioner named Jay Angoff. The month the Affordable Care Act was signed, Sebelius named Angoff to head a new agency that would house the implementation efforts: the Center for Consumer Information and Insurance Oversight.

But Kingsdale, a man of tremendous ego, didn't want to work for someone else. At the same time, he had his own consulting business, and the idea of full-time government work might not make financial sense to him. Kingsdale met with the Office of

Presidential Personnel several times, trying to fashion a deal that would allow him to accept outside clients while working in the White House. Ultimately, he decided he would have to give up too much to help out. DeParle urged him to reconsider; she even offered him her own job.

DeParle had known she wasn't long for the White House. She had ordered only a hundred business cards when she hired on, and she planned to abandon her tiny West Wing office, which she shared with speechwriters Ben Rhodes and Jon Favreau, before the end of 2010. But with one foot out the door, DeParle was sucked back in: Obama asked her to stay on in a more prestigious role, as deputy chief of staff.

DeParle's replacement, Jeanne Lambrew, was given even less power. Health care and climate change, two of Obama's signature issues, were moved under the control of the Domestic Policy Council, once a high-profile panel of advisors but now greatly diminished in stature.

The White House also thought it needed someone capable of leading at HHS, a Sebelius deputy with gravitas and management experience. But the department had trouble recruiting the right person. Throughout 2010, 2011, and 2012, it cycled through a series of folks: Mark Childress, a veteran of Capitol Hill who served as acting general counsel (Childress, a fiery North Carolina native who hasn't met a swearword he's afraid to utter, ended up at the

White House heading up a messaging war room on health care); Joel Ario, a former Pennsylvania insurance commissioner who served as director of the Office of Health Insurance Exchanges; Steve Larsen, who succeeded Angoff at Consumer Information and Insurance Oversight; and Donald Berwick, who served as head of the Centers for Medicare and Medicaid Services. All of them either didn't work out or simply didn't want to stay.

The person who survived was Marilyn Tavenner, Berwick's onetime deputy, who was promoted when Berwick couldn't win Senate confirmation. Tavenner, a former health care executive experienced in the economics of running a hospital, served as acting administrator beginning in late 2011; she wasn't confirmed by the Senate until the middle of 2013. Even then, the administration didn't always keep her in the loop. When the White House decided to delay a provision of the Affordable Care Act that would have required companies with more than fifty employees to contribute to the cost of health insurance, Tavenner told members of Congress that she hadn't been consulted. In fact, when the delay was announced, Tavenner was on vacation.[7]

Two other officials tasked with building the actual website were distracted by a game of musical chairs. Todd Park, the chief technology officer at HHS, and Steve VanRoekel, the federal government's chief information officer, were initially in charge. But Park wanted to go to the White House, to become the federal government's CTO. His departure would have left Jenny Backus, a veteran Democratic communications strategist, in charge of the website. Backus made the case that the website fell under the auspices of the communications office. But the White House had concerns that HHS underestimated what HealthCare.gov needed to be; it was not simply a messaging tool for a campaign, and they insisted that Park maintain oversight. His dual assignments once again ensured that no individual maintained oversight of the project.

Unlike others the administration recruited to help implementation along, Tavenner earned the respect of the White House. But though she was tasked with implementing the law, it was one of a dozen responsibilities that fell under her purview. Even with Tavenner in place, her attention was divided, and without a point person whose sole job was to make sure the law became reality, the law, and the president, were coming into the focus of eager Republican critics.

Republican opponents of the Affordable Care Act wasted no opportunity to make the White House's job more difficult. The already-complicated job of building a federal health insurance exchange was made increasingly complex when most states run by Republicans refused to build their own exchanges. That meant the federal exchange would have to cover more people across state lines. And in fairness to the administration, this wasn't something they'd ever banked on: they really believed that after hemming and hawing, most states would want autonomy over the health care exchanges — after all, when has a governor ever wanted the feds to run anything they could run themselves? But the politics even of expanding Medicaid coverage in these states was so bad for Republicans that almost every state with sole Republican control of the governor's office and legislature decided to sit the entire law out. No expansion of Medicaid, no separate exchanges, and so an extra burden for which the federal government never really had a contingency plan.

After the Supreme Court ruled constitutional the law's individual mandate, requiring the uninsured to enroll or buy plans but striking down a provision requiring states to expand Medicaid to cover more people living near the poverty line, states run by Republican governors and legislatures had even more cover for skipping out on accepting the federal funds. That meant low-income earners in their states would have to buy plans, rather than qualifying for free Medicaid, further burdening the new insurance exchange system. If those expanded Medicaid recipients could have been covered sooner, the exchange could have dealt more easily with the consumers it was meant to serve.

Republicans were so determined to overturn the

law that they refused to fund a reorganization of HHS that would have given more power to the office overseeing implementation, the Office of Consumer Information and Insurance Oversight. The office had more than two hundred employees, but it didn't have the ability to award grants or contracts. Neither did it have the money necessary to build the federal exchange—and congressional Republicans were in no mood to give it to them. Eventually, HHS had to move the office into the larger Centers for Medicare and Medicaid Services (CMS), splintering its locations among Washington, nearby Bethesda, and Baltimore.

At the same time, the White House worried that publicizing regulations and requirements for those state exchanges, rules absolutely required for a state to properly comply with the complex law, would only give Republicans more targets to aim for. Throughout 2011, officials at CMS begged the White House for permission to make public concepts of operation, complex diagrams that would show states how to build their exchanges in order to harmonize with the federal exchange. But Obama advisors remembered the last time a Democratic president had tried to overhaul the nation's health care system: back in the early 1990s, when a task force spearheaded by Hillary Clinton was working on a reform plan, Senate Republican leader Bob Dole had used the task force's complicated charts to mock their work.

The White House's solution was much more complicated. CMS administrators were to praise the work of states whose exchanges were heading in the right direction, without sharing the administration's actual thinking.[8]

By late March 2013, just six months before the exchanges were to open, McKinsey & Company, the well-respected management consulting firm, had begun sounding another alarm. In a report commissioned by HHS, the firm found the exchange's timeline seriously behind the curve. The report concluded that development of the website was falling behind thanks in part to indecision by top policy makers, and in part because the contractors charged with building the site weren't communicating. Perhaps most frightening, the report projected that the department wouldn't have enough time to test the system from end to end before its expected October 1 launch.[9]

White House staff insisted they had made adjustments after the McKinsey report reached their desks. But by late August, weeks before the site was to launch, serious bugs were still popping up. As tensions mounted between CMS and the website's lead contractor, CGI Federal, CMS chief operating officer Michelle Snyder was openly telling colleagues she would have fired the firm if she'd had the option. CMS had sent groups of officials to the company's headquarters, just outside the Beltway, to spot-check new code, much of which failed to work. CMS officials also complained that CGI wasn't working well with an alphabet soup of contractors who had won bids to build other parts of the system.

CGI officials believed the timeline they were given for creating a cutting-edge website was hopelessly compressed. The vision the administration had for a fully integrated site just didn't match what the contractor could pull together in the time allowed.

At a demonstration of the new site on August 27, at CMS's headquarters in Baltimore, some company officials worried that the system would crash in front of their clients. Others hoped it would, so the administration would take seriously their concerns that the time frame wasn't long enough. CGI technicians had compiled a list of more than six hundred bugs that needed to be fixed, a monumental task that scared every computer engineer who read it.

For a system that was supposed to handle thousands of new registrants every day, capacity was becoming one of the biggest issues. By late September, the site was crashing in tests of just five hundred simultaneous users.[10] And yet despite these inauspicious tests, the problems weren't being fully communicated to the White House. In fact, almost simultaneously with those failed tests, White House aides led by senior advisor David Simas were leading detailed briefings about the October 1 launch that didn't merely gloss over the issue of potential bugs in the system, but actually glorified the website, comparing it to popular consumer sites like Kayak and Amazon. Even the president got into the game on September 26, during a campaign-style swing touting the start of the program, bragging about the ease with which the public would be able to shop for insurance, just five days before Health-Care.gov went live.

"Starting on Tuesday, every American can visit HealthCare.gov to find out what's called the insurance marketplace for your state. Here in Maryland, I actually think it's called MarylandHealthConnection.gov. [He's interrupted by applause.] MarylandHealthConnection.gov. But if you go to HealthCare.gov, you can look and they'll tell you where to go. They'll link to your state.

"Now, this is real simple. It's a website where you can compare and purchase affordable health insurance plans, side by side, the same way you shop for a plane ticket on Kayak—same way you shop for a TV on Amazon. You just go on and you start looking, and here are all the options.

"It's buying insurance on the private market, but because now you're part of a big group plan—everybody in Maryland is all logging in and taking a look at the prices—you've got new choices. Now you've got new competition, because insurers want your business. And that means you will have cheaper prices.

"So you enter in some basic information about yourself, what level of coverage you're looking for. After that, you'll be presented with a list of quality, affordable plans that are available in your area. It will say clearly what each plan covers, what each plan costs. The price will be right there. It will be fully transparent.

"Before this law, only a handful of states required insurance companies to offer you instant price quotes, but because of this law, insurers in all 50 states will have to offer you instant price quotes. And so if you've ever tried to buy insurance on your own, I promise you this is a lot easier. It's like booking a hotel or a plane ticket."

That was the president, just five days before the launch. Five days.

On October 1, when the site went live, the full magnitude of the disaster became apparent. Hardly anyone could finish the complicated process of signing up for a plan; in some cases, users couldn't even create accounts because identity verification software didn't work. Software developers began working on individual bug fixes, failing to realize that the problems were systemic. A week into the site's launch, 30 percent of those who applied weren't being directed to screens on which they could input information about their income (critical to qualifying for subsidies) or their identity. A few days later, officials found that the website wasn't calculating those subsidies correctly. There were even questions about data security; one applicant in North Carolina received a letter with personal information about another applicant, from South Carolina.[11]

The administration had a modicum of cover: October 1 was also the day Republicans on Capitol Hill, led by freshman firebrand Ted Cruz of Texas, shut down the government. Polls showed that the GOP was taking a political beating for refusing to come to a budget agreement. While Democrats lambasted Republicans for their recalcitrance, the shutdown was a political godsend, distracting attention from a badly malfunctioning website. In fact, the public was even willing to assume that the shutdown of the government was probably having an impact on the website.

But the shutdown ended a few weeks later, and attention returned to the site. And then the first cancellation notices began arriving.

Throughout his campaign for the Affordable Care Act, Obama had promised that those who liked their health care plans could keep them. But millions of Americans had health care plans with coverage that didn't meet the law's minimum requirements. The White House must have known that those plans would be canceled, making one of Obama's central promises turn into what PolitiFact, a nonpartisan fact-checking organization, later called the "Lie of the Year."

Barack Obama shares a trait with many of his predecessors: he is not one to admit fault readily. But his "if you like your plan, you can keep it" was turning into a national punch line, and congressional Democrats were reeling. They could picture the attack ads coming—shoot, Republican groups in some states were already bashing their Democratic senators for making the same promise—which, by the way, every Democrat who voted for health care reform uttered. So in a November interview with this author broadcast on NBC, the president did something he rarely does—he offered a full mea culpa.

"I regret very much that—what we intended to do, which is to make sure that everybody is moving into better plans because they want them, as opposed to because they're forced into it, that, you know, we weren't as clear as we needed to be in terms of the changes that were taking place," Obama said. "I am sorry that they, you know, are finding themselves in this situation, based on assurances they got from me. We've got to work hard to make sure that they know we hear them, and that we're going to do everything we can to deal with folks who find themselves in a tough position as a consequence of this."

Privately, the White House blamed Sebelius. In

the months after the botched rollout, Sebelius, once the face of health care reform, was barely visible — about the only way this president fires folks. He simply hides them from the media. The administration had originally wanted Tom Daschle, the former Senate majority leader, to run the Department of Health and Human Services; instead, after Daschle's nomination was scuttled, they turned to the former Kansas governor, who had little experience in Washington and who proved virtually unable to recruit a strong manager to oversee her side of the project. Daschle had been expected to lead efforts both at HHS and in the White House on health care reform; relying on Sebelius at HHS and DeParle at the White House further fragmented what should have been a seamless operation.

As early as October 2010, doubts about Sebelius as the lead administrator on this task were already bubbling up in the West Wing. Following another status report meeting by DeParle and Sebelius in Rahm Emanuel's office, when Sebelius left the room, the cold-blooded operator that is Emanuel had wondered aloud whether Sebelius was up to the task. But despite the concern at that point, nothing happened to Sebelius.

That's hardly a surprise: firing people isn't in Obama's DNA. He had let only a handful of officials go, mostly for undermining him. Perhaps the

McChrystal episode hadn't stiffened his spine enough. Politics, too, played a role: Republicans had held up countless nominations, including Berwick's at CMS. There was a virtual guarantee that anyone Obama chose to replace Sebelius would immediately come to embody health care reform writ large, and would run into a Republican roadblock during the Senate confirmation process.

Sebelius knew her job was on the line. The White House was slow in coming to her defense, and some in the West Wing were mystified—and blindsided— when a story appeared in the *New York Times* two weeks after the site's dismal launch, quoting her brother.[12] It was a clear attempt by Sebelius to try to save her own skin and make sure she wasn't totally scapegoated. The president never guaranteed that her job was safe, and indeed in April 2014 she handed in her resignation, in large measure responsible for the train wreck but also partially the scapegoat for a larger problem of communication and leadership.

The tech-savvy president, who couldn't believe that his legacy might be tarnished over an inability to build a functional website, blamed the Washington bureaucracy. He noted that the way the government contracting process works, his campaign experts couldn't even bid on the HealthCare.gov contract. This is yet another example of the promise versus the reality of Obama—bring in new technologies and new people, but instead of trying to change the system, talk about change and continue working within the system that would often get the best of him.

Enrollment numbers improved significantly over the next several months, but the initial shock of such a dismal rollout undercut a central promise of Obama's tenure. There was no CEO in charge of the overall process. Concerns over Obama's re-election delayed regulations and rules that should have been issued years before they finally were. And for too long, no one was held accountable.

For this president's domestic agenda at least, actions, it seemed, kept speaking louder than words. And as the year went on, public polls showed that the administration had inflicted the damage on itself: the public trust Obama had held on to for so long was beginning to slip away.

Senior advisor Dan Pfeiffer's memo, written at the beginning of 2014, had promised a forthcoming year of action. Left unsaid but implicit was the fact that the opportunities of the previous year had been almost entirely squandered. The year 2013, the lost year of the Obama presidency, wore heavily on Obama the human being. Toward the end of the year, one could sense the funk he had slipped into. Between the health care debacle, the NSA, and even the government shutdown, it seemed the president was shrinking in stature by the day.

Obama is someone who can be very introspective; unlike previous presidents who rarely read what was written about them, this one carries his own iPad, and it is loaded with media apps; while he mostly consumes columns — in another life he probably would have been a political columnist instead of a politician — he also reads reports of what's written about him.

By Thanksgiving, the drumbeat about his lost year and perhaps his lost second term was getting louder. He decided he needed his side of the story out, about 2013 and beyond. So he invited his favorite writer, the *New Yorker*'s David Remnick, to travel with him.

His talks with Remnick were as much therapy session as they were a tour of current events. There was even a bit of self-pity. At one point during his sit-down with Remnick, he mused, "It turns out Marlon Brando had it easy [in *The Godfather*]; when it comes to Congress, there is no such thing as an offer they can't refuse." It's a comment that Obama, perhaps, will make again in his own memoirs. Obama truly believes that every single critique of him is rooted in his inability to work with Congress, and he doesn't blame himself, he blames the Republicans.

But it was clear that 2013, with its series of unending and in most cases unresolved crises, was wearing the president down. Remnick quoted Obama at a fund-raiser to which the writer had gained access, where the best advice Obama could offer partisan Democrats boiled down to one word: "patience." "One thing that I always try to emphasize is that, if you look at American history, there have been frequent occasions in which it looked like we had insoluble problems—either economic, political, security—and, as long as there were those who stayed steady and clear-eyed and persistent, eventually we came up with an answer."

It was a long way from Obama the 2008 candidate. Rather than "hope and change," this was Obama pleading with donors that things weren't hopeless.

Later, in his Remnick session, he went further in admitting that he had reached the limits of his influence. "If you're doing big, hard things, then there is going to be some hair on it—there's going to be some aspects of it that aren't clean and neat and immediately elicit applause from everybody. And so the nature of not only politics but, I think, social change of any sort is that it doesn't move in a straight line, and that those who are most successful typically are tacking like a sailor toward a particular direction but have to take into account winds and currents and occasionally the lack of any wind, so that you're just sitting there for a while, and sometimes you're being blown all over the place."

These are the words of a beaten-down president. So concerned was the White House that the public would interpret the Remnick interview as the president throwing in the towel, almost admitting that his days as an effective president were numbered, they quietly reminded people of the timing of his Remnick sit-down: it had taken place at the end of a horrible year for him, and he was venting.

When this interview hit newsstands, in January 2014, the picture of a worn-out president didn't seem to match the man who suddenly seemed to have some energy. Aides now admit that the president probably wasn't in the best place politically to unburden himself the way he had with Remnick.

Getting a full two weeks off over the holidays, without the threat of a budget or health care crisis to delay his Hawaiian sojourn, was exactly what aides say the president needed. He returned to Washington in January somewhat refreshed. Yes, the scar tissue was there, but there was still a little fight left in him. He wanted to prove that his presidency wasn't over, that he still had some political juice and he could rally his party to survive the 2014 midterm elections.

Just as victory and defeat are emblematic of Obama's first five and a half years, they can be used to define this time for the man as well. If Democrats hold the Senate, he can claim victory and use it to make one last attempt to work with Congress on something big, perhaps immigration or even entitlement reform. But if his party loses the Senate, then the l-word (as in "lame duck") will become common Washington vocabulary.

So engaged is Obama now, he has agreed to frequent fund-raisers and political briefings. Normally not someone who could be confused with being a political junkie, he's following the ups and downs of every key Senate race in the country.

He even tailored his State of the Union to a message that Senate Democrats, be they in blue Minnesota or red Arkansas, could rally around. This also explains why the 2014 State of the Union was the least ambitious of his presidency, filled with small, attainable goals and lacking a grand agenda. It was downright Bill Clintonesque, filled with "I'm on your side" types of programs. But for Obama, it was a nod to political reality and one that, for the first time, showed him to be a team player regarding the worries about Congress.

Of course, for Obama, the battle for the Senate is about him, and when his own legacy is on the line and his back is against the wall, he does get competitive. History has shown him to be an operator when he has to be. Harry Reid and the Senate Democrats just hope it isn't too late.

CHAPTER NINETEEN

The Legacy

Barack Obama's place in history was secured the moment he was sworn in to office. No one else will ever be America's first black president.

But that's not the legacy Obama wants. He came to office riding a wave of change, promising to fix a broken Washington and move beyond the partisan politics that disgusted him as much as it did the voters who'd sent him to the White House. Faced with the greatest economic crisis in almost a century, Obama saw the opportunity to re-create while recovering, to revive the economy but also to reduce inequality across socioeconomic boundaries. He would end two wars and attempt to project a new image of America as a source of global tolerance and stability. He had hoped to bridge the divides both Bill Clinton and George W. Bush had forced upon the country. His background was supposed to help bring blacks and whites closer together. Just as Reagan had moved the country squarely to the center-right, Obama hoped he could move it to the center-left.

But hope was one thing, change another. Within days of his arrival at 1600, the president found himself stymied—by Washington institutions like the Pentagon and government bureaucracy, by the petty squabbles among members of his own party, and most of all by Republicans who have sought to block even the most basic steps he wanted to take. Barack Obama wanted to soar above partisanship; instead, his time in office, so far, will be remembered as a nadir of partisan relations. This Obama is a long way from the one who proclaimed in Boston on that now-famous night in 2004 that launched his career, "There's not a black America and white America and Latino America and Asian America; there's the United States of America.... We worship an awesome God in the blue states and we don't like federal agents poking around our libraries in the red states.... We are one people, all of us pledging allegiance to the stars and stripes, all of us defending the United States of America."

The great promise of President Obama was rooted in that 2004 keynote address at the Democratic National Convention. It was shorthand for the outsized expectations that followed him into the White House just four years after delivering it, that he would unite this country again—a country that had been politically divided for nearly twenty straight years.

And now, when he leaves, his legacy will be a generation of political division, not even close to the effect that young, skinny state senator with the funny name wanted to have on the American political landscape.

Of course, history wasn't kind to him. The circumstances into which the Obama presidency was born have meant that for all his efforts, he could not be the president he wanted to be. He has at times hinted at a goal that would, in fact, reposition American politics the way Reagan did. In a commencement address to University of Michigan graduates in 2010, Obama laid out a case for a strong, responsive national government that could help its citizens; perhaps it was a hint at the presidency he wanted to have, not the one that was foisted upon him.

"When America expanded from a few colonies to an entire continent, and we needed a way to reach the Pacific, our government helped build the railroads," he said.

> When we transitioned from an economy based on farms to one based on factories, and workers needed new skills and training, our nation set up a system of public high schools. When the markets crashed during the Depression and people lost their life savings, our government put in place a set of rules and safeguards to make sure that such a crisis never happened

again, and then put a safety net in place to make sure that our elders would never be impoverished the way they had been. When our government is spoken of as some menacing, threatening foreign entity, it ignores the fact that in our democracy, government is us. Government is the police officers who are protecting our communities, and the servicemen and women who are defending us abroad. Government is the roads you drove in on and the speed limits that kept you safe. Government is what ensures that mines adhere to safety standards and that oil spills are cleaned up by the companies that caused them. Government is this extraordinary public university—a place that's doing lifesaving research, and catalyzing economic growth, and graduating students who will change the world around them in ways big and small.

Government shouldn't try to dictate your lives. But it should give you the tools you need to succeed. Government shouldn't try to guarantee results, but it should guarantee a shot at opportunity for every American who's willing to work hard.[1]

That May afternoon in Ann Arbor was a startling defense of government from a politician representing a party that shies away from its reputation as the party of big government. It was also a defense Obama never made again. Perhaps not coincidentally, he gave that speech on one of the slowest news days of the year—a Saturday, and not just any Saturday, but the day Washington turns into wannabe Hollywood, the day of the White House Correspondents' Dinner. That speech got almost *no* media pickup; it never made the evening news beyond the fact that he was in Ann Arbor. Instead, the next day on the Sunday shows, it was Obama's stand-up routine at the dinner that was noted. He says privately he would give the speech again, and make the case for a smarter government of necessity—if his political advisors would let him. But no Democratic consultant would ever advise any president or any major candidate to make the case for government and use it as a centerpiece argument.

Such comments reveal an aspect of Obama that his congressional opponents recognized: no matter his hopes to reform politics, he is deeply political— even if inexpert in politics.

Though his 2008 campaign was based on breaking from the era of George W. Bush, the two men have several traits in common. Both men faced crises early in their first year in office that would come to define them—the September 11 terrorist attacks for Bush, the economic recession for Obama. They both chose to address those crises by tackling something that, though tangentially related, didn't share a direct relationship to the immediate concern: Bush went to war in Iraq as a way to address the global war on terrorism. Obama addressed health care reform, a fundamental element of the economy, in the course of rebuilding from the recession. In explaining their decisions, both made the case that if the challenges they chose to tackle weren't addressed in the short term, they would fester and become long-term threats to the nation. And when their decisions became unpopular and took a political toll on their own parties, both men found they had few allies.

What makes both of their decisions all the more ironic for historians is that neither had run on either issue they took up. Pre-9/11 Bush, campaigning in 2000, talked about a reserved foreign policy, one that did not believe in nation building. Obama stumbled into health care; it was never *the* issue for him, not in the primaries against Clinton and Edwards, both of whom were much more passionate about the topic, nor in the general election. And yet it's now his signature achievement. "Obamacare" is a thing—probably the last issue candidate Obama thought he would be best known for when he was first trudging through the snow in Iowa.

Chief among the political traits Bush and Obama share is the ability to figure out a way to win by any means necessary. At key junctures during Obama's career, he has manipulated the rules in ways that benefit his own ambitions, to the detriment of the higher ideals he espouses. He got a rival for a state senate seat kicked off the ballot. He decided not to take public matching funds for his 2008 campaign, the first post-Watergate candidate to opt out of a system that was supposed to control the amount of money in politics, even after pledging to abide by the rules. He promised to change the tone of politics while running two of the most negative presidential campaigns the nation has ever seen. He strongly opposed Super PACs and outside groups that pledged to spend hundreds of millions of dollars to back their favorite candidates, then tacitly approved of those same groups when it was in his political self-interest to do so.

That doesn't mean Obama has no principles. He feels the need to change Washington at his core. But the paradox that has defined Obama's tenure is that winning office by any means necessary undermined his ability to actually effect that change. During the 2010 health care debate, Obama famously told ABC News, "I'd rather be a really good one-term president than a mediocre two-term president." It's a claim every president makes publicly, but they are just words. Does Obama want to believe that? Of course, but history doesn't look kindly upon any one-term president who fails to win a second term. Still, had Obama been less concerned with winning a second term (which would also have meant being less concerned with his fellow Democrats winning re-election), he would have shown a reformist's courage that, even if it could not possibly have transformed the system, would have served as a beacon for future efforts to do so. And such courage might have resulted in re-election, too; we'll never know, because in politics as in so much in life, there can be no control group. One can't run war-game scenarios when it comes to political what-ifs.

Of course, some things could not have happened without working with Congress and the existing bureaucracy. Whether because of the immediacy of the economic recession, the maneuverings of a clever bureaucracy, or the simple influence of the interest groups that helped him win office, Obama and his team decided to work within the system, rather than blowing it up and starting over from scratch. His legacy in the long run may have bright prospects, but as it stands in the near future he will be a president whose potential wasn't realized. He nudged the political spectrum to the left, without changing it. He began a recovery, without completing it. He passed major legislative initiatives by compromising some of the values he held dear.

Both Clinton, the Democrat who pledged to shrink government, and Bush, the Republican who promised a new era of compassionate conservatism, left office under clouds of partisan division. Obama will almost certainly leave office the same way. And the divide between whites and blacks is as stark as ever, as Democrats rely on growing numbers of minority voters while Republicans become an ever more homogeneous party.

So Obama will never be known as a president who managed Congress effectively. Indeed, some of his legislative successes resulted simply because Republicans on Capitol Hill took their visceral hatred of the president too far. His great victories in Congress — health care reform, financial regulatory reform, the economic stimulus plan — came solely in his first two years in office, when his party controlled the entire apparatus.

Obama himself shoulders some of the blame. He takes personally the criticism that he doesn't play the Washington game, and he knows it's true. The late Meg Greenfield of the *Washington Post* famously compared Washington's political ecosystem to high school, which meant, among other things, that the town is small and suffused with insecurities. That's why things that seem trivial — and did seem trivial to Obama — are actually crucial. Obama did reach out to a small number of Republicans, like Olympia Snowe and, once the GOP won a majority, John Boehner, and he held dinners with small groups of Republican and Democratic senators alike in the first year of his second term. But after the series of cocktail parties held for members of Congress early in his first year in office, and the occasional football game, the White House stopped sending out invitations.

There was never a full-court press, nor the constant flattering of attention or base-touching that has marked legislative relationships between other presidents—and by now it is clear that there will not be. Obama has put in just enough effort to assuage the allies pushing him to do more, but no one would accuse him of being relentless. There's another saying in Washington when things are tough with the other party: you always want to be the one who gets caught trying. The public will reward you for it. But there did come a point when many around the president as well as Obama himself believed they were wasting their time. It really is one of the great differences between Bill Clinton and Obama. Both faced recalcitrant Republicans; Clinton even saw his enemies impeach him. But Clinton was obsessed with winning these Republicans over again, with finding any legislation to pass with them. He just never stopped. Obama's wired differently; he believes the rational should overcome the superficial.

A part of the reason is that Obama doesn't care terribly much if his rivals don't like him. The same insecurities that make most of official Washington need and pine for presidential attention are not in Obama's DNA. While Clinton craved adoration or respect, Obama doesn't share that yearning. Even

Bush, while being wired more like Obama than Clinton, understood the backslapping part of the game; then again, Bush had been a governor who'd had to deal with lots of little state legislator egos. Bush did enjoy the banter, the small parts of the Washington game that, even if he didn't crave them like Clinton, he understood—perhaps because his dad, "Bush 41," actually did have that trait. Certainly those down the way on Capitol Hill, and nearly all of Washington, find it mind-boggling that Obama doesn't get this. More than a few of his advisors, even those closest to him, have wondered how someone who disdains retail politics could have risen so high up in the ranks. "It's like Bill Gates," said one former aide, "not liking computers."

But there's a big difference, of course, and it speaks to an impossible dilemma: Americans believe politics is corrupt, that politicians care about almost nothing beyond their own power, getting rich off the perks of office, and fighting with those who don't agree with them, to the negligence of the country. So, to a great extent, does Barack Obama. But there is no other sandbox to play in, and because he played the political game early, the public began to view him as just another politician.

Obama's big promise on the world stage was to improve America's image around the world, to essentially repent for the sins of the war in Iraq. Certainly the world believed he would do all that and more; why else did the Nobel Committee award him the Peace Prize for feats he had not yet accomplished? The blame does rest on him — that is, if you blame him for raising expectations. For example, his promise to shutter the Guantánamo detention center was abandoned, a hypocrisy that undercut his claims that his would be a more moral and just foreign policy. He wanted to be the president who focused on Middle East peace at the start of his term, not the end. But that didn't work out. He wanted a reset with a former Cold War rival, Russia, but Putin's return to power ended any hopes of doing that. If anything, tensions with Russia are coming to define just about every foreign policy rabbit hole the president finds himself in during his second term.

In a world without twin superpowers, spurred by social media uprisings and growing threats to American dominance in Asia and Europe, America's place is as uncertain as it was before World War II. Of course, no president can handle all conflagrations; there will always be corners of the globe marked by horror and bloodshed and an absence of freedom. And there *were* numerous successes: the most important to the American public, getting out of Iraq and Afghanistan. But even those voter-demanded successes appear questionable. Is it Obama's fault that neither Iraq nor Afghanistan appears ready to stand on its own without U.S. help? Some Republicans want to blame him, but no one can discount the mismanagement of both wars that took place before he took office. To an extent nearly unimaginable only a few years earlier, the United States has engaged Iran. Diplomacy might fail, but it's the first option again. There was progress on arms control, one of those issues that the American public hardly notices but has significant global ramifications. But these successes on the international front also served to reinforce Obama's sense that Congress was hardly worth engaging; he got stuff done when they had little say, and got almost nothing done when they did (internationally, Syria being an example of the latter). And the Middle East is so on fire that it's very likely that the region will actually be more unstable when Obama leaves office than when he took it. Is this Obama's fault or simply historical bad luck? Only time will tell. The second-guessing of his Arab Spring decisions could easily become a big part of the foreign policy debate that will take place in 2016.

So what will the Obama legacy be? Is he simply a minor hiatus in the decades-long feud between the Bush family and the Clinton family that has devolved into the partisan warfare that defines us as a nation, with Jeb Bush and Hillary Clinton simply waiting in the wings to fight the next battle? Or is he something more, an innovator who really has pushed American politics left of center and hastened the evolution—or perhaps even the destruction—of his opponents across the aisle?

The deepest depths of a recession he didn't cause came just a few months into his term, at a time when the government was pumping massive amounts of money into a system in desperate need of the influx. Preventing a depression, in favor of a terrible recession, is the sort of success that is only evident to a select few, often with PhD's, and usually not fully recognized for decades. But it can be a crowning legacy. In the near term, the focus that work required certainly handicapped countless Obama initiatives, as did the tremendous costs of the wars in Afghanistan and in Iraq. It is hard not to wonder about the world Barack Obama might have helped make had he not been tied down by the world he inherited from George W. Bush. This is certainly something that creeps into the president's mind every so often. Then again, would Obama have gotten traction without a public so fed up with traditional politicos like Bush and Clinton?

One thing that seems certain is that Obama has changed the way campaigns are run and elections are won. Obama's team, driven by groundbreaking consumer research and voter targeting based on a nationwide network of volunteers, used the newest technologies to capture and turn out every possible friendly voter they could find. And they adapted to the rapidly changing technologies of the moment:

In 2008, the campaign collected cell phone numbers of volunteers and supporters; by 2012, the techno-wizards were asking those supporters to allow them direct access to their Facebook pages in order to push messages to individual friends, a sort of hub-and-spoke system for the digital age. No presidential campaign will ever again be based on antiquated voter files and paper records. The divides between digital teams, field teams, fund-raising teams, and direct-mail strategists will come down, as they did in the Obama campaigns. Such integration is now the only way to run a national campaign. And Obama's incredible ability to raise money has turned political campaigns into a multibillion-dollar industry as Republicans are now doing whatever it takes to catch up. To think that in 2000, Bush and Gore *together* spent just over $125 million. In 2012, Obama and Romney *together* spent over $2 billion. That's some rate of inflation.

In two ways, the Obama presidency has changed the Democratic coalition. While Jimmy Carter and Bill Clinton relied on a large number of white voters to win the presidency, Obama's focus on lower-intensity voters in traditionally underperforming minority blocs has given Democrats a new advantage in national and statewide elections. The Democratic coalition is increasingly reliant on minority voting groups that are growing rapidly. White voters have declined as a share of the electorate in every election since exit polls began measuring it; Obama's focus on underrepresented minority groups likely sped that decline. Now that less than three-quarters of the electorate is made up of white voters, and given that an increasing share of minorities are voting for Democrats, the coalition Obama has established appears unassailable. Democrats are drawing more and more from a growing pool of voters, leaving Republicans to scramble for a larger share of a shrinking pool. What would have been an inevitable shift toward the Democrats over a period of decades was accelerated by Obama.

Obama will also leave a more homogeneous Democratic Party, ideologically. Once riven by disagreements between liberals and conservative Blue Dogs, the party is now remarkably monolithic in terms of its beliefs. Candidates who just a few years ago were nervous about speaking out for gay rights now openly embrace same-sex marriage. For gay Americans, Obama's administration will go down as being as important as LBJ's was for blacks. Democrats are almost unanimously pro-choice, almost entirely in favor of Obama's health care reform, and almost entirely united on the role of government and the amount it spends.

The ideological divisions that used to exist within the Democratic Party have been driven out, at least in part, by Republicans. The election of

2010, in which voters so handily punished supporters of President Obama's health care overhaul (and
even Democrats who didn't support it), took its
deepest toll among Democrats in marginal seats—
the very members who tended to be the most conservative representatives of the party's House caucus.
Today, there are only a small handful of white Democrats who represent southern House districts; the
vast majority of Southern Democrats hold seats
where minority voters make up a majority of the
voters. Obama has helped unify the Democratic
Party ideologically, ironically, by shrinking the variety of its membership.

Perhaps the only major disagreement that remains
between the Democratic elites is over entitlement
reform. And, in another moment of irony, this time
it's Obama who finds himself out of step with the rest
of his party. Though Obama has long said he would
like to revise the social safety net programs that suck
up so much of the federal government's money (an
issue on which he could find common ground with
Republicans), many Democrats, particularly the ones
in leadership, have made it clear they have no intention of allowing benefit cuts. They have made it clear
that, in that particular case, Obama is the one taking
the more conservative stand. At some point, Republicans are going to rue the day they didn't work with
Obama on Social Security. He was their "Nixon goes
to China" Democratic president.

In the eyes of historians, any president's legacy can be ratified by voters who elect his successor. Since the Civil War, only two presidents, Ulysses S. Grant and Ronald Reagan, have served two full terms then given way to another member of their own party, winning a veritable third term. (Franklin Roosevelt, of course, won four terms on his own and saw Truman, arguably, win a fifth term for him.) And while most presidents have one obvious successor — usually the vice president — Obama has two: his vice president and the woman who almost beat him lo those many years ago.

When Joe Biden was elected to the Senate for the first time, in 1972, Obama was just eleven years old. But Biden and Obama enjoy an unusually warm relationship, and the president likes offering his vice president the occasional advice about how to run in the future. While some vice presidents, like Al Gore, have distanced themselves from their bosses in preparation for their own runs, Biden is much more likely to attach himself to Obama's legacy: Biden's innate loyalty almost requires that he not jump ship, and his political instincts tell him his best chance (scratch that: his *only* chance) to win comes from inheriting the Obama coalition, both in the Democratic primary and in the general election.

The only thing standing in the way of Biden's third run for the White House is Hillary Clinton. Clinton fought the Obama team to a near draw, a bitter contest that, despite outward appearances, continues to fuel grudges within the Democratic Party. Already, the old Obama 2008 team has not been shy about criticizing Hillary's early 2016 moves, warning her that she's making the same mistakes she made in 2006 and 2007, which led to the vacuum that was filled by Obama. But while those differences are there on the staff level, the two principals have patched things up, by necessity: Obama needed Clinton to make sure the Democratic Party wasn't divided as he began governing; and he needed someone of her stature to manage foreign affairs while he handled the economic recovery. (Obama also needed Clinton to be on his team, rather than a constant source of criticism from her powerful perch on Capitol Hill.) Clinton needed Obama, too, to bolster her own legacy, and to leave open the option of running for president once again. Projecting a chummy relationship between the president and his former secretary of state is mutually beneficial, both in the short term and in the future. Interestingly, though, the two have forged a real bond; whether it's a true friendship, only the two of them know for sure. But there is mutual respect. Hillary and Obama are more alike, something the two figured out after spending time together. Realize that all the same criticisms many make of Obama when comparing his political style to Bill Clinton's can easily be made of Hillary. At their core, neither Hillary nor Obama enjoys the game. Hillary, though, came to appreciate the game while watching her husband. Obama, too, has grown to appreciate Bill Clinton's political gifts, but only later in his presidency, perhaps too late to make a big difference in terms of managing Washington.

While Obama may never admit whom he wants as his heir, Hillary or Biden, he did give a hint when at the end of her tenure as secretary of state, he suggested the two sit down for a joint farewell interview with *60 Minutes*. No other cabinet secretary of the modern era was given that kind of presidential treatment before; it's usually reserved for spouses, vice presidents, or ex-presidents. It was Obama's idea, not Hillary's or any staffer's, a gesture that Obama believed Hillary was owed for being a team player.

Their relationship will also be defined by actual accomplishments. The major, lasting impact of the Obama-Clinton partnership on foreign policy will be the redirection of American focus from the Atlantic to the Pacific, a "pivot," in the White House's words, toward the growing markets and militaries in Asia and away from the shrinking European Union. The initiative has focused on engaging China, opening the once-hermit kingdom of Burma to the world, and opening a new military base in northern Australia. Obama may have paid more attention to China than any of his predecessors; his decision to send three high-profile politicians—Jon Huntsman,

Gary Locke, and Max Baucus—to serve as ambassador to Beijing put China on a diplomatic par with Japan, which has historically received prominent American envoys (currently, Caroline Kennedy).

Just as Bush's legacy was shaped by the wars that began under his administration, Obama's international legacy will be shaped in large part by how he shepherded the wars he ended, and by the night in May 2011 when a team of Navy SEALs snuck into Abbottabad, Pakistan, to end the life of the most wanted man in the world, while Obama and his war cabinet watched in the Situation Room.

Since December 7, 1941, when Japanese warplanes attacked Pearl Harbor, the United States has been almost constantly engaged in military operations of one form or another—World War II, the Korean War, the Vietnam War, both Gulf Wars, the war in Afghanistan, countless smaller conflicts everywhere from Grenada to the jungles of Latin America and the mountains of Yugoslavia. The wars in Iraq and Afghanistan of the last decade have especially sapped Americans' interest in spending the money or risking the lives it takes to be the world's police officer. There is an increasing isolationist streak in both political parties, represented by anti-war Democrats and Republican libertarians like Senator Rand Paul, that simply wants the nation out of foreign conflicts.

Obama's failure to intervene in Syria is Example A of the ancillary fallout from America's bloody interventions in Iraq and Afghanistan. The increasing use of drones to kill terrorists and militants in Yemen, Afghanistan, and the tribal regions of Pakistan, rather than using special operations forces, is another extension of war without overt risk to American lives. Yet nobody in the military would say that drones are sufficient to win a war.

Under Obama's watch little has changed in Latin America, save a trade pact with Colombia. There has been little effort to engage or open Cuba, even as the end of the Castro brothers' regime approaches. In fact, Cuba's a great example of Obama's famous caution. While he has been unusually critical of American policy toward Cuba, he won't use his executive power to make a change. Perhaps Florida's 29 electoral votes are more meaningful: is this a case of politics getting in the way of Obama's principles? And while China pours money into new investments in resource-rich Africa, Obama's legacy of engagement there hasn't been nearly as influential as Bush's investments in preventing and combating the AIDS epidemic. Obama's sensitivities regarding an African legacy were on full display in the summer of 2013 when he traveled to the continent as president. Everywhere he turned, folks brought up Bush's AIDS initiative in a positive light; many leaders yearned for something as big and bold as that, if not bigger and bolder. History will decide whether Obama's push to electrify rural Africa is on the level of Bush and AIDS. Right now, it is not seen as that, but in a few decades if the continent's lights are all on, then there's a chance. Of course, Obama's track record in Africa is, happily, nowhere as tragic as Clinton's decision to stay out of the genocide in Rwanda. But it seems highly questionable whether he would get support for intervention in similar circumstances.

Obama, too, has been frustrated by the world leaders with whom he serves, few of whom will go down in history as world-changing visionaries. He gets along well with British prime minister David Cameron, through a mutual understanding that their relationship must work, given the special bond between the United Kingdom and the United States. He thought former French president Nicolas Sarkozy was fun to watch, and Obama and German chancellor Angela Merkel still deeply respect each other, though the NSA disclosures have really frayed their relationship. Obama developed decent ties with Russian president Dmitry Medvedev, a relationship that did not carry over when Medvedev's patron, Vladimir Putin, returned to the presidency.

But Japan, long a close ally of the United States, has gone through five prime ministers since Obama was inaugurated. The structure of the Chinese government and society, and the decennial leadership transition that took place in early 2013, has prevented Obama from forming close personal ties to any particular official. Obama admires Indian prime minister Manmohan Singh, though India has not taken its place on the world stage. "We have not been blessed with the best crop of world leaders," said one top foreign policy aide, offering one specific example: "When Yitzak Rabin is prime minister of Israel, you can accomplish great things." Certainly Obama's relationship with Israeli prime minister Benjamin Netanyahu, who all but openly rooted for Mitt Romney during the 2012 campaign, is strained by a lack of personal chemistry.

At home, Obama's legacy will be defined by the recovery he has built. Obama, Ben Bernanke, and Timothy Geithner were at the wheel of a messy, uneven, and unequal recovery: the unemployment rate lags among minorities even while overall employment is back to pre-Obama levels and the stock market booms; and Congress debates cuts to food stamp programs while increased tax revenues mean the deficit is falling. Income inequality is worse than ever; perhaps Obama's only chance to create change is to highlight the issue and begin a conversation that leads, years if not decades down the road, to real action. Raising the federal minimum wage was a step in that direction, and the Democrats are still seen by most voters as more likely to search for a solution — to an extent. And the problem is massive: During Obama's presidency, the Great Recession fundamentally reshaped the relationship between Middle America and the major cities on both coasts. Many big towns and small cities with populations from 25,000 to 500,000 residents have seen the manufacturing-heavy industries they've relied upon for a century wither and die. As their economic centers collapse, increasing numbers of Americans slip into poverty, with the gap between rich and poor widening. It was only a few years ago that the phrase "the 1%" would have meant nothing to nearly all Americans; now it is recognizable shorthand for a manifestly unjust arrangement.

The transition from manufacturing-based economies to service- and government-based economies, which began decades ago with the dawn of the Information Age, is completing itself under Obama's watch. It's an evolution that is inevitable and, in many places, excruciating. The success/failure divides are stark. Silicon Valley thrives, while nearby Oakland suffers terrifying child poverty rates. Obama speaks at the University of Michigan in flush Ann Arbor, while, not many miles away, Detroit, once one of the largest cities in America, corrodes and reverts to grasslands. Middle America is suffering, angrily so in some places, while the two coasts thrive economically. There are truly two Americas — and it is divided by the 5s, as one Republican consultant likes to say. Between I-5 out west and I-95 back east there is an America that is waiting for the recession to end. West of I-5 and east of I-95 there is an America that is taking off. If the coasts (and some of the thriving *big* cities in between) can't bring the rest of America along, the country's politics is in for a rocky ride for some time.

A full recovery is years, if not decades, away, and there's not much the White House can do about it. One irony of an administration blasted by its Republican critics for growing the size of government in an effort to speed the recovery is that the sheer size of the government workforce when Obama leaves office is likely to be smaller than when he started. But such is the nature of today's Republican opposition: perception trumps reality when espousing a good talking point.

The battle to reform health care didn't end when Obama signed the legislation. As the measure is implemented over the coming years, its success or failure will weigh heavily on the president's legacy. It may be a decade or two before the law's full impact—how much it actually bent the cost curve, how many uninsured Americans were able to get coverage, how many lives were saved in the process—is really measurable. The botched launch of Obama's prime initiative was ample evidence of his management weakness, and implementing the law is going to be made all the more difficult by continued Republican efforts to block the bill. But there is no doubt that a corner has been forever turned, and that in some form national health care will now be part of American life. That the break-through will be known as "Obamacare" may indeed be the president's most lasting legacy, a branding that ultimately obscures so many of the administra-tion's other frustrations and failures. The irony is there: the greatest first aid provided by Obamacare will be to those it helped—and one of those mil-lions may actually be a reputation, that of Barack Obama.

The scandals that marked earlier administrations have been largely absent from the Obama White House. While Obama is clearly ambitious, perhaps even overly so in the way every man who seeks to become the most powerful single person in the world must be, there are no skeletons in his personal closet, and his administration has been careful—some would argue overly so—to avoid the sorts of misuse of power that would get anyone thrown in jail. Obama will go down in history as one of the more decent people to serve in the Oval Office. The scandals that have infected the White House have had their origins far away from 1600 Pennsylvania Avenue. Covering up the roles of CIA operatives in and around Benghazi, Libya, for example, was more a function of the agency trying to maintain the worst-kept secret in foreign policy—that diplomatic facilities are often fronts that spies and operatives can use to hide their true objectives. The close scrutiny the Internal Revenue Service gave to conservative and Tea Party groups over tax-exempt status happened in an agency that has been independent of the White House since Richard Nixon used his IRS to investigate political enemies. And while conservatives railed at the IRS, little attention was given to the many groups that were essentially trying to take advantage of a bad loophole that allowed political groups to get tax-exempt status. The constant investigations led by the zealous Darrell Issa, the California Republican who has used his perch atop the House Oversight and Government Reform Committee to issue hundreds of subpoenas, haven't cost a single political appointee in the administration his or her job. They have only served to undermine one of the more important committees in Congress, which is why Republican leaders have been eager to take the gavel away from him.

Some blame for Obama's challenges has to be apportioned to the proliferation of hyperpartisan cable news channels or political blogs: blame Republicans, blame Democrats, blame anyone and everyone—as long as neither party has an incentive to give in, there's no reason to believe that anyone will be able to break the fever.

And the cynical truth is that the gridlock is in the best interests of many, if not the American people. Candidates, PACs, and lobbying groups financially thrive on discontent. To a great extent, American politics is now defined by declarations of opposition instead of a search for common ground. You run against.

Here, too, Obama's arrogance got the better of him. And at the end of the day, arrogance may be a better description than naïveté. After all, while the presidency was a giant leap for him, he was not entirely a stranger to Washington. He had, albeit briefly, been a senator, and had seen from the inside how things work. He had heard all of his colleagues voice the same platitudes about the process being broken, and seen that none of them had been able to change that. But he would, he just knew it. This was the "hope" he'd spoken about.

Despite it all, Barack Obama believes he has left the country in a position to become a better place, should his vision work. And framed that way, the future is brighter for Obama's place in the history books. Whether it's the energy advancements the stimulus bill funded (simply the aggressive fuel mileage standards might do the trick), the health care benefits that, no matter their birthing pains, will be available to future generations, or the engagement with an emerging China, the administration has put in place building blocks that can become a lasting legacy.

But the grand change Obama promised has not come to pass. The cesspool of Washington stinks more than ever, partisan relations are at a nadir, and more money than ever before is flowing into politics, and we know less about where it comes from. The institutions that existed long before Obama arrived in Washington are stronger than ever, and they will be once he leaves office, too.

When Obama leaves office, it'll be twenty-four straight years of polarizing presidents, all three of whom were elected, in part, to help end some of the acrimony. It is standard for historians to point out that a president could have done more, and surely this will be said about Obama. Presidents ask the same question about themselves.

Because some of the grandest goals candidate Obama had for his presidency, most notably changing Washington and bridging the political divide, will not be fulfilled by him, he can only hope that someday he'll be credited with being the architect of the change he promised. Years from now, it is likely that the two terms of Barack Obama will be seen in a more glowing light than they are now, and if so, that light will put into shadow some of the dysfunction he had to deal with.

Some of that dysfunction was forced upon him,

some of it came from him. If a huge reason for the failure of Washington to get anything done is a focus on means instead of productive ends, Obama's struggles came from his focus on ends to the exclusion of productive means. In that way he was indeed a stranger. In his State of the Union speech in January 2014, he told Congress that he was "eager to work with all of you. But America does not stand still—and neither will I. So wherever and whenever I can take steps without legislation to expand opportunity for more American families, that's what I'm going to do."

The way to get something done, Obama was saying, was to go it alone—just as, to some extent, he always had.

ACKNOWLEDGMENTS

When book agent Matthew Carnicelli cold-called me one day in 2006 (before NBC News was even an idea in my head), little did I know it would lead to me attempting to write a book about one of the more consequential presidencies in a generation. It's been quite a wild ride since my initial coffee with Matthew at a downtown D.C. Starbucks way back when my employer was still *National Journal*. So, first and foremost, I have to thank Matthew for pushing me to do this. I had plenty of book ideas in my head when we met, but I needed someone to focus me, and Matthew did just that.

Of course, figuring out the right book idea and actually completing the book are two different things. And this book would still be in a state of disrepair without my writing, reporting, and research partner, Reid Wilson. I've known Reid since he first came from the *other* Washington to the one we both now call home. His eagerness is contagious. When I'd hit a wall or start losing motivation, it was Reid who provided a shot of enthusiasm that suddenly jumped me out of a writer's block. Of course, Reid did a lot more than play Mr. Motivator. His research and reporting and own set of sources were an integral part of my completing this manuscript. It's fair to say, without Reid, this book would not have been possible. I simply hope that in a few years he'll agree to hire me as *his* research partner when he's churning out a lot more books than I could ever dream of.

And what good is a reported book unless the author has sources? So many folks gave me countless hours of their time (sometimes they knew it, sometimes they didn't!). But without them, this book wouldn't be what it turned out to be. There are some tremendous people who help run our country, be it from a perch on Capitol Hill or at 1600 Pennsylvania Avenue. All of them, I've discovered, truly value the fact that they are witnesses to history in real time. We should all be grateful that they love history enough, love the country enough, to share their observations and experiences to authors and reporters. This country can only get better if we learn from history, and every source who gave me their time had a wonderful "pay it forward" attitude. On behalf of all authors and reporters, thank you.

One of the main challenges of writing this book was trying to do it while I had a day job at NBC News. On one hand, my daily reporting fit hand in glove with my goal of trying to chronicle and understand the historic presidency of Barack Obama. But while editorially the job was a help, my responsibilities consumed a lot of my day-to-day physical and brain power. Trying to juggle reporting for *Nightly News* or the *Today* show and planning *The Daily Rundown* on MSNBC while also conducting two-hour interviews with key administration figures wasn't easy, but NBC and MSNBC were incredibly accommodating and supportive. There are plenty of people who deserve thanks for their patience during the various book black holes that I fell into. But let's start with Albert Oetgen at NBC News and Brooke Brower at *The Daily Rundown,* the two people who probably felt the brunt of this book "distraction" (as they might call it in their not-so-happy moments). Of course, simply giving me the space to do this book is not something that a news organization agrees to lightly, so thank you to my NBC bosses, including executives Pat Fili-Kushel, Deborah Turness, Phil Griffin, and Alex Wallace in New York; Ken Strickland and Meaghan Rady in Washington; and former executives Jeff Zucker and Steve Capus, who initially approved of my attempting this dual assignment.

And then there's Natalie Cucchiara, who, like Reid, deserves an extra place of honor among those folks who got this book into print. As my friends at Little, Brown are well aware, without Natalie, they'd still be waiting for me to actually send in a first draft

of the manuscript, let alone photos, captions, edits—
you name it. Of course, Natalie is much more than
someone who simply helped keep me organized on
the book front. She somehow both kept me employed
at NBC (i.e., making sure I didn't miss new assignments or news) and made sure Little, Brown didn't
totally give up on me. Natalie's a true friend and
confidante and easily one of the most talented and
dedicated colleagues I've ever worked with. Not a
day goes by that I don't wonder how I'd manage
without Natalie.

One of the best decisions Matthew made was
introducing me to the folks at Little, Brown. He
said there was no better place for a first-time author
to go. And boy was he right. I was lucky enough to
work with two editors in particular, Geoff Shandler
and John Parsley. Geoff was a great inspiration
through much of this process, reassuring me that
what I was writing and reporting was new and was
adding to the public discourse. His guidance was
instrumental in getting the book I wanted into print.
John had the unenviable task of coming in toward
the end of this process but was no less helpful. His
fresh eyes helped turn some of my rather dry drafts
into something more readable without losing the level
of detail that I kept insisting on.

The entire Little, Brown team is quite impressive, led by publisher Reagan Arthur. I'd like to single out my chief copy editor, Peggy Freudenthal,

assistant editor Allie Sommer, and audio editor Cheryl Smith, all three of whom are dedicated to churning out the best product they could drag out of me, whether in print or on tape.

There are three other people who sacrificed more than they realized when I committed to writing this book, and that's my immediate family. There are my two kids, Margaret and Harrison; plenty of weekend games and evening practices were missed by their father while I was finishing up an interview or writing a chapter. I hope when they are older and read this, they'll at least have an understanding of what I was up to during some of those days when they would ask their mother, "Is Daddy coming home before bedtime tonight?"

And finally, last but certainly *never* least is my partner, best friend, and wife, Kristian, who was and is my rock. She was my most important writing confidante, honest with me when she thought something didn't make sense, and my greatest cheerleader. Unconditional support is something we can sometimes take for granted; perhaps by admitting that on paper now, I won't do that the next time. In short, thank you, Kristian, for being my biggest champion and my biggest fan.

Notes

1. A Not-So-Fresh Start

1. "As the Ground Shifts, Biden Plays a Bigger Role," Helene Cooper, *New York Times,* December 11, 2010.
2. Jeffrey Toobin, *The Oath* (Doubleday, 2012), p.12.
3. "Biden Urges Passage of Stimulus Despite Voter Backlash," Susan Davis, *Wall Street Journal,* February 6, 2009.
4. Presidential press conference, February 9, 2009.
5. "From the Campaign to the Battlefront," Monica Langley, *Wall Street Journal,* September 22, 2007.
6. "The Choice," George Packer, *The New Yorker,* January 28, 2008.
7. "A Cast of 300 Advises Obama on Foreign Policy," Elisabeth Bumiller, *New York Times,* July 18, 2008.
8. "Man in the Mirror," Michael Crowley, *New Republic,* December 31, 2008.
9. Bob Woodward, *Obama's Wars* (Simon & Schuster, 2010), p. 36.
10. "Toxic Memo," *Harvard Magazine,* May–June 2001.

2. Getting Rolled Early

1. Noam Scheiber, *The Escape Artists* (Simon & Schuster, 2012), p.61; "Inside the Crisis," Ryan Lizza, *The New Yorker,* October 12, 2009.
2. EdSource, U.S. Department of Education.
3. Robert Draper, *Do Not Ask What Good We Do* (Free Press, 2012).
4. Interview sources.
5. U.S. Senate roll call vote 31, 111th Congress, 1st session.
6. U.S. Senate roll call vote 61, 111th Congress, 1st session.
7. U.S. Senate roll call vote 64, 111th Congress, 1st session.

8. Address to a joint session of Congress, February 24, 2009.
9. "Omnibus Spending Bill: Huge Spending and 9,000 Earmarks Represent Business as Usual," Brian Riedl, Heritage Foundation, March 2, 2009.

3. Unplanned Legacy
1. "The time has come for universal health care," Sen. Barack Obama's address to the Families USA Conference, January 25, 2007.
2. "Mandates and Mudslinging," Paul Krugman, *New York Times,* November 30, 2007.
3. "Obama, McCain Tussle on Health Care," *Boston Globe,* October 6, 2008.
4. "Obama, McCain Forged Fleeting Alliance," Paul Kane, *Washington Post,* March 31, 2008.
5. "Remember Obama v. McCain," Chris Donovan, NBC News, January 8, 2008.
6. Press release, Office of Sen. John McCain, February 7, 2006.
7. "McCain, Obama Bury the Hatchet," Jeff Zeleny, *Chicago Tribune,* February 8, 2006.
8. "Obama, McCain Forged Fleeting Alliance
9. "Obama Made a Strong First Impression at Harvard," Ari Shapiro, NPR, May 22, 2012.
10. "Coburn, Obama: Latest Odd Couple," Emily Pierce, *Roll Call,* September 29, 2005.
11. "Health Care Reform from Conception to Final Passage," U.S. Senate Finance Committee.
12. "Grassley: Government Shouldn't 'Decide When to Pull the Plug on Grandma,'" *Iowa Independent,* August 12, 2009.
13. MSNBC, August 17, 2009.
14. "The Origin of Obama's Pastor Problem," James Carney and Amy Sullivan, *Time,* March 20, 2008; "That *Rolling Stone* Article..." Stephen Spruiell, NationalReview.com, April 16, 2008.
15. John Heilemann and Mark Halperin, *Game Change* (Harper, 2010), p. 235.
16. "Spotlight on Alumni: EWC Alumna Ann Dunham—Mother to President Obama and Champion of Women's Rights and Economic Justice," East-West Center, December 9, 2008.

17. "Opponents Paint Obama as an Elitist," Perry Bacon and Shailagh Murray, *Washington Post*, April 12, 2008.

18. Ibid.

19. "Jackson apologizes for 'crude' Obama remarks," CNN, July 9, 2008.

20. Real Clear Politics.

21. Heilemann and Halperin, *Game Change*, pp. 236–37.

22. "Mr. Obama's Profile in Courage," *New York Times* editorial, March 19, 2008.

23. "How Obama Snared the Lion of the Senate," Dan Balz and Haynes Johnson, *Washington Post*, August 3, 2009.

24. "Finance Committee Approves Baucus' America's Healthy Future Act," Senate Finance Committee release, October 13, 2009.

25. "Friends of the Earmark Make Themselves Heard," Jeffrey Birnbaum, *Washington Post*, April 29, 2008.

4. Triage

1. Interview with Robert Gibbs.

2. Interview sources.

3. NBC/*Wall Street Journal* poll, January 23–25, 2010.

4. "Health Vote Caps a Journey Back from the Brink," Sheryl Gay Stolberg, Jeff Zeleny, and Carl Hulse, *New York Times*, March 20, 2010.

5. "Nancy Pelosi Steeled White House for Health Push," Carrie Budoff Brown and Glenn Thrush, *Politico*, March 20, 2010.

6. "Health Care Clincher: The Importance of Being Stupak," Jay Newton-Small, *Time*, March 21, 2010.

7. Interview with Ron Klain.

5. Reluctant Warrior

1. U.S. Senate roll call vote 237, 107th Congress, 2nd session.

2. Speech given by state senator Barack Obama in Chicago, October 2, 2002.

3. Fitzgerald announced he would not seek a second term seven months later, on April 16, 2003. "Illinois Senator Announces He Won't Seek Re-election," Jodi Wilgoren, *New York Times*, April 16, 2003.

4. Obama delivered his speech on Iraq and Afghanistan on July 15, 2008.

5. Bob Woodward, *Obama's Wars* (Simon & Schuster, 2010), p. 33.

6. United Nations Country Profile, Afghanistan.

7. "U.S. Identifies Vast Mineral Riches in Afghanistan," James Risen, *New York Times,* June 13, 2010.

8. MSNBC's *Daily Rundown,* April 6, 2010.

9. Woodward, *Obama's Wars,* pp. 40, 77.

10. "Obama team works on overhaul of Afghanistan, Pakistan policy," Julian Barnes, *Los Angeles Times,* February 11, 2009; Woodward, *Obama's Wars,* p. 88.

11. "Remarks by the President on a new strategy for Afghanistan and Pakistan," The White House, March 27, 2009.

12. "U.S. Fires Afghan War Chief," Yochi Dreazen and Peter Spiegel, *Wall Street Journal,* May 12, 2009; "Gen. David McKiernan Ousted as Top U.S. Commander in Afghanistan," Ann Scott Tyson, *Washington Post,* May 12, 2009.

13. "General Calls for More U.S. Troops to Avoid Afghan Failure," Eric Schmitt and Thom Shanker, *New York Times,* September 20, 2009.

14. "How Obama Came to Plan for 'Surge' in Afghanistan," Peter Baker, *New York Times,* December 5, 2009.

15. "Mullen Calls for More Troops in Afghanistan," Mary Louise Kelly, NPR, September 15, 2009; "Mullen Says More Forces 'Probably' Needed in Afghanistan," Wendell Goler, Fox News, September 15, 2009.

16. "McChrystal: More Forces or 'Mission Failure,'" Bob Woodward, *Washington Post,* September 21, 2009.

17. Memo from Gen. Stanley McChrystal to Secretary Robert Gates, August 30, 2009. First reported by *Washington Post,* September 21, 2009.

18. "How Obama Came to Plan for 'Surge'..."

19. "Obama Considers Strategy Shift in Afghan War," Peter Baker and Elisabeth Bumiller, *New York Times,* September 22, 2009.

20. "McChrystal Rejects Scaling Down Afghan Military Aims," John Burns, *New York Times,* October 1, 2009.

21. Secretary Robert Gates address to the Association of the United States Army, Washington, D.C., October 5, 2009.

22. President Obama's address to the nation on the way forward in Afghanistan and Pakistan, December 1, 2009.

6. THE RE-ELECTION BEGINS...SORT OF

1. William C. Velasquez Institute, Latino Voter Statistics.
2. "Romanoff Confirms White House Job Discussions," Michael Booth, *Denver Post,* June 3, 2010; "White House Defends Using Job Prospect to Sway Romanoff to Quit Colorado Senate Race," Michael Riley, *Denver Post,* June 4, 2010.
3. List posted on BarackObama.com.
4. Interview with Carol Browner.
5. *Meet the Press,* July 11, 2010; "Republicans Could Gain Control of the House in November, Gibbs Says," Associated Press, July 11, 2010.
6. "*The Obamas:* Book Reveals Friction Between Rahm Emanuel, Michelle Obama," Sam Stein and Marcus Baram, *Huffington Post,* January 6, 2012.
7. "Pelosi Vents about Gibbs," Jonathan Allen and John Bresnahan, *Politico,* July 13, 2010.
8. "Obama Rallies for Perriello at the Pavilion," Brian McNeill, *Charlottesville Daily Progress,* September 5, 2010.
9. *The Hotline,* November 3, 2010.

7. THE WINTER THAW

1. "Dean Says Faith Led to Civil Union View," Jim VandeHei, *Washington Post,* January 8, 2004.
2. Illinois Senate debate, C-SPAN 2, 2004.
3. U.S. House of Representatives recorded vote 316, 104th Congress, July 12, 1996.
4. U.S. Senate roll call vote 280, 104th Congress, September 10, 1996.
5. 2008 Democratic Party Platform as adopted, August 25, 2008.
6. "Jim Messina, Obama's Enforcer," Ari Berman, *The Nation,* April 18, 2011.
7. "Top Defense Officials Seek to End 'Don't Ask, Don't Tell,'" Elisabeth Bumiller, *New York Times,* February 2, 2010.
8. "'Don't Ask' Opponents Get a Boost," Ed O'Keefe and Craig Whitlock, *Washington Post,* December 1, 2010.
9. "Senate halts 'don't ask, don't tell' repeal," Dana Bash, CNN, September 22, 2010.

10. "Gay Protesters Interrupt Obama at California Fundraiser for Barbara Boxer," Andrew Malcolm, *Los Angeles Times,* April 19, 2010.

11. "Obama Is Heckled by AIDS Protesters," Sheryl Gay Stolberg, *New York Times,* October 30, 2010.

12. "Gay rights protesters demand Obama end 'don't ask, don't tell,'" Suzanne Malveaux, CNN, November 15, 2010.

13. "House Votes to Allow 'Don't Ask, Don't Tell' Repeal," David Herszenhorn and Carl Hulse, *New York Times,* May 27, 2010.

14. "Senate halts 'don't ask, don't tell' repeal."

15. "Pentagon: Military Ready for 'Don't Ask, Don't Tell' Repeal," Robert Burns, Associated Press, September 20, 2011.

16. "Pentagon Sees Little Risk in Allowing Gay Men and Women to Serve Openly," Elisabeth Bumiller, *New York Times,* November 30, 2010.

17. "Senate Delivers Potentially Fatal Blow to 'Don't Ask, Don't Tell' Repeal Efforts," Ed O'Keefe and Paul Kane, *Washington Post,* December 10, 2010.

18. U.S. House of Representatives recorded vote 638, 111th Congress, December 15, 2010.

19. U.S. Senate roll call vote 281, 111th Congress, December 18, 2010.

8. THE VEEP STEPS UP

1. Recovery.gov.

9. COMING AROUND ON CLINTON

1. "The Surprise Trip to the Briefing Room," Michael Shear, *New York Times,* December 10, 2010.

2. "President Obama & President Clinton on Tax Cuts, Unemployment Insurance & Jobs," The White House, December 10, 2010.

3. "Obama Exits, Clinton Keeps Talking," Carol Lee, *Politico,* December 10, 2010.

4. "Let's Be Friends," Ryan Lizza, *The New Yorker,* September 10, 2012.

5. "Obama plays golf with Clinton, McAuliffe," CNN, December 2, 2012.

10. THE HUNT BEGINS

1. Bob Woodward, *Obama's Wars* (Simon & Schuster, 2010), p.343.

2. "On Defense, a Team, Not Rivals," David Ignatius, *Washington Post,* June 7, 2009.

3. Woodward, *Obama's Wars,* p. 343.
4. "Egypt protesters step up pressure on Hosni Mubarak," BBC, January 31, 2011.
5. Live blog, Egypt protests, Al Jazeera, January 31, 2011.
6. President Obama's address to the Muslim world, June 4, 2009.
7. President Obama remarks on the situation in Egypt, January 28, 2011.
8. Text of Egyptian President Hosni Mubarak's address to the nation, February 1, 2011.
9. "In Arab Spring, Obama Finds a Sharp Test," Helene Cooper and Robert Worth, *New York Times,* September 24, 2012.
10. Ibid.
11. "Remarks by the President on the Situation in Egypt," The White House, February 1, 2011.
12. "How Obama Got Bin Laden: A Detailed Account from *Showdown* by David Corn," *Daily Beast,* April 29, 2012.

11. Trump, bin Laden, and the Craziest Week of the Presidency

1. "Will Boehner's 'Blink' Make a Difference on Tax Cuts? Not Before Lame-Duck," Kate McCarthy, ABC News, September 13, 2010.
2. "And Now, Roy Blunt," Dave Weigel, *Washington Independent,* July 29, 2009.
3. "Donald Trump, Wannabe President: I've Sent Investigators to Hawaii to Look Into Obama's Citizenship," Aliyah Shahid, *New York Daily News,* April 7, 2011.
4. "Poll: 46% of GOP thinks Obama's Muslim," Josh Gerstein, *Politico,* August 19, 2010.
5. The White House posted correspondence between Judith Corley, President Obama's personal attorney, and Loretta Fuddy, Director of the Hawaii Department of Health.
6. "Remarks by the President," The White House, April 27, 2011.
7. "How Obama Got Bin Laden: A Detailed Account from *Showdown* by David Corn," *Daily Beast,* April 29, 2012.
8. "Obama Golfs for the Fifth Weekend in a Row," Keith Koffler, White House Dossier, May 1, 2011.
9. "Press Briefing by Press Secretary Jay Carney and Assistant to the President for Homeland Security and Counterterrorism John Brennan," The White House, May 2, 2011.

10. "Moment of Triumph: 'Visual on Geronimo,'" Michael Scherer, *Time,* May 2, 2011.
11. "The Hunt for 'Geronimo,'" Mark Bowden, *Vanity Fair,* November 2012.
12. "Osama Bin Laden Dead," Macon Phillips, The White House, May 2, 2011.
13. "Press Briefing by Press Secretary Jay Carney..."
14. "The Hunt for 'Geronimo.'"

12. The Chief Executive Learns to Manage

1. "Exclusive: Bill Daley, Unplugged," Roger Simon, *Politico,* October 28, 2011.
2. "Obama/Boehner Jobs Speech Mess: The Buck Stops with Bill Daley," Carol Felsenthal, *Chicago Magazine,* September 2, 2011.
3. WhiteHouseMuseum.org.
4. "Bill Daley, a Weakened White House Chief of Staff, Steps Down," Michael Scherer, *Time,* January 9, 2012.
5. "The Jack Lew You Don't Know," Peter Coy, *Bloomberg Businessweek,* January 10, 2013.
6. "The Runaway General," Michael Hastings, *Rolling Stone,* June 22, 2010.
7. "On Monday Night, McChrystal Called Biden to Apologize for Remarks in Profile," David Gura, NPR, June 23, 2010.
8. "McChrystal article renews attention to split with Biden over Afghanistan," Anne Kornblut, *Washington Post,* June 23, 2010.
9. "Press Briefing by Press Secretary Robert Gibbs," The White House, June 22, 2010.
10. General Stanley McChrystal, *My Share of the Task: A Memoir* (Portfolio, 2013), p. 387.
11. Ibid., pp. 387–88.
12. "Statement by the President in the Rose Garden," The White House, June 23, 2010.
13. McChrystal, *My Share of the Task,* p. 388.

13. A Challenger Emerges

1. National Exit Polls, 2008.
2. "VP Biden to Target Ohio, Pennsylvania, Florida for 2012," Associated Press, November 28, 2011.

3. "When Obama and Romney First Met: the 2004 Winter Gridiron Dinner," Lynn Sweet, *Chicago Sun-Times,* September 30, 2012.

4. "Romney: Obama Called After Wife Fell Ill Recently," Associated Press, January 4, 2009.

5. "Remarks by the President at the Congressional Gold Medal Ceremony for Senator Edward William Brooke," The White House, October 28, 2009.

6. "Briefing by White House Press Secretary Robert Gibbs, March 22, 2010," The White House.

7. "Why I Vetoed Contraception Bill," Mitt Romney, *Boston Globe,* July 26, 2005.

8. FEC filing by RickPerry.org Inc., October 2011 quarterly report.

9. "White House Aides Bill Burton and Sean Sweeney to Form Consulting Firm," Jeanne Cummings, *Politico,* February 16, 2011.

10. "RNC Close to Calling Romney Presumptive Nominee," Reid Wilson, *National Journal,* April 19, 2012.

11. 2012 election results, Kansas Secretary of State's office.

12. A speech delivered at the dedication of John Brown Memorial Park in Osawatomie, Kansas, Theodore Roosevelt, August 31, 1910. Transcript courtesy TeachingAmericanHistory.org.

13. "Remarks by the President on the Economy in Osawatomie, Kansas," The White House, December 6, 2011.

14. Ibid.

15. "As Romney's Firm Profited in SC, Jobs Disappeared," Jack Gillum, Associated Press, December 19, 2011.

16. "Companies' Ills Did Not Harm Romney's Firm," Michael Luo and Julie Creswell, *New York Times,* June 22, 2012.

17. "Mitt Romney: 'I Have Some Friends Who Are NASCAR Team Owners,'" Ariel Edwards-Levy, *Huffington Post,* February 26, 2012.

18. "Mitt Romney Talks About NFL Owner Friends," Shira Schoenberg, *Boston Globe,* March 13, 2012.

19. "Mitt Romney Says 'Corporations Are People,'" Philip Rucker, *Washington Post,* August 11, 2011.

20. "Obama's Speech in Columbus, Ohio, May 2012," Council on Foreign Relations, May 5, 2012.

21. "Surrogate for Obama Denounces Anti-Mitt Romney Ad," Raymond Hernandez, *New York Times,* May 20, 2012.

22. "Is This Obama's Party?" Zeke Miller, *BuzzFeed,* May 22, 2012.

23. "Romney supporters drown out David Axelrod at Boston press conference," Sarah Boxer, CBS News, May 31, 2012.

24. "So the Voters May Choose: Reviving the Presidential Matching Fund System," Campaign Finance Institute.

25. Total advertising buys in August 2004 according to filings with the Internal Revenue Service.

26. "Behind the Scenes in the 2012 Campaign," Robert Schlesinger, *U.S. News,* December 5, 2012.

27. "Master Campaigner Summons the Spotlight for Obama (and Himself)," Peter Baker, *New York Times,* September 10, 2012.

28. "Transcript of Bill Clinton's Speech to the Democratic National Convention," *New York Times,* September 5, 2012.

29. "Obama says all-day debate prep 'is a drag,'" Mark Knoller, CBS News, October 1, 2012.

30. "How a Race in the Balance Went to Obama," Adam Nagourney, Ashley Parker, Jum Rutenberg, and Jeff Zeleny, *New York Times,* November 7, 2012.

31. Ibid.

32. KDVR weather reports.

33. White House press pool reports from November 5–6, 2012.

14. If He Had a Son

1. "Genealogy for a Nation of Immigrants," Alessandra Stanley, *New York Times,* February 9, 2010.

2. "News Conference by the President," The White House, July 22, 2009.

3. "Health Care Front-And-Center on Public's News Agenda," Pew Research Center, July 30, 2009.

4. "Obama 'Surprised' by Controversy over Remark about Arrest of Black Scholar," Associated Press, July 23, 2009.

5. "Beer Summit Begins: Obama Sits Down With Crowley, Gates," Ben Feller, Associated Press, August 30, 2009.

6. "Remarks by the President on the Nomination of Dr. Jim Kim for World Bank President," The White House, March 23, 2012.

7. "Remarks by the President on Trayvon Martin," July 19, 2013.

8. "How Mitch McConnell Enabled Barack Obama," Isaac Chotiner, *New Republic,* May 15, 2013.

9. "When Did McConnell Say He Wanted to Make Obama a 'One-Term President'?" Glenn Kessler, *Washington Post,* September 25, 2012.

10. "McConnell: I Take Obama 'At His Word' That He's a Christian," Sam Stein, *Huffington Post,* May 25, 2011.

11. "Obama Woos GOP with Attention, and Cookies," Jeff Zeleny, *New York Times,* February 4, 2009.

12. "In President's Outreach to GOP, Past Failures Loom," Jackie Calmes, *New York Times,* March 11, 2013.

13. U.S. Sen. Tom Coburn, Barack Obama Form Unlikely Friendship," Chris Casteel, *The Oklahoman,* March 8, 2009.

14. "In President's Outreach to GOP, Past Failures Loom."

15. "Obama Tells Donors Europe to Blame for Weak Job Growth," Kate Anderson Brower, *Bloomberg,* June 2, 2012.

16. "Does President Obama Have a Second-Term Strategy?" Glenn Thrush, *Politico,* July 17, 2013.

17. "Obama Flashes Irritation in Press Room," Jonathan Martin and Carrie Budoff Brown, *Politico,* January 22, 2009.

18. David Mendell, *Obama* (HarperCollins, 2009), p. 278.

19. Ibid., p. 277.

20. "Obama Dines with Conservative Columnists," Helene Cooper, *New York Times,* January 13, 2009.

21. "Obama Meets with Liberal Columnists," Michael Calderone, *Politico,* January 14, 2009.

22. In 2009, Obama chose Louisville, North Carolina, Memphis, and Pitt for the Final Four. In 2010, he chose Kansas, Kansas State, Kentucky, and Villanova. Obama chose Ohio State, Duke, Kansas, and Pitt in 2011, and North Carolina, Kentucky, Ohio State, and Missouri in 2012.

15. THEY WERE FIRST-GRADERS

1. "Sources: No Movement in President Obama, John Boehner Cliff Talks," Jake Sherman and Carrie Budoff Brown, *Politico,* December 13, 2012.

2. President Obama's daily schedule, White House Dossier, December 13, 2012.

3. "Newtown School Shooting: Transcript of Police, Fire Radio Dispatch," *New Haven Register,* December 14, 2012.

4. "Noah Pozner's Family Remembers and Mourns," Naomi Zeveloff, *Jewish Daily Forward,* December 26, 2012.

5. "A Timeline of Mass Shootings in the U.S. Since Columbine," Aviva Shen, ThinkProgress, December 14, 2012.

6. "Chicago Police Confirm 'Tragic Number' of 500 Homicides," Jeremy Gorner and Peter Nickeas, *Chicago Tribune,* December 28, 2012.

7. "Shaken Obama Says Hearts 'Broken,' Pledges Action," Jared Favole and Carol Lee, *Wall Street Journal,* December 14, 2012.

8. "President Obama Makes a Statement on the Shooting in Newtown, Connecticut," The White House, December 14, 2012.

9. "White House Describes Gun Control Measures Obama Supports," Jeff Mason and Matt Spetalnick, Reuters, December 18, 2012.

10. NRA release of Wayne LaPierre's remarks, December 21, 2012.

11. Democratic Party Platform, 1996. Archived by The American Presidency Project at U.C. Santa Barbara.

12. Democratic Party Platform, 2000. Archived by The American Presidency Project at U.C. Santa Barbara.

13. "Kerry on Hunting Photo-Op to Help Image," Jodi Wilgoren, *New York Times,* October 22, 2004.

14. Data compiled by the Center for Responsive Politics.

15. "What President Obama Said About Gun Control in the 2012 Campaign," Chris Cillizza, *Washington Post,* December 16, 2012.

16. "Senate rejects expanded gun background checks," Ted Barrett and Tom Cohen, CNN, April 18, 2013.

17. "Senate Blocks Gun-Control Legislation in Blow to Obama," John Whitesides and David Lawder, Reuters, April 17, 2013.

16. THE LOST YEAR

1. "Obama Makes His Immigration Push," Zachary Goldfarb and Rosalind Helderman, *Washington Post,* January 29, 2013.

2. "Senate, 68 to 32, Passes Overhaul for Immigration," Ashley Parker and Jonathan Martin, *New York Times,* June 27, 2013.

3. Ibid.

4. "NSA Collecting Phone Records of Millions of Verizon Customers Daily," Glenn Greenwald, *Guardian,* June 5, 2013.

5. "Snowden Used Low-Cost Tool to Best NSA," David Sanger and Eric Schmitt, *New York Times,* February 8, 2014.

6. "Spying Scandal: Obama Owes Us an Explanation," Gregor Peter Schmitz, *Der Spiegel,* July 2, 2013.

7. "Northern Ireland and Germany Trip 2013," The White House.

8. "Merkel Calls Obama About Alleged U.S. Monitoring of Her Phone," Scott Wilson and Michael Birnbaum, *Washington Post,* October 23, 2013.

9. "Readout of the President's Phone Call with Chancellor Merkel of Germany," The White House, October 23, 2013.

10. "Merkel, Hollande to Discuss European Communication Network Avoiding U.S.," Erik Kirschbaum, Reuters, February 15, 2014.

11. "Reception for Obama Is More Sober Than in 2008," Alison Smale, *New York Times,* June 19, 2013.

12. "Brazil Leader Postpones Trip to U.S. Over Spying," Bradley Brooks, Associated Press, September 17, 2013.

13. "Remarks by the President on the Deaths of U.S. Embassy Staff in Libya," The White House, September 12, 2012.

14. "What They Said, Before and After the Attack in Libya," *New York Times,* September 12, 2012.

15. Second Presidential Debate, Federal News Service, Hempstead, N.Y., October 16, 2012.

16. "House Republican report slams WH for Benghazi attack," Stephanie Condon, CBS News, February 11, 2014.

17. "Statement by the President," The White House, May 14, 2013.

17. A Thick Red Line

1. "Jaco Report: Full Interview with Todd Akin," Charles Jaco, Fox2Now St. Louis, August 19, 2012.

2. "Remarks by the President to the White House Press Corps," The White House, August 20, 2012.

3. "Obama's Uncertain Path amid Syria Bloodshed," Mark Mazzetti, Roberth Worth, and Michael Gordon, *New York Times,* October 22, 2013.

4. Ibid.

5. Ibid.

6. Ibid.

7. "Statement by Deputy National Security Advisor for Strategic Communications Ben Rhodes on Syrian Chemical Weapons Use," The White House, June 13, 2013.

8. "President Obama: 'I have not made a decision' on Syria," *PBS NewsHour,* August 28, 2013.

9. "Syria crisis: No clear winner in Russia-U.S. G20 duel," Bridget Kendall, BBC News, September 6, 2013.

10. "Joint Statement on Syria," The White House, September 6, 2013.

11. "Remarks with United Kingdom Foreign Secretary Hague," U.S. State Department, September 9, 2013.

12. "Sen. Corker slams Obama on credibility," Dana Bash, CNN, September 11, 2013.

18. Control-Alt-Delete

1. "President Hosted Obamacare Watch Party," Nikki Schwab, *U.S. News,* September 18, 2013.

2. "How They Did It," Jonathan Cohn, *New Republic,* May 21, 2010.

3. Ibid.

4. "President Hosted Obamacare Watch Party."

5. "Healthcare.gov: How Political Fear Was Pitted Against Technical Needs," Amy Goldstein and Juliet Eilperin, *Washington Post,* November 2, 2013.

6. Ibid.

7. "Health Site Puts Agency and Leader in Hot Seat," Sheryl Gay Stolberg, *New York Times,* October 28, 2013.

8. "Healthcare.gov: How Political Fear..."

9. "Officials Were Warned About Health Site Woes," Sharon LaFraniere and Eric Lipton, *New York Times,* November 18, 2013.

10. "Tension and Flaws Before Health Website Crash," Eric Lipton, Ian Austen, and Sharon LaFraniere, *New York Times,* November 22, 2013.

11. "Notes Reveal Chaotic White House Talks on Health Care Site," Robert Pear, *New York Times,* November 5, 2013.

12. "Sebelius Stands Firm Despite Calls to Resign," Robert Pear, *New York Times,* October 16, 2013.

19. The Legacy

1. "Remarks by the President at University of Michigan Spring Commencement," The White House, May 1, 2010.

ABOUT THE AUTHOR

Chuck Todd is the NBC News Political Director and the moderator of *Meet the Press,* the flagship Sunday morning public affairs program and longest-running broadcast in television history. Prior to taking the helm of *Meet the Press* in September 2014, Todd served as NBC News Chief White House Correspondent (2008–2014) as well as host of MSNBC's *The Daily Rundown* (2010–2014). Todd has held the role of Political Director since March 2007, leading all aspects of the news division's political coverage and analysis across every platform. He is also the editor of *First Read,* NBC's must-read guide to political news and trends in and around Washington, D.C.